Online Health and Safety

Online Health and Safety

From Cyberbullying to Internet Addiction

Bernadette H. Schell

Library of Congress Cataloging-in-Publication Data

Names: Schell, Bernadette H. (Bernadette Hlubik), 1952–
Title: Online health and safety : from cyberbullying to internet addiction / Bernadette H. Schell.
Description: Santa Barbara : Greenwood, 2016. | Includes bibliographical references and index.
Identifiers: LCCN 2015032650 | ISBN 9781440838965 (hardback : alk. paper) | ISBN 9781440838972 (ebook)
Subjects: LCSH: Cyberbullying. | Internet addiction.
Classification: LCC HV6773.15.C92 S36 2016 | DDC 303.48/33—dc23 LC record available at http://lccn.loc.gov/2015032650

ISBN: 978-1-4408-3896-5
EISBN: 978-1-4408-3897-2

20 19 18 17 16 1 2 3 4 5

This book is also available on the World Wide Web as an eBook.
Visit www.abc-clio.com for details.

Greenwood
An Imprint of ABC-CLIO, LLC

ABC-CLIO, LLC
130 Cremona Drive, P.O. Box 1911
Santa Barbara, California 93116-1911

This book is printed on acid-free paper ♾
Manufactured in the United States of America

Contents

Preface

Generally speaking, an internet (lowercase) is a network connecting computer systems. "The Internet" that we are all familiar with today dates back to 1969 when it was pioneered in the United States. Then, the Internet was a high-speed network built by the U.S. Department of Defense as a digital communications experiment that linked hundreds of defense contractors, universities, and research laboratories. This powerful computer network belonging to the U.S. Advanced Research Projects Agency, or ARPA, allowed highly trained artificial intelligence (AI) researchers in dispersed locations to transmit and exchange critical information with incredible speed.

To keep the United States and its citizens physically safe, especially in times of crisis, government agents working in isolated pockets could continue to transmit critical information over the ARPAnet rather than have agents physically move from one geographic location to another in order to have an information exchange. This "networked" tribe arrangement that was developed back in 1969 continues to exist in the more sophisticated online world today, allowing people to connect remotely.

Nowadays, the Internet refers to a collection of networks connected by routers. The Internet is the largest network in the world and comprises backbone networks such as MILNET, mid-level networks, and stub networks. Though the pioneering ARPAnet was dedicated to the U.S. military and selected contractors and universities partaking in defense research, without question, the ARPAnet hugely advanced the emerging field of information technology (IT).

Today, Internet users come from all walks of life—students and teachers, businesspeople, medical professionals, bankers, police, social agencies, and government officers. There is little question that the Internet has brought many conveniences to modern-day online users, such as doing online banking without leaving home, engaging in online games with players around the globe with the flick of a clicker, surfing the Net on any topic of interest, communicating in online social networks for relationships or entertainment, or booking a flight to a wonderful destination in the sun without having to go out into a raging snowstorm.

However, since about 1995 mental health practitioners have recognized that an obsession with the virtual world can and does lead to harmful Internet and gaming addictions, as well as other harmful person-related behaviors like cyberbullying and cyberstalking, and online predation. Even corporate and government network hacks, identity theft, and Internet fraud have become present-day, hugely costly phenomena.

On a larger, societal scale, in recent years, there has been an incredible rise in social media Web site usage among online users, connecting individuals to friends and coworkers anywhere around the world; copyright infringement, placing the authors of creative works at risk; and real-time file sharing among online users capitalizing on peer-to-peer (P2P) networks. What is more, the police, lawyers, and mental health practitioners have noted a rapid rise in obscene and offensive content on the Internet, as well as online censorship—setting off a raging debate about what constitutes information freedom and what prevents it. And while the Internet seems to be viewed by many as somewhat bittersweet, or vice-versa depending on one's perceptions, individuals in developed countries are expecting more readily available and convenient access to online health records and health services—which were formerly heavily land-based rather than virtually based.

Online Health and Safety: From Cyberbullying to Internet Addiction explores all of these topics—concerns of experts, known prevalence rates, remedies for dealing with the problem areas, and prevailing controversies and real-world challenges—leading to opportunities for future research solutions. The topics are divided into two main sections: (1) the online issues involving harm to persons, and (2) the macro-system issues regarding online health and safety.

THE ONLINE ISSUES INVOLVING HARM TO PERSONS

Chapter 1 covers the many facets of Internet and gaming addictions. On a very basic level, any kind of activity that one engages in while online can eventually present as a computer or Internet addiction. The chapter focuses on these two addictions, their definitions, the controversies surrounding them, cases of clients who have gone for therapy because of persistent and bothersome Internet and gaming obsessions, and treatments commonly employed to help clients overcome their addictions.

Chapter 2 opens with the case of Amanda Todd, a 15-year-old girl who was cyberbullied and cyberharassed after she posted a video on YouTube with flash cards and this message, "I've decided to tell you about my never ending story." Amanda told her story about being abused, bullied, harassed, stalked online, and stalked in person by some as yet unidentified person. To relieve herself of the pain, Amanda eventually committed suicide. This chapter focuses on the two concepts of cyberbullying and cyberstalking—their definitions, their measurement and conceptualization, controversies surrounding them, cases that have been well publicized and/or investigated by mental health experts, and treatments or remedies that have been employed to counteract these mounting and heinous problems in society.

Chapter 3 deals with the many dark sides of online predators. The chapter focuses on the concept of online predation, how it is defined, the assessed prevalence of the problem, controversies surrounding online predation and online victims, the Internet's role in advancing online sexual predation and grooming, the process of online predation, the typologies of online predators, the typologies of victims, and the various legal remedies, mental health treatments, or other remedies that have been employed to counter this virtual-world problem that easily blends into a real-world problem.

Chapter 4 opens with the concerns of U.S. president Barack Obama following online breaches like the massive kind that targeted the networks of large companies like Sony, Target, and Home Depot in 2014. This chapter focuses on the three main topics of corporate/government network hacks, identify theft, and Internet fraud. Discussions focus on the known breadth of these problems and some solutions provided by experts on not only preventing the problems but recovering from these very costly realities.

THE MACRO-SYSTEM ISSUES REGARDING ONLINE HEALTH AND SAFETY

Chapter 5 discusses the interesting topic of technology and social behavior: the rise of social media Web sites. In 2015, without question, social media Web sites like Facebook, YouTube, Twitter, LinkedIn, Instagram, Pinterest, Vine, Snapchat, and Tumblr—to name just a few—were flourishing. This chapter focuses on the rise of social media and social marketing by looking at some recent statistics, including the Pew Research Center's *Social Media Update for 2014*. Controversies surrounding social media Web sites are also discussed, starting with what is known about social media addiction. What is known about some harms affiliated with social media usage on a broader scale is discussed—particularly sexting. The chapter goes on to discuss some legal, mental health, and policy resolutions for dealing with these harms and closes by looking at some recent business challenges to social media Web sites, as well as concerns about criminals lurking in social media Web sites in order to target vulnerable users.

Chapter 6 deals with the rather complex modern-day issues of copyright infringement, legal and illegal file sharing, and peer-to-peer (P2P) networks. The protection of intellectual property rights (IPR) from attack by online users or cybercriminals has been a major concern for many corporations for more than 15 years, because taking the creative works of someone else without paying a legitimate fee costs industry billions of dollars annually in lost revenues and jobs. This chapter looks at the fascinating controversies surrounding online copyright infringement, P2P networks, and file sharing in the United States and elsewhere. The chapter opens with defining these terms and then discusses recent file-sharing trends in various jurisdictions. The next focus is on legislation aimed at curbing copyright infringements and illegal file sharing through P2P networks, followed by a section on understanding the intentions behind illegal downloading. Next, the chapter looks at how the criminal arm uses P2P networks to share illegal files, including child pornography. The chapter closes with policy implications of technology for detecting P2P and copyright violations.

Chapter 7 deals with online obscene and offensive content and censorship. This fascinating chapter defines what is meant by obscene content (including pornography and child pornography), offensive content/hate speech transmitted through the Internet, and online censorship. Then the chapter discusses the topic of why, even in jurisdictions like the United States that support freedom of speech and Internet openness, there will never be total freedom of the press or a lack of press and Internet censorship. The media headline cases of Assange, Manning, and Snowden are detailed, along with salient points of concern at the macro-system level for society. The methods used by governments to censor online users and content are then described. The chapter closes with the results of the *Freedom on the Net 2014* findings.

Chapter 8 deals with online personal health records and health services. This final chapter looks closely at the benefits and controversies surrounding online health records and online health services, primarily by disclosing key research findings in the United States, the European Union, and Japan. The chapter opens with definitions for online health records and online health services and then discusses the opportunities and concerns of online citizens and health care professionals regarding these concepts. Particular concerns from legal, privacy, security, and trust perspectives are detailed for particular patient groups, including adolescents, those seeking mental health assistance, and the elderly. Suggested institutional remedies for dealing with these concerns are then outlined, along with the relevance of the U.S. legislation known as HIPAA, or the Health Insurance Portability and Accountability Act of 1996. The chapter closes by discussing policy issues regarding online health records and online health services, and how lessons learned from Japan might be applied to other jurisdictions, including the United States.

Part I

Online Issues Involving Harm to Persons

Chapter 1

Internet and Gaming Addictions

While the condition called "Internet addiction" is not yet fully recognised as an established disorder and the controversial debate is still on-going, Internet Gaming Addiction (IGA) has been listed as an emerging disorder worthy of further investigation in the latest version of the Diagnostic and Statistical Manual of Mental Disorders–V (DSM–V).

—Lawrence T. Lam

OVERVIEW

On a very basic level, any kind of activity that one engages in while online can eventually present as a computer or Internet addiction. These addictions are broad and could involve watching online pornography, viewing obscene or offensive content online, acting as an online predator, engaging in obsessive computer hacking, spending tons of money in online gambling, sending and receiving an excessive number of e-mails, or becoming obsessed with online gaming. As some of these topics are covered in other chapters in this book, we will focus in this chapter on Internet and gaming addictions—their definitions, the controversies surrounding them, cases of clients who have gone for therapy because of persistent and bothersome Internet and gaming addictions, and treatments commonly employed to help clients overcome their addictions.

Experts generally agree that acknowledgment of the scope of relationship problems caused by Internet addiction has been undermined by its current popularity and the advanced utilities the Internet brings at work and at home. Young (1996) found that serious relationship problems were reported by 53% of Internet addicts surveyed. Marriages, dating relationships, parent-child relationships, and close friendships have been noted to be seriously disrupted by those so inclined to "Net binges." A common pattern tends to emerge: "Net bingers" gradually spend less time with people in their real-world lives in exchange for solitary time spent in front of a computer. For adult heavy Internet users, their marriages often appear to be the most affected, as Internet use interferes with many responsibilities and obligations at home, and the spouse not Internet-addicted will often voice feeling like a "cyberwidow(er)" (Young 1998).

Therapists have also heard of heavy online users forgetting to get their children after school is over, forgetting to prepare them dinner, or delaying to put them in bed at the appropriate hour. Though loved ones at first commonly rationalize that the heavy user in the family is just "in a phase," when addictive behaviors of the family member continue, arguments about the excessive time spent online follow—with the inevitable denial of such behavior by the individual so addicted (Young 1998).

Furthermore, family lawyers have recently reported seeing a rise in divorce cases because of cyberaffairs. Though individuals may initially form online relationships as an innocent pastime, over extended periods of time, such relationships inevitably eclipse the time spent with real-life people or loved ones. The addicted spouse often socially isolates himself or herself from the family and refuses to engage in once-enjoyed events, such as going out to dinner, traveling together, or just spending time chatting with one another (Quittner 1997).

In teens and adolescents, massively multiplayer online role-playing games, or MMORPGs as they are often called, are one of the most rapidly growing forms of Internet addiction. Like those addicted to alcohol or drugs, MMORPG gamers show several classic signs: they lie about their heavy gaming use, they lose interest in other activities or withdraw from family and friends in order to game, and they use gaming as a means of psychological escape rather than forming intimate relationships in the real world.

It is difficult to estimate how widespread the game addiction problem is, but according to the American Medical Association, as many as 90% of American children and adolescents play video games, and of that population, as many as 15% of them—more than 5 million children—may be addicted in the United States alone. In fact, problems rooted in excessive gaming have become so serious that in some countries—such as in the Netherlands in 2006—detox centers for those addicted to games have opened their doors (Young 2009b).

Chapter 1 focuses on computer and gaming addictions—how they are defined, the difficulties in measuring them, and strategies for helping clients to deal with their addictions.

ADDICTION, COMPUTER ADDICTIONS, AND INTERNET ADDICTIONS DEFINED

Addiction Defined

What is an addiction, in general, and a computer addiction or an Internet addiction, specifically? In the mental health community, "an addiction" is generally defined as "a compulsive, continued use of a substance or behavior that is known by the user to be harmful physically and/or psychologically." In this context, an addiction is often described by mental health practitioners to be symptomatic of an impulse control disorder—characterized by a tendency to gratify a desire or impulse, despite the negative consequences that such gratification may create for oneself or for significant others (Lesher 1997; American Psychiatric Association 2000).

When mental health experts talk about the constellation of traits typically seen in addicted clients, it tends to include these seven behavioral traits (Young 1996): (1) withdrawal from daily activities, (2) tolerance issues, (3) a preoccupation with the substance or behavior in question, (4) heavier or more frequent use of the substance or behavior than intended, (5) centralized activities to procure more of the substance or to engage in the behavior, (6) loss of interest in other social or work or recreational activities formerly enjoyed, and (7) denial—outright disregard for the physical or psychological consequences caused by the use of the substance or addiction in question.

However, it is important to note that among the mental health experts there are purists who believe that the term *addiction* should only be applied to cases involving chemical substances and not to Internet or gaming addictions (e.g., Rachlin 1990; Walker 1989).

A review of the literature on Internet or gaming addictions tends to indicate a more liberal rather than a strictly conservative perception of these concepts. For example, increasingly in the mental health literature, experts publish research findings on the following diverse areas of Internet or gaming addictions: pathological gambling (Griffiths 1990; Walters 1996), eating disorders (Lacey 1993; Lesieur and Blume 1993), sexual addiction (Goodman 1993), technological addiction of a general nature (Griffiths 1995), and video game and online gaming addiction (Griffiths 1992; Keepers 1990).

Computer and Internet Addiction Defined

The term *Internet addiction* was first coined, it is generally believed, in 1995 when a psychiatrist from the United States, Dr. Ivan Goldberg, used it as a joke to describe his avid use of the Internet when communicating with fellow psychiatrists. Goldberg (1996) later more seriously suggested that the diagnostic criteria for an Internet addiction disorder (IAD), if it were to be more broadly received by the mental health expert community, would likely be based on the diagnostic criteria for substance abuse disorder (SAD) found in the fourth edition of the *Diagnostic and Statistical Manual of Mental Disorders* (aka the *DSM)* and would tend to focus on symptoms related to tolerance, withdrawal, and forgoing or reducing important social and occupational activities. The *DSM*, it should be noted, is widely used for mental disorder diagnosis by mental health experts in many countries.

Furthermore, Dr. Kimberly Young presented the term *computer addiction* at the 1996 American Psychological Association annual convention in Toronto, suggesting that Internet addictions are not unlike other addictions—such as those involving substance abuse—in that they can cause a number of negative life side effects for those so addicted, such as loss of control, social isolation, dysfunctional marital and family relationships, or impaired academic or work achievements (Young 1996). In her talk, Young noted that not only do "computer-addicted" or "computer-obsessed" types tend to neglect their loved ones and their chores, but they also tend to have odd sleeping patterns and poor eating habits. Of all the diagnoses referenced in the *DSM-IV*, published in 1995, she shared that "pathological gambling" can be viewed as most closely related to the pathological nature seen in Internet "extreme users." By using pathological gambling as a model, "Internet addiction" could be defined, she said, as "an impulse-control disorder which does not involve an intoxicant." She also noted that computer- or Internet-addicted types are generally not able to maintain a task- and socially/emotionally balanced regimen over the longer term, and that there are often related psychological cravings or physical withdrawal symptoms when an extreme user is unable to get his or her online "fix."

In a 1996 academic paper outlining the psychology of computer use and addictive use of the Internet, Young reported that "computer-addicted" types tend to spend, on average, 38 hours a week online, compared to the "non-addicted" types who spend, on average, 5 hours a week online (Schell, Dodge, and Moutsatsos 2002).

Types of Computer Addictions, Including Gaming

Gaming in general and online gaming in particular are placed in the broader life activity of play. The activity of play has been present throughout human history, because it is generally perceived by the players to be pleasurable and entertaining. Simply put, play is a way of relaxing and of departing from one's daily routine in order to enjoy something unique.

Huizinga (1938), in his cultural analysis of play, referred to this phenomenon as a free activity outside of one's ordinary life that is not perceived to be serious but is absorbing and intense. Play tends to proceed within its own defined boundaries of time and space, according to fixed rules and in an orderly fashion. Its purpose is often to promote the creation of social groupings, which tend to surround game players with special secret codes or behaviors particular to any given game, thus stressing the game players' difference from others in "the common world" through disguise or by other legitimate means of game play. In short, play in general and game play in particular is generally seen to be enjoyable pastime activities that do not detract from a normal, healthy life but rather add to its enjoyment by bringing together like-minded people, fostering task and emotionally balanced sociocultural protocols of behavior.

Within the last few decades, a new kind of virtual playground has emerged, because the Internet affords online players a huge variety of games and game genres. These include, for example, casual browser games like DarkOrbit or FirstPerson, ego-shooters like Counterstrike, massively multiplayer online role-playing games (MMORPGs) like World of Warcraft, and simulation games like Second Life. Other online games like Neocron combine distinct genres within one game (Kuss and Griffiths 2012).

To say that online games are seriously engaging for the players is an understatement. For example, not only are MMORPGs simultaneously played by hundreds of thousands of users globally, but online players often socialize in guilds, cooperating with one another to reach game-relevant goals. Furthermore, players take on virtual personae known as "avatars." Thus, players can depart from their typical life roles by taking on the life of, say, avatar magicians or warriors. Finally, simulation games mimic real life in a type of metaverse, where any behaviors doable in actual life can be done in a virtual world (Kuss and Griffiths 2012).

The broad appeal of these Internet games is outlined by the NPD Group's 2010 software sales ranking, indicating that the public's current preference is for MMORPG and real-life simulations. This preference may be explained by the fact that online players are provided with the capability to move between the real and the imagined, the self and the other. In short, when engaging in online games, players are given a practically boundless license to explore themselves and others in society before returning to the real world (Kuss and Griffiths 2012).

As Silverstone (1999) earlier remarked, in sophisticated online games, players can not only investigate culture, but also create it. The latest software sale rankings demonstrate that Internet games attract tons of gamers worldwide, but, without question, there is a minority of people who play excessively; they are the online gaming addicts. Recent research suggests that this minority of gamers experiences symptoms traditionally associated with substance-related addictions, such as mood modification, tolerance, and behavioral salience (Mehroof and Griffiths 2010; Young 2009b).

One of the most dramatic and highly publicized stories worldwide of online gaming addiction occurred in August 2005 when a 28-year-old South Korean man died—not because he committed suicide, but because he played the game Starcraft at an Internet cafe for 50 hours straight. He had not slept properly and had eaten very little in that period of time. While no autopsy was ever performed, he is believed to have died from heart failure stemming from exhaustion (Young 2009b).

Experts warn, however, that it isn't just the addicted gamers who suffer from their obsessions. There could be other innocent victims. In South Korea, a couple was arrested when their four-month-old daughter died of suffocation after the couple left her unattended in their apartment for several hours while they played World of Warcraft at a nearby Internet cafe. In Reno, Nevada, a couple was so obsessed with video games that they left their babies starving and suffering from other health problems. According to authorities, Michael and Iana Straw's children—a 22-month-old boy and an 11-month-old girl—were so badly malnourished that they were near death when social workers found them and took them to a hospital. The couple pleaded guilty to child neglect and faced a 12-year prison sentence (Young 2009b).

Current Problems with the Internet Addiction and Gaming Addiction Definition and Measurement

Despite the many studies completed in recent years on Internet overuse or gaming addiction, to this day there remain no consistent diagnostic criteria or measurement scale for either of these. This lack of criteria has resulted in inconsistent reporting related to the prevalence, progress, and adequate treatment of Internet or gaming overuse (Cho et al. 2014).

Dr. Jerald Block (2008) forcefully argued that Internet addiction, or Internet use disorder (IUD), appeared to be a common disorder in the general population, meriting full inclusion in the *DSM–V* when it would eventually be published. Conceptually, he maintained, an IUD diagnosis in the *DSM* would be defined as a compulsive-impulsive spectrum disorder that involves online and/or offline computer usage consisting of at least three subtypes: (1) excessive gaming, (2) online behaviors indicating a sexual preoccupation, and (3) excessive e-mail/text messaging. All of these variants, he said, share the following four components:

- *Excessive use*, often associated with a loss of sense of time or a neglect of basic drives,
- *Withdrawal*, including feelings of anger, tension, and/or depression when the computer is inaccessible,
- *Tolerance*, including the need for better computer equipment, more software, or more hours of use, and
- *Negative repercussions*, including arguments, lying, poor achievement, social isolation, and fatigue resulting from excessive online behaviors. (Block 2008)

Interestingly, Internet gaming disorder (IGD), not IUD, has been identified in Section III of the *DSM–V*, released in 2013, as a condition warranting more clinical research and experience before it might be considered for full inclusion in the main mental health diagnostic book as a recognized disorder. The *DSM–V* stated that Internet gaming disorder is most common in male adolescents aged 12 to 20 years, and that mental health experts believe it is more prevalent in Asian countries than in North America and Europe, but this belief requires further study before it can be more readily accepted. Notably, Internet-based gambling is not included in the diagnostic criteria for IGD, because Internet-based gambling was already included in the gambling disorder diagnostic criteria in earlier versions of the *DSM* (Sarkis 2014).

Accepting these points, the *DSM–V* (American Psychiatric Association 2013) proposed the ongoing consideration and review of nine diagnostic criteria for Internet gaming disorder, based on many of the criteria earlier outlined by Dr. Block (2008) for IUD:

1. Having a preoccupation with Internet gaming,
2. Having withdrawal symptoms when the Internet is taken away or is not available,
3. Developing tolerance—having the need to spend increasing amounts of time engaged in Internet gaming,
4. Having unsuccessful attempts to control Internet gaming use,
5. Having ongoing, excessive Internet use despite knowledge of the negative psychosocial problems,
6. Experiencing a loss of interests, previous hobbies, or real-life entertainment as a result of excessive Internet gaming use,
7. Escaping or relieving a dysphoric (i.e., downward) mood by relying on Internet gaming,
8. Deceiving family members, therapists, or others regarding the amount of Internet gaming one is actually engaged in, and
9. Jeopardizing or losing a significant relationship, job, or educational or career opportunity because of excessive Internet gaming use. (American Psychiatric Association 2013)

To fill the absence of a measurement tool to properly assess Internet and gaming addictions, in 2014, researchers Cho and colleagues developed one for assessing game addiction in youth, in particular, based on the nine IGD criteria cited above. In all, 41 items were developed for the inventory using a 4-point Likert scale (ranging from 1 = not at all to 4 = always).

Sample items relevant to the nine criteria were developed by Cho and colleagues (2014), including the following:

- Preoccupation: "I feel like I am on the Internet even when I am not";
- Withdrawal: "I feel bored and joyless when I cannot be online";

- Tolerance: "I want to be online more when I am doing more";
- Unsuccessful attempts: "I cannot control the number of hours that I use the Internet";
- Continued excessive Internet use: "I want to go online even if I am scolded";
- Loss: "I don't want and can't be bothered to think of things other than the Internet";
- Escape: "I forget my problems when I am online";
- Deceive: "I hide my online history that shows what I did online"; and
- Jeopardize: "I stopped my daily routine due to Internet use." (Cho et al. 2014)

FURTHER CASE EXAMPLES OF INTERNET AND GAMING ADDICTION

Internet Addiction Case

In a 1996 academic article, Young (1996) reported the case of a 43-year-old, married homemaker who took part in her computer addiction studies. This woman said that, quite unlike the stereotypical young male computer geek who becomes computer-addicted because of his computer savviness, she was basically computer illiterate. She was able to go online by using the family's recently acquired personal computer only because of the menu-driven applications that were provided by her Internet service provider. At first, she said, she spent just a few hours online entertaining herself in chat rooms, defined as virtual communities where online users can chat with one another in real time. However, she affirmed, within just three months, she began to increasingly immerse herself in the virtual world, spending as much as 50 to 60 hours per week there.

The woman said that she developed a sense of community in the chat room. Though she often intended to spend at most 2 hours there in the mornings, she wound up spending as much as 14 hours in a single sitting. Besides partaking in online chats, she also confessed to constantly checking her e-mail. Eventually, she said, she would be online all night, finally cutting herself off from the virtual world in the early morning hours. The woman said that she experienced feelings of depression, anxiety, and irritability when she was not able to be on her computer; so, in order to avoid these adverse feelings, she tried to stay in the virtual world as long as she could. She stopped visiting with her friends, she cancelled appointments, and she reduced the amount of time spent with her family. Not only did she stop doing enjoyable activities like playing bridge with colleagues in her bridge club, but she stopped performing the normal routine chores of buying groceries or cleaning the house. Yet, despite this vast change in her behavior, the woman did not view her Internet addiction to be a problem that needed resolving (Young 1996).

Other family members began to complain about the woman's changed behaviors. Her two teenage daughters said that they felt ignored by her, and her husband of 17 years complained about the high Internet service provider fees that they were paying because of his wife's excessive time spent online—as much as $400 a month. He was extremely concerned, he openly shared with her, about her lack of interest in their marital relationship. Nonetheless, the woman insisted that her online behavior was normal, she was simply not addicted to the Internet, and she refused to get medical assistance for the so-called problem defined by her family members. In just one year from the family's purchase of the personal computer, the woman had become legally separated from her husband and was separated emotionally from her two daughters (Young 1996).

The woman finally admitted that she would need some kind of intervention by a mental health professional, because on her own, she said, she was unable to completely stop going online. She further admitted to still being unable to form a healthy, open relationship with her family members (Young 1996).

Gaming Addiction Cases

Freeman (2008) describes four brief scenarios of individuals who sought medical help for gaming addiction either because of their own recognized addiction to gaming or because of someone else's addiction to gaming. Interestingly, for all four individuals, there was an element of addiction to MMORPG. What makes MMORPG so addictive in nature?

For starters, MMORPG game players can be anywhere in the world, as long as they are connected by the Internet. Second, in MMORPG, game players can create their own characters that then interact with other players' characters in the virtual game as though they were in the real world. Third, the game objective for players is of a compelling nature; players engage in the online game to gain points so that they can buy powers, thereby advancing in the game, which can go on forever and is "addictively" played in real time.

One of the MMORPG-addicted players was a 30-year-old man named Bill with a college degree who went for medical treatment after his wife told him that he needed a psychiatric evaluation because of the inordinate amount of time he spent in the virtual world rather than in the real world. Another individual who sought help was a 41-year-old computer programmer named Jim. He said that he suffered from severe depression and suicidal ideation caused, in large part, because he was convinced that his wife of 13 years was having an online affair with another player in a MMORPG. The third person seeking help was a 39-year-old woman named Michelle. She admitted to being a recovering alcoholic, but she was seeking medical intervention for her depression, which she noted was worsening because of her fiance's inordinate amount of time spent playing MMORPGs with his brother. The fourth individual was a 27-year-old man named George who lived with his mother because he did not have steady employment. He sought medical help because he often would pass out in front of his computer. He tried to combat his fatigue by using methamphetamines so that he could play for up to 32 hours at a time, and he admitted to having a medical history of obsessive behaviors, depression, and substance abuse—including alcohol and drugs (Freeman 2008).

Worldwide Cases and Concerns

Though we have viewed a handful of Internet- and gaming-addicted cases presented by two authors, the number of reported concerns around the issue is growing annually and is worldwide in scope. Because as of yet there is no consistent definition or means to effectively assess the severity of Internet and gaming addiction in clients seeking medical assistance, it is difficult at this stage to determine actual prevalence rates for these addictions in the general population.

However, certain countries, particularly those in Asia, have attempted to publish estimates of the prevalence of these addictions in their populations. After data from the China Internet Network Information Center showed that 103 million people had gone online as of June 2005—of whom 15.8% were teenagers younger than 18 years—the problem of Internet addiction, particularly in these young "netizens," immediately attracted considerable attention from Asian psychiatrists and educators.

Researchers like Chou and Hsiao (2000) reported that the incidence rate of Internet addiction among Taiwan college students had been projected to be 5.9%, while Wu and Zhu (2004) projected that 10.6% of Chinese college students were Internet addicts.

In a more recent study by Cao and Su (2006), in their assessment of 2,620 Chinese adolescents having a mean age of 15 years, the estimated rate of their Internet usage was 88%, and their incidence of Internet addiction was projected to be 2.4%. These researchers also reported a significant gender difference in Internet addiction rates: of the 64 study participants identified as having an Internet addiction, 53 were males (83%), while 11 (17%) were females.

A study completed by Morahan-Martin and Schumacher in 2000 using 277 U.S. college students similarly found that pathological Internet users were more likely to be males than females. The males also tended to use online games and to be drawn to technologically sophisticated Web sites, compared to college students who did not present as Internet-addicted.

Along with a burgeoning interest in Internet and gaming addictions as a research topic, there is little question that patient-assist intervention centers are growing increasingly visible globally. As a case in point, the Chinese government not only placed a ban on opening new Internet cafes for its citizens but financed a treatment center for netizens with perceived addiction problems at the Beijing Military Region Central Hospital. In the United States, there are a number of addiction centers specifically focusing on the Internet and gaming, including the Illinois Institute for Addiction and the Impulse Control Disorders Clinic at Stanford University. In Amsterdam, there are many Internet addiction specialists affiliated with the Smith & Jones Addiction Consultants firm, and in Ecuador, The Center, Inc. serves clients with specialized treatment programs for online addictions. Web sites have also been developed by a number of these agencies to provide additional information and online support for addicted gamers and their concerned families and friends (Freeman 2008).

TRENDS AND CONTROVERSIES RELATED TO INTERNET AND GAMING ADDICTION

Is the Internet in and of Itself Addictive?

With the apparent rise in online and gaming addictions, experts are wondering if the Internet is in and of itself addictive. Take, as a case in point, the married, non-tech-savvy woman who became addicted to online chat rooms and e-mail reading once her family acquired their personal computer. Young (1996) spoke to this trend and controversy by noting, first, that with the recent surge in access to information technologies due to greater computer affordability and online service availability for the bulk of citizens in the developed world, there is a new generation of diverse computer users—and Internet and gaming addicts—who do not necessarily match the computer addict stereotype of a young, tech-savvy male.

Accepting the severity of the symptomology seen in the non-tech-savvy woman's case described by Young (1996) and in the four client cases provided by Freeman (2008), as well as in the increasing number of Internet and gaming addiction cases documented worldwide, there is little question that present and future research needs to focus on the prevalence, characteristics, consequences, and effective treatments for these types of addictive behaviors. However, mental health experts, at least at this stage, are reluctant to suggest that the Internet is addictive in and of itself.

The case of the non-tech-savvy woman further suggests, affirmed Young (1996), that certain risk factors may be associated with the development of addictive use of the Internet. First, the type of application used by the online user may be associated with a higher risk of Internet abuse. The woman in this case became addicted initially to online chat rooms, consistent with earlier research findings by Turkle (1995) indicating that highly interactive applications available online (like chat rooms and MMORPGs) likely play a more significant role in Internet- and gaming-abuse formation rather than simply having Internet access. Second, this woman reported a *sense of excitement* from her online activities when asked by her family members why she spent so much time in the virtual world. Thus, besides type of application, a special sense of arousal is also likely responsible for the various forms of Internet and gaming addictions as a result of clients' engaging in these arousing activities (Young 1996).

Keepers (1990) reported a similar high experienced and voiced by game addicts, as did Griffiths (1990) for gambling addicts. Taken as a composite, noted Young (1996), such relatively consistent findings imply that the level of excitement experienced by online users engaged in certain types of activities may be associated with the creation of and longer-term fueling of online addictions. However, affirmed Young (1996), present and future research needs to be undertaken to determine whether this type of online addictive behavior is implicated in or acts as a substitute for other established addictions currently detailed in the *DSM*, such as chemical dependencies, pathological gambling, and sexual addictions. Further research also needs to be undertaken to determine if Internet or gaming addictions act as a comorbid factor with other psychiatric disorders, notably, depression and obsessive-compulsive disorders.

Are Certain Kinds of Games More Controversial and Addictive Than Others?

Are certain kinds of games like MMORPG more controversial, more addictive, and thus more marketable to young people and adults than other games? Mental health experts have been trying to determine an answer to this very question for years.

As Freeman (2008) suggested, role-playing games from the early tabletop versions to the now hugely popular MMORPGs (which, again, can be played 24 hours a day by anyone anywhere in the real world) have been linked to controversy for quite some time—even in 1998 when the term MMORPG was initially believed to have been coined by the creators of the game Everquest. What's more, in the 1980s, the game Dungeons and Dragons was believed by many to be tied somehow to satanism, to an increase in suicide attempts by active game players, and to cultlike activity practices by some avid players in this genre. But despite these alleged links to aspects deemed quite controversial or even socially questionable, MMORPGs, in particular, continued to build on their early popularity globally. By 2006, the revenues for MMORPGs reached the billion-dollar level.

In looking at the four game-addicted cases earlier presented by Freeman (2008), readers might suspect that MMORPG players are particularly at risk for game addiction. Yet Freeman warns that just as not everyone who consumes alcohol will become an alcoholic, clearly not everyone who plays MMORPGs develops problematic behaviors or an outright addiction. While anyone with a predisposition can eventually become addicted to game play, Freeman (2008) notes that individuals born between 1977 and 1997 seem to be the most vulnerable, primarily because these individuals have been raised with readily available access to computers, video games, and the Internet. Regardless of the particular game genre, he posits, anyone who spends a considerable amount of his or her time online during waking hours—whether it be in chat rooms, in online game play, or checking e-mail—is already exhibiting signs of an addictive predisposition.

Freeman (2008) concludes that regardless of the particular kind of activities one is engaged in online, it is more important to note the equivalent amount of time spent online versus in real-world activities. When the equivalent amount of time spent online equals a full-time job but for nonessential purposes—then, reasonably, this pattern of behavior could lead to problems with one's ability to function in other areas of life. Thus, the line between healthy and pathological behaviors has historically been described as this: When the performance of life activities becomes a problem for an individual in question—whether this performance issue is related to drugs, alcohol, gambling, sex, shopping, eating, gaming, or online activities—then there is clearly a pathological and not a healthy behavioral and psychological pattern emerging.

As for gaming, the bottom line, affirmed Freeman (2008), is this critical point: Intense gamers often describe entering a zone—a flow experience where hours may be perceived to be seconds. Those who tend to experience this phenomenon seem, on record, to be more prone to game addiction, regardless of the game they are engaged in, but odds are that it is a MMORPG because of its very appealing psychological attachment. On the whole, MMORPG-addicted individuals tend to lie about or misrepresent the amount of time that they spend online. They inevitably lose interest in other routine life activities, enabling them to continue playing games online, despite the negative consequences.

According to Yee, (2002), more than 40% of online game players consider themselves to be addicted to MMORPGs, and, of these, about 5% to almost half said that they were unsuccessful at quitting their online playing.

PSYCHOLOGICAL AND PSYCHIATRIC COFACTORS UNDERLYING INTERNET AND GAMING ADDICTIONS

Cofactors of a Psychiatric Nature

The high percentage of psychiatric comorbidity in the substance-abusing or addictive population has been well documented in the mental health literature (Shapira et al. 2000). By definition, comorbidity is the extent to which two pathological conditions occur together in a given population. However, the documented percentage of comorbidity with Internet addiction, while the subject of considerable research being undertaken at this time, is not yet known (Freeman 2008).

From the literature established to date, documented comorbidity has been cited for gaming addiction and four psychiatric pathological conditions in particular (Christensen et al. 2001; Volkow 2004):

1. Mood disorders (including depression, bipolar disorders, and substance-induced mood disorders),
2. Anxiety disorders (including social phobias and generalized anxiety disorder),
3. Attentional disorders (including attention deficit disorder and attention deficit hyperactivity disorder), and
4. Substance use disorder (including amphetamine abuse or dependence and cocaine abuse or dependence).

Mood Disorders

Let us look more closely at how mental experts define mood disorders. It is important to note that the central notion in cognitive models of emotional disorders is that it is not events per se, but an individual's appraisal of events that is responsible for the production of anxiety, depression, and anger in human beings. In depression, the individual's interpretations that are considered to be important relate to perceived loss of a relationship, status, or competence (Schell 1997).

The term *depression* is used in a number of ways, but three are especially important: as a description of mood, to describe a syndrome, or to describe an illness. As a mood, depression is part of the normal range of experience, usually developing in response to some frustration or disappointment in life. The syndrome of depression consists of a depressive mood, together with other outward signs of distress like weight loss, inability to concentrate, and so on. Clinical depression is an illness involving the presence of the syndrome of depression and also implying that the state is not transitory but that it is associated with significant functional impairment. Individuals thus affected often cannot complete their daily living routines. Often, clinically depressed individuals are unable to work or are only able to do so with significantly reduced efficiency. Finally, excessive intake of substances like alcohol or drugs not only acts as a breeding ground for depression, but often exacerbates it (Schell 1997).

It is often claimed by mental health experts that there are actually two distinct types of depression, one known as psychotic or endogenous depression (which includes the depressive phase of a bipolar or manic-depressive illness) and the other known as neurotic or reactive depression. Endogenous depressions are further subdivided into unipolar (i.e., recurrent depression) and bipolar (manic-depressive types of illness), each having distinctive genetic and gender differences. Though the evidence for this dichotomy between endogenous and neurotic or reactive depression remains tenuous, experts globally often classify "cases" by it. In short, probably the best way to look at depression is via a continuum, with the typical psychotic stereotype placing at one end of the pole, the typical neurotic stereotype placing at the other pole, and the majority of depression sufferers placing somewhere between the two poles (Schell 1997).

Anxiety Disorders

In anxiety, the important cognitions center on perceived physical or psychosocial danger. Thus, in chronic anxiety states, individuals systematically overestimate the danger inherent in any given situation. Such overestimates automatically activate the anxiety program, which is a type of "flight" or "fight" response. Common behaviors include changes in an individual's autonomic arousal as preparation for fleeing, fighting, or fainting (which is a form of escape from the threatening stimulus).

Moreover, with chronic anxiety, there is typically an inhibition of ongoing and aspiring behaviors; thus, there is selective scanning of the environment for possible sources of danger. By definition, then, anxiety is "an unpleasant emotional experience varying in degree from mild unease to intense dread that is associated with the anticipation of impending or future disaster" (Schell 1997).

Research suggests there are two different types of anxiety: (1) recurrent panic attacks, and (2) generalized anxiety disorder, which is unrealistic or excessive worry. In recurrent panic attacks, which can occur unexpectedly and in almost any situation, individuals experience a sudden, intense feeling of apprehension or impending doom that is associated with a wide range of outward signs of distress, including the following: breathlessness, palpitations, chest pain, dizziness, tingling in the hands and feet, hot and cold flashes, sweating, faintness, trembling, and feelings of unreality. The unexpected and highly distressing nature of these outward signs leads the sufferers to think that they are in danger of some physical or mental disaster such as fainting, having a heart attack, losing control, or going insane. Whereas some sufferers experience calmness between the storms of panic, most sufferers remain chronically stressed between attacks, primarily because they ruminate about when the next attack will occur and where. Panic disorder often starts suddenly, with onsets commonly occurring in the mid- to late twenties (Schell 1997).

In generalized anxiety disorder arising out of basic life experiences, individuals suffer such wide-ranging outward signs of distress as muscle tension, twitching and shaking, restlessness, easy fatigue, breathlessness, palpitations, sweating, dry mouth, dizziness, nausea, diarrhea, flushes or chills, frequent urination, feeling on edge, difficulty concentrating, sleep disturbances, and irritability. Although thoughts associated with excessive worry and anxiety vary between individuals, they generally involve an appraisal of not being able to cope, of receiving negative evaluations from others at work or at home, and of experiencing diffuse health state concerns. Generalized anxiety states generally begin in the early teens or later (Schell 1997).

Attentional Disorders

Children and adolescents with an excess of hyperactive, inattentive, and impulsive behaviors are diagnosed currently to have attention deficit/hyperactivity disorder (ADHD). Currently, the third facet of ADHD, impulsivity, has become the focus of considerable research effort, and it has been strongly argued by mental health experts that "disinhibition" is central to distinguishing this disorder from others. Disinhibition is currently best operationalized as a failure by certain individuals to suppress inappropriate responding in, say, a go/no-go life task (Sergeant 2000).

Substance Abuse

The National Institute on Drug Abuse (NIDA) defines "addiction" as a chronic, reoccurring brain disease characterized by compulsive drug-seeking and use, despite its known harmful consequences. Simply put, drugs change the brain by changing its structure and how it works. Such changes not only can last for an extended period, but they often result in a number of self-destructive behaviors. Recent estimates indicate that American citizens' addiction to substances like alcohol, nicotine, and illegal and prescription drugs, as a composite, results in more than $700 billion a year in health care costs, crimes, and lost productivity in the workplace. An estimated 90,000 Americans die annually from legal and illegal drug abuse, and tobacco abuse results in 480,000 deaths annually (National Institute on Drug Abuse 2014).

Addiction is not a specific diagnosis in *DSM–V*, because in 2013, the American Psychiatric Association (APA) replaced the categories of substance abuse and substance dependence with one category: substance use disorder. Symptoms affiliated with this disorder include impaired control, impaired social relationships, risky use of substances, and the pharmacological aspects of tolerance and withdrawal. Furthermore, the *DSM–V* operationalizes "clinically-impairing or clinically-distressing" substance use as obvious client distress when at least two or more of the following item presentations manifest, as previously discussed (National Institute on Drug Abuse 2014): the user takes larger amounts of the substance or over a longer period than intended; the user either has a persistent desire to cut down or limit the use of the substance—without success; or the user has an intense craving or urge to use the substance.

How Mood Disorders, Anxiety Disorders, and ADHD Are Comorbid with Game Addiction

In the case studies described earlier in this chapter, it was quite clear that some of the clients experienced episodes of depression, anxiety, and mood disorders. However, since none of the cases talked about the presence of attention deficit disorders being present in the clients, first, we will look more closely at what mental health experts have reported is a possible link between ADHD and game addiction. Then, we will look at how mood disorders, anxiety disorders, and ADHD are comorbid with game addiction.

Without question, children's and adolescents' use of computer and video games is becoming highly popular, with dramatic increases seen in such game play over the last decade. In fact, researchers now report that the amount of time children spend in Internet, video game, and social media activities involves about three hours per day in the general population—with growing evidence of a high prevalence of computer game and video game addiction among children worldwide (as noted earlier in this chapter). There is also emerging evidence of an association between computer and video game addiction and ADHD, but it is not clear yet whether computer game and video game addiction meets the strict criteria for a syndrome, thus having it defined in *DSM–V*.

It is also not clear yet whether gaming addiction actually qualifies as a clinically significant pattern of behavioral, psychological, and physical symptoms causing inordinate amounts of distress or impairment in the addicted individuals. To the point: In 2007, the American Psychiatric Association (APA) considered whether or not video game addiction should be added to the *DSM–V*, but the mental health reviewers concluded that there was insufficient evidence to include computer game addiction as a psychiatric disorder, as earlier noted. Though experts tend to agree that recent studies are indicating that ADHD is a risk factor for the duration of time children and adolescents spend playing computer games and video games, what is less well understood are the physiological and neuropharmacological mechanisms that underlie both disorders—which may shed light on future diagnosis and treatment issues, once clarified (Weinstein and Weizman 2012).

Of the first three disorders defined above (i.e., depression, anxiety, and ADHD), it is becoming increasingly clear that ADHD is the most common psychiatric disorder among adolescents with Internet addiction who have been referred for psychiatric treatment. Further, it is becoming clear that ADHD can predict the occurrence of Internet addiction two years later in adolescents. Mental health experts now believe that several rather complex bio-psycho-social mechanisms might explain the coexistence of Internet or game addiction and ADHD (Yen et al. 2014).

First, since Internet behavior is generally characterized by rapid response and immediate rewards, this environment may provide immediate stimulation and rewards for individuals with ADHD—who become easily bored and have an aversion to delayed rewards. Second, since most individuals with ADHD tend to be attracted to enhanced stimulations with quick reward paths, Internet games with their "get to the next game level" incentives present a very attractive quick reward path for players with ADHD. Third, since, as noted, adolescents with ADHD have abnormal brain activities associated with impaired inhibition, and they have difficulty in controlling or limiting their Internet use, they are more vulnerable to Internet and game addiction relative to others in the general population. Fourth, because ADHD symptoms can also negatively impact adolescents' interpersonal relationships, they may choose to form social relationships in a virtual world rather than in the real world. Taken as a composite, the association between ADHD and Internet and game addiction suggests that adolescents with ADHD seem like a sound target group for understanding preventive scheduling for Internet and game addictions (Yen et al. 2014).

Besides ADHD, anxiety and depression are two psychological symptoms prevalent in individuals with Internet and game addiction, but some of the key issues linking the relationships of Internet and game addiction with anxiety and depression in adolescents diagnosed with ADHD have not been investigated in depth. However, research studies have found that more than one-third of adolescents with ADHD have comorbid anxiety disorders, and that generalized anxiety disorder but not social phobia is the most prevalent diagnosis co-occurring with ADHD in children and adolescents. Furthermore, from 5% to 40% of children and teens with ADHD meet the criteria for major depression (Yen et al. 2014).

To help fill this void, the research team of Yen and colleagues (2014) investigated the relationships of Internet and game addiction with multiple dimensions of anxiety and depression in adolescents clinically diagnosed with ADHD. A total of 287 Taiwan adolescents between the ages of 11 and 18 years who had been diagnosed with ADHD and Internet addiction symptoms—and accompanying kinds of anxiety (i.e., physical anxiety symptoms, harm avoidance, social anxiety, and panic), depression symptoms (i.e., depressed affect, somatic or bodily symptoms, and interpersonal problems), and self-esteem issues—were given a battery of tests including the Chen Internet Addiction Scale, the Taiwanese version of the Multidimensional Anxiety Scale for Children (MASC-T), the Center for Epidemiological Studies Depression (CES-D) Scale, and the Rosenberg Self-Esteem Scale (RSES).

The study results indicated that higher physical symptoms and lower harm-avoidance scores on the MASC-T anxiety scale, higher somatic and bodily discomfort scales on the CES-D depression scale, and lower self-esteem scores on the RSES were significantly associated with more severe Internet addiction symptoms. The researchers concluded that future prevention and intervention programs for adolescents with Internet and gaming addictions as well as ADHD should take into serious consideration clients' anxiety, depression, and self-esteem treatment (Yen et al. 2014).

How Substance Abuse Is Comorbid with Game Addiction

Several recent studies have reported that the risk of Internet and game addiction is associated with an increased prevalence of substance dependence (Bakken et al. 2009; Padilla-Walker et al. 2010).

However, note researchers, the participants in most of these studies have been adults, not adolescents—the population that has been identified as being at particular risk for these kinds of addictions (Young 2009b; Freeman 2008). Adolescence alone, regardless of the involvement in the Internet, is an extremely challenging and complex transition for young individuals. Put bluntly, exploring and trying to discover one's identity as an adolescent can be an overwhelming stage in one's life. If the adolescent is using online gaming or some other substance as an escape, it is more than likely that many more obstacles will be encountered. Consequently, the teen will struggle with unmanageable physical and emotional consequences (Kelly 2004; Young 2009b).

Furthermore, in these studies focusing on the comorbidity of game and substance addiction, the number of participants surveyed typically has not been sizable enough to show significant comorbidity with these two kinds of addictions.

From a substance-addiction angle, since adolescence is a critical time in individuals' lives commonly characterized by risk-taking behavior, greater novelty-seeking, and intimate personal relationships, it seems reasonable that recent estimates by experts indicate that 12% of U.S. 8th graders (i.e., children 13–14 years old) and 22% of U.S. 10th graders (i.e., young adults 15–16 years old) admitted to episodes of heavy alcohol drinking within the past two years (Johnston et al. 2004).

It seems reasonable, then, to conjecture that an overlap between Internet addiction or gaming addiction and substance abuse may be due to similar characteristics predisposing adolescents with similar temperaments toward—and their developing brain regions responding to—Internet heavy use or substance heavy use with alcohol or cocaine. In fact, in a recent study of 686 high school students, Cho, Kim, Kim, Lee, and Kim (2008) reported that Korean adolescents with problematic Internet use showed higher self-directedness and cooperativeness and lower scores in novelty-seeking and self-transcendence when they were administered a temperament and character inventory.

Furthermore, in a study of 166 high school students, Lee and colleagues (2008) reported that adolescents manifesting excessive Internet use also showed higher harm avoidance relative to healthy comparison adolescents. In another recent study by Ando and colleagues (2012), 88 adolescents having pronounced alcohol dependence and higher harm avoidance were unable to abstain from drinking excessively for a considerable period of time.

Mental health experts now believe that adolescents having both Internet and substance addiction may also share similar vulnerable brain regions, particularly the dorsolateral and orbitofrontal cortices (Crockford et al. 2005; Han, Hwang, and Renshaw 2010).

Given these study findings indicating considerable overlap and similar traits in adolescents with Internet and substance abuse, the research team of Lee, Han, Kim, and Renshaw (2013) investigated possible overlapping substance abuse and Internet addiction in a large, uniformly sampled population of Korean students ranging in age from 13 to 18 years. Just over 73,000 students from 400 middle schools and 400 high schools in 16 cities within South Korea participated in the Web-based survey. The majority of students, 85.2%, were considered to be general Internet users (GU), 11.9% were considered to be Internet users with potential risk for addiction (PR), and 3.0% were considered to be at high risk for Internet addiction (HR).

In the GU group, 20.8% of the respondents admitted to drinking alcohol, 11.7% admitted to smoking, and 1.7% admitted to using drugs. In the PR group, 23.1% of the respondents admitted to drinking alcohol, 13.5% admitted to smoking, and 2% admitted to using drugs. In the HR group, 27.4% of the respondents admitted to drinking alcohol, 20.4% admitted to smoking, and 6.5% admitted to using drugs. After adjusting for sex, age, stress, depressed mood, and suicidal ideation, the researchers reported that smoking and drug use, in particular, seem to predict a high risk for Internet addiction. They concluded by saying that because students with a high risk for Internet addiction have vulnerability for addictive behaviors, comorbid substance abuse should be evaluated and, if found, treated in adolescents with Internet and possibly gaming addictions (Lee et al. 2013).

TREATMENTS FOR INTERNET AND GAMING ADDICTION

Treatments for Internet Addiction

Cognitive behavioral therapy (CBT) has been shown to be an effective treatment for compulsive disorders, such as pathological gambling, as well as for substance abuse, emotional disorders like recurrent panic attacks, and eating disorders (Hucker 2004; Beck et al. 1993). In CBT, clients are taught not only to monitor their thoughts in order to identify those provoking addictive feelings and actions, but to hone new coping skills and other means to prevent relapses from occurring.

For example, because anxiety is a cognition disorder coupled with inappropriate behavior, effective treatments for this disorder usually include some form of cognitive behavioral therapy. CBT aims to reduce anxiety, generally, and panic attacks, specifically, by teaching individuals how to identify, evaluate, control, and modify their negative thoughts as a means of decreasing impending feelings of doom; this protocol typically requires CBT sessions lasting from 5 to 20 weeks. An illustration of the cognitive procedures used for "breaking" chronic panic attacks is presented below. In this example, the therapist (Th) is Dr. David Clark from the University of Oxford, one of the world's leading experts on effectively using CBT for treating anxiety. He is attempting to help the client (Cl) challenge his erroneous belief that he will faint and collapse during a panic attack.

Cl: In the middle of a panic attack, I usually think I am going to faint or collapse.

Th: How much do you believe that sitting here right now and how much would you believe it if you had the sensations you get in an attack?

Cl: 50% and 90% in an attack.

Th: OK, let's look at the evidence you have for this thought. Have you ever fainted in an attack?

Cl: No.

Th: What is it then that makes you think you might faint?

Cl: I feel faint and the feeling can be very strong.

Th: So, to summarize, your evidence that you are going to faint is the fact that you feel faint?

Cl: Yes.

Th: How can you then account for the fact that you have felt faint many hundreds of times and have not yet fainted?

Cl: So far, the attacks have always stopped just in time or I have managed to hold onto something to stop myself from collapsing.

Th: Right. So, one explanation of the fact that you have frequently felt faint, had the thought that you will faint, but have not actually fainted, is that you have always done something to save yourself in time. However, an alternative explanation is that the feeling of faintness that you get in a panic attack will never lead you to collapsing, even if you don't control it.

Cl: Yes, I suppose so.

Th: In order to decide which of these two possibilities is correct, we need to know what has to happen to your body for you to actually faint. Do you know?

Cl: No.

Th: Your blood pressure needs to drop. Do you know what happens to your blood pressure during a panic attack?

Cl: Well, my pulse is racing. I guess my blood pressure must be up.

Th: That's right. In anxiety, heart rate and blood pressure tend to go together. So, you are actually *less* likely to faint when you are anxious than when you are not.

Cl: That's very interesting and helpful to know. However, if that's true, [why] do I feel so faint?

Th: Your feeling of faintness is a sign that your body is reacting in a normal way to the perception of danger. Most of the bodily reactions you are experiencing when anxious were probably designed to deal with the threats experienced by primitive man, such as being approached by a hungry tiger. What would be the best thing to do in that situation?

Cl: Run away as fast as you can.

Th: That's right. Now, on the basis of what we've discussed so far, how much do you believe you might faint in a panic attack?

Cl: Less, say 10%.

Th: And if you were experiencing the sensations?

Cl: Maybe 25%. (Clark 1989, 76–77)

The typical range for CBT for most disorders is from three to four months, or about 12 weekly sessions with a mental health professional. At the early stages of CBT, the therapy is behavioral in nature, with a focus on specific behaviors or life situations where a client's impulse control disorder causes the greatest difficulty. As the CBT sessions evolve, the focus tends to move to the cognitive assumptions and distortions that have become ingrained in the user, triggering the compulsive behavior and various adverse effects. For Internet addiction, in particular, the therapist will advocate moderated and controlled use of the Internet by the user, with the primary goal of abstaining from problematic applications of Internet behavior (such as watching online pornography), while retaining controlled use of the computer for legitimate employment purposes (Orzack 1999; Greenfield 1999).

As a case in point, a lawyer who seeks help for Internet addiction would be encouraged by the therapist to abstain from visiting adult Web sites, while still being able to access the Internet to conduct legal searches and to e-mail clients (Young 2009a).

Near the beginning, suggestions for a routine change may be in order. If, say, a client's Internet habit involves checking e-mail first thing in the morning, the therapist may suggest that the client take a shower or start breakfast first thing instead of going online. If the client tends to use the Internet nightly and has a pattern of returning home from work and then sitting in front of the computer for the rest of the night, the therapist might suggest waiting until after dinner and after the news broadcast before heading online. If the user goes online every weeknight, have him or her wait until the weekend, or if he or she is an all-weekend user, have him or her shift to just weekdays (Young 2007).

Moreover, the goal-setting plan must be specific, structured, and reasonable. To avoid relapse, the therapist may encourage the client to spend 20 hours online (instead of a current 40 hours) by scheduling those 20 hours in specific time slots and writing them into a weekly planner. The client should keep the Internet sessions brief but frequent to help avoid cravings and withdrawal. As an example of a 20-hour schedule, the client might plan to use the Internet from 8 to 10 p.m. every weeknight and from 1 to 6 on Saturday and Sunday (Young 1999).

If this online goal-setting moderation plan is not effective, then abstinence from particular applications may be required. If a particular trigger (like chat room, interactive games, or e-mail) is the most problematic for the user, then abstinence from that particular application is the next appropriate intervention. While the client must stop all online activity involving that application, less appealing online applications can still be allowed.

Generally, abstinence is most applicable for the client who also has a history of a prior addiction, such as alcoholism or drug use, where he or she often finds the Internet to be a physically "safe" substitute addiction. Unfortunately, while the client justifies the Internet as a "safe" addiction, he or she still avoids dealing with the compulsive personality or the unpleasant situation triggering the addictive behavior. In these cases, such clients may feel more comfortable working toward an abstinence goal, as their prior recovery from substance abuse likely involved this model (Young 1999).

In CBT, there are also noncomputer or non-Internet behavior goals that are reinforced, such as helping clients to take on positive lifestyle changes not involving online activities—such as trying new "off-line" hobbies, attending social gatherings in the real world instead of the virtual world, and becoming more involved in family activities that have fallen by the wayside (Young 2009a).

To help the client work toward a new, general lifestyle routine that is less computer intensive, the therapist may recommend that the client develop a personal inventory of what he or she has cut down on or cut out completely because of the time spent online. Perhaps the client is spending less time hiking, golfing, fishing, camping, or dating. Or maybe the client puts off trying new things like attending a fitness club.

The therapist should have the client rank each new desired life activity using a scale from 1 (very important) to 3 (not very important). The client should genuinely reflect on how life was before the Internet, particularly the very important items. By having the client focus on how these activities improved the quality of his or her life, this exercise will assist the client in becoming more aware of the choices he or she made regarding the Internet and, thus, rekindle the lost activities that were once enjoyed. This is a means of helping clients recultivate pleasant feelings about real-life activities rather than engaging in virtual world activities that are euphoric and emotionally fulfilling (Young 1999).

To be less anxious in the "real world" so that the client feels less disposed to escape into the virtual world, besides CBT, Young (2009a) suggests that other remedies such as assertion training, behavioral rehearsal, coaching, support groups (like those found at the McLean Hospital in Belmont, Massachusetts, and Proctor Hospital in Peoria, Illinois), and relaxation training have been shown to be effective. Finally, family therapy should be recommended for marriages and family relationships that have been disrupted and negatively influenced by Internet addiction (Young 1999).

In 1998, Young first reported that catastrophic thinking might most strongly contribute to compulsive Internet use in providing a nice psychological escape mechanism to avoid the real world and its perceived problems. Subsequent studies have reinforced the notion that other maladaptive cognitions such as overgeneralizing or catastrophizing, fixating on negative core beliefs, and living in a real world with cognitive distortions all contribute to compulsive use of the Internet. There is little question that CBT can be effectively used to address this constellation of negative core beliefs, cognitive distortions, and rationalizations (i.e., "just a few more minutes online will not hurt") so that the client can once again feel comfortable living in the real world rather than in the virtual world (Young 2009a).

Treatments for Gaming Addictions

Young (2009b) points out that when deciding upon a sound regimen for treating clients with gaming addictions, therapists need to take into special consideration the determined protocol if the client is an adolescent instead of an adult. While most adults voluntarily seek therapy for their gaming addictions, for most adolescents, referral to treatment is involuntary and is usually mandated by parents, teachers, or the judicial system. When asked of adolescent or teen clients in "Intake" what the problem is, the most common answers are: "Don't know" or "Somebody (such as a family member, teacher, or policeman) just overreacted." When pressed, most adolescents would say that not only are they doing nothing different from their peers, they often will then go on to explain that they are not online as much as other friends of theirs who play the same or similar games.

Therefore, Young (2009b) posits, successful treatment must not only address the gaming behavior but also assist an adolescent in navigating the normal developmental tasks of identity formation, so often neglected while using gaming as a means of coping with life's problems. Treatment for adolescents should thus focus on effective problem-solving and social skills necessary to build self-esteem in clients. For example, therapists may want to increase communication skills among adolescent clients by enlisting the help of an older, trusted friend or sibling to engage an adolescent client in short conversations and to help develop his or her real-world social interaction skills. Therapists often use books, magazines, and television to teach an adolescent client about facial expressions by having them learn others' body language in order to better understand what the other person is feeling. Role-playing conversations are also helpful in building client confidence; here, clients can practice using eye contact when speaking to other people and to hone their active listening skills—which they cannot typically do online.

Parents often fall into an enabling role with a gaming-addicted adolescent, since they may tend to make excuses for their children when they skip school or fail to meet deadlines. It is important for parents to learn effective intervention efforts that support but do not enable addictive behavior. To this point, therapists need to focus energy here as well as on the client. Parents also need to establish clear time limits with the teen or child about what is an appropriate time spent online. Though obvious at first glance, this is an important step in the intervention protocol. Because adolescence is a time of experimentation with new freedoms (such as going out with friends late at night or learning to drive), freedom to use the Internet at will is considered by many parents to be a normal part of growing up—making it even harder for parents to establish clear time limits. But parents need to set limits around online game-playing time. There is special software available to help parents monitor and control their children's Internet use, if other less invasive means seem to fail (Young 2009b).

Furthermore, besides these behavioral interventions, notes Freeman (2008), when comorbid disorders with Internet and gaming addictions are present, client outcomes are greatly improved if they are addressed concurrently. As with other addictions or dependencies, the most effective treatments are a combination of psychopharmacology and psychotherapy, such as CBT. A number of twelve-step programs have also shown promise in their effectiveness for clients (see, for example, Wieland 2005). Also, the role of the neurotransmitters norepinephrine and dopamine when there is a concurrent addiction to gaming and to substances is widely accepted.

However, when the client's addiction is primarily a behavior (like excessive gaming) and does not involve substance abuse, research has shown dopamine and serotonin involvement to be useful. Both selective serotonin reuptake inhibitors and antipsychotic medications, given alone or in combination, have been shown to be effective in a number of recent published clinical trials and case studies. Other treatment options studied by researchers for impulse control disorders are wide-ranging and frequently useful—including lithium and mood stabilizers, opioid antagonists, tricyclic antidepressants, selective serotonin and norepinephrine reuptake inhibitors, benzodiazepines, the norepinephrine dopamine reuptake inhibitor bupropion, and beta-blockers (Freeman 2008).

Sometimes in gaming addictions, other features of the illness will be focused on by the therapist. For example, although not necessarily related to all MMORPGs, the strong sexual nature of some games has been noted and, thus, attended to by mental health experts. In the mental health field, "cybersex" is often referred to as the "crack cocaine of sex addiction," so a specially devised addiction model of treatment is applied therapeutically. Moreover, the function of the monoamine neurotransmitters, serotonin, norepinephrine, and dopamine, are frequently used by therapists as the model for treating addictions and other compulsive behaviors. Without question, this area of research appears to be the future of pharmacologic psychiatric treatment, and this area is developing rapidly as a means of providing relief to addicted gamers (Freeman 2008).

For readers interested in knowing what treatment protocols were followed for the four client cases earlier described by Freeman (2008), and their effectiveness for these clients, what follows are brief updates. For some of these clients, there were medication regimens that were tried but were unsuccessful, so the therapist continued to search for improved regimens. It needs to be underscored that not all of these cases were success stories, because some of the clients were at times noncompliant with either their prescribed medications or with the psychotherapy regimens. The "bottom line," affirms Freeman, is that addictions are many times difficult to treat. Countertransference issues (defined as the incompletely recognized emotional reactions a physician has toward a patient or his or her circumstances) also make dealing with this population difficult for many practitioners. In short, therapists' understanding of the chronic nature and psychopathology of addictions can help them better manage clients' protocols.

As to the four clients earlier described, Bill has required inpatient treatment in a psychiatric facility twice because of severe depression, suicidal ideation, and auditory hallucinations. His medical condition was eventually diagnosed as a bipolar disorder. He is currently stable on duloxetine, aripiprazole, and zolpidem. His family relationships have improved, and he is doing well in his studies in game technology and creation. Although the therapist recommended to Bill that he undergo CBT, he said that he was not interested.

Jim has filed for divorce and has moved into his own apartment. He appears to have resolved most of his issues, although he continues CBT. He is considering filing for custody of his three children, and he says that his wife continues to partake in online game activities. Consequently, he says that he doubts he can trust her again. He was treated with escitalopram for one year, at which point Jim decided to stop taking medication. He appears to be doing well.

Michelle takes her medication in a compliant manner, as she has been diagnosed as having bipolar disorder. She remains with her fiancé, who has agreed to spend less time online because he is now working full-time and he will no longer play games while she is in the home. Her medications are oxcarbazepine and citalopram. Although couples therapy was recommended, they have not tried to find a therapist.

Finally, George remains unemployed. He denies any illegal drug use, and he is still abusing alcohol periodically. The amount of time he spends playing online games has decreased, primarily because his mother no longer has Internet service in the home. He is intermittently compliant with taking his prescriptions of citalopram, bupropion, and divalproex, but he has not shown an interest in a recommended CBT option.

For readers wanting additional insights about effectively treating clients with Internet and gaming addictions, see the interview with Dr. Kimberly Young presented in the Interview with an Expert sidebar.

INTERVIEW WITH AN EXPERT

Dr. Kimberly Young, Expert in Internet Addiction

In 1995, Dr. Kimberly Young started the Center for Internet Addiction to treat clients who are addicted to the Internet in a number of dysfunctional ways. Dr. Young developed a specialized form of cognitive behavioral therapy

(CBT) for internet addiction, the first evidence-based Digital Detox™ recovery program, known as CBT-IA. A registered psychologist in the United States, Dr. Young's practice includes private sessions for clients with Internet addictions, workshops for therapists on the latest techniques that produce positive results, forensic assessments for legal matters, and corporate consulting. Her Web site, Netaddiction.com, is a valuable educational resource providing online users academic articles, books for further reading, and self-assessment inventories like the Internet Addiction Test, or IAT, to help them ascertain if they have an Internet addiction problem.

Q You are a recognized expert in Internet addictions. Why and how did you become interested in this field?

A Internet addiction began as a pet project in a young researcher's one-bedroom apartment in Rochester, New York. I was that young researcher. It was 1995 and the husband of a friend of mine was seemingly addicted to AOL chat rooms, spending 40, 50, 60 hours online at a time when it was still $2.95 per hour to dial into the Internet. Not only did they suffer financial burdens but their marriage ended in divorce when he met women in online chat rooms.

Q In 1996, you gave a talk in Toronto at the American Psychological Association's annual convention and used the term "computer addiction," and you later referred to "computer-addicted types" as spending, on average, 38 hours per week online. Given today's technology, do you think that this number is still valid?

A The first study on Internet addiction shortly followed, as I collected over 600 similar case studies of people who suffered from relationship problems, academic problems, financial problems, and job loss because they were unable to control their Internet use. This study was the one presented at the APA entitled "Internet Addiction: The Emergence of a New Disorder," now a cited paper. Studies in China, Korea, and Taiwan emerged in the early 2000s. Historically, this was a pivotal moment, as the research led to the development of inpatient treatment facilities.

Today, no one looks at time as a symptom, but rather it is a set of criteria [it would be like counting the number of drinks to diagnose alcoholism—it is not quantified as much as looked at as a set of behaviors]. Today, the widely used Internet Addiction Diagnostic Questionnaire is on the homepage of our center's Web site at http://netaddiction.com.

Q If someone thinks that he or she is computer-addicted, what would be your proposed strategy nowadays for helping them deal effectively with such?

A In 2006, the first inpatient center to treat Internet addiction opened in Beijing, China. The Asian cultures seemingly had significant problems dealing with problem Internet use compared to the rest of the world, although we have been treating Internet addiction all this time and we look at CBT-IA as the main form of treatment. You can read more on our first steps in this approach online at http://netaddiction.com/wp-content/uploads/2012/10/JCP.CBT-IA.pdf.

Q So, is the Internet bad because it can result in addiction? Please explain.

A No, I don't think it is bad. The Internet is a practical tool. We use it each day, and I think we have more productive uses of it [than harms]. I am pro-Internet.

Q How does the fact that most people must use the Internet for school or work complicate the treatment process?

A We use terms like *digital diet* and *digital nutrition* with clients and tell them to see the Internet as a practical tool that one must *balance*. With that said, we do not have people use online porn who are addicted to porn, or if they are addicted to games, they can't game again, but they can check e-mail for work, do homework online for school, and make online travel plans. Healthy digital nutrition is like healthy eating—there is a distinct difference between eating healthy fruits and veggies or eating a bag of chips or doughnuts.

Q Do you think that society condones or encourages Internet addiction—and why?

A I think the United States is way behind other countries who have advanced this "pro" and "con" debate to find ways that people can use technology without being consumed by it. Korea, for instance, has this entire master plan for the prevention and treatment of Internet addiction. It is very comprehensive and starts teaching young children the pros and cons of technology at early ages. In the United States, we do nothing. We need to bring awareness to our schools and our children that technology can be misused and addictive.

Q Where do you think that the future research focus on Internet addiction will likely be?

A I think it will focus on early childhood development and the impact of technology on our brains. There is significant research already on the role of the prefrontal cortex in Internet addiction (see http://ncbi.nlm.nih.gov/pmc/articles/PMC4034340/).

So, as young children use technology, we will worry and study the social, developmental, and cognitive impact.

CONCLUSION

This chapter looked at the intricacies between Internet and gaming addictions and how they might be related to other addictions, such as alcohol and drugs. What became obvious early is that mental health professionals are still grappling with whether or not these disorders need to be included in mental health diagnostic manuals like the *DSM*, despite the fact that there are mounting concerns worldwide that there is quickly becoming an epidemic on this addiction front that needs some real answers in definition, in measurement, and in treatment. Even the American Psychiatric Association suggests that future issues of the *DSM* may find it useful and appropriate to define one or both of these addictions as a recognized mental health disorder. Meanwhile, further research needs to be conducted that more clearly defines the comorbidity features and appropriate treatment regimens for those who suffer from Internet and gaming addictions.

REFERENCES

American Psychiatric Association. (2000). *Diagnostic and statistical manual of mental disorders* (4th ed., text rev.). Washington, DC: Author.

American Psychiatric Association. (2013). *Diagnostic and statistical manual of mental disorders* (5th ed.). Washington, DC: Author.

Ando, B., Must, A., Kurgyis, E., Szkaliczki, A., Drotos, G., Rozsa, S., et al. (2012). Personality traits and coping compensate for disadvantageous decision-making in long-term alcohol abstinence. *Alcohol and Alcoholism, 47*, 18–24.

Bakken, I. J., Wenzel, H. G., Gotestam, K. G., Johansson, A., & Oren, A. (2009). Internet addiction among Norwegian adults: A stratified probability sample study. *Scandinavian Journal of Psychology*, *50*, 121–127.

Beck, A. T., Wright, F. D., Newman, C. F., & Liese, B. S. (1993). *Cognitive therapy of substance abuse*. New York, NY: Guilford.

Block, J. (2008). Issues for DSM-V: Internet addiction. *American Journal of Psychiatry, 165*, 306–307.

Cao, F., & Su, L. (2006). Internet addiction among Chinese adolescents: Prevalence and psychological features. *Child: Care, Health and Development, 33,* 275–281.

Cho, H., Kwon, M., Choi, J-H., Lee, S-K., Choi, J. S., Choi, S-W., & Kim, D-J. (2014). Development of the Internet addiction scale based on the Internet gaming disorder criteria suggested in DSM-5. *Addictive Behaviors, 39,* 1361–1366.

Cho, S. C., Kim, J. W., Kim, B. N., Lee, J. H., & Kim, E. H. (2008). Biogenetic temperament and character profiles and attention deficit hyperactivity disorder symptoms in Korean adolescents with problematic Internet use. *Cyberpsychology, Behavior, and Social Network, 11,* 735–737.

Chou, C., & Hsiao, M. C. (2000). Internet addiction, usage, gratification, and pleasure experience: The Taiwan college students' case. *Computers and Education, 35,* 65–80.

Christensen, M., Orzack, M., Babington, L., & Patsdaughter, C. (2001). Computer addiction: When monitor becomes control center. *Journal of Psychosocial Nursing and Mental Health Services, 39,* 40–47.

Clark, D. M. (1989). Anxiety states: Panic and generalized anxiety. In K. Hawton, P. Salkovskis, J. Kirk, & D. M. Clark (Eds.), *Cognitive behavior therapy for psychiatric problems: A practical guide* (pp. 53–96). Oxford: Oxford University Press.

Crockford, D. N., Goodyear, B., Edwards, J., Quickfall, J., & el-Guebaly, N. (2005). Cue-induced brain activity in pathological gamblers. *Biological Psychiatry, 58,* 787–795.

Freeman, C. B. (2008). Internet gaming addiction. *Journal for Nurse Practitioners, 4,* 42–47.

Goldberg, I. (1996). Internet addiction disorder (IAD): Diagnostic criteria. Retrieved from http://www.rider.edu/~suler/psycyber/supportgp.html

Goodman, A. (1993). Diagnosis and treatment of sexual addiction. *Journal of Sex and Marital Therapy, 19,* 225–251.

Greenfield, D. (1999). *Virtual addiction: Help for netheads, cyberfreaks, and those who love them.* Oakland, CA: New Harbinger.

Griffiths, M. (1990). The cognitive psychology of gambling. *Journal of Gambling Studies, 6,* 31–42.

Griffiths, M. (1992). Pinball wizard: The case of a pinball machine addict. *Psychological Reports, 71,* 161–162.

Griffiths, M. (1995). Technological addictions. *Clinical Psychology Forum, 71,* 14–19.

Han, D. H., Hwang, J. W., & Renshaw, P. F. (2010). Bupropion sustained release treatment decreases craving for video games and cue-induced brain activity in patients with Internet video game addiction. *Experimental and Clinical Psychopharmacology, 18*, 297–304.

Hucker, S. J. (2004). Disorders of impulse control. In W. O'Donohue & E. Levensky (Eds.), *Forensic psychology*. New York, NY: Academic Press.

Huizinga, J. (1938). *Homo ludens: A study of the play-element in culture*. Boston: Beacon Press.

Johnston, L. D., O'Malley, P. M., Bachman, J. G., & Schulenberg, J. E. (2004). *Monitoring the future, national survey results on drug use, 1975–2004* (NIH Publication No. 05–5727 1). Secondary school students.

Keepers, C. A. (1990). Pathological preoccupation with video games. *Journal of the American Academy of Child and Adolescent Psychiatry, 29,* 49–50.

Kelly, R.V. (2004). *Massively multi player online role playing games. The people, the addiction, and the playing*. Jefferson, NC: McFarland and Co., Inc.

Kuss, D. J., & Griffiths, M. D. (2012). Internet gaming addiction: A systematic review of empirical research. *International Journal of Mental Health and Addiction, 10,* 278–296.

Lacey, H. J. (1993). Self-damaging and addictive behavior in bulimia nervosa: A catchment area study. *British Journal of Psychiatry, 163,* 190–194.

Lam, L. T. (2014). Internet gaming addiction, problematic use of the Internet, and sleep problems: A systematic review. *Current Psychiatry Reports, 16,* 444–453.

Lee, Y. S., Han, D. H., Kim, S. M., & Renshaw, P. F. (2013). Substance abuse precedes internet addiction. *Addictive Behaviors, 38,* 2022–2025.

Lee, Y. S., Han, D. H., Yang, K. C., Daniels, M. A., Na, C., Kee, B. S., et al. (2008). Depression-like characteristics of 5HTTLPR polymorphism and temperament in excessive internet users. *Journal of Affective Disorders, 109,* 165–169.

Lesher, A. I. (1997). Addiction is a brain disease, and it matters. *Science, 278,* 807–808.

Lesieur, H. R., & Blume, S. B. (1993). Pathological gambling, eating disorders, and the psychoactive substance use disorders. *Comorbidity of Addictive and Psychiatric Disorders, 12,* 89–102.

Mehroof, M., & Griffiths, M. D. (2010). Online gaming addiction: The role of sensation seeking, self-control, neuroticism, aggression, state anxiety, and trait anxiety. *Cyberpsychology & Behavior, 13,* 313–316.

Morahan-Martin, J., & Schumacher, P. (2000). Incidence and correlates of pathological Internet use among college students. *Computers in Human Behavior, 16,* 13–29.

National Institute on Drug Abuse. (2014). The science of drug abuse and addiction: The basics. Retrieved from http://www.drugabuse.gov/publications/media-guide/science-drug-abuse-addiction-basics

Orzack, M. (1999). Computer addiction: Is it real or is it virtual? *Harvard Mental Health Letter, 15,* 8.

Padilla-Walker, L. M., Nelson, L. J., Carroll, J. S., & Jensen, A. C. (2010). More than just a game: Video game and Internet use during emerging adulthood. *Journal of Youth and Adolescence, 39,* 103–113.

Quittner, J. (1997, April 14). Divorce Internet style. *Time,* 72.

Rachlin, H. (1990). Why do people gamble and keep gambling despite heavy losses? *Psychological Science, 1,* 294–297.

Sarkis, S. (2014). Internet gaming disorder in *DSM-5*. Retrieved from http://www.psychologytoday.com/blog/here-there-and-everywhere/201407/internet-gaming-disorder-in-dsm-5

Schell, B. H. (1997). *A self-diagnostic approach to understanding organizational and personal stressors: The C-O-P-E model for stress reduction*. Westport, CT: Quorum Books.

Schell, B. H., Dodge, J. L., & Moutsatsos, S. S. (2002). *The hacking of America: Who's doing it, why, and how.* Westport, CT: Quorum Books.

Sergeant, J. (2000). The cognitive energetic model: An empirical approach to attention-deficit hyperactivity disorder. *Neuroscience and Biobehavioral Reviews*, *24,* 7–12.

Shapira, N. A., Goldsmith, T. D., Keck, P. E., Khosia, U. M., & McElroy, S. L. (2000). Psychiatric features of individuals with problematic internet use. *Journal of Affective Disorders, 57,* 267–272.

Silverstone, R. (1999). Rhetoric, play, performance: Revisiting a study of the making of a BBC documentary. In J. Gripsrud (Ed.), *Television and common knowledge* (pp. 71–90). London: Routledge, 2010.

Turkle, S. (1995). *Life behind the screen: Identity in the age of the Internet.* New York, NY: Simon & Schuster.

Volkow, N. D. (2004). The reality of comorbidity: Depression and drug abuse. *Biological Psychiatry*, *56,* 714–717.

Walker, M. B. (1989). Some problems with the concept of "gambling addiction": Should theories of addiction be generalized to include excessive gambling? *Journal of Gambling Behavior, 5,* 179–200.

Walters, G. D. (1996). Addiction and identity: Exploring the possibility of a relationship. *Psychology of Addictive Behaviors, 10,* 9–17.

Weinstein, A., & Weizman, A. (2012). Emerging association between addictive gaming and attention-deficit/hyperactivity disorder. *Current Psychiatry Reports*, *14,* 590–597.

Wieland, D. M. (2005). Computer addiction: Implications for nursing psychotherapy practice. *Perspectives of Psychiatric Care*, *41*, 153–161.

Wu, H. R., & Zhu, K. J. (2004). Path analysis on related factors causing internet addiction disorder in college students. *Chinese Journal of Public Health*, *20*, 1363–1364.

Yee, N. A. (2002). Understanding MMORPG addiction. Retrieved from http://www.nickyee.com/hub/addiction/home.html

Yen, C-F., Chou, W-J., Liu, T-L., Yang, P., & Hu, H. F. (2014). The association of Internet addiction symptoms with anxiety, depression and self-esteem among adolescents with attention-deficit/hyperactivity disorder. *Comprehensive Psychiatry*, *55*, 1601–1608.

Young, K. S. (1996). Psychology of computer use: XL. Addictive use of the Internet: A case that breaks the stereotype. *Psychological Reports*, *79*, 899–902.

Young, K. S. (1998). Internet addiction: The emergence of a new clinical disorder. *Cyberpsychology and Behavior*, *1*, 237–244.

Young, K.S. (1999). The controversial nature of Internet addiction. Paper presented at the 107th Annual Meeting of the American Psychological Association, Boston, MA., August 21, 1999.

Young, K.S. (2007). Treatment outcomes with Internet addicts. *CyberPsychology & Behavior*, 10, 671–679.

Young, K. (2009a). Internet addiction: Diagnosis and treatment considerations. *Journal of Contemporary Psychotherapy*, *39*, 241–246.

Young, K. (2009b). Understanding online gaming addiction and treatment issues for adolescents. *American Journal of Family Therapy*, *37*, 355–372.

Chapter 2

Cyberbullying and Cyberstalking

How is it that your story has impacted us in this way? Some may differ in opinion but it was so brave of you to make and put your video out for the world to see. Even if your intentions was just a small world. You took courage and strength to do that. Unfortunately, you got knocked down with words such as 'attention seeker', 'psycho', 'crazy person', 'porn star' and more. None of it true (in your family's opinion or those that cared/care about you). There are still those out there that harass for pleasure. But I use those as examples so we can learn from them. (I am not talking today to write about those that bullied, cyberbullied or sextorted you for obvious reasons. This is your BIRTHDAY!)

—Carol Todd, mother of Amanda Todd and founder, The Amanda Todd Legacy (2014)

OVERVIEW

In 2012, when 15-year-old Amanda Todd posted a video on YouTube with flash cards and this message, "I've decided to tell you about my never ending story," it clearly appeared to be a "cry for help." Amanda Todd, a young woman born in 1997 in British Columbia, Canada, was, like most teens her age, looking forward to eventually graduating from high school. In the video Amanda told her story about being abused, bullied, harassed, stalked online (known as cyberstalking), and stalked in person by some yet unidentified person. She simply relayed her version of how she unsuccessfully tried to cope with the extreme pain experienced as a result of the ongoing cyberbullying: she harmed herself, took drugs, self-mutilated her body, and drank alcohol. She was clearly desperate for someone to understand her, to listen to her, and, perhaps, to provide some remedies for her—which is why she made the video.

For all intents and purposes, according to her mother, Amanda was a happy, normal teen before her tragedy unfolded. Her problems began after she was introduced to some anonymous person on Facebook, who allegedly flattered her for her beauty and then convinced her to flash her topless body to him. A year later, either this person or some other anonymous person sent her the picture online, and it went viral. As a result, Amanda became the target of massive bullying and teasing at school and online. Even after Amanda changed high schools several times, the bullying followed her. Amanda's troubles, she thought, were never-ending: her reputation was totally tarnished, and she was assaulted by classmates. As the drugs and alcohol she took were not long-lasting, Amanda then decided to consume large quantities of bleach to end the pain, but she was saved in her final moments. Months later, Amanda committed suicide to end the pain once and for all. This time her efforts did not fail her.

One would think that this would be the end of Amanda's tragedy. But after her suicide, more than 17 million people worldwide watched her video. Some online viewers started accusing her even after her death of attention-seeking by producing the video, of being a "psycho," or of being a porn star because of her bare-chest exposure on the Web sent through a webcam. These were the pain-inducing accusations that her mother Carol referred to in the opening quote of this chapter.

But who was the perpetrator? To find out, the Canadian police began a massive investigation, and the infamous Anonymous hacker cell went on their own massive cyberinvestigation, along with Facebook's internal security team. Eventually, in January 2014, a 35-year-old man was charged in the Netherlands in connection with Amanda's suicide. The originally unnamed suspect, said to have lived alone in a holiday home in Oisterwijk, was charged with extortion, Internet luring, criminal harassment, and child pornography, Canadian police said. Dutch prosecutors said that they believe the man approached underage women through the Internet and then seduced them into performing sexual acts in front of a webcam (BBC 2014).

Later identified as Aydin Coban, the imprisoned man wrote a four-page letter addressed to the *Globe and Mail* and a Dutch television station, claiming in 2015 that he was innocent of the charges and was really a victim of bad press and shoddy investigations naming him as the perpetrator (White 2015).

Clearly, Amanda never did make it to her high school graduation. Her mother, Carol, has since spoken publicly about the cruelty of cyberbullying and cyberstalking and has made an appearance on the Dr. Phil television show. She also created The Amanda Todd Legacy to help find solutions to these heinous acts that would help save other young victims.

How prevalent are the harm-inflicting behaviors known as cyberbullying and cyberstalking? In the last five years, a number of research studies have demonstrated that cyberbullying, in particular, has become an important global phenomenon, with an estimated prevalence among adolescents somewhere between 20% to 70% (Tokunaga 2010).

Results vary from country to country, but the variance remains consistently large. For example, in Germany, empirical studies have found cybervictim prevalence for cyberbullying and cyberstalking to be somewhere between 3% to 36%, and cyberperpetrator prevalence to be somewhere between 5% to 42% (Katzer, Fetchenhauer, and Belschak 2009; Pieschl and Porsch 2012; Wachs and Wolf 2011). Part of the variance in these findings can be attributed to methodology (Menesini and Nocentini 2009). Generally, self-reported prevalence is lower if adolescents have to report their online experiences over a short period of time, relative to a longer time period, and if it is measured with a single item instead of more items.

Besides this basic problem with methodology, there is also an ongoing controversy around what cyberbullying and cyberstalking are conceptually (Pieschl et al. 2013).

We will focus in this chapter on the two concepts of cyberbullying and cyberstalking—their definitions, their measurement and conceptualization, controversies surrounding them, cases that have been well publicized and/or investigated by mental health experts, and treatments or remedies that have been employed to counteract these mounting and heinous problems in society.

CYBERBULLYING AND CYBERSTALKING DEFINED

Cyberbullying Defined and Differentiated from Real-World Conventional Bullying

"Conventional bullying" is defined as an intentional aggressive act perpetrated by a group or an individual repeatedly and over time against a victim who cannot easily defend himself or herself (Olweus 1996). Thus, three defining characteristics for conventional bullying include:

- An intention to cause harm to another,
- Repetition of the harmful act, and
- The presence of a power imbalance—setting conventional bullying apart from simple roughhousing, fights between friends, or single acts of peer aggression.

By applying this definition to the virtual world, cyberbullying can be said to be bullying via electronic communication tools—including these three defining characteristics (Li 2006).

Recently, some researchers have questioned whether Li's (2006) definition for cyberbullying is totally accurate, as there is growing empirical evidence supporting the notion that it is not just bullying in the virtual world but quite a unique and distinct behavioral pattern. In fact, from a statistical vantage point, the linear correlation between "conventional bullying" and cyberbullying seems to be only of a moderate size effect, thus indicating that there are a significant number of individuals in the adolescent population who are involved not just in cyberbullying but in conventional bullying as well. Moreover, there are very specific risk factors for cyberbullying that are not implied for conventional bullying—such as the greater computer proficiency needed to be both a cybervictim and a cyberbully, more frequent Internet use by both victim and perpetrator, and more frequent Internet risky behavior undertaken by both parties (Erdur-Baker 2010; Huang and Chou 2010; Utsumi 2010).

"Conventional bullying" has consistently been viewed in the mental health literature as a relationship in which an individual or a group of individuals intentionally and repeatedly perpetrate aggressive behaviors toward someone unable to defend himself or herself (Olweus 1993; Salmivalli 2010). Thus, conventional bullying commonly consists of physical, verbal, and covert forms of aggressive behaviors.

The phenomenon of cyberbullying has included online aggressive and offensive behaviors involving harassment, cyberstalking, spreading rumors about the target, intimidating the target relentlessly, and bombarding the target with technologically generated capabilities such as e-mails, instant messaging, blogs, and chat room discussions of a demeaning nature regarding the target (Menesini, Calussi, and Nocentini 2012). Previous studies have reported that from a gender perspective, males were mainly engaged in conventional physical bullying, while females were mainly engaged in indirect bullying. However, to date, no clear gender difference has emerged for cyberbullying (Slonje and Smith 2008; Williams and Guerra 2007).

Several recent studies have advanced the argument that traditional bullying and cyberbullying have different life phase proclivities. For traditional bullying, its intensity tends to begin and gradually increase during childhood, have its peak during preadolescence, and decrease later in adolescence (Brown, Birch, and Kancherla 2005; Fitzpatrick, Dulin, and Piko 2007). However, cyberbullying seems to be committed mainly by preadolescents and adolescents who are increasingly using new technologies to engage in relationship-building as well as in harassing targeted peers (Hinduja and Patchin 2008; Ybarra and Mitchell 2004; Goldbaum et al. 2003).

One consideration in favor of the posited equalization in definition between cyberbullying and conventional bullying by Li (2006) is that one of the most replicated findings in cyberbullying research suggests that the same adolescents are frequently involved in both conventional bullying and cyberbullying at various phases of their lives (Dempsey et al. 2011; Li 2007). In Germany, the research team of Katzer and colleagues found a correlation of .55 between victims of conventional bullying and victims of cyberbullying, and a correlation of .59 between perpetrators of conventional bullying and perpetrators of cyberbullying (Katzer, Fetchenhauer, and Belschak 2009)—indicating a significant overlap on both the victim and perpetrator poles for conventional bullying and cyberbullying.

Another consideration in favor of equating conventional bullying and cyberbullying is that some risk factors are the same for both kinds, though most of these risk factors are unspecific. For example, victims of cyberbullying report more personal problems, more peer relationship problems, more family-related problems, and more depressive and somatic symptoms (i.e., bodily flare-ups during high-stress periods, such as increased bouts of asthma) than nonvictims (Schultze-Krumbholz and Scheithauer 2009; Utsumi 2010).

Furthermore, bullying perpetrators seem to show more aggression in the cyberworld as compared to others not so predisposed, a more positive attitude toward aggression aimed at others, less empathy toward the targets, a less positive parent-child relationship, less perceived peer support, more delinquency, and more smoking and drinking abuse than nonperpetrators (Ang and Goh, 2010; Calvete et al. 2010; Utsumi 2010).

In summary, because of a number of similarities existing between conventional bullying and cyberbullying, researchers generally contend that it might be warranted to transfer defining common characteristics between conventional bullying and cyberbullying. Nevertheless, this transfer of definition has been a point of controversy in the mental health field. To this end, alternative definitions have been suggested in the literature—a point discussed later in this chapter.

Accepting that there are growing numbers of recent research undertakings investigating cyberbullying per se, it is important to underscore the fact that research involving specific aspects of cyberbullying is still very much in the early stages (Pieschl et al. 2013).

Cyberstalking Defined and Differentiated from Conventional Stalking

By definition, cyberstalking means using the Internet as part of a targeted online campaign against someone with the intent of causing fear, distress, or alarm (Ogilvie 2000). Since about 2000, the notion of cyberstalking (aka "online stalking") has gained lots of media and public attention as a new form of disturbing online behavior that can have tremendously harmful and damaging psychological—and even physical—consequences not dissimilar to the harms seen in traditional forms of stalking (aka "off-line stalking") (Maple, Short, and Brown 2011). Furthermore, as Internet use increases and as more personal information becomes readily available online—often because the victims themselves post very personal information, which in earlier years they would not have had the means of doing—it appears likely that more people will turn to cyberstalking either to pursue relationships or to get revenge for relationships turned sour (Parsons-Pollard and Moriarty 2009).

It is important to also note that cyberstalking overlaps considerably with similar kinds of online behaviors causing harm like cyberbullying, cyberharassment, and "trolling"—defined as intentionally trying to provoke an emotional response through online comments or posts, many of which can be outright maddening or "flaming" in nature (Hardaker 2010). The common piece among all of these behaviors is that they are unwanted, and they commonly evoke fear or distress in the victims. There is, however, a thread of distinction differentiating these cyberbehaviors. For example, cyberstalking is differentiated from trolling in that the former is targeted toward a specific person or persons, whereas the latter is not. Also, cyberstalking is differentiated from cyberharassment primarily because as a behavioral pattern, the former continues over a considerably more prolonged period of time than the latter (Ogilvie 2000; Sheridan and Grant 2007).

Mental health experts warn that given the rapidly changing domain of technology, the types of repetitive threats manifested in cyberstalking will likely continue to expand over time. To date, behaviors identified as cyberstalking include, but are not limited to, a perpetrator's performing the following (Cavezzaa and McEwan 2014; Sheridan and Grant 2007):

- Sending repeated and unwanted e-mails or instant messages to a target;
- Posting false or hostile information online about the victim;
- Using social networking sites like Facebook to harass the victim;
- Subscribing to online services or products—not in the perpetrator's name, but in the victim's name;
- Hacking the victim's personal online accounts;
- Impersonating the victim online, thus engaging in online identity theft;
- Spamming the victim with unwanted e-mails or sending the victim files containing computer viruses; and
- Recruiting others to harass or threaten the victim through the Internet.

Before giving specific illustrations of cyberstalking, it is important to emphasize that *both* off-line and online stalking involve harassing or threatening behaviors that a perpetrator engages in repeatedly, and that a perpetrator can include both kinds of activities in the fear campaign—such as following the target from place to place in the real world, appearing at the target's home or business in the real world, making harassing telephone calls in the real world, sending threatening messages online, and assuming the victim's identity both in the real world and in the virtual world. While some of this off-line and online annoying or menacing behavior may fall short of the legal definition of the crime of stalking (known as "criminal harassment" in Canada), such behaviors may actually be a prelude to stalking and violence.

At a minimum, stalking and cyberstalking result in varying degrees of psychological harm to the target experiencing such episodes. In the more extreme cases, stalking and cyberstalking can result in physical harm, including kidnapping of the target (or the target's significant others) and murdering the target (or the target's significant others). The stalker or cyberstalker may even choose to take his or her own life (Schell, Dodge, and Moutsatsos 2002; Schell and Lanteigne 2000).

Two Cases Illustrating Cyberstalking

Perhaps it would be useful at this stage to present two real-life cases of cyberstalking that caught the media's attention at two different times. The first case is that of a young adult named Eric Burns, who was a cyberstalker first and a computer hacker second, and who went by the online moniker of Zyklon. Eric's case came to the media's attention in 1999, when reporters documented the particulars of the cyberstalking/hacking case in the *Washington Post* and the *Seattle Times*. Simply stated, Eric developed an obsession with a young woman named Crystal. The computer and his hacking exploits became a way that Burns could advertise worldwide, using the Internet, his unrelenting "love" for her—hopefully to get her attention, if not her commitment. Eric's claim to fame was that he attacked the Web pages of about 80 businesses and government offices (including the *Toronto Star* newspaper in Canada, the Chinese government, NATO, U.S. vice president Al Gore, and the U.S. Information Agency (USIA), whose pages were hosted by Laser.Net in Fairfax, Virginia). The 19-year-old hacker designed a computer program called "Web bandit" to identify computers on the Internet vulnerable to attack. Then he used the vulnerable systems to advertise his proclamation of love for Crystal. With each hit, Eric included the phrase, "Crystal, I love you" and occasionally other details of his apparent obsession (Schell, Dodge, and Moutsatsos 2002).

Ironically, with Crystal's assistance, Eric Burns was eventually identified as being Zyklon. He was charged by the FBI with three counts of computer intrusion related to the last three incidents, given a $250,000 fine, and ordered to fulfill a restitution repayment of $40,000–$120,000 for system damage caused over a two-year period. However, in the end, the prosecutors agreed to drop two of the charges in exchange for a guilty plea by Eric to one count of computer intrusion and an agreement to pay $36,240 in restitution.

As for Crystal, she came out of this cyberstalking case relatively unscathed. She said that she had never really talked to Eric in high school; she simply took one law class with him in her senior year. After that class, Crystal said, she began to receive letters from him, then gifts. Court records indicate that she received a crystal bell and a diamond necklace from Eric, which her family returned. She admitted that she did not go to the police at the time or seek a legal restraining order to have him keep his distance from her, because she didn't feel that Eric represented a real threat to her. She didn't even know that he was hacking computer networks to declare his love for her. Halfway through her senior year, Crystal said, someone phoned her home and told her to view a certain Web address to see some of Eric's handiwork. However, Crystal admitted that she couldn't be bothered to do so (Schell, Dodge, and Moutsatsos 2002).

The second cyberstalking case illustrates much more harm and undue distress reported by the victim. This case appeared in the media in 2013 and entailed the following. In August 2013, a U.S. man pleaded guilty to stalking his ex-partner after he impersonated her online. After their relationship soured, the man sent her multiple e-mails and repeatedly telephoned her, finally pretending to be her spouse. In this role, he convinced the telephone company and the Internet service provider to disconnect her services. Consequently, the woman applied for and got a legal restraining order (Jouvenal 2013; Provence 2013).

However, the man did not stop his concerning behaviors. Over an eight-month period, he continued to impersonate her in various online forums—by advertising items/services allegedly for sale by her or wanted by her. For example, he posted in her name fake ads for casual sex partners and for pornography, and when men showed interest in these ads, he told them to ignore the "no trespassing" signs in her yard and the security gate she had installed to keep herself safe, but to continue with the missions they went there for. Even more disturbing, in some instances, the perpetrator directed the interested buyers to perform specific sexual acts on the woman once they arrived at her house. According to the victim, she was receiving as many as six visits a day from interested men, some of whom refused to leave. There was even one man who rammed his car through her security gate. It is understandable that the woman feared that her ex-partner would become violent toward her, or that one of the men answering the fake ads would sexually assault her (Jouvenal 2013; Provence 2013).

CURRENT PROBLEMS AND CONTROVERSIES CONCERNING CYBERBULLYING AND CYBERSTALKING

Controversies Concerning Cyberbullying

Medium Involved in the Act(s)

A unique aspect of cyberbullying and one major controversy that has been reported because of it is the particular medium involved in the act. For example, Smith and colleagues (2008) categorized cyberbullying along seven different media or communication tools, because different high-tech media have different characteristics, given their variety: (1) text messages, (2) e-mails, (3) cell phone calls, (4) photo or video clips, (5) instant messages, (6) Web site comments, and (7) chat room conversations.

Recent research studies have shown, for example, that different media have been used with varying frequencies and effectiveness against cyberbully targets. While these different media have had noticeably varying effects on cybervictims' experiences and their perceived harm as a result of the acts, there is not a consistent finding from one study to another as to which medium produces the most harmful results (Slonje and Smith 2008). In fact, as of late, researchers have argued that this kind of media categorization is outdated, given the huge popularity of smartphones. The issue, they affirm, is that smartphones have caused earlier kinds of media to converge. Thus, the previously cited media and their role in cyberbullying cannot realistically be clearly distinguished anymore (Ortega, Mora-Merchán, and Jäger 2007).

Accepting this thesis, researchers like Pieschl, Porsch, Kahl, and Klockenbusch (2013) have argued that even though the hardware and technical applications converge in smartphones, other aspects of the media do not. Consequently, these researchers proposed that one relevant dimension for explaining varying media effects is the "representational code" rather than the software applications per se. Specifically, what may be more important in terms of causing harm to victims through cyberbullying acts is verbal codes (i.e., written or spoken text), compared to visual codes (i.e., pictures and videos)—depending on how the particular target in question is predisposed to these vulnerabilities and, thus, processes them. In short, verbal and visual codes are assumed to be processed differently (Paivio 1986), and, therefore, they seem to have quite different effects on the threat experience perceived by victims. Clearly, more research needs to be done in this area relating verbal and visual codes to the psychological and information-processing predispositions of the victims.

Measurement Issues Regarding Cyberbullying

We have already established that researchers continue to clarify what makes conventional bullying the same as or different from cyberbullying, but as long as this debate continues, it will be difficult to get a real sense of the pervasiveness of cyberbullying in student and adult populations, as well as its accurate measurement, since there is no agreed-upon inventory for assessing such.

Having said this, there is mounting evidence that cyberbullying appears to be a conceptually distinct subarea of bullying behavior, and that it differs from traditional bullying in two important ways. First, cyberbullying extends the reach of the perpetrator beyond the school or the workplace, allowing bullying perpetrators to follow victims into their homes or other social settings, including through electronic contact. Second, cyberbullying allows a degree of anonymity for the offender that is absent in traditional bullying (Patchin and Hinduja 2006; Tokunaga 2010). Although in its formative stages, an increasing body of literature has demonstrated the pervasive nature of cyberbullying, which needs to be taken into account when developing tools to measure this phenomenon.

While conventional bullying is often subdivided into three main expressions of bullying (i.e., verbal, physical, and relational bullying), for cyberbullying, Willard (2007) proposed eight types of activities and other forms of online social cruelty that should be considered. However, these tend not to be incorporated in all investigations. Given this lack of a universal measurement tool, researchers in various countries have taken different approaches for assessing the pervasiveness and harm caused by cyberbullying.

For example, the German research team of Pieschl, Porsch, Kahl, and Klockenbusch (2013) considered only five of these eight types of activities to be distinctive to cyberbullying:

1. Harassment (using insults or threats against the victim),
2. Denigration (spreading damaging rumors to harm the victim's reputation),
3. Impersonation (assuming a fake identity to impersonate the victim and behaving in an embarrassing or damaging way),
4. Outing and trickery (gaining and then violating the trust of the victim by publicly announcing private and embarrassing secrets via photos or videos), and
5. Exclusion (systematically excluding the victim from online activities or online groups). (Pieschl et al. 2013)

This research team excluded the other categories of Willard's (2007) taxonomy from their conceptualization of cyberbullying, primarily because these activities concerned arguments between equally powerful peers (earlier defined as flaming), were more related to online harassment than to cyberbullying, or were more closely related to sexual harassment or to cyberstalking than to cyberbullying. Pieschl, Porsch, Kahl, and Klockenbusch (2013) conducted two studies with experimental methods. Their first study findings showed that power imbalance in terms of perceived popularity of the perpetrator was relevant for the affective, cognitive, and behavioral experience of the target. In other words, according to the targets, cyberbullying by a "popular" bully was experienced as more distressing than cyberbullying by an "unpopular" bully. Their second study findings showed that medium factors unique to cyberbullying are also relevant for the experience of the target. Depending on the medium used and on whether it primarily involved video-based or text-based incidents, different types of harm were found to be related to different patterns of coping strategies in the victims. Therefore, the researchers concluded that cyberbullying seems to be both a unique phenomenon and one closely related to conventional bullying.

In the United States, the research team of Stewart, Drescher, Maack, Ebesutani, and Young (2014) argued that if research teams want to develop more accurate assessments of cyberbullying, which are critical for intervention planning and evaluation of victims, then the limitations of many currently available self-report measures of cyberbullying victimization—a lack of psychometric information and a limited scope—need to be accounted for. To address these limitations, the U.S. team developed and investigated the psychometric properties of a broad self-report measure of cyberbullying, which they named the Cyberbullying Scale (CBS).

Stewart, Drescher, Maack, Ebesutani, and Young (2014) examined the factor structure and reliability of the CBS across 736 students in grades 6 to 12 in six northern Mississippi schools. Exploratory statistical results indicated that the structure of the CBS was best represented by a one-factor model. The finding of a single-factor structure suggests, therefore, that cyberbullying is a one-dimensional construct, which is consistent with other previous study findings. The researchers concluded that the CBS demonstrated strong psychometric properties, including excellent internal consistency (Cronbach's $\alpha = .94$) and significant positive correlations with the cyberbullied victims' constructs of anxiety, depression, and loneliness. Their study results, they found, provided support for the CBS as a sound measure of adolescent cybervictimization.

These researchers also pointed out that no significant differences were observed in the CBS scores across age groups, suggesting that cybervictimization was experienced equally often by adolescents across middle school and high school. However, differences were noted between genders, with females reporting significantly greater CBS total scores than males. This difference, the authors noted, suggests that females are more likely to experience cybervictimization than males, but the impact of this larger volume of cyberbullying experiences on females remains the task of future studies to determine. Further, the authors said that the large number of students who reported being cyberbullied is, indeed, evidence of the pervasive nature of this phenomenon. Finally, the prevalence rate of cybervictimization (i.e., the percentage of youth with nonzero endorsement on the CBS) found in the present study was toward the high end of that typically reported (i.e., approaching 60%).

Traits of Cyberbullies and the Psychological Harm Caused to the Victims

Researchers have consistently pointed out that, besides a lack of agreement on how best to quantify cyberbullying, there is also a paucity of information on the traits of cyberbullies and the psychological harm caused to victims. If, as recent estimates indicate, from 20% to 70% of adolescents experience some degree of cyberbullying, this crime has the potential to be a significant public health issue affecting the majority of youth in ways that the field does not yet fully understand (Stewart et al. 2014). Further, the research findings that exist relating the experience of cyberbullying to psychopathology suggest a negative impact of the experience—similar to that experienced by traditional forms of overt and relational aggression (Crick 1996).

The latter have been associated with psychosocial difficulties of victims, including social anxiety (Juvonen and Gross 2008); mind-body somatic complaints, like increased asthma flare-ups (Gradinger, Strohmeier, and Spiel 2009); clinical depression and suicidal ideation and attempts (Hinduja and Patchin 2010); substance abuse (Mitchell, Wolak, and Finkelhor 2007); loneliness (Sahin 2012); and academic difficulties (Beran and Li 2007). The negative aftermath of cyberbullying clearly underscores the serious nature of this kind of activity, thus emphasizing the need and importance for ongoing research in this area.

There is, without question, a known shortage of research studies completed on cyberbullies' traits and on their psychological predispositions (Baroncelli and Ciucci 2014). With a few exceptions (for example, Ang and Goh 2010), research has disproportionately focused on traditional forms of bullying, while the role of emotions in cyberbullying has been hardly explored. Nonetheless, there are several reasons to expect differences in emotional characteristics of cyberbullies and on-land bullies, considering that these perpetrators—children or adults—are removed from face-to-face interactions with their victims (Dooley, Pyzalski, and Cross 2009).

The role of emotions in traditional bullying has emerged from the debate about bullies' social information processing; namely, whereas aggressive children have been reported to have problems at the initial stages of information processing (i.e., encoding and interpreting social cues), many bullies seem to not only accurately perceive their social world but to possess more advanced levels of mind skills, particularly the ability to recognize others' emotions, intentions, beliefs, and goals. Importantly, in traditional bullying, the perpetrators seem to consistently display a "biased" response evaluation style, choosing self-oriented, self-fulfilling goals regardless of the harmful consequences for others in the real-world environment (Arsenio and Lemerise 2001; Camodeca and Goossens 2005; Gini 2006).

Furthermore, a number of studies investigating the link between empathy and bullying have reported that affective empathy (by definition, the ability to share others' affective states), rather than cognitive empathy (by definition, the ability to read and understand others' feelings) appeared to be at the core of bullies' deficiencies, especially in males (Caravita, Di Blasio, and Salmivalli 2009; Jolliffe and Farrington 2011). Also, bullies are reportedly more prone to display a "cold cognition," defined as a mind that formulates ideas in instrumental terms and lacks empathic understanding of others. Consequently, for bullies, the intensity of their experienced emotions, along with their rather scarce capacity to regulate them (as displayed by their ongoing proneness to anger, emotional outbursts and negativity, and low levels of fear reactivity) are the key emotional processes appearing to influence both the generating and the performing of their bullying behaviors. In short, the mental health literature, to date, seems to indicate that traditional bullies seem as skilled as their peers in emotional display rule knowledge (Camodeca and Goossens 2005; Garner and Hinton 2010).

But what about cyberbullies? A recent study in Italy by Baroncelli and Ciucci (2014) investigated whether different components of trait emotional intelligence (or trait emotional self-efficacy) were uniquely related to traditional bullying and cyberbullying in a sample of 529 preadolescents (having a mean age of 12 years and 7 months), while controlling for other forms of bullying/victimization. Their findings showed that the dimensions concerning appraisal of one's own and others' emotions were not deficient in children performing bullying and/or cyberbullying behaviors. Some of these researchers' study findings were useful in understanding what likely goes on in the minds of cyberbullies. Many aspects of bullying behavior (i.e., intentionality, repetition over time, and cold cognition) suggest that traditional bullies may not have a deficient emotional functioning, and they may actually be fully aware of this reality. This awareness may then help to reinforce the amount of effort that they consequently invest in identifying their target's body language and facial expression. Moreover, this awareness could further promote the bully's monitoring of his or her peers' reactions not only to handle "assistants" and "reinforcers" in the bullying activities but to obtain a dominant role within the class-group.

In this 2014 Italian study, traditional bullies also declared not being particularly impaired in accurately monitoring and regulating their emotional states; in fact, bullies in cyberspace may actually use their information to plan and enact online their bullying behaviors. This information may also help them to select the most effective way of attacking their victims without incurring sanctions. Like traditional bullies, the cyberbullies in this study did not declare deficits in their basic emotional processes—again supporting the notion that self-evaluation about their abilities may help them more effectively plan and act out their cyberbullying plots. Finally, though cyberbullies lack face-to-face interactions with their victims, they still have to effectively plan how to remotely hurt them. Given this reality, cyberbullies may have to anticipate their target's emotional reactions—thus relying only on their own reactions to their acts (i.e., excitement) and their sense of expectation to gain "an edge" over the targets.

Baroncelli and Ciucci (2014) concluded that, despite a high concurrency between traditional and online bullying, their study results suggest that these two forms are distinct phenomena, and that they involve different personality traits in the perpetrators. Thus, they argued that different interventions by mental health practitioners are needed for cyberbullies, as compared to those commonly administered for traditional bullies.

Legislation Challenges in Cyberbullying

In 2008, the U.S. Congress passed the Protecting Children in the 21st Century legislation, which, among other concerning issues, addressed cyberbullying. In addition, by 2011, at least 44 U.S. states had legislation in place addressing school bullying, harassment, and intimidation. The main challenge in addressing cyberbullying through current antibullying legislation in the United States or elsewhere typically lies in some of the previously stated differences between traditional face-to-face bullying and cyberbullying. These include online anonymity, power differentials between the bully and the victim, an intent to harm, and the repetitive nature of the unwanted act.

The task of demonstrating that an instance of cyberbullying qualifies under current legislation is often a challenge. In response to this reality and as a fruitful means of remedying this situation, some U.S. states are developing specific cyberbullying legislation. For example, North Carolina has enacted the Protect Our Kids/Cyberbullying Legislation (S.L. 2009-551), making it a misdemeanor to engage in cyberbullying. In Missouri, cyberbullying is a crime that can result in jail time, fines, or both for the perpetrators of such acts. Other states, including Ohio and Virginia, have amended existing legislation to address cyberbullying per se.

Controversies Surrounding Cyberstalking

Measurement Issues Regarding Cyberstalking

Accepting that considerable controversy exists over how best to measure cyberbullying in order to get a fair assessment of the prevalence rates in vulnerable populations, the same can be said about measurement issues regarding cyberstalking. We earlier looked at the cyberstalking case of Eric Burns. He was caught, charged by the FBI on hacking-related charges rather than on cyberstalking charges, and was issued a penalty for the harms caused to company and government networks. But how many cyberstalkers are in the virtual world?

The bottom line is that mental health experts maintain that no reliable estimates of the prevalence of cyberstalking exist. In fact, the most detailed epidemiological studies of "traditional stalking" victimization, in general, were actually completed in the late 1990s and the beginning of 2000—at the time when everyday online users had access to and began to explore the fascinating world of the Internet (Budd and Mattinson 2000; Purcell, Pathé, and Mullen 2002; Tjaden and Thoennes 1998).

More recent surveys seem to still report only broad "traditional stalking" prevalence rates, rather than focusing on the prevalence rates of cyberstalking per se (Smith et al. 2011). For example, Baum, Catalano, Rand, and Rose (2009) said that 26% of those who reported being victimized by a stalker in the 2006 United States National Crime Victimization Survey reported receiving unsolicited or unwanted e-mails from their on-land stalkers, but other types of cyberstalking behavior were either not investigated or not reported.

Again, a contributing factor leading to the lack of prevalence rates worldwide for cyberstalking lies in the fact that mental health practitioners affirm that there is no readily available means for measuring this complex phenomenon, but advancements are being made in empirically assessing some relevant aspects. As noted earlier in this chapter, experiencing harassment, threats, and unwanted sexual advances by others while online are some of the component behaviors of cyberstalking; thus, cyberstalking can be and has been broadly defined as "the repeated pursuit by a stalker who uses electronic or Internet-capable devices."

The "repeated pursuit behaviors" aspect includes and can be measured by persistent and unwanted electronic communications containing messages laced with coercive or intimidating wording or sexual overtones. The "repeated communications" aspect can be measured by given messages sent through e-mails, blogs, instant messenger messages, text, and video messages. These communications can occur in chat rooms, in online social networks, or on other Web sites that the victim is known to frequent, and can be measured accordingly (Reyns 2010).

Even though cyberstalking is a crime in many jurisdictions worldwide, including the United States, Australia, and Canada, the few estimates of cyberstalking victimization that have been published have varied widely across studies, in large part due to measurement issues, as noted by many researchers (Reyns, Henson, and Fisher 2011; Holt and Bossler 2009; Sheridan and Grant 2007; Spitzberg and Hoobler 2002). The reality is that few estimates of cyberstalking offending from studies employing sound methodologies have been published (Parsons-Pollard and Moriarty 2009). These limitations vary by study, but most of these reported studies have relied on a convenience sample rather than on a random sample, or they have very small sample sizes and definitional ambiguities concerning what behaviors actually constitute cyberstalking. Nonetheless, these studies provide a starting point from which to consider the scope of cyberstalking victimization (Reyns, Henson, and Fisher 2011).

Without question, the study and measurement of cyberstalking is in the early stages of its development. This evolution is understandable, given that the first acknowledged incident of cyberstalking occurred just 10 years ago (Henson 2010; McQuade 2006). By examining the limited body of studies attempting to estimate the magnitude of cyberstalking, researchers need to continue their efforts to better define and measure this type of pursuit-based victimization (Parsons-Pollard and Moriarty 2009).

Estimates of Cyberstalking Victimization

Accepting this reality, reported estimates of cyberstalking victimization are broad, ranging from 1% to 32%. This wide range suggests that cyberstalking is a potentially more widespread problem than "traditional stalking," whose reported estimates have ranged from 2% to 13% for males and from 8% to 32% for females (Spitzberg and Cupach 2007). Furthermore, it needs to be underscored that while no estimates of cyberstalking offending have been published to date, the limited information available indicates that offenders are usually males who have had a previous relationship with the victim (as in the case of Eric Burns and Crystal).

Stalkers and Cyberstalkers: Are They Distinct Populations and Do These Stalking Processes Vary?

Given that there is relatively little empirical research regarding cyberstalking, it is extremely difficult to ascertain whether stalkers and cyberstalkers are distinct populations, let alone determine if these processes vary considerably.

A very recent Australian study tried to fill this identified gap in the mental health literature by comparing 36 cyberstalking offenders with an age- and gender-matched sample of 36 off-line stalkers (Cavessa and McEwan 2014). Because the sample size used in this study was quite small, the researchers used nonparametric statistics to analyze their data. In the end, these researchers reported few between-group differences between stalkers and cyberstalkers. Compared to off-line stalkers, cyberstalkers were reportedly more likely to be ex–intimate partners of their victims (75% vs. 47%) and were less likely to approach their targets (56% vs. 78%), though they did engage in other off-line stalking behaviors.

Further examination of specific cyberstalking behaviors by the Australian research team suggested that cyberstalkers with various motivations used the Internet in distinct ways, indicating that in terms of the off-line and online stalking process, there are similarities when one takes into account the perpetrator's motivations. In short, noted Cavessa and McEwan (2014), once the motivation of the stalker is considered and strongly entrenched, whether the acts occur off-line or online, the treatment and management strategies for dealing with the aftermath are likely to be similar.

To this important point, stalking and cyberstalking cases are classified in a motivational sense as being "relational" or "revengeful." At the core of "relational" stalking (online or off-line) is a one-sided attempt by the perpetrator to create or maintain a close, if not romantic, relationship with the target. In "revenge" stalking (online or off-line), the perpetrator's actions are characterized by intimidation and threats. No active relational claim is typically invoked. If allowed to escalate, relational stalking can turn into revenge stalking (Schell and Lanteigne 2000).

In relational stalking, the two parties (stalker and target) are either completely unacquainted or only superficially acquainted, as in the case of Eric Burns and Crystal. Relational stalking cases include three variations along this basic "stranger" theme (Schell and Lanteigne 2000):

1. The pursued target can be a stranger initially encountered in some public or semipublic place, giving rise to "unacquainted stalking";
2. The pursued target can be a publicly identified figure, often an official or a celebrity with whom the pursuer has come to feel that he or she has a special understanding or emotional attachment: known as "pseudo-acquainted stalking"; and
3. The pursued target can be a contact from the past (i.e., a former classmate or a date), or a contact in the present: known as "semi-acquainted stalking."

Whereas a relational stalker may initially advise a target "I would never do anything to hurt you" (despite behavior that may later vitiate this stated sentiment), a revenge stalker's explicit spirit and aims are just the opposite. Revenge stalkers are intent on hurting their targets psychologically and/or physically, right from the beginning (Schell and Lanteigne 2000).

The Six Stages of Stalking in the Real World and (Presumably) in the Virtual World

Six stages of stalking engaged in by perpetrators have been consistently reported by law enforcement and mental health experts. Because these behaviors are visible even to outsiders, they can be documented by targets and other witnesses and used as evidence, if needed, in court proceedings. While not all targets experience all of these stages, when stalking as a process escalates, the activities of the perpetrators tend to move from one stage to the next. In some cases, several stages may occur simultaneously (Schell, Dodge, and Moutsatsos 2002).

These six stages move from the pleasant through the very unpleasant in relational stalking, and from the unpleasant to the very unpleasant in revenge stalking. The more advanced both types of stalking, the greater the violence potential by the perpetrators. The six stages of stalking are as follows, and in recent years, have included both on-land and online acts (Schell, Dodge, and Moutsatsos 2002):

1. *Courtship*: The stalker sends the target flowers, love letters, treats, and other signs of caring.
2. *Surveillance*: The stalker tracks, watches, and follows the target around known territories.
3. *Communication*: The stalker leaves repeat telephone and/or e-mail messages for the target, or creates an online link with the target in a social network like Facebook or LinkedIn.
4. *Symbolic Violence*: The stalker may send death threats to the target or affiliates, may send suicide notes to the target or verbally threaten suicide, or may send by snail mail or e-mail devaluing notes to the target or about the target to colleagues and/or employers.
5. *Physical Violence*: The stalker may get physical, even attempting to assault or kidnap the target, family members, or work affiliates.
6. *Transference Violence*: If the stalker cannot reach the target, she or he may transfer anger and violence onto others believed to be obstructing access.

Of the six phases described, Eric Burns was obviously in the earlier "courtship" stage in his pursuit of Crystal. It is important to note that stalking exists on a continuum of severity. In fact, even in the early stages, the acts may be so subtle that targets may not even know that it is happening—as was the case with Crystal. Her friends had to warn her about what Eric was doing online to get her attention. On a final note, the severity of any set of acts related to stalking must be appropriately assessed by law enforcement agents or mental health experts on an individual basis, and a careful assessment must be made as to the likelihood that the stalker's activities may move beyond a noncriminal threshold (Schell, Dodge, and Moutsatsos 2002).

Stalking and Cyberstalking Legislation

Accepting that a methodological limitation underlying both stalking and cyberstalking victimization research is the problem of definitional consistency, this issue arises in terms of current stalking and cyberstalking legislation—primarily because definitions vary across state-level criminal statutes in the United States and in various jurisdictions worldwide. In general, the legal criteria for prosecuting a series of incidents or behaviors as stalking or cyberstalking include the following elements (Nobles et al. 2014):

- An unwanted pattern of conduct or behavior (e.g., following, spying on, and making unwanted phone calls),
- The victim or a "reasonable person" would expect to experience fear or a comparable emotional response (e.g., torment, distress, and annoyance), and
- There exists a credible threat of harm to the victim.

Given that the definitions vary from one jurisdiction to another, researchers have generally adopted a relatively broad definition of stalking victimization that encompasses many types of pursuit behaviors. For instance, Fisher and Stewart (2007) defined stalking as being repeatedly pursued in a manner that causes a reasonable person to fear for his or her safety, while Black and colleagues (2011) stated that stalking victimization involves a pattern of harassing or threatening tactics used by a perpetrator that is both unwanted and causes fear or safety concerns in the victim.

An additional challenge in operationalizing stalking in a legal sense concerns the context and nature of the technology used. While the Internet, as a whole, has grown in its capability to facilitate social networking sites like Facebook, these trends have also fundamentally changed opportunities for cybercrimes to occur—which affects how prosecutors actually frame their arguments in court. For example, because the Internet lacks centralization in spatial or temporal terms, asymmetric interactions are much more feasible, since offenders and their targets need not be in direct contact for one-on-one communication to occur. Furthermore, social networking sites can be easily misused by stalkers as instruments of terror. Stated succinctly, with the proliferation and ubiquity of present-day forms of personal technology, experts trying to make a conceptual differentiation between stalking and cyberstalking in either a mental health or a legal context find it extremely difficult. For this reason, legislatures have tried to adapt to this high-tech trend. While most states in the United States or in other jurisdictions elsewhere do not have cyberstalking statutes per se, cyberstalking can be and has been prosecuted under existing stalking and harassment statutes (Nobles et al. 2014).

Traits of Stalkers and Differences in Behaviors for Stalking and Cyberstalking Victims

Accepting that the first cyberstalking case was documented only a decade ago, there is a paucity of research not only detailing the mental health traits of stalkers (particularly in an online environment) but also in outlining the differences in behaviors for stalking and cyberstalking victims. Considering that there is a greater number of research findings reported for off-line stalkers, adult stalkers appear to be narcissistic and self-centered individuals with significant mental health issues. For example, former studies have reported major mental health illness in 63% of the stalkers for which data were complete. Further, 85% of the stalkers reportedly had a combined psychiatric and personality disorder, and substance abuse or substance dependence was further noted in 35% of the cases. A mood disorder was reported in 25% of the stalking cases (Schell, Dodge, and Moutsatsos 2002).

The most frequent personality disorders reported for stalkers are borderline, narcissistic, histrionic, and dependent. Generally, stalkers have poor stress-coping habits and a sparse toolkit of well-honed interpersonal skills, and their interpersonal relations are marked by repeat rejection by adults because of their odd communication and stress-coping styles (Schell, Dodge, and Moutsatsos 2002).

A recent study by Nobles, Reyns, Fox, and Fisher (2014) used a large nationally representative sample of adults in the United States to examine more closely stalking and cyberstalking and to compare stalking and cyberstalking victimization. As discussed, whether cyberstalking represents a distinct form of pursuit-based victimization or is a variant of stalking is not well understood, and convincing arguments have been made on both sides of this debate. This study further examined the seriousness of the offense (i.e., whether it involved a physical attack, a threat, or a financial cost to the victim), the duration of the stalking episode, the degree of experienced fear by the victim, and an acknowledgment of adopting self-protective behaviors by the victims. Investigating these effects was considered to be the next logical step in advancing the understanding of stalking and cyberstalking victims' decision making about and the actual use of self-protection against the stalker.

The univariate statistics of the victimization dimensions revealed some interesting similarities and highlighted some noteworthy differences between stalking and cyberstalking victims. The mean number of self-protective behaviors adopted was higher for cyberstalking victims (1.52) than for traditional stalking victims

(1.08), despite a shorter mean duration of victimization (651.91 days vs. 768.81 days). Cyberstalking victims also less frequently reported fear at onset (22.64% vs. 28.41%) and fear over time (13.60% vs. 15.46%), relative to traditional stalking victims. However, the reporting of threats (23.40% for cyberstalking victims vs. 22.02% for traditional stalking victims), the number of attacks (8.78% for cyberstalking victims vs. 7.76% for traditional stalking victims), and the number of stalking behaviors (43.99% vs. 38.28%) for the cyberstalking victims and the stalking victims, respectively, were all higher for the former as compared to the latter (Nobles et al. 2014).

The bivariate statistics revealed further differences in victimization characteristics between the traditional stalking and the cyberstalking targets. The levels of several situational characteristics were significantly greater in the latter group, including the number of protective acts taken in response to the victimization in general and the out-of-pocket costs associated with victimization in particular. Other situational characteristics of victimization, particularly the total duration of the episode, were not significantly different between the two groups. While the occurrence of self-reported fear at onset was significantly different for the two groups, the distribution findings indicated higher counts in the opposite direction suggesting that at onset, the traditional stalking victims actually perceived greater fear than did the cyberstalking victims. Finally, the demographic variables revealed several significant differences. The mean age was lower for the cyberstalking victims as compared to the traditional stalking victims, and more cyberstalking victims were male and white, compared to the traditional stalking victims. Finally, cyberstalking victims reported significantly higher household incomes and education level than did the traditional stalking victims (Nobles et al. 2014).

The findings from this recent U.S. study (Nobles et al. 2014), affirmed the researchers, hold promise for future criminal justice policy, as follows:

- First, given that cyberstalking is associated with negative factors and outcomes (such as costs, fear, and physical attacks), this study underscores the importance for stalking legislation to specifically mention cyberstalking either as part of the legal stalking code or as a separate crime. Presently, only three U.S. state statutes (Florida, Illinois, and Rhode Island) specifically outlaw cyberstalking or "stalking by computer" within their antistalking codes.
- Second, since there appear to be substantial financial costs associated with cyberstalking victimization that exceeds those associated with traditional stalking, tailoring laws to address financial needs with mechanisms such as court-imposed restitution may assist cyberstalking victims.
- Third, these results suggest that, for both traditional stalking and cyberstalking victims, self-identifying their experience as "stalking" is associated with

an increase in undertaking self-protective behaviors—thus having considerable implications for policy and programming. A minority of victims of both traditional stalking (38.3%) and cyberstalking (44.0%) actually considered their experiences to be "stalking." This finding suggests that victims are more likely to take action to protect themselves when they acknowledge that "the pursuit behaviors" are serious enough to be dealt with through legal means. Clearly, greater education is needed to have adolescents and adults better understand the process of stalking—and why they need to take appropriate actions in the earlier stages before the process escalates to a dangerous zone.

TREATMENTS AND SUGGESTED INTERVENTIONS FOR CYBERBULLYING AND CYBERSTALKING

Suggested Interventions for Cyberbullying

School Policies and Other School Prevention Remedies

Most authorities agree that it is important for schools to develop policies on traditional bullying and cyberbullying to address the seriousness of the problem and the consequences for perpetrators intent on engaging in such behaviors. For example, policies prohibiting the use of the school or district Internet system for "inappropriate" communication among school peers can be easily enacted. It must be made clear to all students that there is a limited expectation of privacy when using technology on school premises.

However, it is important to also note that there has been considerable controversy as to what authority schools have in the regulation of student behavior occurring outside of the school system. As such, schools generally have limited jurisdiction over bullying and cyberbullying acts, although this has not prevented some schools from developing policies that hold students accountable for their online behavior, even when not at school. Often the material used in cyberbullying is created outside of the school setting, sometimes in the home environment. Regardless of where the harmful material is produced, once it becomes known to others, it can have a significant adverse impact in many ways, including disrupting the learning environment for many and advancing the victimization of a particular target (Snakenborg, Van Acker, and Gable 2011).

U.S. federal legislation generally maintains that school administrators can discipline students for bullying other students in class or outside of it, which for any reason—whether it stems from time, place, or type of behavior—meaningfully disrupts classwork or involves substantial disorder or the invasion of the rights of others. Thus, those who cyberbully others may think that they are "immunized" by the U.S. constitutional guarantee of freedom of speech, but this is, arguably, not often the case.

While teachers and administrators may act to confiscate and search student cell phones, laptop computers, and technological devices used in such cyberbullying campaigns, they do risk challenges of violating the First and Fourth Amendments of the U.S. Constitution related to a "chilling effect on otherwise innocent communication" and "search and seizure" regulations, respectively. State and federal wiretap laws and invasion of privacy violations have also been levied against school districts attempting to intervene in suspected acts of cyberbullying. Moreover, without careful policies and procedures in place to preserve a "chain of custody" when confiscating items from a student or saving cyberbullying content, important evidence may be suppressed by the court as a result of illegal search and seizure, thus undermining an otherwise sound prosecution. It needs to be underscored, therefore, that care should be taken to develop a legally defensible policy and approach for addressing cyberbullying in schools (Snakenborg, Van Acker, and Gable 2011).

In addition to policies and procedures related to cyberbullying, school administrators should consider making efforts to educate students on the proper use of electronic media and sound ways to prevent cyberbullying. Curriculum-based programs specifically made to address cyberbullying in U.S. schools have included the iSAFE Internet Safety Program; Cyber Bullying: A Prevention Curriculum; Sticks and Stones: Cyberbullying; and Let's Fight It Together: What We All Can Do to Prevent Cyberbullying. The protocols used in these programs are wide-ranging and commonly include videos or "Webisodes" related to cyberbullying, as well as scripted lessons to help students discuss issues related to cyberbullying—particularly, how to prevent it and how to address it once it has been identified. Each of these programs has the potential to be used as a stand-alone intervention to help prevent cyberbullying, or it can be part of a broader antibullying program. Because there is a strong overlap between victims and perpetrators of traditional bullying and cyberbullying, as noted, a comprehensive prevention and intervention program may be a preferred approach to searching and seizing (Snakenborg, Van Acker, and Gable 2011).

School administrators should also consider incorporating antibullying strategies like cooperative learning, peer mediation, and social skills into the mainstay of daily classroom instruction. Moreover, when bullying or cyberbullying behaviors occur and are reported to authorities by either the victims or by others, the victims may need immediate and comprehensive counseling. In short, administrators and faculty need to establish a holistic culture in which bullying and cyberbullying are not tolerated—and then immediately act to heal the victim once these heinous acts have been reported. Engaging in these positive interventions early indicates to students that the problem of cyberbullying is taken very seriously and will not be tolerated. There is little question that a routine reinforcement of appropriate social norms should be implemented in the school system (Mason 2008).

Using Successful Mental Health Protocols for Cyberbullying Victims

A recent study by Gámez-Guadix, Orue, Smith, and Calvete (2013) has contributed a better understanding of the relationship between cyberbullying and psychological/behavioral health problems in victims. First, given the reported relationship of cyberbullying to other risk behaviors such as substance abuse, it seems advisable to include strategies to prevent cyberbullying within interventions being applied to other identified behavioral problems experienced by adolescents. For example, as depressive symptoms appear to predict cyberbullying victimization, prevention programs promoting self-esteem or increasing social support (perhaps through peer support schemes) should prove beneficial for assisting cyberbullying victims. Second, providing counseling services for problematic Internet use (PIU) or Internet addiction (see chapter 1) could prove to be very useful for assisting cyberbullying victims.

Suggested Interventions for Cyberstalking

Useful Web Sites and Suggested Interventions for Helping Cyberstalking Victims

According to the recent study assertions by researchers Cavezzaa and McEwan (2014), there is no reason to think that treatments and suggested interventions aimed at victims of traditional stalking should fail to work for victims of cyberstalking.

First, a number of Internet victim abuse resources exist online to help targets manage their situations and get protection and prevention advice from the police and mental health practitioners. These include the following Web sites with content on cyberbullying, cyberstalking, and online child abuse:

- CyberAngels (http://www.cyberangels.org/security/stalking.php);
- GetNetWise (http://kids.getnetwise.org/safetyguide/);
- Kids Internet Safety Alliance (KINSA) (http://www.kinsa.net)

- National Center for Victims of Crime Stalking Resource Center (http://www.victimsofcrime.org/our-programs/stalking-resource-center);
- National Coalition Against Domestic Violence (http://www.ncadv.org/);
- National Domestic Violence Hotline (http://www.thehotline.org/);
- National Organization for Victim Assistance (http://www.trynova.org/);
- PREVNet (Promoting Relationships and Eliminating Violence Network) (http://www.prevnet.ca)
- WiredSafety (https://www.wiredsafety.org/); and
- Working to Halt Online Abuse, or WHOA (http://www.haltabuse.org/).

Each of the above organizations (and their Web site content) varies in the amount of assistance provided to victims, but most include educational programs, referral services, and law enforcement assistance (Parsons-Pollard and Moriarty 2009). When consulted, a number of the above groups would generally advise targets that if they are receiving unwanted cyber contact, they should make it clear to the perpetrator not to make contact again. Targets should also take care to save all communications for evidence, in case legal proceedings are initiated, and they should also block or filter unwanted messages. Importantly, if the episodes continue, the cyberstalking target should contact the perpetrator's Internet service provider (ISP), as well as enforcement agents. If the target is feeling psychologically harmed or stressed, a mental health practitioner should be consulted immediately (Schell, Dodge, and Moutsatsos 2002).

To prevent cyberstalking attacks, many of these groups would also generally recommend the following actions be taken in order to prevent becoming a traditional or a cyberstalking victim (Schell, Dodge, and Moutsatsos 2002):

1. Not sharing personal information in public spaces online or giving personal information to strangers online, including in e-mail or in chat rooms.
2. Not using one's real name as the user ID but instead using a gender- and age-neutral online moniker.
3. Being cautious about meeting online acquaintances in real-life settings, and if one chooses to meet an online acquaintance, doing so in a public place is sound advice, as well as taking along a trusted friend.
4. Making sure that one's ISP and Internet relay chat (IRC) network have an acceptable use policy prohibiting cyberstalking—and if one's network fails to respond to complaints of such a nature, one should immediately switch to a more responsive provider—all in the name of staying safe online.
5. Making sure that if an online situation becomes hostile, one immediately logs off, and if a situation places the online user in fear, he or she should contact a law enforcement agent immediately.

More Effectively Dealing with Cyberstalking Underreporting Issues

Mental health and law enforcement agents know that cyberstalking is, unquestionably, underreported for a number of reasons. In earlier studies cited in the mental health literature, about 75% of cyberstalking victims failed to report the offense, because they did not think that it was serious enough, they were not sure if the incident was actually criminal in nature, or they believed that the police would not think that the reported behaviors involved a serious offense.

Because of these critical issues, Working to Halt Online Abuse (WHOA) is currently one of the few online organizations actively collecting data on cyberstalking victims. WHOA maintains that they have approximately 50 to 75 victims contacting them weekly, and of the thousands of online users who have contacted them, WHOA has been able to obtain very useful data through a self-report survey. While many cyberstalking victims do not want to provide their personal information, WHOA has successfully gathered demographic data from approximately 280 victims yearly (Parsons-Pollard and Moriarty 2009).

In addition, there is no clear knowledge in the United States or elsewhere of how many law enforcement agencies are actually capable of handling these types of cyberstalking cases once victims present themselves to authorities. Thus, victims of cyberstalking may find themselves in a situation where a responding officer has no idea that a stalking or cyberstalking law even exists in that jurisdiction. An informal survey of law enforcement agencies found that most agencies do not investigate or prosecute cyberstalking cases, and often victims are told to return once they have been physically threatened. A likely source of this dilemma is that while there have been some grant funds available for law enforcement training in cyberstalking victim services, a considerable number of these funds have been diverted to domestic violence and sexual assault response (Parsons-Pollard and Moriarty 2009).

CONCLUSION

This chapter focused on the many harms caused by cyberbullying and cyberstalking, along with key issues regarding definitional problems related to these concepts, prevalence rate issues related to various methodological weaknesses, and the underreporting of both of these crimes by victims—who, by and large, feel that their cries for help from authorities or caring others will likely fall on deaf ears.

Although cyberbullying and cyberstalking are relatively new crimes, there is ample evidence that as technology advances, these crimes will also increase in frequency and intensity. Therefore, it is critical that law enforcement, the legal community, researchers, and mental health experts better conceptualize these concepts. More effective laws and increased enforcement in jurisdictions in the United States and globally will also lead to more reliable definitions and data collection methods for cyberbullying and cyberstalking—and more reliable estimates of their prevalence. It is only when more effective laws are in place, along with these other noted advancements, that victims will begin to feel more comfortable reporting such incidents earlier in the process rather than later when death to oneself or to others can result.

For some additional thoughts on problems with cyberbullying and cyberstalking in society—as well as legal measures for dealing with these in various jurisdictions—readers are referred to the Interview with an Expert sidebar, an interview with Warren Bulmer, a Canadian police officer, criminal investigator, and trainer in online safety.

INTERVIEW WITH AN EXPERT

Detective Constable Warren Bulmer, Police Officer, Criminal Investigator, and Trainer in Online Safety

With a career spanning more than 25 years, Detective Constable Warren Bulmer has become a leader in the investigation and prosecution of Internet-facilitated crimes online. His policing career has been predominantly spent within the field of criminal investigation, including 12 years assigned to major crime, fugitive, and child exploitation investigations. Detective Constable Bulmer is an international instructor in the area of computer-facilitated crime; he has lectured to more than 4,000 police and prosecutors from 32 different countries. He also has testified in court as an expert in various capacities relating to digital evidence, including as an expert in Facebook. Detective Constable Bulmer has specialized in the area of social networks and is called upon by police all over Canada to teach them how law enforcement can balance the right to investigate with the protections afforded to citizens under the Canadian Charter. He is a published writer of articles and is a contributing author to a book entitled *Evidence and Investigation: From the Crime Scene to the Courtroom.*

Q Could you discuss how in the virtual world cyberbullying and cyberstalking may be related concepts or are distinctly different—as they are both clearly unwanted forms of online aggression?

A I would suggest that they are distinctively different but from a legal point of view, often one crosses the line into the other. Cyberbullying in Canada and many other jurisdictions has had no legal definition or criminal context. Stalking in many forms is defined in Canadian law and elsewhere. These two concepts can also be somewhat related; it has been my experience that in many cases, an incident starting out with some sort of cyberbullying then graduates into a stalking or criminal harassment situation—thereby crossing the threshold into criminality.

The impact of either of these on the victim is not mitigated by whether or not the case becomes a criminal investigation.

Q PREVNet findings* indicate that 25% of Canadian kids admit to cyberbullying behavior, and 1 in 3 report that they have been cyberbullying others. Do these Canadian statistics reflect similar trends in the United States and elsewhere around the world—and why?

A It is difficult to quantify these types of statistics, because they are often published to serve or benefit a specific entity, institution, or agenda. Research shows widespread numbers globally for "reported" statistics. For example, these statistics from the Stop a Bully Canadian reporting agency seem to demonstrate trends in reporting from 2009; however, they are only reported by schools that are members of this agency's program.

Realistically, you could walk into two local high schools, geographically separated by, say, three kilometers, and students from one school will tell you that they have been a victim of cyberbullying or have cyberbullied and even report to being both victim and perpetrator. The students at the second school, however, may report zero to a low number of incidents.

There are many key factors at play determining why or why not, statistically, these trends don't correlate globally by geography alone. Demographics such as culture and wealth play a key role. In many parts of the world, access to technology is a challenge. Internet penetration has to become a part of the equation if one wants to effectively compare reported statistics on cyberbullying. Let's compare Canada versus the United States. In 2014, statistics showed that the Canadian population was about 34,834,841, with about 33,000,381 users of the Internet—equating to a 94.7% penetration rate. The United States during the same time period had a population of 318,892,103, with about 277,203,319 users of the Internet—equating to an 86.9% penetration rate. Yet Canada's reported cyberbullying statistics are significantly lower than those of the United States.

---

* Promoting Relationships and Eliminating Violence Network (PREVNet). (2015). Retrieved from http://prevnet.ca

Should we expect that reported incidents of cyberbullying would be higher when and where more people use the Internet? That is a key question that has not yet been answered.

Q PREVNet findings also indicate that nearly half of Canadian youth in distress have reported involvement in traditional bullying or cyberbullying. Can you comment on the broader relationship and known trends between distress in youth and being a victim or perpetrator of traditional bullying or cyberbullying?

A Socioeconomic status is one of the stereotypical indicators looked at when analyzing the root causes of bullying and cyberbullying. Other historical predictors that have been considered include bullying and cyberbullying victims becoming the perpetrators, youth being targeted because of a lack of religious or racial deference shown by the perpetrators, or youth being targeted by perpetrators because of their sexual orientation or gender identification. Youth who are in one or more of these categories or classifications tend to be the target of bullies. There are no rules and there are no exceptions, meaning anyone can be a victim and/or a perpetrator of bullying. The traditional bullying of people has become less tolerated in society, and those who witness a physical or verbal assault of someone on the street are more apt to get involved. The cyberbullying phenomenon is significantly less defended, because the Internet offers avenues such as anonymity and is generally considered to be not as harmful or indicative of violence.

Q PREVNet findings also indicate that more than half of youth who participate in cruel online behavior like bullying or stalking have said that "they are just joking around." Do you think that society condones or encourages cyberbullying and cyberstalking—and why?

A I think there is a higher tolerance for cyberbullying and harassment in social media use by all ages. We have seen lots of examples where someone on the street was bullied or targeted by others, and often bystanders get involved in many land-based cases. In fact, they have created a television show that focuses on this very thing entitled *What Would You Do?*

When it comes to the virtual world, people seem to think that because cyberbullying is occurring online, it's not as serious as if it were occurring on land. The term "free speech" gets added to the online situation. So, things that people may not say to someone's face in the presence of others in a land-based situation become acceptable when similar things are posted on Facebook. Then it is labeled as "free speech."

There has also been a lack of legislation to support enforcement, education, and prevention of cyberbullying per se.

Q U.S. federal legislation generally allows school administrators to discipline students for bullying or stalking others—whether it be in an online or off-line environment. Administrators have risked challenges of violating the First and Fourth Amendments of the U.S. Constitution. Can you comment on present-day Canadian legislation, and how it is similar to or different from the U.S. legislation aimed at curbing bullying and stalking in schools?

A In comparing the United States and Canada, there are some legal components that are parallel and others that cannot be fairly compared. In the United States, the First Amendment of the Constitution affords free speech. This is constantly challenged and is currently a topical issue before the U.S. Supreme Court in a case called *Elonis v. United States*, 13-983 U.S. (2015). Here, the petitioner is defending his right to free speech by threatening to kill his wife, absent of the intent to actually carry it out.

In Canada, we have the Charter of Rights and Freedoms, and Section 2 provides similar "freedom of expression" principles. To date, we have not seen a constitutional challenge to the same level, but it is coming.

Like those in the United States, Canadian schools are governed by provincial (similar to state) legislation, and the laws vary across Canada. In Ontario, for instance, we have the Education Act R.S.O. 1990, Chapter E.2. Bullying is defined in section 1(1), and cyberbullying is defined in section 1.0.0.2. Its intent is to create schools that are safe, inclusive, and accepting of all pupils, to address inappropriate pupil behavior and promote early intervention, and to establish disciplinary approaches promoting positive behavior. This bill also imposes a number of mandatory reporting provisions for school staff and states that a school principal *shall* investigate any reported matter.

Unlike in the United States, Canada has only one criminal law, the Criminal Code R.S.C., 1985, c. C-46. There is no criminal offense for "cyberbullying" or "cyberstalking," but there are substantive offenses where charges are laid by police when the facts could be described as "cyberbullying."

In December 2014, the government of Canada passed Bill C-13, assenting it into law on December 9, 2015. Labeled the "cyberbullying bill," it includes amendments to the Criminal Code in the areas of new offenses, as well as police powers. Bill C-13, overall, is an attempt to close the gap between antiquated law and modern technologies.

Q Where do you think that the future research focus on cyberbullying and cyberstalking by youth will be?

A It is difficult to imagine how research into cyberbullying and cyberstalking by youth can really be effective. It is an underreported event, and it is fluid—meaning that as technology evolves in the form of new apps or new social sites, the youth move very quickly to use the technology. As an example, a study conducted on Facebook use in teens today would be completely different from what it would have been even 12 months ago. During this period, teens' use of Facebook has dropped significantly.

Q How does the fact that most kids use the Internet for school complicate the intervention or treatment process for victims or perpetrators of cyberbullying and cyberstalking?

A Access to technology in today's digital environment in many circles is thought of as a basic human right and not a privilege. It is an issue for debate that will remain unresolved for a long time to come. In June 2011, the United Nations published a report stating that disconnecting people from the Internet is a human rights violation and against international law.

In some criminal cases in Canada, we have seen judges impose court-ordered conditions both preconviction and postconviction, restricting or limiting people's use of or access to technology and the Internet. In a criminal context, judges weigh the hardship placed on a person before they impose such a condition. It is challenging, indeed, when an accused person facing serious allegations involving technology needs to be restricted from continuing to commit offenses or have their ability to do so mitigated. Yet, this same individual is employed in a field of work that requires them to use a computer as a condition of their employment.

As school curricula have progressed, modern-day students have a greater need, and in many cases, a mandatory one to use technology in their everyday learning, projects, and assignments. School regulators, I surmise, would have to undertake the same careful analysis as a judge would in a court of law before doling out punishments to students.

REFERENCES

Ang, R. P., & Goh, D. H. (2010). Cyberbullying among adolescents: The role of affective and cognitive empathy, and gender. *Child Psychiatry and Human Development, 41*, 387–397.

Arsenio, W. F., & Lemerise, E. A. (2001). Varieties of childhood bullying: Values, emotion processes, and social competence. *Social Development, 10*, 59–73.

Baroncelli, A., & Ciucci, E. (2014). Unique effects of different components of trait emotional intelligence in traditional bullying and cyberbullying. *Journal of Adolescence 37,* 807–815.

Baum, K., Catalano, S., Rand, M., & Rose, K. (2009). *Stalking victimization in the United States*. Washington, DC: U.S. Department of Justice.

BBC. (2014). Man charged in Netherlands in Amanda Todd suicide case. Retrieved from http://www.bbc.com/news/world-europe-27076991

Beran, T., & Li, Q. (2007). The relationship between cyberbullying and school bullying. *Journal of Student Wellbeing, 1,* 15–33.

Black, M. C., Basile, K. C., Breiding, M. J., Smith, S. G., Walters, M. L., Merrick, M. T., et al. (2011). *The national intimate partner and sexual violence survey (NISVS): 2010 summary report.* Atlanta, GA: National Center for Injury Prevention and Control, Centers for Disease Control and Prevention.

Brown, S. L., Birch, D. A., & Kancherla, V. (2005). Bullying perspectives: Experiences, attitudes, and recommendations of 9- to 13-year-olds attending health education centers in the United States. *Journal of School Health, 75,* 384–392.

Budd, T., & Mattinson, J. (2000). *The extent and nature of stalking: Findings from the 1998 British Crime Survey.* London: Home Office.

Calvete, E., Orue, I., Estévez, A., Villardón, L., & Padilla, P. (2010). Cyberbullying in adolescents: Modalities and aggressors' profile. *Computers in Human Behavior, 26,* 1128–1135.

Camodeca, M., & Goossens, F. A. (2005). Aggression, social cognitions, anger and sadness in bullies and victims. *Journal of Child Psychology and Psychiatry, 46,* 186–197.

Caravita, S. C. S., Di Blasio, P., & Salmivalli, C. (2009). Unique and interactive effects of empathy and social status on involvement in bullying. *Social Development, 18,* 140–163.

Cavezzaa, C., & McEwan, T. E. (2014). Cyberstalking versus off-line stalking in a forensic sample. *Psychology, Crime & Law, 20,* 955–970.

Crick, N. R. (1996). The role of relational aggression, overt aggression and prosocial behavior in the prediction of children's future social adjustment. *Child Development, 67,* 2317–2327.

Dempsey, A. G., Sulkowski, M. L., Dempsey, J., & Storch, E. A. (2011). Has cyber technology produced a new group of peer aggressors? *Cyberpsychology, Behavior and Social Networking, 14,* 297–302.

Dooley, J. J., Pyzalski, J., & Cross, D. (2009). Cyberbullying versus face-to-face bullying: A theoretical and conceptual review. *Journal of Psychology, 217,* 182–188.

Erdur-Baker, Ö. (2010). Cyberbullying and its correlation to traditional bullying, gender and frequent and risky usage of Internet-mediated communication tools. *New Media & Society, 12,* 109–125.

Fisher, B. S., & Stewart, M. (2007). Vulnerabilities and opportunities 101: The extent, nature, and impact of stalking among college students and implications for campus policy and programs. In B. S. Fisher & J. J. Sloan III (Eds.), *Campus crime: Legal, social and policy issues* (2nd ed., pp. 210–230). Springfield, IL: Charles C. Thomas.

Fitzpatrick, K. M., Dulin, A. J., & Piko, B. F. (2007). Not just pushing and shoving: School bullying among African American adolescents. *Journal of School Health, 77,* 16–22.

Gámez-Guadix, M., Orue, I., Smith, P. K., & Calvete, E. (2013). Longitudinal and reciprocal relations of cyberbullying with depression, substance use, and problematic Internet use among adolescents. *Journal of Adolescent Health, 53,* 446–452.

Garner, P. W., & Hinton, T. S. (2010). Emotional display rules and emotion self-regulation: Associations with bullying and victimization in community-based after school programs. *Journal of Community & Applied Social Psychology, 20,* 480–496.

Gini, G. (2006). Social cognition and moral cognition in bullying: What's wrong? *Aggressive Behavior, 32,* 528–539.

Goldbaum, S., Craig, W. M., Pepler, D. J., & Connolly, J. (2003). Developmental trajectories of victimization: Identifying risk and protective factors. *Journal of Applied School Psychology, 19,* 139–156.

Gradinger, P., Strohmeier, D., & Spiel, C. (2009). Traditional bullying and cyberbullying: Identification of risk groups for adjustment problems. *Zeitschrift für Psychologie/Journal of Psychology, 217,* 205–213.

Hardaker, C. (2010). Trolling in asynchronous computer-mediated communication: From user discussions to academic definitions. *Journal of Politeness Research, 6,* 215–242.

Henson, B. (2010). Cyberstalking. In B. S. Fisher and S. P. Lab (Eds.), *Encyclopedia of victimology and crime prevention* (pp. 253–256). Thousand Oaks, CA: Sage.

Hinduja, S., & Patchin, J. W. (2008). Cyberbullying: An exploratory analysis of factors related to offending and victimization. *Deviant Behavior, 29,* 129–156.

Hinduja, S., & Patchin, J. W. (2010). Bullying, cyberbullying, and suicide. *Archives of Suicide Research, 14,* 206–221.

Holt, T. J., & Bossler, A. M. (2009). Examining the applicability of lifestyle-routine activities theory for cybercrime victimization. *Deviant Behavior, 30,* 1–25.

Huang, Y. -Y., & Chou, C. (2010). An analysis of multiple factors of cyberbullying among junior high school students in Taiwan. *Computers in Human Behavior, 26,* 1581–1590.

Jolliffe, D., & Farrington, D. P. (2011). Is low empathy related to bullying after controlling for individual and social background variables? *Journal of Adolescence, 34,* 59–71.

Jouvenal, J. (2013). Stalkers use online sex ads as weapons. Retrieved from http://www.washingtonpost.com/local/i-live-in-fear-of-anyone-coming-to-mydoor/2013/07/14/26c11442-e359-11e2-aef3-339619eab080_story.html?tid= pm_local_pop

Juvonen, J., & Gross, E. F. (2008). Bullying experiences in cyberspace. *Journal of School Health, 78,* 496–505.

Katzer, C., Fetchenhauer, D., & Belschak, F. (2009). Cyberbullying: Who are the victims? A comparison of victimization in Internet chatrooms and victimization in school. *Journal of Media Psychology, 21,* 25–36.

Li, Q. (2006). Cyberbullying in schools: A research of gender differences. *School Psychology International, 27,* 157–170.

Li, Q. (2007). New bottle but old wine: A research of cyberbullying in schools. *Computers in Human Behavior, 23,* 1777–1791.

Maple, C., Short, E., & Brown, A. (2011). *Cyberstalking in the United Kingdom. An analysis of the ECHO pilot survey*. Luton: National Centre for Cyberstalking Research, University of Bedfordshire.

Mason, K. L. (2008). Cyberbullying: A preliminary assessment for school personnel. *Psychology in the Schools, 45,* 323–348.

McQuade, S. C. (2006). *Understanding and managing cybercrime*. Boston, MA: Allyn & Bacon.

Menesini, E., Calussi, P., & Nocentini, A. (2012). Cyberbullying and traditional bullying: Unique, additive and synergistic effects on psychological health symptoms. In Q. Li, D. Cross, & P. K. Smith, *Cyberbullying in the global playground: Research from international perspectives* (pp. 245–262). Oxford: Wiley-Blackwell.

Menesini, E., & Nocentini, A. (2009). Cyberbullying definition and measurement: Some critical considerations. *Zeitschrift Für Psychologie/Journal of Psychology, 217,* 230–232.

Mitchell, K. J., Wolak, J., & Finkelhor, D. (2007). Trends in youth reports of sexual solicitations, harassment, and unwanted exposure to pornography on the Internet. *Journal of Adolescent Health, 40,* 116–126.

Nobles, M. R., Reyns, B. W., Fox, K. A., & Fisher, B. S. (2014). Protection against pursuit: A conceptual and empirical comparison of cyberstalking and stalking victimization among a national sample. *Justice Quarterly, 31,* 986–1014.

Ogilvie, E. (2000). *Cyberstalking. Trends and issues in crime and criminal justice.* Canberra: Australian Institute of Criminology, 2000.

Olweus, D. (1993). *Bullying at school. What we know and what we can do.* Oxford, UK: Blackwell.

Olweus, D. (1996). *Gewalt in der Schule: Was Lehrer und Eltern wissen sollten—und tun können [Violence in school: What teachers and parents should know—And can do].* Bern: Huber, 1996.

Ortega, R., Mora-Merchán, J. A., & Jäger, T. (Eds.). (2007). Acting against school bullying and violence. In *The role of media, local authorities and the Internet.* Landau: Verlag Empirische Pädagogik, 2007.

Paivio, A. (1986). *Mental representations: A dual coding approach.* New York, NY: Oxford University Press, 1986.

Parsons-Pollard, N., & Moriarty, L. J. (2009). Cyberstalking: Utilizing what we do know. *Victims & Offenders, 4,* 435–441.

Patchin, J. W., & Hinduja, S. (2006). Bullies move beyond the schoolyard: A preliminary look at cyberbullying. *Youth Violence and Juvenile Justice, 4,* 148–169.

Pieschl, S., & Porsch, T. (2012). *Schluss mit Cybermobbing! Das Trainings- und Präventionsprogramm 'Surf-Fair' [Stop cyberbullying! The training and prevention program 'Surf-Fair'].* Weinheim: Beltz, 2012.

Pieschl, S., Porsch, T., Kahl, T., & Klockenbusch, R. (2013). Relevant dimensions of cyberbullying—Results from two experimental studies. *Journal of Applied Developmental Psychology, 34,* 241–252.

Provence, L. (2013). Intent to harass: Stalker pleads guilty to fake Craigslist sex ads. Retrieved from http://www.readthehook.com/109983/intent-harass-stalker-pleadsguilty-fake-craigslist-sex-ads

Purcell, R., Pathé, M., & Mullen, P. E. (2002). The prevalence and nature of stalking in the Australian community. *Australian and New Zealand Journal of Psychiatry, 36*, 114–120.

Reyns, B. W. (2010). A situational crime prevention approach to cyberstalking victimization: Preventive tactics for Internet users and online place managers. *Crime Prevention and Community Safety, 12,* 99–118.

Reyns, B. W., Henson, B., & Fisher, B. S. (2011). Being pursued online: Applying cyberlifestyle routine activities theory to cyberstalking victimization. *Criminal Justice and Behavior, 38,* 1149–1169.

Sahin, M. (2012). The relationship between the cyberbullying/cybervictimization and loneliness among adolescents. *Children and Youth Services Review, 34,* 834–837.

Salmivalli, C. (2010). Bullying and the peer group: A review. *Aggression and Violent Behavior, 15,* 112–120.

Schell, B. H., Dodge, J. L., & Moutsatsos, S. S. (2002). *The hacking of America: Who's doing it, why, and how.* Westport, CT: Quorum, 2002.

Schell, B. H., & Lanteigne, N. M. (2000). *Stalking, harassment, and murder in the workplace: Guidelines for protection and prevention.* Westport, CT: Quorum, 2000.

Schultze-Krumbholz, A., & Scheithauer, H. (2009). Social–behavioral correlates of cyberbullying in a German student sample. *Zeitschrift für Psychologie/ Journal of Psychology, 217,* 224–226.

Sheridan, L. P., & Grant, T. (2007). Is cyberstalking different? *Psychology, Crime & Law, 13,* 627–640.

Slonje, R., & Smith, P. K. (2008). Cyberbullying: Another main type of bullying? *Scandinavian Journal of Psychology, 49,* 147–154.

Smith, K. E., Coleman, K., Eder, S., & Hall, P. (2011). *Homicides, firearms offences and intimate violence 2009/10 (Home Office Statistical Bulletin).* London: Home Office.

Smith, P. K., Mahdavi, J., Carvalho, M., Fischer, S., Rusell, S., & Tippett, N. (2008). Cyberbullying: Its nature and impact in secondary school pupils. *Journal of Child Psychology and Psychiatry, 49,* 376–385.

Snakenborg, J., Van Acker, R., & Gable, R. A. (2011). Cyberbullying: Prevention and intervention to protect our children and youth. *Preventing School Failure, 55,* 88–95.

Spitzberg, B. H., & Cupach, W. R. (2007). The state of the art of stalking: Taking stock of the emerging literature. *Aggression and Violent Behavior, 12,* 64–86.

Spitzberg, B. H., & Hoobler, G. (2002). Cyberstalking and the technologies of interpersonal terrorism. *New Media & Society, 4,* 71–92.

Stewart, R. W., Drescher, C. F., Maack, D. J., Ebesutani, C., & Young, J. (2014). The development and psychometric investigation of the cyberbullying scale. *Journal of Interpersonal Violence, 29,* 2218–2238.

Tjaden, P., & Thoennes, N. (1998). *Stalking in America: Findings from the national violence against women survey.* Washington, DC: National Institute of Justice.

Todd, C. (2014). 18 roses for my daughter Amanda's would-be 18th birthday. Retrieved from http://www.huffingtonpost.ca/carol-todd/amanda-todd_b_6233200 .html

Tokunaga, R. S. (2010). Following you home from school: A critical review and synthesis of research on cyberbullying victimization. *Computers in Human Behavior, 26,* 277–287.

Utsumi, S. (2010). Cyberbullying among middle school students: Association with children's perception of parental control and relational aggression. *Japanese Journal of Educational Psychology, 58,* 12–22.

Wachs, S., & Wolf, K. D. (2011). Zusammenhänge zwischen Cyberbullying und Bullying—erste Ergebnisse aus einer Selbstberichtsstudie [Correlates of cyberbullying and bullying—First results of a self-report study]. *Praxis der Kinderpsychologie und Kinderpsychiatrie, 60,* 735–744.

White, P. (2015, January 29). Suspect in Todd case proclaims innocence. *The Globe and Mail*, p. A3.

Willard, N. E. (2007). *Cyberbullying and cyberthreats. Responding to the challenge of online social aggression, threats, and distress.* Champaign, IL: Research Press, 2007.

Williams, K., & Guerra, N. G. (2007). Prevalence and predictors of Internet bullying. *Journal of Adolescent Health, 41*, S14–S21.

Ybarra, M. L., & Mitchell, K. J. (2004). Online aggressor/targets, aggressor and targets: A comparison of associated youth characteristics. *Journal of Child Psychology and Psychiatry, 45,* 1308–1316.

Chapter 3

Online Predators

> *I never realized how dangerous MySpace could be. It was foolish of me to put that suggestive picture of me in my bikini up. One day a guy sent me a message saying that he wanted to "do it" with me, and if I didn't he would tell everyone at school that I'm a little whore. I called the police after crying all day and talking to my parents. (15-year-old girl from Canada)*
>
> —Patchin and Hinduja (2010, 1)

OVERVIEW

In chapter 2, we focused at the start on the tragedy of Amanda Todd, a 15-year-old who was lured on the Internet by a man who encouraged her to send pictures of herself bare-chested and then was cyberbullied by her peers for doing so. The unfortunate ending was that Amanda successfully committed suicide as a means of ending the excruciating psychological pain. However, Amanda's story is increasingly becoming a familiar one that has found its way to the media headlines.

In 2002, CBS News ran a story about a sixth-grader named Christina Long—a 13-year-old adolescent who seemed to have two sides to her life. At her Catholic elementary school in Danbury, Connecticut, Christina was a good student, she led the cheerleading squad, and she served as an altar girl in her church. But when she went on the Internet, according to police reports, she would often use provocative screen names like "Hot es300," and in the real world, Christina engaged in sexual relationships with partners that she met in online chat rooms. Eventually she was strangled by a married restaurant worker, Saul Dos Reis, then 25 years old, an immigrant from Brazil who confessed to killing Christina and who afterward led police to a remote ravine where he had placed her dead body. Dos Reis was charged with using an interstate device—the Internet—to entice a child into sexual activity, and he was sent to prison for 30 years. Police said that Christina had had sexual relations with Dos Reis on several occasions. Two years before her death, Christina had gone to live with her aunt in Danbury, because her parents had substance abuse issues (Hancock 2002).

Particularly since about 2000, law enforcement and mental health experts in North America have increasingly voiced serious concerns about the potential harms that can occur in cyberspace—an environment increasingly available to adults and minors as more families procure computers and Internet services at reasonable costs. Clearly, posit these experts, the Internet facilitates access to child exploitation materials that were once difficult to locate, thereby providing adults instant access to children from all over the world or within any given jurisdiction (Choo 2008).

Similar concerns about the Internet's inadvertent promotion of online predation were raised in a 2009 report by the Australian Government Attorney-General's Department, positing that it is relatively easy to actually engage minors in sexual activities without being in the physical presence of the minor—with the assistance of the Internet. For example, an offender may use the Internet to groom or procure a minor to perform a sexual activity using a webcam device, or the offender may e-mail a child asking him or her to masturbate in front of a webcam, while the offender (or other adults with similar motivations) watches the minor perform the acts over the Internet (Australian Government Attorney-General's Department 2009).

Other examples of online child exploitation have been reported in various jurisdictions around the globe—and the perpetrators are not just adult men. As a case in point, in the United States in December 2011, a husband and wife team were charged with sex trafficking of teenage females. Prosecutors alleged that both of the accused adults recruited teenage females by promising money, drugs, and a "family-like environment." Sadly, the predators maintained control over their teen victims by providing them with drugs, by using physical force or threats of force against them, and by fostering a climate of fear. The pair used the Internet to advertise their prostitution enterprise to other interested adults in the California area (FBI 2011).

There is little question that online predation is a global phenomenon. In 2014, an international online child abuse organized crime group was discovered and shut down after a joint investigation by the United Kingdom's National Crime Agency (NCA), the Australian Federal Police, and U.S. Immigration and Customs Enforcement. The multicountry 2012 undercover operation, under the code name Operation Endeavour, resulted in 29 arrests of online predators in 12 countries worldwide (Leyden 2014).

In Germany, for example, during the period 2004–2007, a case was referred to mental health experts in which the father had "organized" the sexual abuse of his daughter. The experts reported that, first, the father sexually abused her and filmed the abuse. He then invited other men to sexually abuse her before she went off to school in the mornings. Her father went to the length of generating a customer list.

To make sure that his daughter was appealing, he made sure that she was dressed in "sexy" lingerie and that she wore makeup. He put her under pressure by saying that he had a contract, and if this contract were not fulfilled, the entire family would be in serious danger (Weber, Haardt-Beker, and Schulte 2010).

Because of these kinds of online abuses of minors, online chat rooms and social networking Web sites like MySpace have in recent years received a significant amount of negative attention from the media and many concerned parents or authority figures, who point to incidents like that of Christina and of other minor victims—where predators have contacted, become involved with, and assaulted or murdered children or adolescents whom they met online. Moreover, concerned parents have voiced their extreme discontent with the amount and type of personal and private information adolescents seem to be disclosing on their Facebook profile pages and on other online channels.

To get a clearer understanding of whether these worries are well founded, in 2006, researchers Patchin and Hinduja completed an extensive content analysis of approximately 2,400 randomly sampled adolescent MySpace profiles. Contrary to voiced concerns, this research team reported that the vast majority of youth were actually making responsible choices with the information that they posted online and were limiting access to their profiles—a finding that was replicated a year later. Moreover, a significant number of adolescents seem to be abandoning their online profiles and/or choosing not to visit social networking sites altogether because of the potential risks involved (Hinduja and Patchin 2008).

At about the same time that Hinduja and Patchin published their research findings, U.S. federal prosecutors warned parents and teachers through media campaigns that the Internet is becoming an increasingly dangerous place for children and adolescents, because their online profiles often attract aggressive sexual predators. The U.S. Department of Justice warned that personal information posted online could lead to innocent targets being abducted or sexually exploited in the real world, because pedophiles are not only finding innovative ways to exploit their targets but are using the Internet to share information on how best to lure and exploit. At one of the campaign news conferences, U.S. federal agents warned that "seemingly friendly" Web sites like MySpace or Facebook are often employed by sexual predators as "victim directories"; thus, adolescents who think that they are innocently posting very personal information or their identities on these "friendly" sites are actually setting themselves up for disaster (Filosa 2007).

We will focus in this chapter on the concept of online predation, how it is defined, the assessed prevalence of the problem, controversies surrounding online predation and online victims, the Internet's role in advancing online sexual predation and grooming, the process of online predation, the typologies of online predators, the typologies of victims, and the various legal, mental health treatments, or other remedies that have been employed to counter this virtual-world problem that easily blends into a real-world problem.

ONLINE PREDATION DEFINED

A famous cartoon by Peter Steiner, published in the *New Yorker* on July 5, 1993, had this caption: "On the Internet, nobody knows you're a dog." This observation pretty much encapsulates what has since become a truism about the virtual world—that everybody's online identity can be very easily manipulated. For example, online users can use fake names instead of their given names online (called monikers) or pretend to be someone other than who they really are—such as portraying themselves as teenagers when they are really middle-aged adults. The malleability of online identity is demonstrated clearly in the relatively new phenomenon of "Second Life" and similar virtual worlds, where online users interact through "avatars." Although it is impossible to quantify the actual degree of misrepresentation of identity and personal characteristics occurring in the online environment, the potential for criminals to exploit innocent young victims there is becoming increasingly obvious (Urbas 2010).

In contrast, there is little question that the bulk of adult online users are keenly aware of the phenomenon of fraudulent communications floating daily in the virtual world. For example, most online adults have in recent years received e-mails sent by others claiming to be from close relatives of Nigerian ministers who desperately need to transfer large sums of money to some trustworthy online party, or e-mails by so-called lottery officials who claim to be notifying online winners of their unexpected good fortune. To the extent that spam filters and other technological protections do not effectively do their job of dealing with this online "trash" invisibly, when these annoying e-mails do arrive, most online-savvy adults just delete them manually or skip reading them altogether, knowing full well that more of the same genre will be generated. This deleting or nonattention exercise, while a waste of time and often humor-producing, tends to result in little harm on the receiving end.

However, for some more vulnerable online targets, the harm caused by Internet-based criminals known as "online predators" can be far more serious. A particularly concerning area of online offending relates to the sexual exploitation of children and young adults.

In fact, police globally find that the Internet crimes they most often investigate involve "online predation"—defined as the exploitation by online adult users of vulnerable younger online users through child pornography or by attempts to make contact with these young victims for sexual purposes. Online predation is known by various labels and stages, including child or adolescent predation, grooming, and luring. This activity may involve the use of pornography in the adult user's attempt to exploit a child's or a teen's sexual curiosity, or to break down his or her resistance or reluctance to perform sex acts. Indeed, many examples of child grooming begin with quite innocuous contact through a chat room with a conversational focus between the online parties on sports, music, beauty, or any topic that would typically appeal to targets in this younger age group. The "grooming" by the online predator then moves on to more intimate and sexually oriented communications. Importantly, to gain a child's or young adult's trust and to establish a relationship that can be exploited for the desired sexual contact, online offenders often assume an identity different from their own. The frustrating reality is that most children have been taught about "stranger danger" in the real world, but they are far more trusting of others their own age or older when they go online. It is little mystery, then, that a common strategy used by online predators is adopting the pseudo-identity of a younger person when seeking out and grooming targets (Urbas 2010).

With increasing reports of solicitation and exploitation experienced by young people online, the use of the Internet by adults seeking to initiate contact with children for sexual purposes is of concern and requires immediate attention from mental health experts and law enforcement alike. However, a major problem in the legal field is that currently there is no agreed-upon definition for the term "Internet offending"; therefore, this label is used to describe a range of Internet-facilitated offenses, including online predation and child or adolescent grooming.

This range includes Internet-offending behaviors such as exchanging child pornography; locating potential victims for sexual abuse intentions; engaging in inappropriate sexual communications with minors, including showing them sexually explicit material for desensitizing and grooming purposes, functioning to "normalize" certain sexual activity as a means to lower the victim's inhibition; and corresponding with other adults who have a deviant sexual interest in children (Taylor and Quayle 2010).

Although the concept of sexual grooming in the physical world and online has been factored into meta-analyses in the literature of the broader field of Internet offending behaviors, "sexual grooming" is seen as the initial setup phase for full-blown online predation. Often, researchers use this term to define the early circumstances when an offender seeks contact with a child for the production of child pornography. Thus the term "grooming"—whether it involves an online or off-line environment—has generally been used to describe offenders' actions during the preparatory stages of sexual abuse and is broadly defined in the meta-analytic literature as the situation whereby a potential offender will set up opportunities to abuse by gaining the trust of the child in order to prepare him or her for abuse either directly or through computer-mediated communication (McAlinden 2006).

Despite the significance of sexual grooming in the onset of sexual abuse, the mental health literature varies in its consideration of both the onset and the termination of the grooming process, with Gillespie (2002) positing that it would not be feasible to precisely define when grooming starts or when it ends, for it is a protracted process involving various stages and acts. For this reason, the process of sexual grooming as an underlying dynamic in online offender–victim interactions remains largely unexplained. Consequently, the mental health literature in this specific area is sparse. This outcome is a major void, considering the rapidly increasing number of incidents of adults using the Internet to befriend and exploit children in various ways—whether it is for sexual gratification, for the production and distribution of images of a sexually explicit nature, or for contact that may facilitate or lead to sexual offenses (Craven, Brown, and Gilchrist 2006, 2007).

THE INTERNET'S ROLE IN ADVANCING ONLINE SEXUAL PREDATION AND GROOMING—AN ENABLER OR A DETERRENT?

The Internet as an Enabler

Because the Internet has proven to be a very attractive tool for predators to view sexually abusive images of children and identify potential victims, its lethal use in this manner has been a major concern for legal authorities and mental health experts globally. However, attempting to quantify exactly how many indecent images are available online is not so straightforward. Not only are authoritative statistics unavailable to gauge the present scale of Internet sex crimes against children, but the lack of authoritative quantitative data is a key limitation in truly understanding the prevalence rates.

Nonetheless, Taylor and Quayle (2006) suggest that the steady flow of court cases in the United Kingdom and in the United States, in particular, involving indecent images suggests a relatively high level of activity by online users, with the high demand for these images leading to an increase in real-life sex abuse cases of children who are used in the image production process to be later shared with others online. Moreover, in 2008, the International Policing Agency (Interpol) reported that there were in excess of 512,000 child abuse images on their database—with submissions from 36 member countries.

So, what makes the Internet environment so attractive to online predators? Accepting that Internet sex offenders, like off-line sex offenders, are a rather diverse group, the reason why they access sexually explicit images of children also seems to vary, note experts in both the mental health and law enforcement fields (Taylor and Quayle 2003).

Cooper (1998) refers to three basic components of Internet use (known as the triple "A" engine) that are applicable to the prolific downloading of indecent images of children from the Internet:

- *Accessibility*—the Internet, being a virtual world, is available 24 hours, 7 days a week.
- *Affordability*—Internet users can find "free" material matching their whims and needs.
- *Anonymity*—Internet users' sense of freedom and openness to experimenting are virtually endless, enhancing their ability to talk openly and pointedly about their sexual desires while online.

Other mental health researchers have affirmed that the Internet can serve as an enabler for online predators to engage in their harmful behaviors because of the following noted features of this online environment (Aslan 2011):

- The Internet permits online users easy access to vast quantities of sexually explicit images, allowing the online user to become sexually aroused by viewing the images and to use them in a number of ways—including for sexual gratification, as an aid to masturbation, or to provide stimulation for further sexual fantasies (Bates and Metcalf 2007; Howitt and Sheldon 2008).
- The Internet also enables online users interested in having sex with minors to organize, maintain, and increase the size of their collections of sexually explicit images by capitalizing on these relationships with their victims. Images custom-made are particularly desired in the online predator adult community, giving the online predator who contributes "new" material to the trading community a "special status" (Quayle and Taylor 2007).
- The Internet lets online predators not only access and establish contact with potential victims but also use sexually explicit pictures to seduce minors, encouraging them to cooperate in the sexual demands of the adult and to create a sense of sexual arousal in them (Durkin 1997; Quayle and Taylor 2002).
- The Internet enables online predators to form their own "virtual communities," where the use, production, and transmission of sexually explicit images of minors is both acceptable and normal; in this community, the users' sexual attraction to minors is seen as a perverted expression of "love," as opposed to an expression of "abuse"—which is how mainstream society views such acts (Taylor 1999; Quayle and Taylor 2002).
- The Internet enables online predators to experiment with new ways of relating to others, adopting different roles in an anonymous fashion (with a reduced risk of being identified), and procuring or creating new and unique sexual stimuli to

facilitate their sexual curiosity and that of other online users by morphing existing images with those involving real-world contact with victims (Talamo and Ligorio 2001; Quayle and Taylor 2002; Wolak, Finkelhor, and Mitchell 2005).

- The Internet enables new ways of completing "old" crimes, such as the trafficking of children for sexual exploitation and recruiting child prostitutes—often by using the personal information posted by minors to locate them. The Internet is then used to blackmail the exploited minors to ensure their silence regarding the criminal acts committed by (1) the "stranger" adult, (2) by a peer in the minor's age group, or (3) by a so-called trusted relative or family friend (McCabe 2008; Filosa 2007; Mitchell, Finkelhor, and Wolak 2005; Quayle and Taylor 2002).
- The Internet enables the child sex tourism trade in a number of ways, by providing a convenient marketing channel through various specially designed Web sites; by providing potential child sex tourists with pornographic accounts written by other child sex tourists detailing their sexual exploits with minors; by providing information on sex establishments with adults-minors—including prices and top destinations worldwide; and by providing key information on how to procure child prostitutes (Council of Europe 2007; Stanley and Tomison 2001; Sutton and Jones 2004).

The Internet as a Deterrent

Some mental health and law enforcement experts have suggested, in contrast, that the Internet may actually have some benefits in deterring child abuse. For example, if masturbating to indecent images of children can act as a substitute for the sexual abuse that could occur in the real world—because the action has fulfilled the online predators' desires or needs—then the Internet can be seen as a deterrent that has prevented actual sexual abuse of minors in the real world from occurring (Quayle and Taylor 2002).

To this point, Riegel (2004) has posited that viewing child erotica online is useful as a substitute for actual sexual contact with minors. Other experts, as noted above, loudly counter the so-called "positive function" of the Internet in deterring offender behavior by suggesting that such assertions fail to acknowledge that the actual creation, distribution, and collection of sexually explicit images causes real and extreme psychological and physical harm to minors—which has the potential to further victimize other children by making it an attractive arousal tool. It is important to reiterate, say these experts, that viewing indecent images of children is *not* a victimless crime, and that such images (including pseudo/morphed images) represent a form of heinous victimization that should be viewed as very psychologically and physically harmful to the victims.

THE PROCESS OF ONLINE PREDATION, BEGINNING WITH GROOMING

Grooming and the Process of Online Predation

Gillespie (2002) maintains that while sexual grooming is not new, the Internet provides new and distinct opportunities for predators to sexually exploit minors, for which grooming is often a prerequisite. For example, in Finkelhor's (1984) Precondition model, there are four preconditions leading to possible sexual offending against minors: (1) a predator's motivation to sexually abuse, (2) a predator's overcoming his or her own inhibitors, (3) a predator's overcoming external inhibitors, and (4) a predator's overcoming the resistance of the targeted minor.

The Precondition model further proposes that an offender's motivation to sexually abuse a minor appears to be linked to three distinct internal motives within the predator (Finkelhor 1984): (1) emotional congruence, referring to a predator's emotional identification with minors—given that the former has not been able to meet his or her emotional needs fully with other adults; (2) deviant sexual arousal, with a proclivity of the adult to arousal with minors; and (3) blockages (temporary or persistent), in terms of the adult's not being able to meet both emotional and sexual needs in adaptive ways—often the aftermath of stressful or unusual situations; these may be developmental in nature (e.g., fear of intimacy), situational in nature (e.g., relationship problems), or both. As a result of these three motivational aspects, the predator may find the Internet to be a particularly effective medium for finding sexual gratification in an anonymous virtual environment.

Predators' overcoming external inhibitors in the Precondition model (Finkelhor 1984) refers to their bypassing hurdles in the online and real-world environments to more effectively create opportunities for engaging in the sexual abuse of minors. Often this phase involves grooming potential victims online as well as in the online environment in which they spend considerable amounts of time. Accepting this reality of online predation, minors who spend considerable time in chat rooms and in other online venues are, through probabilities alone, possible targets of predators.

In terms of an adult's overcoming a minor's resistance to engage in sexual acts, O'Connell (2003) affirms that preparatory activities predators commonly use include compiling a nonthreatening online "minor" profile—with the primary goal of attracting other online users of a similar age but likely of opposite gender. The predator then waits for the targeted minor to be "baited" into starting a conversation with him or her. The predator may, instead, decide to lurk in the chat room—first observing and assessing other conversations taking place there and then choosing to start a conversation with a particular "vulnerable" minor by sending a private, custom-designed, "baiting" message to him or her.

However, O'Connell (2003) underscores the fact that many online predators will use their own adult persona to lure their victims, rather than pretend to be a minor or someone else. Thus, many minors are aware that they are conversing with an adult or someone older than they—which is often perceived by the minors to be a positive force. To this point, Williams, Elliot, and Beech (2013) said that there are two types of online predators regarding online personae: true representation of themselves versus deceptive representation of themselves. Obviously, whichever persona of this pair the perpetrator chooses to use affects the way that the minor is approached online.

The Process of Online Predation

According to O'Connell (2003), six stages employed by online predators give insights into both their patterns of online predation activities and their underlying motivators. These six stages of online predation are as follows:

1. *Friendship-forming stage*. Purpose of this stage: to get to know the minor by exchanging pictures so that the predator can verify that the conversation is with a minor and meets the preference criteria for victimization being sought.
2. *Relationship-forming stage*. Purpose of this stage: to lengthen the friendship-forming phase by talking about topics like the minor's home or school life as a means of being the minor's "best friend."
3. *Risk-assessment stage*. Purpose of this stage: to identify the location of the minor and to identify usage of the computer by other adults as a possible means of being detected.
4. *Exclusivity stage*. Purpose of this stage: to have the minor think that he or she is "so special," thus fostering the feeling of being "best friends" and of being a trustworthy online adult. The adult builds trust through a variety of means, including the gradual introduction of sexual topics, followed by an increased intensity of sexual topics; through gift-giving to the minor (such as concert tickets, video games, or clothing); and by apologies for upsetting the minor if there is obvious initial resistance or guilt. These apologies serve as a superficial means of rebuilding the shaken "trust" between online adult and online minor.
5. *Sexual stage*. Purpose of this stage: to have the nature of the conversation with the minor vary from slight suggestions of sexual activity to overt sexual activity requests, along with a range of explicit descriptions of the desired activities by the predator—often "sold" to the minor as serving a valuable mentoring or educating purpose that she or he should be proud of.
6. *Concluding stage/damage limitation/hit-and-run tactic*. Purpose of this stage: for the predator to lavish the minor with praise for performing the desired

sexual activities and to pretend to want to maintain or to reestablish a trusting relationship—which is solely motivated by the predator's trying to escape getting caught for his or her actions. The truth is that the predator has no genuine interest in either damage limitation or in maintaining a caring relationship with the minor but is looking for a safe "hit-and-run" tactic to escape being detected.

In short, in the early stages of grooming, the online predator tries to get to know the minor by discussing common interests, hobbies, or daily routines. This effort sets the foundation for the later main purpose: to become sexually active with the minor. Prior to this main goal, however, the online predator is apt to engage the minor in sexualized talk through persuasion, threats or coercion, or bribes—monetary or otherwise. Moreover, the predator will typically engage the minor in watching sexually explicit visuals, videos, and/or live performances via webcam or streaming to serve as a means of desensitizing the minor to the shock value of such acts and to "normalize" what the minor is seeing. Following the actual sexual exploitation of the minor, the online predator may terminate the interaction by half-heartedly trying to maintain or reestablish the relationship with the victim or by quickly abandoning the relationship altogether as a quick means of escape.

TYPOLOGY OF ONLINE PREDATORS

With recent developments of the Internet, different typologies have been proposed by mental health experts and law enforcement to categorize online predators by their online activities and their likely motivations for these behaviors. These typologies predominantly focus on the predator's offending behavior relating to child pornography per se, with a smaller emphasis on online sexual grooming—seen as part of the larger picture of offending behaviors (Kloess, Beech, and Harkins 2014). Before looking at some proposed typologies of online predators, we will look first at some key factors facilitating and contributing to online offending behavior.

Factors Facilitating and Contributing to Online Offending Behavior

Research on the publications of pedophile organizations in particular and on the content of pedophilic Web sites and message boards supports the notion that accessing minor-related sexual content not only serves to validate one's own dysfunctional interests but helps those of this persuasion to communicate and network through the Internet. This online support system lowers would-be predators' inhibitions and helps them to justify their behaviors by "normalizing" them in this virtual environment of like-minded deviants (Quayle and Taylor 2001; Wolak et al. 2008).

Quayle and Taylor (2001) further maintain that the anonymous nature and "playful" quality of the Internet adds to the disinhibiting effects of offending behaviors, along with the reality that online predators can openly express to others online their non–socially approved sexual interests and fantasies—thus highlighting the compounding driving force of unique contextual and motivational factors aiding and abetting online predators in their crimes.

For some individuals, prolonged engagement in online activities has been posited by some researchers to contribute to the actual replacement of real-world social interactions, exacerbating problems with social isolation and intimacy deficits and causing considerable harm to family life and other real-world, previously appreciated relationships by the perpetrator (Elliott and Ashfield 2011). Consequently, online predators tend to justify their inordinate amounts of time spent online in what is perceived by them to be a "safe" and "controlled" way of relating to people. This so-called "safe" and "controlled" virtual world may include cybersexual interactions by one adult with other adults of similar ilk or the sexual exploitation of minors by the online predator. Clearly, without social sanctions, these online interactions act to diminish moral attitudes, while simultaneously providing for sexual need gratification (Elliott and Ashfield 2011).

The broad range of activities adults partake in through the virtual world is largely determined by their reasons for going online. Some adults may go online to prevent being bored, anxious, or depressed (Quayle, Vaughan, and Taylor 2006), while other adults may conduct their social relations online instead of with real-world partners for a variety of personal reasons, including dissatisfaction with one's current state, early sexualized experiences, and/or inadequate adolescent socialization (Lambert and O'Halloran 2008).

Simply put, for adults and adolescents with intense feelings of social inadequacy, the virtual world may be far less threatening than the real world. Mental health experts generally believe that cybersexual interactions allow adults searching for sexual gratification through computer-mediated communications to operationalize their sexual fantasies that prior to the Internet would have been self-extinguished. However, research findings increasingly show that, despite the hope that socially insecure adults and adolescents place in their online social and sexual relationships, as Internet-addicted online users continue to justify their being engaged online as an "innocent pastime," the reality is that they remain unchallenged with their decreasing off-line social contacts—which intensifies their need to lengthen the amount of time that they spend online. This vicious circle, affirm researchers, actually increases rather than decreases the Internet-obsessed adult's levels of depression and feelings of loneliness—and this same logic also appears to describe the vicious circle for online predators (Quayle and Taylor 2003).

Typology of Online Predators and a Comparison with Off-line Predators

Typologies of Internet sexual offenders should be seen as existing along a broad spectrum of individuals who engage in a diverse set of problematic Internet usage. Recently, Lanning (2012) distinguished between (1) situational-type sexual offenders and (2) preferential-type sexual offenders, based on their motivations and on the specific-need driven behavioral patterns. For online predators using the Internet to sexually exploit minors, Lanning (2012) differentiated between (1) pedophiles (hebephiles), (2) diverse offenders, and (3) latent offenders.

According to this researcher, the diverse offender displays a variety of deviant sexual interests rather than a strong sexual preference for children and adolescents. Pedophiles, in contrast, display a keen and deviant sexual interest in children and adolescents in particular. Latent offenders tend to be adults with potentially illegal but previously latent sexual preferences that have more recently begun to manifest, often after their inhibitions are weakened by arousal patterns fueled and validated through online communications with others. Situational-type offenders tend to include adults and adolescents who search online for pornography and eventually find themselves engaging in cybersexual interactions or other sexual acts of a criminal nature. The latter may include individuals trafficking in child pornography for financial gain (Lanning 2012).

Clearly, while Lanning's (2012) typology of online predators lists a variety of categories of offenders engaging in the more deviant forms of online offending behavior, it also highlights the fact that some individuals become interested in criminal online activities following their arousal with more legal kinds of online sexual activities, such as adult pornography and consenting cybersex. In short, both law enforcement and mental health experts maintain that the Internet may actually facilitate online users' (minors', adolescents', and adults') engagement in certain illegal sexual activities by, first, fueling their sexual arousal and, second, by lowering their previously set inhibitions following access to an extensive array of sexual content and online communities with sexually deviant normative values and behaviors.

Reported Similarities and Differences in Off-line and Online Sexual Predators

There has been an ongoing debate among experts as to whether Internet child predators are similar to or different from their off-line peers and individuals in the general population. A recent meta-analysis by Babchishin, Hanson, and Hermann (2011) looked at the extent to which online and off-line offenders differed in terms of demographics (particularly age and level of education) and psychological characteristics—including their degree of empathy for their victims, defined as the perpetrator's awareness of and understanding of the harmful impact of sexual offending on the victim.

The meta-analytic study findings suggest that online sexual predators tend to be Caucasian single males who are slightly younger and more likely to be unemployed, compared to the general population. In terms of educational level, online sexual predators did not differ significantly from those in the general population.

Regarding psychological characteristics of child predators, the meta-analysis identified relatively few statistically significant differences between online and off-line offenders. Importantly, both online and off-line offenders reported greater rates of childhood physical and sexual abuse than the general population—thus indicating that an "abuse cycle" from one generation to the next may be an important contributing factor. Online predators, compared to off-line predators, tended to have greater victim empathy, greater sexual deviancy, and lower impression management. The researchers concluded that the few differences observed between online and off-line offenders can be explained by the fact that online offenders had greater self-control and more psychological barriers to acting on their deviant motivations, compared to their off-line counterparts (Babchishin, Hanson, and Hermann 2011).

CURRENT PROBLEMS AND CONTROVERSIES CONCERNING ONLINE PREDATION

Prevalence Rates and Known Victim Risk Factors

It is important that mental health experts have a sound understanding of the prevalence rates associated with online predation for a number of practical reasons. First, mental health practitioners need an accurate assessment of the nature and prevalence of online child molestation, because they are likely to encounter related issues in a variety of contexts. For example, psychologists working with children or teens may receive referrals regarding actual victims of online predation or those in danger of becoming a victim because of the youth's online sexual risk-taking. Second, school psychologists may have to respond to the concerns of parents or teachers who have received publicity about Internet-initiated sex crimes—and who want clarification about whether such publicity is exaggerated or not. Third, in cases in which youths have been victimized, are being targeted, or are at risk to become victimized, mental health experts need to plan sound strategies for helping victims to heal from the experienced harm or to attempt to thwart harm to potential victims. Fourth, some psychologists may be hired to assist adults caught in the "web" of sexually compulsive online behaviors that may include potential or actual illegal conduct with young online users. Such adults may be referred to treatment because they have been caught by law enforcement, or they may seek treatment voluntarily. Fifth, Internet-related predation problems may become obvious only after adults receive mental health assistance for individual, couples, or family therapy; however, once these predation issues become revealed, the onus is on the mental health practitioner to intervene in a professionally responsible manner (Wolak et al. 2008).

The underreporting of sexual abuse has been a long-standing challenge (Brackenridge et al. 2008)—a factor that also applies to the Internet environment. Estimating the prevalence of online sexual exploitation of children is dependent on several key factors, including the young victim's awareness and recognition of the problem, as well as knowledge of or the availability of support mechanisms to facilitate the young victim's reporting of problematic or negative online experiences. Furthermore, an overlap between online sexual grooming and general online relationship-forming and sexual experimentation may further enhance the recognition of the problem—particularly in cases where youth are not aware of conversing with an adult or with someone having blatant sexual motives. Additionally, the interactions may never progress to become sexually explicit, or in cases where concerns or suspicions actually arise, the offender may employ coercive, threatening strategies to prevent disclosure by the child that sexual activities are being sought (Bryce 2010).

Despite these potential difficulties in recognizing and reporting online sexual grooming, prevalence estimates worldwide have recently been reported by those in law enforcement. For example, between 2009 and 2010, of a total of 2,391 reports received from the public to the Child Exploitation and Online Protection Centre in the United Kingdom (CEOP, 2010), 64% of the reports related to grooming, making it the most reported activity. This figure is consistent with the reported rates of problematic online experiences by adolescents elsewhere.

In 2004, Ybarra, Leaf, and Diener-West reported that 97% of U.S. youth between the ages of 12 and 18 said that they use the Internet, and about 20% of them said that they received online sexual solicitations between 1999 and 2000 alone. Furthermore, in Sweden in 2006, 82% of children between the ages of 9 and 11, and 95% of adolescents between the ages of 12 and 16, used the Internet; of these, a concerning 32% reported receiving online sexual solicitations (Shannon 2008).

Although actual incidence rates of exploited children in the real world and online remain largely unknown and severely underreported (Berson 2003), regardless of the methodology employed, the increase in reported problematic or negative experiences online regarding the actual receipt of sexual solicitations by children and adolescents illustrates a bothersome level of prevalence regarding intended contact-seeking and potential sexual exploitation. Furthermore, accepting the reality that 66% of adolescents regularly use the Internet to access chat rooms (Lambert and O'Halloran 2008), this heavy use rate provides further evidence of the many challenges surrounding early detection and intervention by law enforcement and mental health practitioners regarding online predation in its many forms.

Patterns of Risky Online Behaviors as a Risk Factor for Online Predation of Minors

Multiple mental health experts support the notion that there is increased risk associated with a pattern of different kinds of potentially risky online behaviors—including posting online personal information, interacting with unknown people, having unknown people on a "buddy list," talking to unknown people about sex, seeking pornography, and being rude or nasty to other users.

As the number of different types of these behaviors increases, so do the odds of online interpersonal victimization, including sexual solicitation or harassment. Youths who had engaged in three or four different types of these online behaviors have been reported to be somewhere between 5 to 11 times more likely to report online interpersonal victimization than those who had not engaged in risky behavior to this degree. Further, youths who interacted online with unknown people and also engaged in a high number of different risky online behaviors were much more likely to receive aggressive sexual solicitations than were youths who interacted online with unknown people but restrained their risky behavior. This profile of Internet victims as youths who take risks online is consistent with research from off-line environments showing risk-taking youths to be more vulnerable to victimization in general (Jensen and Brownfield 1986; Lauritsen, Laub, and Sampson 1992; Wolak et al. 2008).

The reality is, note law enforcement and mental health experts, that wherever in the world they reside, children and adolescents are often unsupervised online—an observation reported in the *State of the Net* survey (Consumer Reports Magazine 2011), which found that among young online users, more than 5 million were aged 10 and under, and they admitted that their online accounts were largely unsupervised by their parents. Given these study findings, experts say that younger online users are particularly vulnerable to exploitation in cyberspace, due to two key factors: (1) there is a lack of visual cues in cyberspace to assist minors in making more appropriate judgment calls about the suitability, trustworthiness, or sincerity of those with whom they are communicating online; and (2) children aged 10 and under, in particular, are often at an early stage of learning in terms of how to communicate effectively with others online. Thus, relative to the more socially skilled online adults, children are particularly vulnerable to being exploited.

It is important to underscore that online child sexual exploitation can take many forms, and that minors themselves may also engage in illegal behaviors, such as taking or sending explicit sexual images or videos of themselves before forwarding the images or videos to others—a relatively more recent Internet activity known as "sexting." While there is as yet little research into the exact nature and prevalence of sexting (Bluett-Boyd et al. 2013), several surveys conducted in the United States have recently suggested that sexting is an important emerging issue there and elsewhere.

For example, a U.S. study commissioned by the National Campaign to Prevent Teen Pregnancy (2008) found that 20% of respondents between 13 and 19 years, and 33% of respondents between 20 and 26 years, have reportedly electronically sent, or posted online, nude or seminude pictures or videos of themselves. In another study encompassing 20 European countries, 14,946 respondents aged 11 to 16 were interviewed; of these, between 0.9% and 11.5% of the respondents in each of the 20 countries reportedly engaged in sexting activities (Baumgartner et al. 2014).

Gender and Lifestyle Risk Factors

Mental health experts tend to agree that female youths are considerably more at risk than male youths for victimization by Internet-initiated sex crimes as well as for statutory rape in general (Cheit and Braslow 2005; Troup-Leasure and Snyder 2005; Wolak et al. 2008). Also, female youths who become sexually active during early adolescence may be especially vulnerable, because they are more likely to be involved with more mature partners (Leitenberg and Saltzman 2000, 2003) and to partake in risky sexual behaviors in the real world (Ponton and Judice 2004). Although female youths represent a higher proportion of victims than male youths, in the latter category, those who identify as gay or questioning their sexual orientation appear to be another youth segment particularly susceptible to online victimization—and later real-world victimization.

Male youths seem to constitute about 25% of the victims in Internet-initiated sex crimes, and virtually all of their offenders are mature males (Wolak et al. 2008). While being sexually victimized by male offenders does not confirm with large degrees of accuracy that male victims are gay, recent reports have shown that the bulk of Internet-initiated cases involving male youths had elements making it overt that the victims were gay or questioning their sexual orientations, in that they would often meet offenders in gay-oriented chat rooms. Other research has shown that hostility and social stigma toward homosexuality per se (Tharinger and Wells

2000; Williams et al. 2005), as well as feelings of isolation and loneliness (Martin and D'Augelli 2003; Sullivan 2002), may impair the ability of male youths identifying as gay or questioning their sexuality to form age-appropriate, intimate relationships—both online and off-line. Concerns about confidentiality and feelings that problems are "too personal to disclose" can also limit these male youths' willingness to get information about sexual matters from trusted adults (Dubow, Lovko, and Kausch 1990). Therefore, they turn to the Internet to either find answers to their questions about sexuality or to meet potential romantic partners. In these online environments, the vulnerable youths may encounter adults who can readily exploit them.

LEGAL AND MENTAL HEALTH INTERVENTION STRATEGIES AND NONPROFIT ORGANIZATIONS TO DETER OR DEAL WITH ONLINE PREDATION

Legal Strategies Aimed at Curbing Grooming in the United States and in the United Kingdom

Grooming by predators is a criminal offense in the United States. Here, § 2421 and § 2422 under Title 18 of the U.S. Code criminalize the persuading, inducing, enticing, or coercing of a minor to travel to and meet to engage in any sexual activity for which a person can be charged with a criminal offense. Both of these sections also include a perpetrator's attempt to do any of the online actions listed. However, when there is no documented meeting that occurs in the real world between an offender and a victim, sexually exploitative interactions such as those used on the Internet can only be brought to the attention of authorities or mental health experts when a victim actually comes forward and discloses the abuse to authorities or mental health practitioners. Another way that online predation is discovered follows from some undercover police investigation (Kloess, Beech, and Harkins 2014).

It is important to note that in the United Kingdom, there is not separate legislation for online minor exploitation as compared to off-line minor exploitation; in fact, these sexual abuse offenses have been drafted widely in order to apply to a variety of situations. The Sexual Offences Act of 2003 is the United Kingdom's key piece of legislation regarding sexual abuse and grooming of victims in general; while this law applies to sexual offenses having adult victims, minors as victims are treated differently and are covered by a number of other specific criminal offenses. Furthermore, the United Kingdom does not legislate separately for predation actions committed outside of its legal jurisdiction (Hillman, Hooper, and Choo 2014).

In the United States, although clearly causing or inciting a minor to engage in sexual activity is a criminal offense under Title 18 of the U.S. Criminal Code, third-party watching of such sexual acts is considered to be heinous in nature and is, therefore, covered by additional criminal statutes in some U.S. states—such as in California, Florida, and New York (Kloess, Beech, and Harkins 2014).

It is obvious that approaches to constructing and providing an adequate legal response in the United States and in the United Kingdom as a means to combat grooming, in particular, are still in their infancy, particularly when extending the problem to newer forms of technology like cell phones (Kloess, Beech, and Harkins 2014).

Legal Strategies Aimed at Curbing Online Predation in Australia, Canada, and South Africa

Australia

In Australia, under the Criminal Code Act 1995 and by more recent amendments in 2014, what qualifies as a "child sex offense" for the purposes of the Crimes Act of 1914 may be found under three broad headings (Hillman, Hooper, and Choo 2014):

- Sex Tourism Offenses,
- Child Pornography and Child Abuse Material Offenses, and
- Sexual Offenses against Children in Australia.

In this jurisdiction, sex tourism is defined as the commercial sexual exploitation of children (persons under the age of 16 at the time of the alleged offense) by individuals who travel from developed countries to meet children in developing countries for sexual activities. Adults engaging in sex tourism can receive prison sentences of from 12 to 15 years upon conviction.

Regarding pornography and child abuse material offenses, Section 474.26 of the Australian Criminal Code—namely, using a carriage service to procure persons under 16 years of age for sexual activities—was introduced in 2004. Consequently, three separate offenses were created, each resulting in a maximum prison sentence of 15 years, where the perpetrator is convicted of using a carriage service to send a communication to another person with the intention that the receiver will (1) engage in sexual activity with the perpetrator; or (2) engage in sexual activity with another person; or (3) engage in sexual activity with another person who is or whom the perpetrator believes is under 18 years of age.

Regarding sexual offenses against children, the Australian Criminal Code differentiates between "child abuse material" and "child pornography material" in Section 473.1, whereby the former includes images or representations of persons who are or seem to be under the age of 18 as being the victim of torture, cruelty, or physical abuse. The latter includes images or representations of minors engaged in sexual activity with adults or as involving activities associated with the sexual organs or breasts. It is an offense under the Australian Criminal Code to possess, control, distribute, obtain, attempt to obtain, or facilitate the production or distribution of such sexually explicit material involving minors. These terms were given a broad meaning in the Australian Criminal Code in order to deal with both print and online media, as well as data stored in data centers in overseas jurisdictions. It is important to note that the Code exempts from liability law enforcement officers involved in investigations of this nature. Sections 474.19(1) and 474.22(1) of the Australian Criminal Code make it an offense for an individual to access any of the material described above using the Internet. Child grooming, in particular, is covered under Section 474.27 of the Australian Criminal Code.

Canada

The law in relation to child exploitation in Canada was recently amended (February 2014) with the intention of increasing the sentencing options available to judges upon conviction relating to cases of child predation and exploitation. For sexual offenses against minors, the Canadian Criminal Code of 1985 maintains that direct and indirect touching of a person under 16 for a sexual purpose, as well as an invitation to a minor to touch the offender for a sexual purpose, is illegal. There is also special provision under the Canadian Criminal Code for an aggravated offense, whereby the perpetrator is in a trust or authority position relative to the minor, making it illegal to sexually assault a person under age 18. There is an increased penalty in cases where a weapon was found to be employed in carrying out the sexual assault of the minor. Furthermore, Section 170 of the Canadian Criminal Code creates a specific offense covering circumstances where a parent or guardian of a child procures that child for the purposes of having him or her engage in sex with a third party. The Canadian Criminal Code also makes it a criminal offense to communicate with a minor through a telecommunications service (such as the Internet) with the intent of committing or facilitating any of the child predation crimes outlined. It is also an offense under Section 212(4) of the Canadian Criminal Code to pay a minor for sex. Finally, Section 163.1(1) of the Code defines "child pornography" very similarly to the definition found in Australian legislation, making it an offense under Section 171.1 to make sexually explicit material available to a child—online or off-line (Hillman, Hooper, and Choo 2014).

South Africa

South African law considers sexual exploitation of minors in a single section of the Sexual Offences Act, Section 17. This section includes both giving money to a minor or to a third party for allowing sexual activity with a minor, and making the offering of these kinds of services, criminal offenses. This section also makes it an offense if an adult fails to prevent the sexual exploitation of a minor, especially when the perpetrator is the parent or guardian. Section 17 is seen as a catch-all section that makes it a criminal offense to engage in sexual exploitation of minors in a variety of ways—especially as a facilitator or as a legal guardian of the minor. Section 20, in particular, makes it a criminal offense to benefit from minor pornography.

Furthermore, Section 18 deals with grooming offenses, making it a criminal act to engage in any means of coercing a minor into sexual activity, including using pornography or pictures of sexual objects to lower the minor's inhibitions. Under Section 18, it is a criminal offense to share such sexually explicit acts involving a minor with a third party. While, theoretically, South African law intends to provide a great deal of protection to minors and the ability to punish those involved in predation behaviors, legal experts have argued that by affording in this troubling area only a single chapter of legislation (spanning just five pages) of the Sexual Offenses Act, there is a dreadful lack of commitment by South Africa to attend to this heinous predation issue—which could have been and should have been articulated much more fully and forcefully in the law (Hillman, Hooper, and Choo 2014).

Closing Remarks

Given the relatively new phenomenon of online child exploitation, it has quickly become an extremely important area of legal, mental health, and public policy concern in jurisdictions worldwide. The main reason is that such acts have a traumatic psychological and physical impact on the young victims. Unfortunately, it is currently difficult for experts to obtain realistic long-term trend data on reported convictions on a global scale. Part of the problem, as shown in this section, is that existing legislative and prosecution-based approaches, while important, vary considerably from one jurisdiction to another and are, legal experts posit, grossly lax and inadequate. This analysis clearly highlights the need for clearer national and international definitions regarding online predation, for in its present state, the apparent lack of consistency in the international legislative environment creates needless opportunities for the ongoing sexual exploitation of minors, particularly in the ever-expanding online and mobile phone environment (Hillman, Hooper, and Choo 2014).

E-Safety Programs for Dealing with Online Predation and Mental Health Experts' Reflections on Dealing with Online Predation Victims

E-Safety Education

By definition, "e-safety" refers to the way that young people are taught about risks online, how to protect themselves, and to whom they should report "concerning" activity while online. Education of minors about online or e-safety is considered to be a key deterrent to online predation. Thus, in the United States, Canada, the United Kingdom, and elsewhere in the developed world, teams of law enforcement, mental health experts, private sector leaders, educators, and legal experts are developing comprehensive online safety strategies and programs for minors—often distributed in schools and online. E-safety information is commonly cascaded to parents through their children's schools. Through e-safety initiatives, both children and their parents/guardians are made responsible for taking appropriate steps to increase minors' safety while online.

Mental health experts affirm that a key ingredient in keeping minors safe in an online environment is to ensure parental involvement in the e-safety educational process. Parents need to emphasize in an age-appropriate way that there is no single profile of a child who will become the victim of sexual abuse, and that, most often, authorities maintain that the perpetrator of such acts is someone the child likely knows and cares about—such as a relative, a friend, or a so-called "trusted" authority figure like a coach, teacher, or minister.

Parents also need to understand themselves the important fact that most child predation victims report feeling unprotected, unable to resist their perpetrators on their own, and isolated by what has happened to them. While most e-safety programs in schools and other community organizations encourage open discussions between parents and their children about the difference between "good touches" and "bad touches," national surveys have found that this basic teaching as a solo strategy does little to help children do something to prevent being victimized and, in some cases, actually makes the situation worse. What is even more alarming, these national surveys have shown that children who had undergone this basic education but who subsequently became victims of sexual abuse were half as likely to report it as were children who had no basic program at all (Corley 2005).

In contrast, children given additional training, particularly in social and emotional skill development, were better able to protect themselves against the threat of being victimized—because they were more apt to say that they wanted to be left alone, they were more willing to yell or fight back when approached by an adult with sexual demands, and they would actually threaten to tell on the perpetrator if something bad did happen to them. In short, parents need to emphasize this strong message to their children: You need [the self-awareness] to know that when a situation feels wrong, you can trust that feeling, and then you need [enough self-confidence and assertiveness] to trust and act on your experienced feelings of distress—even in the face of an adult who may be trying to reassure you that "it's okay to do what is being demanded" (Corley 2005).

In short, mental health experts posit that the more effective e-safety programs that have been developed enlist the participation of parents who teach their children to assert what they want, to assert their rights as worthy individuals rather than to be passive, and to not blame themselves if something did or does happen to them by an untrustworthy adult. Children need to know what their body boundaries are and to be ready to defend them. Furthermore, they need to know that their parents form part of a critical network of support to whom they can turn in times of trouble. Critical to the safety of the child when online and off-line is emotional coaching, emotional support, and emotional skill building. Age-appropriate messages have been developed by Corley (2005) for parents to share with their children in a boundary-setting exercise as a means of helping to deter sexual abuse and online predation.

So, where might a model e-safety education program be found? In the United Kingdom, for example, some of the most commonly used, well-designed, and widely disseminated e-safety education materials were produced by the Child Exploitation and Online Protection Centre (CEOP). Here, CEOP is primarily responsible for digitally mediated surveillance in its law enforcement functions. Created in 2006, CEOP was also meant to be a cross-agency department of the Serious Organized Crime Agency (SOCA) in the United Kingdom. The e-safety education program developed by CEOP was created by a knowledgeable team of experts comprised of police officers, staff seconded from charities, and a broad range of strategic private sector partners interested in keeping minors safe online, including Visa Europe and Microsoft (Barnard-Wills 2012).

The normative discourse of the materials is that it not only gives minors a sound, basic understanding of the online environment and information technology (IT), including the opportunities afforded to users because of it, but that it has a further priority of helping minors to be aware of certain common online threats—such as cyberbullying, cyberstalking, and online predation. Such material, then, should clearly convey the behavioral and motivational tactics of the perpetrators likely to be involved in such acts. Another message that tends to be present is the push for minors' privacy protections—thus sending a strong warning to minors not to disclose their personal information in online forums or with individuals with whom they are communicating online. Today, e-safety materials available to minors globally are dominated by the threat of child sexual abuse per se; consequently, these tend to be very much harm- and loss-based from a content perspective.

As a case in point, CEOP has created its ThinkuKnow material, designed to be both emotionally engaging for its young audience and impactful in terms of getting key online safety messages to minors. The pedagogy of ThinkuKnow is also very interactive and uses a number of powerful short films to educate minors about the risks that they may encounter when using the Internet. The main goal is to empower children to know how to recognize and report an online problem, particularly child sexual abuse. To this end, the CEOP discourse constructs two linked sets of dangerous behaviors arising from minors' wrongly assessing their online and off-line environments: first, that minors should not wrongly assume that the online and off-line environments are the same; and second, that minors should not wrongly assume that the two environments are totally different (Barnard-Wills 2012).

To this end, the CEOP discourse tends to portray the online environment as being more dangerous than the offline environment for three main reasons: (1) online users can and do lie, (2) it is easy for online users to remain anonymous in this environment, and (3) online users can circulate sexually explicit images more freely online than in the real world because the virtual world tends to be less guarded. Another key point delivered by the ThinkuKnow material is that Internet addiction, defined as spending too much time online to the extent that one is neglecting one's off-line personal and social life, is by many counts very psychologically and physically harmful. Yet another key point delivered by the ThinkuKnow material pertains to wrongly assuming that online activity exists in a vacuum unrelated to off-line life; this message is exemplified by online users' posting images online that they would not want people in the off-line world to see (Barnard-Wills 2012).

Experts' Reflections on Dealing with Online Predation Victims

Recently, an insightful study conducted in Germany by the research team of Weber, Haardt-Beker, and Schulte (2010) included reflections from mental health practitioners about the care and treatment of victims of online child pornographic exploitation (known as CPE in Germany). These researchers contacted all specialized institutions nationwide dealing with sexually abused children—both online and off-line. Using a combined questionnaire and interview methodology with the mental health professionals from these institutions, the study team's database included 245 cases of confirmed CPE (197 female children and 48 male children), as well as 280 suspected cases of CPE.

The researchers reported that the cases of CPE were of not only of a higher complexity than the off-line cases, but that the former were significantly more demanding for mental health practitioners to conquer effectively—thus raising scores of intervention questions about appropriate professional involvement and strategy planning. Two key concerns expressed by these experts involved challenges such as (1) the intense long-term guilt maintained by the victims after the online exploitation occurred, and (2) the issue of permanence once the sexually abusive images were distributed online. The lingering harm, these experts noted, made it very difficult for their young clients to adhere to the "coping" strategies designed with their assistance so that they could move forward with greater resilience. Furthermore, a key issue consistently making it difficult for victims to even disclose the CPE to authorities was a combined intense feeling of guilt over their own behavior and a fear of the threats made by their perpetrators (Weber, Haardt-Beker, and Schulte 2010).

The type of abusive images dealt with during counseling or therapy included mainly sexual acts between minors and adults, including the touching of genitals, vaginal abuse in the females, oral abuse, posing for nude pictures, and photographing or filming of the genitals. About half of the professionals said that they did not know whether the child-abusive images of the victimized females had actually been distributed to others over the Internet. This uncertainty was even greater, they affirmed, with the male victims. Of the study group, 15 female victims and 5 male victims knew that their abusive images had been publicized on the Internet, and of this subset, 6 of the female victims and all 5 of the male victims said that they had seen their pictures online (Weber, Haardt-Beker, and Schulte 2010).

The professionals who took part in the study also tended to agree on the following points: (1) that there are gender differences in terms of coping with CPE, (2) that special training is needed in order to provide effective and lasting counseling/therapy for victims of CPE, (3) that the number of unreported cases of CPE is undoubtedly higher than those unreported for off-line cases, and (4) that professionally intervening with victims of CPE is extremely complex and often fraught with setbacks. Regardless of gender, the victims of CPE seemed to present with different symptoms of trauma than victims otherwise traumatized.

The researchers concluded that even though CPE is talked about a lot in the mental health literature as a major problem to be attended to in society, there is still a major void existing about how to effectively identify CPE victims, how to properly approach them, and how to design sound interventions to help them move on to live a normal, healthy, productive life free of guilt and fear (Weber, Haardt-Beker, and Schulte 2010).

To give readers additional insights about the challenges forensic psychologists encounter when dealing with online predation, an interview with Dr. Angela Eke, coordinator of the Research Unit within the Behavioural Sciences and Analysis Services of the Ontario Provincial Police (OPP) in Canada, is included. Her areas of research include sexual offending and child exploitation, with a focus on offender risk assessment.

INTERVIEW WITH AN EXPERT

Dr. Angela Eke, Expert in Online Child Exploitation

Dr. Angela Eke is the coordinator of the Research Unit within the Behavioural Sciences and Analysis Section of the Ontario Provincial Police (OPP) in Canada. Her degrees are in psychology, and her areas of research include sexual offending and child exploitation, with a focus on offender risk assessment. Many of her research projects are collaborative efforts involving other mental health and criminal justice professionals.

Dr. Eke has given numerous presentations and has conducted workshops on child pornography offending, recidivism, and risk assessment for various audiences, including mental health practitioners, victim services, police, and other criminal justice professionals. She has also helped organize and deliver in-house training on topics relating to mental health and has assisted in the development of a formal safeguard program for those working in the area of online child exploitation. She is the recipient of the Kids' Internet Safety Alliance (KINSA) Heroes of the Fight Award.

Q You are a recognized expert in online child exploitation. For your contributions in this area, you have been awarded the KINSA Heroes of the Fight Award. Can you speak more about this award and why you were the recipient?

A I feel very fortunate to have received the KINSA Heroes award in 2010 for my research in the area of child pornography offending. There were seven people who were honored that year, including colleagues D/S/Sgt Frank Goldschmidt of the Ontario Provincial Police and Dr. Michael Seto of the Royal Ottawa Health Care Group. KINSA is a not-for-profit organization that was created by a group of dedicated and experienced criminal justice and business professionals. They have a global impact, in part through their provision of training relating to identifying, rescuing, and protecting children from online and off-line sexual abuse, as well as their work relating to cyberbullying and child advocacy. They have a publicly accessible Web site for those interested in learning more about KINSA.

Q Dr. Michael Seto has reported that about 5% of online sexual offenders commit a new sexual offense of some kind during a 1.5- to 6-year follow-up. Can you say more about this finding and your views on what may be an effective mental health intervention to reduce this recidivism rate?

A This finding came from a meta-analysis [by definition, a research study that analyzes and combines findings from a number of studies] that Dr. Seto conducted with colleagues and published in 2011. The majority of the samples involved child pornography offenders. These types of studies are helpful, as they combine many findings to give us a more generalized understanding of the data trend. One of our studies was included in that research team's analysis; we separated out findings of sexual recidivism (i.e., subsequent offending) based on other offender characteristics (i.e., history of other offending), demonstrating heterogeneity within the group.

When reviewing research and discussions relating to recidivism rates, researchers believe that it is important to consider where this information comes from. Usually, research is based on official data, such as reports of sexual offending to police. Data collected based on new contacts with police provides us with an idea of how many offenders will be identified as repeat offenders and allows us to examine risk factors for future offending. However, it is also understood to be an underestimate of true offending, including sexual recidivism. Contact sexual offending among child pornography offenders is also examined in other ways, including *prior* offending that is known to police, as well as self-reported prior offending.

Self-report research helps us understand undetected (i.e., unreported) offending. For example, in Seto and colleagues' 2011 meta-analysis, 12% of child pornography offenders had a current or prior known contact sex offense, whereas self-report data suggested approximately 50% of child pornography offenders admit to having committed a contact sex offense against a child in the past, so self-report numbers were much higher than officially reported numbers.

Regarding the second part of your question, knowledge about factors associated with the onset of contact sexual offending, as well as risk factors for recidivism among child pornography offenders will help us to better understand treatment and management targets; consequently, mental health experts can better direct resources to, hopefully, reduce subsequent offending. Some treatment and management considerations can include sexual motivation (e.g., paraphilias), personality characteristics, substance use, impulsive behaviors, and coping strategies, along with many others.

Q Dr. Michael Seto also suggests that there may be a distinct subgroup of online-only offenders who pose relatively low risk of contact sexual offenses in the future. Can you outline where this subgroup places, relative to other online and off-line child predator typologies?

A Whether some online child pornography offenders represent a distinct group of offenders has been a key topic of conversation in the literature. As stated in my previous answer, not all child pornography offenders are the same. Just recently, a number of articles have been published examining child pornography offenders with and without contact sexual offenses. There are some interesting differences between the two. This work may inform us regarding expectations for subsequent offending (i.e., risk)—which is important in both how we approach our use of resources and considerations for sentencing. For example, offenders considered to be at higher risk for reoffending may receive more intensive supervision and treatment, as well as longer sentences in general.

For any child pornography offender, regardless of his or her prior or current offending, the child pornography offense arrest provides the opportunity for intervention. Many child pornography offenders involve themselves with this material because they have a sexual interest in children. Their arrest allows for an opportunity to provide assistance, to help them manage this sexual interest and criminal behavior (namely, accessing child pornography)—with the goal of reducing the risk of subsequent sexual offending and, thus, reducing the future victimization of children.

Q The potential for child predators to misuse mobile phone technology (especially the iPhone) is highlighted by the fact that there are five billion mobile phone connections worldwide—comprising 77% of the global population.* How do mental health experts perceive this threat, and what strategies might be used to combat it?

A All technology has the potential for misuse, and mobile phones are now very common, easy to use, and have multiple applications (or features) that aid us in documenting and sharing with others images and information. So, yes, these forms of technology can have a prominent place in offenses involving electronic media. As mobile and computing technology amalgamate into single devices, this reality might become even more

---

* McCartan, K. F., & McAlister, R. (2012). Mobile phone technology and sexual abuse. *Information and Communication Technology Law, 21*, 257–268.

relevant. Mobile technology also comes into play when we consider youth exposure to pornography; in particular, some of the research examining adolescent access to mainstream pornography suggests that their first exposure to pornography is online, often via their cell phones. And, as touched on in this chapter, concerns about sexting among teens relates commonly to mobile devices.

Q Where do you think that the future research focus on online predation will likely be and why?

A There will be many research directions that influence and assist in what we know about Internet-facilitated sexual offending and the impact on society. A few that come to mind include a continuation of research into child pornography offenders themselves, as well as offender risk. Currently, a very practical interest is how we work with offenders, how best practices in relation to treatment and behavior management can be developed. So, I expect that we will start to see more research examining the efficacy of programs used with child pornography offenders.

In the emerging literature, we are seeing new lines of research that compare offenders who have been arrested versus those in the community (e.g., via anonymous online studies), as well as issues relating to how offenders are detected and the associations between contact sex offending and the content of offender pornography collections. I expect that these threads will also continue.

Importantly, there is new work examining best practices to assist victims, including setting up centers that can assist families through the court system, as well as provide all levels of social and psychological support. There is also interesting sociological research examining the role of pornography and social norms in the ever-evolving social media and technology age. At the same time, we are seeing more research relating to the wellness of individuals who are involved in these investigations, to support their own mental and general health.

A very important piece to all of this is primary prevention: How might we prevent offending and prevent victimization in the first place? Across professional groups, there have been a variety of discussions regarding primary prevention. For example, interested readers can access resources on various Web sites in this regard, including going to the "Prevention" tab of the Association for the Treatment of Sexual Abusers (ATSA) Web site.

Q Are laws making online predation and grooming a criminal offense in the United States, Canada, and elsewhere effective—why or why not?

A In many instances, the offenses are illegal off-line, too, but there are nuances that matter regarding online use. For example, there are new offenses, such as *accessing* child pornography, that relate specifically to online activities. Efficacy could be measured in a number of ways; for example, the impact on the rates of victimization, the impact of new legislation on reporting, what happens with offenders (i.e., do they desist), and so forth. Since a lot of legislation in this area is quite new, time will matter in how we understand—and how we can assess—the impact or influence of these charges. I expect that researchers will examine these offenses from a variety of perspectives; for example, how well the laws work (i.e., whether they meet their intended goals), the meaning of these laws in terms of correctional issues (i.e., sentencing, probation, and treatment), and how we can better provide assistance and support to victims.

CONCLUSION

This chapter looked at the criminal activities associated with online predation. What is obvious is that while online predation is a global phenomenon of extreme concern to the authorities and to mental health practitioners because of the severe harm caused to the victims—who are children and adolescents—there are many questions remaining about the typology of the perpetrators and the types of effective counseling that would help to heal the young victims in the short-term as well as over the longer term. Moreover, though many developed countries have developed criminal statutes regarding off-line and online predation, legal experts posit that existing legislation not only falls short of the optimum but varies considerably from one jurisdiction to another. Consequently, understanding the global prevalence rates of this societal problem remains a relative mystery. Finally, the authorities predict that the problem will increase as predators begin to exploit their victims using smartphone technologies.

REFERENCES

Aslan, D. (2011). Critically evaluating typologies of internet sex offenders: A psychological perspective. *Journal of Forensic Psychology Practice, 11*, 406–431.

Australian Government Attorney-General's Department. (2009). Proposed reforms to Commonwealth child sex-related offences. Canberra, ACT: Attorney-General's Department.

Babchishin, K. M., Hanson, R. K., & Hermann, C. A. (2011). The characteristics of online sex offenders: A meta-analysis. *Sexual Abuse: Journal of Research and Treatment, 23,* 92–123.

Barnard-Wills, D. (2012). E-safety education: Young people, surveillance and responsibility. *Criminology and Criminal Justice, 12,* 239–255.

Bates, A., & Metcalf, C. (2007). A psychometric comparison of Internet and non-Internet sex offenders from a community treatment sample. *Journal of Sexual Aggression, 13,* 11–20.

Baumgartner, S. E., Sumter, S. R., Peter, J., Valkenburg, P. M., & Livingstone, S. (2014). Does country context matter? Investigating the predictors of teen sexting across Europe. *Computer and Human Behavior, 1,* 157–164.

Berson, I. R. (2003). Grooming cybervictims: The psychological effects of online exploitation for youth. *Journal of School Violence, 2,* 5–21.

Bluett-Boyd, N., Fileborn, B., Quadara, A., & Moore, S. (2013). *The role of emerging communication technologies in experiences of sexual violence: A new legal frontier?* (Research report no. 23.) Melbourne, Australia: Australian Institute of Family Studies.

Brackenridge, C. H., Bishopp, D., Moussalli, S., & Tapp, J. (2008). The characteristics of sexual abuse in sport: A multidimensional scaling analysis of events described in media reports. *International Journal of Sport and Exercise Psychology, 6,* 385–406.

Bryce, J. (2010). Online sexual exploitation of children and young people. In Y. E. Jewkes & M. E. Yar (Eds.), *Handbook of Internet crime* (pp. 320–342). Cullompton, England: Willan.

Cheit, R. E., & Braslow, L. (2005). Statutory rape: An empirical examination of claims of "overreaction." In N. Dowd, D. G. Singer, & R. F. Wilson (Eds.), *Handbook of children, culture, and violence* (pp. 85–112). Thousand Oaks, CA: Sage.

Child Exploitation and Online Protection Centre (CEOP). (2010). *Annual review 2009–2010.* 2010 Retrieved from http://ceop.police.uk/Publications/

Choo, K-K. R. (2008). Organised crime groups in cyberspace: A typology. *Trends in Organized Crime, 11,* 270–295.

Consumer Reports Magazine. (2011, June). That Facebook friend might be 10 years old, and other troubling news. Retrieved from http://www.consumerreports.org/cro/magazinearchive/2011/june/electronics-computers/state-of-the-net/facebook-concerns/index.htm

Cooper, A. (1998). Sexuality and the Internet: Surfing into the new millennium. *Cyber Psychology and Behavior, 1,* 187–193.

Corley, M. D. (2005). Sexplanations II: Helping addicted parents talk with their children about healthy sexuality, sexual addiction, and sexual abuse. *Sexual Addiction and Compulsivity, 12,* 245–258.

Council of Europe. (2007). *Convention on the protection of children against sexual exploitation and sexual abuse.* Strasbourg, France: Council of Europe.

Craven, S., Brown, S., & Gilchrist, E. (2006). Sexual grooming of children: Review of literature and theoretical considerations. *Journal of Sexual Aggression, 12,* 287–299.

Craven, S., Brown, S., & Gilchrist, E. (2007). Current responses to sexual grooming: Implication for prevention. *Howard Journal of Criminal Justice, 46,* 60–71.

Dubow, E. F., Lovko, K. R., & Kausch, D. F. (1990). Demographic differences in adolescents' health concerns and perceptions of helping agents. *Journal of Clinical Child Psychology, 19,* 44–54.

Durkin, K. (1997). Misuse of the Internet by pedophiles: Implications for law enforcement and probation practice. *Federal Probation, 61,* 14–18.

Elliott, I. A., & Ashfield, A. (2011). The use of online technology in the modus operandi of female sex offenders. *Journal of Sexual Aggression, 17,* 1–13.

Federal Bureau of Investigation (FBI). (2011, December 6). Husband and wife team charged with sex trafficking of teenagers. Media release.

Filosa, G. (2007, March 24). Online profiles attracting sexual predators, feds warn: Teen sites being used as victim directories. *The Times Picayune.* Retrieved from LexisNexis.

Finkelhor, D. (1984). *Child sexual abuse: New theory and research.* New York, NY: Free Press.

Gillespie, A. (2002). Child protection on the Internet: Challenges for criminal law. *Child and Family Law Quarterly, 14,* 411–426.

Hancock, D. (2002). The two faces of a 13-year-old girl. Retrieved from http://www.cbsnews.com/news/the-two-faces-of-a-13-year-old-girl/

Hillman, H., Hooper, C., & Choo, K-W. R. (2014). Online child exploitation: Challenges and future research directions. *Computer Law and Security Review, 30,* 687–698.

Hinduja, S., & Patchin, J. W. (2008). Personal information of adolescents on the Internet: A quantitative content analysis of MySpace. *Journal of Adolescence 31,* 125–146.

Howitt, D., & Sheldon, K. (2008). Sexual fantasy in paedophile offenders: Can any model explain satisfactorily new findings from a study of Internet and contact sexual offenders? *Legal and Criminological Psychology, 13,* 137–158.

Interpol. (2008). Databases. Interpol Fact Sheet, COM/FS/2008-07/GI-04. Retrieved from http://www.interpol.int/Public/ICPO/FactSheets/GI04.pdf

Jensen, G. F., & Brownfield, D. (1986). Gender, lifestyles, and victimization: Beyond routine activity. *Violence and Victims, 1,* 85–99.

Kloess, J. A., Beech, A. R., & Harkins, L. (2014). Online child sexual exploitation: Prevalence, process, and offender characteristics. *Trauma, Violence, and Abuse, 15,* 126–139.

Lambert, S., & O'Halloran, E. (2008). Deductive thematic analysis of a female paedophilia website. *Psychiatry, Psychology and Law, 15,* 284–300.

Lanning, K. V. (2012). Cyber "pedophiles": A behavioral perspective. In K. Borgeson & K. Kuehnle (Eds.), *Serial offenders: Theory and practice* (pp. 71–87). Sudbury, MA: Jones & Bartlett Learning.

Lauritsen, J. L., Laub, J. H., & Sampson, R. J. (1992). Conventional and delinquent activities: Implications for the prevention of violent victimization among adolescents. *Violence and Victims, 7,* 91–108.

Leitenberg, H., & Saltzman, H. (2000). A statewide survey of age at first intercourse for adolescent females and age of their male partner: Relation to other risk behaviors and statutory rape implications. *Archives of Sexual Behavior, 29,* 203–215.

Leitenberg, H., & Saltzman, H. (2003). College women who had sexual intercourse when they were underage minors (13–15): Age of their male partners, relation to current adjustment, and statutory rape implications. *Sexual Abuse, 15,* 135–147.

Leyden, J. (2014, January 17). International child abuse webcam ring smashed after routine police check. *The Register.* Retrieved from http://www.theregister.co.uk/2014/01/17/webcam_abuse_ring_dismantled/

Martin, J. I., & D'Augelli, A. R. (2003). How lonely are gay and lesbian youth? *Psychological Reports, 93,* 486.

McAlinden, A.-M. (2006). "Setting 'em up": Personal, familial and institutional grooming in the sexual abuse of children. *Social and Legal Studies, 15,* 339–362.

McCabe, K. A. (2008). The role of Internet service providers in cases of child pornography and child prostitution. *Social Science Computer Review, 26,* 247–251.

Mitchell, K. J., Finkelhor, D., & Wolak, J. (2005). The Internet and family and acquaintance sexual abuse. *Child Maltreatment, 10,* 49–60.

National Campaign to Prevent Teen Pregnancy. (2008). Sex and tech: Results from a survey of teens and young adults. *Computer Law and Security Review, 30,* 687–698.

O'Connell, R. (2003). A typology of child cybersexploitation and online grooming practices. Retrieved from http://www.jisc.ac.uk/uploaded_documents/lis_PaperJPrice.pdf

Patchin, J. W., & Hinduja, S. (2010). Trends in online social networking: Adolescent use of MySpace over time. *New Media & Society, 12,* 197–216.

Ponton, L. E., & Judice, S. (2004). Typical adolescent sexual development. *Child and Adolescent Psychiatric Clinics of North America, 13,* 497.

Quayle, E., & Taylor, M. (2001). Child seduction and self-representation on the Internet. *CyberPsychology and Behavior, 4,* 597–608.

Quayle, E., & Taylor, M. (2002). Child pornography and the Internet: Perpetuating a cycle of abuse. *Deviant Behavior*, *23,* 331–361.

Quayle, E., & Taylor, M. (2003). Model of problematic Internet use in people with a sexual interest in children. *CyberPsychology and Behavior, 6,* 93–106.

Quayle, E., & Taylor, M. (2007). *Internet and child pornography*. London: Psychology Press.

Quayle, E., Vaughan, M., & Taylor, M. (2006). Sex offenders, internet child abuse images and emotional avoidance: The importance of values. *Aggression and Violent Behavior, 11,* 1–11.

Riegel, D. L. (2004). Effects on boy-attracted pedosexual males of viewing boy erotica [Letter to the editor]. *Archives of Sexual Behavior*, *33,* 321–323.

Shannon, D. (2008). Online sexual grooming in Sweden: Online and off-line sex offences against children as described in Swedish police data. *Journal of Scandinavian Studies in Criminology and Crime Prevention, 9,* 160–180.

Stanley, J., & Tomison, A. M. (2001). *Strategic directions in child protection: Informing policy and practice*. Unpublished report, South Australian Department of Human Services.

Sullivan, M. (2002). Social alienation in gay youth. *Journal of Human Behavior in the Social Environment, 5,* 1–17.

Sutton, D., & Jones, V. (2004). *Position paper on child pornography and Internet related sexual exploitation of children*. Brussels, Belgium: Save the Children Europe Group.

Talamo, A., & Ligorio, B. (2001). Strategic identities in cyberspace. *CyberPsychology and Behavior*, *4*, 109–120.

Taylor, M. (1999). *The nature and dimensions of child pornography on the Internet*. Paper presented at the International Conference on Combating Child Pornography on the Internet, Vienna. Retrieved from http://www.asem.org /Documents/99ConfVienna/pa_taylor.html

Taylor, M., & Quayle, E. (2003). *Child pornography: An Internet crime*. New York, NY: Brunner-Routledge.

Taylor, M., & Quayle, E. (2006). The Internet and abuse images of children: Search, pre-criminal situations and opportunity. In R. Wortley & S. Smallbone (Eds.), *Situational prevention of child sexual abuse* (pp. 169–195). New York, NY: Criminal Justice Press/Willan.

Taylor, M., & Quayle, E. (2010). Internet sexual offending. In J. M. E. Brown & E. A. E. Campbell (Eds.), *The Cambridge handbook of forensic psychology* (pp. 520–526). New York, NY: Cambridge University Press.

Tharinger, D., & Wells, G. (2000). An attachment perspective on the developmental challenges of gay and lesbian adolescents: The need for continuity of caregiving from family and schools. *School Psychology Review, 29,* 158–172.

Troup-Leasure, K., & Snyder, H. N. (2005). Statutory rape known to law enforcement. Juvenile Justice Bulletin. Retrieved from http://www.ncjrs.gov/pdffiles1/ojjdp/208803.pdf

Urbas, G. (2010). Protecting children from online predators: The use of covert investigation techniques by law enforcement. *Journal of Contemporary Criminal Justice, 26,* 410–425.

Weber, J., Haardt-Beker, A., & Schulte, S. (2010). Care and treatment of child victims of child pornographic exploitation (CPE) in Germany. *Journal of Sexual Aggression, 16,* 211–222.

Williams, R., Elliott, I. A., & Beech, A. R. (2013). Identifying sexual grooming themes used by Internet sex offenders. *Deviant Behavior, 34,* 135–152.

Williams, T., Connolly, J., Pepler, D., & Craig, W. (2005). Peer victimization, social support, and psychosocial adjustment of sexual minority adolescents. *Journal of Youth and Adolescence, 34,* 471–482.

Wolak, J., Finkelhor, D., & Mitchell, K. (2005). The varieties of child pornography production. In E. Quayle & M. Taylor (Eds.), *Viewing child pornography on the Internet: Understanding the offense, managing the offender, helping the victim.* Lyme Regis, UK: Russell House.

Wolak, J., Finkelhor, D., Mitchell, K. J., & Ybarra, M. L. (2008). Online "predators" and their victims: Myths, realities, and implications for prevention and treatment. *American Psychologist, 63,* 111–128.

Ybarra, M. L., Leaf, P., & Diener-West, M. (2004). Sex differences in youth-reported depressive symptomatology and unwanted Internet sexual solicitation. *Journal of Medical Internet Research, 6,* 1–5.

Chapter 4

Corporate/Government Network Hacks, Identity Theft, and Internet Fraud

> *As cybersecurity threats and identity theft continue to rise, recent polls show that nine in 10 Americans feel they have in some way lost control of their personal information—and that can lead to less interaction with technology, less innovation and a less productive economy.*
>
> —Shear and Singer (2015)

OVERVIEW

On Monday, January 12, 2015, U.S. president Barack Obama announced that he would call for new U.S. federal legislation to make companies more forthcoming when credit card data and other personal consumer data are hacked in an online breach like the massive kind that targeted the networks of Sony, Target, and Home Depot in 2014.

These high-profile breaches in 2014 illustrate not only how businesses are unprepared to protect data on their systems, but also that Sony Pictures Entertainment, producer of the controversial lampoon film *The Interview*—portraying the assassination of North Korean leader Kim Jong-un—may have been the victim of the worst corporate hack in history. The Sony network hack occurred in late November 2014, just before the planned release of this film during the holiday season. Everything from key business intellectual property (IP)—corporate "trade secrets"—to employees' private personal information was obtained by highly skilled hackers and then put on the Internet for online users around the world to see. Even more frightening from an IT security point of view, the experts brought in by Sony to respond to the targeted hack attack posited that there might have been little that Sony could have done to prevent it because the attack was unprecedented in nature in terms of complexity. According to the FBI, the malware used, eventually tied to North Korean state-sponsored hackers, was undetectable by industry-standard antivirus software (Dingman 2014; Holland and Spetalnick 2014; Silcoff 2014).

At the start of January 2015, President Obama publicly announced that North Korea, angry about the film, appeared to have acted alone and that their actions fell outside the bounds of "acceptable state behavior." In fact, the North Korean regime denounced the film as "an act of war" and said that it would "mercilessly destroy" anyone associated with it (Wente 2014). Immediately, Washington, viewing the cyberattack on Sony as a serious U.S. national security matter and in need of a proportional "response," began consultations with Japan, China, South Korea, and Russia, seeking their help in constraining North Korea in their rogue cyberactivities—and perhaps sending a strong message that a planned retaliatory cyberwar could be in the making. By definition, a cyberwar is an information war (Schell and Martin 2006) fought in cyberspace rather than on land (Dingman 2014; Holland and Spetalnick 2014; Silcoff 2014).

There is little question that these corporate hack attacks are costly on a number of fronts—to employees of the firms regarding exposure of their personal information, to clients regarding potential exposure on the Internet of their personal financial information (including credit card numbers or PIN numbers), and to the industry itself regarding loss of revenue and consumer trust. By the end of December 2014, initial projected costs of the Sony hack attack were pegged at around $200 million, and insiders in the firm said that Ms. Amy Pascal, the highest-ranking woman in Hollywood, would likely soon be fired from the company's helm because of the mounting costs related to the exploit (Wente 2014).

By January 16, 2015, updated cost and revenue estimates for the Sony Corporation as a whole were announced, with the troubling issues encountered by the corporation in 2014 producing a negative impact on the fiscal year bottom line at more than US$2.1 billion. Part of this cost was linked to the November hack attack, and part was linked to a downgrading of the corporation's mobile phone market share. Consequently, Sony Corporation announced at the start of 2015 that it would close all of its 14 retail stores in Canada over the next two months as the company tried to recover from this twofold "hit" (Marlow 2015).

The damage and costs affiliated with the Target and Home Depot hack attacks were costly, as well, to the corporations and to their clients. The Target hack, for example, exposed customers' personal information by targeting point-of-sale systems—costing the retailer $200 million in gross costs and likely costing the CEO, Gregg Steinhafel, his job (Dingman, Silcoff, and Greenspan 2014).

The Aftermath of Government and Corporate Network Hack Attacks: Fear

Following these high-profile network attacks, a 2014 survey of Canadian business executives indicated that their 2015 IT security budgets would be increased significantly, as well as their network firewall protections. Anxiety among these executives focused on their firms becoming the possible target of a looming hack attack (Blackwell 2014). Moreover, market research firm Gartner Group has estimated that worldwide information security spending would grow to US$86 billion by 2016 from a significant $62 billion in 2012. But, it seems, the exploit business is even better for the bad guys. According to the Washington-based Center for Strategic and International Studies, the annual cost of cybercrime to the global economy now exceeds $400 billion—and this number is climbing exponentially year after year (Dingman, Silcoff, and Greenspan 2014).

But companies are not alone in their fear of having their networks attacked, for governments have recently reported being the targets of hack attacks by other nations. For example, in late July 2014, a state-sponsored hacker group broke into Canada's National Research Council's network (the country's premier scientific research agency), which was connected to other Canadian government service computers. Senior government officials said they were aware of the hacking effort for several days before they acted to shut down the research agency's network, but they used the time to lurk in the background to gather information on the cyberintruders. Apparently, the Canadian government was able to take its time because the hackers were probing rather than stealing data (Chase 2015).

The reason that the hackers were successful in gaining entry is that the firewall, or network security system, was not as strong as the ones protecting the other government computers. Thus, the hackers were successful in gaining access to the "weak link in the fence"—which is a common hack-attack strategy. In previous cyberespionage incidents involving the Canadian government's Finance Department and Treasury Board networks, the Canadian government officials only privately blamed the Chinese government for financing the hack attacks. However, after this network attack, Canadian prime minister Stephen Harper publicly fingered the Chinese government. To better safeguard the data stored on Canadian government computers, Canada is now investing more than $100 million to rebuild and enact broader network safeguards (Chase 2015).

Given these high-profile corporate hacks, recent U.S. polls suggest that 9 in 10 Americans feel that in some very important way they have lost control of their personal information—with the possibility that their identities could be stolen, or that they could become the victims of Internet fraud (Shear and Singer 2015).

An interesting real-life example is that of Martin Knuth, one of Home Depot's most loyal customers and, in his mind, a likely victim of the September 2014 Home Depot hack attack, when hackers accessed the confidential credit card information of 56 million North American customers. This retired Canadian admitted that though he had not yet noticed any fraudulent charges on his credit card account, the risk of his data being compromised and used by "the bad guys" was probably quite high, since he shops at his nearby Home Depot about 10 times more often than the average person (Dingman, Silcoff, and Greenspan 2014).

The Need for More "Protections" Legislation

As a means of better safeguarding U.S. citizens who engage in online activities, in January 2015, President Obama announced that he would be proposing new legislation. One proposed new piece of legislation was the Personal Data Notification and Protection Act, which would demand a single, national standard that would make companies tell their clients within 30 days after they discover that their industry data network had been hacked. In making his announcement, President Obama posited that the existing "patchwork of state laws" does not adequately protect Americans and their personal information stored in company networks. Furthermore, this patchwork places an unnecessary burden on companies operating in the United States (Shear and Singer 2015).

Calling on Congress to get behind him in a bipartisan way, Obama also outlined a forthcoming bill known as the Student Digital Privacy Act, which would require educational institutions to use the data they collect on students for educational purposes only. They would not be allowed to sell student data to third parties for unrelated purposes or to send targeted ads to students based on the data they collected (Carson 2015).

Commenting further that the United States pioneered both the Internet and the Bill of Rights, President Obama affirmed that U.S. citizens—whether they communicate on land or online—should have a strong sense that they have "a sphere of privacy" that should not be breached by the U.S. government or by any commercial interests. He noted that it was also time to present a revised federal Consumer Privacy Bill of Rights that would uphold this important tenet. Earlier, in February 2012, the White House released a consumer privacy white paper that called for a comprehensive Consumer Privacy Bill of Rights. The Commerce Department has completed its multiple-year public consultations on the draft of the bill. The bill was released in February 2015 so that Congress could begin serious consideration of a revised Consumer Privacy Bill of Rights (Carson 2015). The highlight of the bill is that its requirements are based on the notion of the fair information practice principles—requiring transparency, individual control, respect for context, focused collection and responsible use, security, access and accuracy, and accountability.

As is the case with any proposed piece of federal legislation, there are proponents and there are opponents for any new wording. For example, a senior policy director at the Center for Democracy and Technology in the United States suggested that President Obama's privacy announcement would generally be applauded by consumers and students alike, but that congressional approval of a breach notification law would be more difficult to get. A new breach notification law would likely be opposed by companies that have dealt with the rigors of breach reporting in accordance with state privacy breach laws; thus, they would likely not as easily support or be looking forward to a new national standard regarding breach notification (Carson 2015).

There is little question that during the past 15 years, the Internet has dramatically transformed the world—many things for the better and some things for the worse. We will focus in this chapter on defining key terms and understanding the interrelationships between the cybercrimes known as (1) corporate and government network hacking; and (2) Internet fraud and identity theft (including loss of privacy). By definition, a "cybercrime" is a crime related to technology, computers, and the Internet (Schell and Martin 2004), and by its very nature, cybercrime typically involves the stealthy infiltration of malicious software into corporate or government networks—followed weeks, months, or even years later by the electronic extraction of coveted data (Silcoff 2014).

There is little doubt that cybercrime, as illustrated by the costly 2014 data breaches at Target, Home Depot, Sony, and the Canadian government network, have become a serious concern for corporations and government agencies alike. Citizens, too, are becoming concerned that their personal information stored on networks is increasingly at risk. Various legislative and other suggested technological remedies for dealing with these costly global issues will also be discussed.

HACKERS, HACKING, AND CYBERWARFARE DEFINED

Hackers

The word *hacker* has taken on many different meanings and narratives over the years, recently ranging from an individual who enjoys learning the details of computer systems and how to stretch their capabilities to a malicious or inquisitive meddler who tries to discover information by poking around networks, possibly by deceptive or illegal means (Steele et al. 1983). Interestingly, when originally used, the word *hacker* in Yiddish stood for an inept furniture maker—not exactly the kind of individual who instills fear in the hearts of many or is sought after by government authorities as a dangerous criminal (Schell, Dodge, and Moutsatsos 2002).

Hacking

It is important to emphasize that the ability to conduct hacking is a skill involving the manipulation of technology in some way, shape, or form. Initially, hacking played a key role in the development of computer systems and the very first Internet—the U.S. ARPAnet systems of the 1950s and 1960s, described in the preface of this book. "Hacking" to many in the computer underground back in the late 1950s originally was used to define the act of immersing oneself in computer systems' details to optimize their capabilities. Often, hackers were computer programmers who worked at universities (like MIT) or in government agencies, responsible for speeding up computers' then-slow processing times and creating work-arounds to improve the overall user experience (Holt and Schell 2013).

Thus, from the beginning, hacking was seen by those who engaged in such acts to result in a positive outcome. That is why those who see themselves in this light refer to themselves as "White Hats." Using a computer to cause harm to networks, data, or people, on the other hand, has more recently been termed "cracking." Those who see themselves in this light refer to themselves as "Black Hats" (Schell and Martin 2006).

Today, the dominant narrative of hacking tends to involve a broad range of cybercrimes involving malicious computer use. This range includes digital trespassing, identity theft, Internet fraud, doxing (i.e., the act of identifying a person from a bit of information like an e-mail address and then using this information to find the real-world address and phone number of that person), cyberwarfare, and corporate and government network hacking (Fisk 2013).

The terms "hacker" and "hacking" are both closely tied in the media's present-day portrayal regarding the risks and unknowns of daily computer use. Thus, with even minute technical glitches, IT experts might declare that a network has been illegally intruded into or "hacked" (Fisk 2013).

Cyberwarfare

The concept of cyberwarfare—defined as conducting an information war in the cyberworld rather than on land—began to become a more popular term in mainstream society following the 9/11 terrorist attacks on U.S. soil as well as with increasing threats to personal and national security throughout the 2000s (Fisk 2013).

One of the first internationally reported cases of cyberwar occurred in March 2005 between Indonesia and Malaysia over a dispute regarding the Ambalat oil fields in the Sulawesi Sea, an information war that incorporated university network hacking and threatened corporate network hacking. Officials in Kuala Lumpur were apparently upset over an intrusion into Malaysian waters by an Indonesian naval vessel after Indonesian president Yudhoyono ordered the military to present itself in the Sulawesi Sea jurisdiction under dispute. Just 24 hours later, the website of Universiti Sains Malaysia was under cyberattack and plagued with aggressive anti-Malaysian messages having an Indonesian twist. Two days after this cyberattack, documents seized from members of the Lashkar-e-Toiba terrorist group killed in an encounter with Indian police indicated that they had planned a "suicide hack attack" on the network of companies producing software and computer chip design outlets in the Karnail Singh area of the Indian city of Bangalore, which houses high-profile companies like Intel, Texas Instruments, and IBM. Their motive was to cyberattack these companies to hinder the economic engine of India. The companies back then said they not only had tight entry requirements in their highly secure environments but also well-designed disaster recovery plans in the event of such an attack (Schell 2007).

By 2008, with the Internet's amazing potential and powers, the world witnessed a full-blown cyberwar when Georgia and Russia briefly went to war online as distributed denial of service (DDoS) attacks brought down Georgian Web sites and caused considerable economic damage. Even to this day, it is not clear who the perpetrator of the cyberattacks actually was; according to the media, Russia was the obvious perpetrator. After these attacks were analyzed by IT experts, it seems that they likely came from around the world, not just from Russian hackers. Thus, it seems that rather than acting alone, a loose coalition of third-party actors—and likely a diaspora—achieved Russia's ends of causing harm to Georgia. A key point that is becoming increasingly clear globally is that the line between a digital war and a land-based war is difficult to differentiate. Moreover, instead of acting directly, governments are increasingly hiring talented hackers from within or outside their jurisdiction to produce results that can build extreme chaos and unpredictability in targeted nations or businesses (Schell 2014; Tossell 2012).

GOVERNMENT/CORPORATE NETWORK HACKING DEFINED, TYPES OF EXPLOITS, HOW HACKING IS DONE, THE MOTIVES OF DATA RAIDERS AND THE HARMS CAUSED BY HACKING, ATTACK COSTS, AND RECENT COSTLY INCIDENTS

Government/Corporate Network Hacking Defined

In recent years, media headlines have become laden with real-world hacking exploits targeting government networks—known as government hacking—or industry networks—known as corporate hacking.

Common Types of Exploits

Hacking exploits targeting computer systems or data in either setting can be viewed as acts of trespass, deception, or theft through a variety of cracking techniques used by hackers, such as the following (Schell and Martin 2004; Holt and Schell 2013):

- **Flooding/Denial-of-Service:** A form of cyberspace vandalism resulting in denial-of-service (DoS) to authorized users of a Web site or system. A DDoS attack is designed to disrupt a computer system or Web site by bombarding the site with so much Web traffic that it "crashes." Botnets—a large network of virus-infected computers—can be used by Black Hats to generate spam, spread viruses, conduct "click fraud," or conduct attacks on other networks (Dingman, Silcoff, and Greenspan 2014).
- **Virus and Worm Production and Release:** A form of cyberspace vandalism causing corruption and possibly erasing of data.
- **Spoofing:** The cyberspace appropriation of an authentic user's identity by non-authentic users, causing fraud or attempted fraud in some cases and critical infrastructure breakdowns (such as air or traffic control) in other cases.
- **Phreaking**: A form of cyberspace theft or fraud (or both) consisting of using technology to make free long-distance telephone calls.
- **Infringing Intellectual Property Rights and Copyright:** A form of cyberspace theft involving the copying of a target's information or software without consent.
- **Phishing:** A form of fraud where the offender sends prospective victims an e-mail from a financial institution or service indicating that the user will be cut off from services if the user does not respond in a timely fashion. The information provided is then stolen and used by the offender.

How Hacking Is Done

More sophisticated types of hacking, or cracking, typically involve methods of bypassing the entire security system by exploiting gaps in the system's programs (i.e., the operating systems, the drivers, or the communications protocols) that run the computer system. The more talented cracks often use vulnerabilities in commands and protocols, such as the following (Schell and Martin 2004):

- FTP (file transfer protocol)—a protocol used to transfer files between systems over a network.
- TFTP (trivial file transfer protocol)—a network protocol allowing unauthenticated transfer of files.

- Telnet and SSH—two commands used to remotely log into a UNIX computer.
- Finger—a UNIX command providing information about users that can be utilized to retrieve the .plan and .project files from a user's home directory. These text files are used to store information about the user's location, near-future plans, and the projects currently being worked on.
- NFS (network file system)—one method of sharing files across a local area network or through the Internet.
- The e-mail system.
- UUCP (an acronym for UNIX to UNIC copy)—a protocol used for the store-and-forward exchange of e-mail.

In the recent past, after gaining access to a system, a Black Hat could then install code (i.e., a portion of the computer program that can be read, written, and modified by humans) directly into the computer system or add a transmitter device for later installation.

That said, it needs to be emphasized that Black Hat hackers are constantly updating and changing their methods. Year by year, they are becoming more clever. Generally speaking, today's Black Hats have become quite adept at launching hack attacks gradually and methodically, sometimes leaving malware (i.e., malicious software infecting a computer network and forcing it to do an attacker's bidding—using viruses, Trojan horses, spyware, or key loggers) dormant on unsuspecting machines for months before ordering them to carry out their missions. Tactics used by sophisticated Black Hats can be quite diabolical, and they tend to get a great return on investment (ROI).

One such tactic includes "spear phishing"—an e-mail masquerading as being from a trusted source but sent with the goal of obtaining sensitive information, often by downloading data-sniffing and computer-controlling malicious software. Spear phishing is exemplified by e-mails claiming to be from UPS, FedEx, or some other "trusted" company about a package awaiting delivery to the online user but instead delivering malware in an attachment or link that the user responds to. Other kinds of malware used by Black Hats are especially nefarious because they can capture online users' keystrokes, network activities, screen shots, audio files, Skype conversations, and documents, which are later used for mal-inclined purposes. Furthermore, ransomware (i.e., malicious software designed to block access to a system or account until a sum of money is paid) is especially dangerous, because it locks a computer or network with an unbreakable encryption and then demands payment to release the data (Dingman, Silcoff, and Greenspan 2014).

Then there are the prebuilt "exploit kits" available through the Internet and used for cracking systems; the going rate is only about $2,000. Also popular among

Black Hats wanting to crack networks are malware programs enabling rooting (a system for removing security protection from computers), the denial of service attacks (where, as noted, company Web sites are flooded with questionable network traffic), and the use of proxy server and virtual private network hosting services to actually disguise the origin of the hack attack. But the most valuable tool in the Black Hat's toolbox remains the Zero-Day Exploit—a previously undetected software vulnerability used to crack affected systems before the software developers or manufacturers can address or fix the problem (known as "patching"). The vulnerability period can last anywhere from days to years, and two major and very costly "zero days" in 2014 included Heartbleed and Shellshock. What is very interesting is that Rand researchers have reported that Zero-Day exploits can be sold in the criminal world for several hundred thousand dollars (Dingman, Silcoff, and Greenspan 2014)!

The Motives of Data Raiders and the Harms Caused by Hacking

The motives of Black Hat "data raiders" tend to range from credit card fraud and intellectual property (IP) theft to planting chaos in society. Furthermore, the hackers themselves can be far-ranging in age and in hacking talent, including young teens who download tools from the Internet, known as Newbies; disgruntled but tech-savvy employees of companies or government agencies; or a shadowy mix of organized criminals, state-sponsored corporate spies (like those affiliated with the Canadian government's National Research Council), or tech-savvy terrorists.

An interesting study, for example, conducted by Panda Security in May 2009 surveying 4,100 teenage online users found that about 67% of the respondents said that they tried at least once to hack into their friends' instant messaging or social network accounts by acquiring free tools and content through the Internet. Some respondents admitted to using Trojans to spy on friends, to crack the servers at their schools, or to steal the identities of acquaintances in social networks (Schell 2011).

In both government and corporate hacking, as previously discussed, harm is caused—making these acts in a legal technical sense a "cybercrime." When defining conventional crimes, Anglo-American law bases criminal liability on the coincidence of four key elements, as outlined by Susan Brenner (2001):

1. A culpable mental state (*mens rea*).
2. A criminal action or a failure to act when one is under a duty to do so (*actus reus*).

3. The existence of certain necessary conditions or "attendant circumstances." With some crimes, it must be proved that certain events occurred, or certain facts are true, for an individual to be found guilty of a crime.
4. A prohibited result, or harm.

In a conventional crime like bigamy (i.e., having multiple marriages), all four of these elements must combine to warrant the imposition of liability. First, an individual must enter into a marriage knowing either that he or she is already married or that the person whom he or she is marrying is already married. The prohibited act is the redundant marriage (*actus reus*). The culpable mental state (*mens rea*) is the perpetrator's knowledge that he or she is entering into a redundant marriage. The attendant circumstance is the existence of a previous marriage still in force. Finally, the prohibited result, or harm to persons, is the threat that bigamous marriages pose to the stability of family life. Simply stated, crimes involve conduct perceived to be unacceptable by society's standards. Thus, society, through its laws, imposes criminal liability (Schell and Martin 2004).

Now let's look at how these four elements apply to the cybercrime of hacking in the instance of "cybertrespass" (Wall 2001). To begin, a hacker enters a computer or computer system in, say, a government agency or corporation and unlawfully takes, or exercises unlawful control over, the property—the information or the software belonging to someone else (*actus reus*). He or she enters the network with the purpose of committing an offense once inside and acts with the intention of depriving the lawful owner of the software or information (*mens rea*). By society's standards, the hacker has no legal right to enter the computer or the network in question, or to take control over what is contained therein (attendant circumstances). The hacker is, therefore, liable for his or her acts. The hacker unlawfully entered the computer network (i.e., criminal trespass) to commit an offense (i.e., theft) once inside, and as a result, the target is deprived of his or her software or information (i.e., harm is done).

Black Hat hacking results in harm. Harm can be done to property (such is the case by flooding, virus and worm production and release, spoofing, phreaking, and infringing intellectual property rights and copyright), to persons (such as in cyberstalking and online predation), or both. In the cyberworld, there are also, by law, technical nonoffenses, which are commonly politically motivated and controversial in nature, but noncriminal. Hacktivism, whereby hacker activists, or hacktivists, pair their activism interests with their hacker skills to promote their platforms and missions, is a technical nonoffense (Schell and Martin 2004).

In the United States, if caught and convicted for hacking exploits, the offenders are often charged with "intentionally causing damage without authorization to a protected computer." A first offender faces up to five years in prison and pays fines of up to $250,000 per count, or twice the loss suffered by the victim, with the courts deciding according to the range prescribed in the legislation as well as by the strength of evidence provided in court. The victim may also seek civil penalties (Schell and Martin 2004).

Estimated Harm Costs

There is little question, as seen from the cases discussed so far, that data breaches are costly to targeted government agencies and corporations. In fact, data breaches caused by malware—software designed by Black Hats to infiltrate or damage a computer system without the owner's informed consent and including such cyber-destroyers as viruses, worms, spyware, adware, and Trojan horses (a particular kind of network software application developed to stay hidden on the computer where it was installed but made to access personal information and then send it to a remote party via the Internet)—are extraordinarily costly (Schell and Martin 2006).

In 2010, for example, the Ponemon Institute reported that the costs of a data breach reached $214 per compromised record and averaged $7.2 million per data breach event, including the direct costs of the data breach (i.e., notification to clients and legal defense costs) and indirect costs, such as consumer loss of trust and lost business. According to this report, since 2005, security breaches have compromised well over 500 million records, not including government agency and corporation data losses attributable to employee human error or negligence—which has been another major problem found within these environments (Eschelbeck 2012).

Twelve Recent Costly Government and Corporation Hacking Incidents Globally

Some of the largest government and corporate hacks in recent history have compromised millions of records per attack. Following are the particulars (the millions of records exposed and the kind of exposure) about some of the 12 biggest corporate and government known hacks occurring globally from June 1984 to September 2014. These particulars clearly show the growth of the problem globally with each passing year. But how much is "too much" of this kind of cybercrime? Though there are no clear-cut answers to this question, McAfee's Net Losses report on the cost of cybercrime globally suggests that most countries will tolerate malicious activity like government and corporate hacking as long as it remains at acceptable levels—less than 2% of the national income. Here is the sampling of 12 global hack attack particulars (Dingman, Silcoff, and Greenspan 2014):

1. TRW (June 1984): 90 million records exposed; hack exposed credit-reporting databases.
2. TJC (January 2007): 94 million records exposed; hack exposed credit cards and transaction details of consumers who shop at Winners, HomeSense, and Marshalls.
3. Heartland Payment Systems (January 2009): 130 million records exposed; hack and related malicious software exposed clients' credit cards at the processor.
4. Shanghai Roadway (March 2012): 150 million records exposed; this firm may have illegally bought and sold their customers' personal information.
5. Unknown South Korean firms (June 2013): 140 million records exposed; it is believed that North Korean hackers exposed e-mail addresses and personal identification numbers.
6. Adobe Systems (October 2013): 152 million records exposed; hack of company network exposed information related to customer orders.
7. Target (December 2013): 110 million records exposed; hack exposed customers' personal information by targeting point-of-sale systems.
8. Korea Credit Bureau (January 2014): 104 million records exposed; fraud committed by an "insider" employee exposed 104 million people's credit card information.
9. eBay (April 2014): 145 million records exposed; hack exposed the names, encrypted passwords, and personal information of clients.
10. NYC Taxi & Limousine (June 2014): 173 million records exposed; hack exploited weak anonymized trip details and personal information of taxi drivers.
11. JP Morgan (August 2014): 83 million records exposed; hack exposed the personal information (names, addresses, phone numbers, and e-mails) of the clients of household and small business accounts.
12. Home Depot (September 2014): 56 million records exposed; using malware, hackers stole debit and credit card information from the point-of-sale systems.

THE NEED FOR SECURITY POLCIES/CHECKLISTS AND A CLOSER LOOK AT HOW ENTERPRISES DEAL WITH NETWORK INTRUSION PREVENTION, NETWORK INTRUSTION AND DETECTION, AND NETWORK RECOVERY

The means by which enterprises try to detect and prevent network intrusions and to recover from them vary widely. Some less conventional means include recent attempts by major software companies like Microsoft, Google, Mozilla Firefox, and Facebook to "outbid" the bad guys by increasing what they are willing to pay for what has become known as "bug bounties." By definition, a bug bounty program is one where cash rewards are offered to talented hackers to find and report exploitable vulnerabilities in software before they can be capitalized on by cybercriminals. For example, during 2013–2014, Microsoft allegedly paid two "bug finders" $100,000 each (Dingman, Silcoff, and Greenspan 2014).

More conventional means employed to prevent network intrusions include (1) the need for security policies and security policy checklists in government agencies and businesses, and (2) the importance of providing intrusion prevention and intrusion detection systems in place as well as ensuring fast intrusion recovery. Let us look more closely at these.

The Need for Security Policies and Security Policy Checklists

As a general means of protecting their networks, government agencies and businesses need to develop security policy checklists that are developed by security experts and that use questions dealing with a number of security-related issues. Before outlining these questions, one other major item needs an answer first: Are all of the items on the checklist to be distributed to all employees and fully understood by them? If so, the following set of questions dealing with the network's safety and with the employees' privacy needs to be discussed and set as a form of organizational policy, for both of these notions are intricately connected in virtual space (Schell and Martin 2006):

1. *Administrator's rights and responsibilities* (employee privacy): Under which conditions may a system administrator examine an employee's online account or his or her e-mail, and which parts of the system should the system administrator not examine (e.g., favorite Web site bookmarks)? Can the system administrator monitor network traffic, and, if so, which boundaries exist?
2. *Backups*: Which systems are backed up and how often? How are backups secured and verified (network safety)?
3. *Connections to and from the Internet* (network safety): Which computers should be seen from the outside? If computers are outside the firewall (i.e., bastion hosts), how securely are they separated from computers inside the firewall? Are connections from the Internet to the internal network allowed to go outside the internal network? If there is traffic across the Internet, how is it secured, and what protection is in place against various forms of malware?
4. *Dial-up connections* (network safety): Are dial-up connections allowed, and, if so, are they authenticated? Which access level to the internal network do dial-up connections provide? How are the modems distributed within the company? Can employees set up modem connections to their home or desktop computers?

5. *Documentation* (network safety): Does a map of the network typology exist, and is it clearly stated where each computer fits on that map? Along these same lines, is there an inventory of all hardware and software, and does a document exist detailing the preferred security configuration of every system?
6. *Emergency procedures* (network safety): Which kinds of procedures exist for installing security "patches" or handling exploits? In cases of system intrusion from hackers, is it company policy to shut down the network immediately, or does the company intend to monitor the system intruder for a while? How and when are employees notified of system exploits (employee privacy), and at which stage and at what time are law enforcement agencies called in to investigate?
7. *Logs* (network safety): Which information is logged, how, and where? Are the information logs secure from tampering, and if so, are they regularly examined—and by whom?
8. *Physical security* (network safety): Are systems physically protected from "outsider" hackers (nonemployees) and adequately secured, where needed, from "insider" hackers (employees)?
9. *Sensitive information* (network safety): How is sensitive and proprietary government agency or government information protected online, and how are the backup tapes protected?
10. *User rights and responsibilities* (network safety): What degree of freedom do employees have in terms of selecting their own operating system, software, and, say, games for their computers? Can employees send and receive personal e-mail or do personal work on company computers? Which policies exist regarding "insider" abuse (accidental and intentional) of IT services? Furthermore, which penalties are applied, when, say, an employee brings down a server?

The Key: Intrusion Prevention, Intrusion Detection, and Intrusion Recovery

Because of the dangers of experiencing a network intrusion by both insider and outsider hackers, intrusion prevention is a priority for government agencies and corporations. Unlike in the recent past, enterprises are moving away from the very time-consuming process of detecting intrusions whereby system administrators react to them manually, and are rapidly moving toward implementing automated mechanisms found in marketed intrusion prevention systems (IPS). Furthermore, three key criteria are normally considered as providing a useful network and host-based IPS application. These are as follows (Holt and Schell 2013):

1. *The IPS must not disrupt normal operations.* When the IPS is put online, it must not place unacceptable or unpredictable latency into a network. Also, it

should not use more than 10% of a system's resources, so that network traffic and normal processes on the servers can continue to run.

2. *The IPS must block exploits using more than one algorithm* to operate at both the application level and the firewall-processing level.
3. *The IPS must have the capability to distinguish "real attack events" from "normal events."* Because no IPS currently on the market is totally effective at this task, trained analysts must continue to flag and more thoroughly investigate suspicious traffic activity on the network.

While intrusion prevention is important, so is intrusion detection. Nowadays, an intrusion detection system (IDS) is put into place—a security appliance or software running on a device that tries to detect and warn of ongoing system "cracks" or attempted "cracks" in real time or near real time. IDSs come in three varieties: anomaly based, pattern based, and specification based.

By definition, an anomaly-based IDS treats all exposed behavior of systems on the network unknown to them as a potential attack, so these systems require extensive training of the IDS so that "good traffic" can be distinguished from "bad traffic." By definition, a pattern-based IDS assumes that the attack patterns are known and can therefore be detected in the current network. However, because an IDS cannot detect new attack types, it requires constant maintenance to incorporate new attack patterns as they are discovered. By definition, a specification-based IDS searches for states of the system known to be undesirable, and upon detecting such a state, reports that there has been a network intrusion (Schell and Martin 2006).

All three types generate logs and other key network information that indicate the state of the safety health of the network: traffic patterns, unusual open ports, or unexpected running processes, which are then routinely reviewed by highly trained security analysts, who search for suspected or real intrusions. Because this log review process is extremely time-consuming, enterprises are nowadays investing in automated systems (such as Hewlett-Packard's Virus Throttler software, which identifies and alerts system analysts of suspicious network traffic and causes some of the network's functions to slow down so that the malware is impeded) (Schell and Martin 2006).

Finally, as discussed in this chapter, if a network is under attack, or if the damage is known to have occurred, intrusion recovery is extremely important in order to maintain consumer trust and to save the government agency or the corporation money. For this reason, government agencies and companies need to have an appropriate disaster recovery plan. A disaster recovery plan is defined as a strategy outlining both the technical and the organizational factors related to network security. Such plans tend to begin with a comprehensive assessment of the network to determine acceptable risk levels for the system. These can then be used to produce a set of IT security policies and procedures for assisting employees and work groups within the enterprise to cope effectively if a network becomes disrupted or stops altogether. Also, appropriate decisions need to be made by system administrators as to which methods and systems will be required so that the enterprise can implement its security policies and procedures quickly and effectively—the primary goal of intrusion recovery (Schell and Martin 2006).

HOW EFFECTIVE HAVE ENTERPRISES BEEN IN THEIR NETWORK PREVENTION, NETWORK INTRUSION DETECTION, AND NETWORK RECOVERY EFFORTS?

The 2010/2011 CSI Computer Crime and Security Survey

Richardson (2012) in his 2010/2011 survey provided some insights into how well enterprises seem to be doing in terms of staying ahead of the cybercriminals or of rapidly recovering from exploits if these intrusions could not be prevented. He discussed the effectiveness of fighting against and then recovering from hack attacks by looking through the lens of a three-axis model: Basic Attacks, Malware Attacks, and Attacks 2.0—the advanced persistent threats. The 350 IT Security experts and system administrators in the United States who responded to this Computer Crime and Security Survey shared these views (Richardson 2012):

1. *Basic Attacks*. The basic core of unelaborate attack vectors accounts for the bulk of basic attacks on networks—phishing, rudimentary port scans, brute-force attacks on password-protected accounts (defined as a trial-and-error exhaustive effort by application programs to decrypt encrypted data, such as passwords), and the more conventional viruses. Though these attacks are generally basic, they can still cause considerable damage. They are very much like smash-and-grab attacks on retail storefronts during riots. The IT security respondents believed that their organizations could protect their networks from these basic attacks, because they had taken the appropriate protection measures. Overall, the respondents tended to view basic attacks more as a nuisance than as any real threat.
2. *Malware Attacks*. The middle core of the three-axis model represents a layer of extended versions of previous attacks. This realm includes malware created from generational and customized toolkits, phishing attacks using real company or government agency names known to online victims to capitalize on the scam, and tools scanning for unpatched systems with known vulnerabilities. This is where "insider" hackers tend to focus, because they have access. The findings showed that enterprises are less successful in preventing these kinds

of attacks—not because of their sophistication, but because existing tools are not keeping up with the threats.

3. *Attack 2.0 Layer*. The outermost axis, the Attack 2.0 layer, includes the "advanced persistent threats," or APTs. It is at this level that the threats with the highest sophistication are found—malware that is customized to be more effective in targeted attacks. According to the survey findings, about 22% of the respondents said that at least some of their security incidents involved targeted attacks, and about 3% of them said that their networks experienced more than 10 targeted attacks. The bottom line is that this layer remains a major problem for government agencies and corporations.

Taken as a composite, concluded Richardson (2012), the findings indicate that government agencies and companies are in a "cyber arms race" against cybercriminals. Broadly speaking, at the core or basic level, the good news is that attacks persist, but they are largely rebuked with a suite of protections in place—firewalls, intrusion prevention systems, and intrusion detection systems. In the middle, companies and government agencies are holding their own but struggling against the inventiveness of cybercriminals and their funding sponsors—often nations or nation-states. At the advanced Attack 2.0 level, the picture is blurry about whether government agencies and corporations are effectively winning the fight in the race.

The Price Waterhouse Coopers (PWC) 2014 U.S. State of Cybercrime Survey Findings

Fast forward now to 2014 when the world heard about the enormously costly hacks in the corporate world. The summary findings of this more recent U.S. survey regarding the state of cybercrime exploits in 2013–2014 are quite grim. This report, which included the responses of more than 500 respondents in U.S. organizations, law enforcement, and government agencies, posits that as cybersecurity incidents have grown in frequency and cost over the last five years, the network protection programs currently in place in U.S. enterprises are losing ground in the cyber arms race to the enemy, primarily because they are not adequately addressing "insider" vulnerabilities, and they are not assessing the security practices of third-party partners and supply chains. Furthermore, most do not invest adequately in cybersecurity, ensuring that it is an integral part of and in alignment with their overall enterprise strategies (Mickelberg, Pollard, and Schine 2014).

Particularly worrisome are attacks by tremendously skilled threat actors trying to steal highly sensitive—and often very valuable—intellectual property, private communications, and other strategic assets and data. It is little wonder that in 2014, the U.S. director of National Intelligence ranked cybercrime as the top national security threat to the United States, higher than that of terrorism, espionage, and weapons of mass destruction. The threat is underscored by the FBI's having notified in 2013–2014 at least 3,000 U.S. companies—ranging from small banks to major defense contractors and leading retailers—that they had been victims of serious and extremely costly cyberintrusions. In today's highly volatile virtual world, nation-states and other very tech-savvy criminals continually and rapidly update their strategic moves to maintain a formidable lead against advances in security safeguards implemented by businesses and government agencies. For example, some highly skilled hackers created a new version of DDoS attacks that can generate traffic rated at a staggering 400 gigabits per second, the most powerful DDoS assaults known to date (Mickelberg, Pollard, and Schine 2014).

What is more alarming, the report's findings highlight the reality that in 2013 alone, about 7% of U.S. organizations lost $1 million or more because of data breach incidents, and about 20% reportedly lost from $50,000 to $1 million. In the wake of recent 2014 U.S. data breaches among U.S. retailers, the risk of legal liability and costly lawsuits will likely escalate. Clients and employers concerned about the loss of privacy and personal information will not accept the rather empty claims of businesses that they are unaware of cyber risks—and that they are not prepared to invest enough resources into securing their networks, their employees, and their clients (Mickelberg, Pollard, and Schine 2014).

In a similar 2014 survey conducted in Canada (Blackwell 2014), 60% of the executives surveyed said that they have boosted their cybersecurity budgets in the past two years, and a significant 87% of the respondents said that they are now prepared for threats. However, only 23% of the respondents said that they are "very well" prepared.

THE CASE FOR STRONG DATA BREACH NOTIFICATION AND BROAD-BASED CONSUMER PROTECTIONS

In 2003, California enacted the first comprehensive data breach notification legislation in the United States, known as the California Security Breach Notification Act. The legislation was passed as a result of a massive breach at a California state agency when the names, addresses, and Social Security numbers of employees were put at risk. Under the original statute, information triggering a network breach notification included a first and last name, along with any of these: the Social Security number, the driver's license number, or an account, debit, or credit card number combined with any security information that could be used by a cybercriminal to authorize a transaction illegally. To put it mildly, this was landmark legislation, for it was one of the first attempts in the United States to codify personal information whose unauthorized use could result in harm to consumers (Salane 2013).

This law recognized that organizations collecting and storing sensitive consumer information had an obligation to safeguard that information and to expediently inform consumers when a network was compromised. That way, consumers were put on notice that they might want to protect themselves. Furthermore, in 2008, California updated the legislation to include medical records and health insurance, and since then, the state has updated its law to include notice to the attorney general (Salane 2013).

In recent years, other states have followed suit, and by August 2012, similar breach notification was available in 46 states, the District of Columbia, Guam, Puerto Rico, and the Virgin Islands. Annually, state laws seem to evolve to address new risks to consumers, and from the evidence to date, most state legislatures tend to side with consumers when there is a serious known data breach. Without question, data breach legislation is a broad-based form of consumer protection. Importantly, data breach notification imposes a penalty for data loss—not just through notification but through the simple fact that such breaches cannot be kept secret. In short, breach notification requirements ensure that organizations include consumers in the event information sharing and provide incentives for organizations to share breach information with possible victims in as timely a fashion as possible (Salane 2013).

President Obama's proposed new legislation on data breach notification, announced in January 2015, will apparently impose a 30-day deadline on enterprises to notify possible victims once a data breach has occurred.

IDENTIFY THEFT AND INTERNET FRAUD

Internet Fraud Defined and the Role of the United States' IC3

The Internet provides new opportunities for criminal activities. It may be used to support existing criminal activities, provide new ways of conducting these, extend the geographic reach of criminal activities, or create all new types of criminal activity. Part of the reason that the Internet is a favorite place to operate, in the criminal mind, is that it offers a great degree of anonymity. Ten years ago, few upstanding members of society would have thought that gift cards—whose amount is loaded in the retail store by cashiers—would be a hot commodity for organized crime. But in Canada alone, criminals are now using gift cards to launder some of their profits from drugs, fraud, or other illegal activities—with estimates pegged at somewhere between $5 billion and $55 billion a year. Their main asset: anonymity. Experts say that criminals can buy a stack of gift cards from retailers and transfer them to "an associate," who redeems the products for things like high-end electronics that can be exchanged for cash—thus providing ongoing funds for criminal activities (Gray 2014).

Media stories abound worldwide about how online users have become victims of Internet fraud in general and identity theft in particular—so much so that identity theft was labeled by Newman (1999) more than fifteen years ago as "the crime of the millennium." By definition, "Internet fraud" encompasses a wide range of online criminal activities—cybercrimes—that bring harm to the targets—such as stealing intellectual property rights (IPR), conducting computer intrusions (i.e., hacking), engaging in economic espionage (i.e., the theft of trade secrets) or online extortion, laundering money internationally, conducting credit card or online auction fraud, spamming online users, and committing identity theft or a growing list of other Internet-facilitated crimes. Because the harms produced by Internet fraud can be extensive, in the United States, the Internet Fraud Complaint Center (IFCC) was created. The IFCC is a partnership between the FBI and the National White Collar Crime Center (NW3C). As of 2003, this center has been referred to as the Internet Crime Complaint Center, or IC3. The Web site for the center can be found at http://www.ic3.gov/about/default.aspx.

The role of the IC3 is to deal with Internet-related fraud by providing a user-friendly reporting mechanism to alert law enforcement agents of a likely criminal or civil breach. As a service to law enforcement and regulatory bodies, the IC3 maintains a centralized repository for Internet fraud complaints and maintains statistics related to fraud trends (Schell and Martin 2006).

The IC3 also issues public service announcements when Internet fraud has been identified, as well as the likely targets. As a case in point, on January 13, 2015, there was an advisory on the IC3 Web site saying that college students in the United States were targeted to be part of a work-from-home scam. Students would receive e-mails in their school accounts recruiting them for payroll or human resource positions with fake companies. If the student were interested in such a position, he or she would have to provide a bank account number to receive a deposit and then transfer a portion of the monies to another bank account. The student didn't know that the other bank account was involved in the scam that the student inadvertently helped to perpetuate. In fact, the funds the student would receive and redirect elsewhere were stolen by cybercriminals. Sadly, students who chose to participate in the scam became unknowing criminals themselves—leading them to have their bank accounts possibly closed because of fraudulent activities, to face federal charges, and to have a blemish on their credit records. Though the e-mails received by the students had grammar, capitalization, and tense errors, some of the students who responded to the e-mails were naïve and, consequently, were duped by these non-native-English-speaking scammers.

An earlier case of Internet fraud investigated by the FBI took place in 2003 and involved a then 19-year-old hacker named Adil Yaha Zakaria Shakour, a native of Los Angeles, California. Following the investigation, on March 13, 2003, this "outsider hacker" pleaded guilty to cracking government and corporate networks and, later, carrying out credit card fraud on victims as a result of the breaches. Shakour committed a series of intrusions into four separate computer systems: a server at an Air Force base in Florida (after which he defaced the Web site), computers at Accenture (a management consulting and technology services company in Illinois), an unclassified network computer at the Sandia National Laboratories in California, and a server at Cheaptaxforms.com in North Carolina. After he cracked the latter, Shakour obtained customers' credit card information and other personal information, which he then used to buy more than $7,000 worth of items for his personal use. He was sentenced to one year and one day in federal prison, a three-year term of supervised release, and a $200 special assessment. He was also ordered to pay $88,253.47 for damages, investigation, and repairs in restitution. Also as part of his sentence, the court restricted Shakour's computer use during the supervised release period following his federal prison term (Schell and Martin 2004).

Since many of the laws that experts believe can help deter Internet fraud and identity theft are similar, let us now look more closely at identity theft before reviewing these.

Identity Theft Defined, Its Projected Prevalence, and Tips for Preventing It

By definition, "identity theft" is the malicious stealing of and consequent misuse of someone else's identity (Holt and Schell 2013). Without question, the Internet enables traditional identity theft to be extended to many more targets in multiple jurisdictions. Generally, land-based identity theft tends to be smaller-scaled because of less jurisdictional "opportunity."

By 2013, for the 13th consecutive year, identity theft topped the U.S. Federal Trade Commission's (FTC's) list of consumer complaints. The FTC received more than two million complaints in 2012, and during that year, about 20% of the complaints were about identity theft involving the misuse of personal information like a Social Security number, credit card number, or bank account number to commit theft. According to the FTC, the thieves were most likely to grab people's wages, government benefits, tax refunds, or credit card and bank accounts. Other criminals opened utility accounts, received medical care, took out loans in other people's names, or rented apartments. Often, consumers are first alerted that they are the victims of identity theft only after they check their credit ratings and note some abnormality (Small 2013).

While at first glance this broad definition would seem to be adequate to help researchers determine the prevalence of this problem in society, the reality is that the vagueness of this definition has actually contributed to the lack of reliable data regarding identity theft prevalence—as evidenced by the varying crimes that scholars have placed under this heading. These crimes have included, for example, checking and credit card fraud, counterfeiting, forgery, mail fraud, mortgage fraud, human trafficking, and terrorism, to name just a few (Copes, Kerley, Huff, and Kane 2010).

A rather recent study conducted by the research team of Copes, Kerley, Huff, and Kane (2010) attempted to assess the prevalence rate of identity theft in the United States by using data from the National Public Survey on White Collar Crime. The objectives of the study were to determine the degree to which this crime, including credit card fraud as a type of identity theft, affects victim profiles that include demographic characteristics, risky activities, and reporting decisions. Specifically, the researchers compared victim profiles for victims experiencing existing credit card fraud, new credit card fraud, and existing bank account fraud. Findings from their exploratory study suggest that including existing credit card fraud may actually obscure the fact that those who are female, black, young, and low-income are disproportionately victimized by existing bank account fraud, the type of identity theft that is most financially damaging and the most difficult type to clear for victims so affected.

Regardless of any demographic factor, because far too often gullible online users share their personal data with others in the virtual world, they become victimized by online thieves. It is interesting how many people worldwide have naïvely responded to 419 scams or to phishing exploits—a form of Internet fraud where the offender sends prospective victims an e-mail from a "legitimate" financial institution or service indicating that the user will be cut off from services if he or she does not respond in a timely fashion. The information provided by the online user is then used illegally by the offender to commit some form of identity theft. The 419 scams, in particular, may appear to come from Nigeria or northern Africa and are called "419 scams" in reference to the legal code for fraud in Nigeria (Holt and Schell 2013).

Here is an example of a 419 scam that may have been delivered to readers' e-mail boxes. Look closely at all of the errors in spelling and grammar. Then ask yourself: Would I likely have responded to this request for my personal information?

From: KOFU GEORGE kofu.george@btinternet.com
Reply-to: kofu.george@yahoo.com
Subject: From Master George Kufo
Date: 03/01/2010 04:05:37 AM (Mon, 1 Mar 2010 09:05:37 +0000 (GMT))
From Master George Kufo

Permit me to inform you of my desire of going into business relationship with you. I got your contact from the International web site directory. I prayed over it and selected your name due to your esteeming nature and the recommendations given to me as a reputable and trust worthy person I can do business with and by their recommendations I must not hesitate to confide in you for this simple and sincere business.

I am George Kofu the only Son of late Mr. and Mrs. Maxwell Kufo My father was a very wealthy cocoa merchant in Abidjan, the economic capital of Ivory Coast, before he was poisoned to death by his business associates on one of their outing to discuss on a business deal. When my mother died on the 21st October 1998, my father took me special because I am Motherless. Before the death of my father on 30th June 2006 in a private hospital here in Abidjan

He secretly called me on his bedside and told me that he has a sum of $15.5M (Fifteen Million, five hundred thousand United States dollars) left in a suspense account with one of the Bank here in Abidjan, that he used my name as his only Son for the next of kin in a deposit of the fund. My Father also explained to me that it was because of this wealth and some huge amount of money his business associates supposed to balance him from the deal they had, that was why he was poisoned to by his business associates, that I should seek for a God fearing foreign partner in a country of my choice where I will transfer this money and use it for investment purpose, (such as real estate management).

Dear One I am honorably seeking your assistance in the following ways. 1) To provide a Bank account where this money would be transferred to. 2) To serve as the guardian of this since I am a Boy of 19 years.

Moreover, I am willing to offer you 20% of the sum as compensation for effort input after the successful transfer of this fund to your designate account overseas. If you are interested on this deal kindly get back to me.

Thanks and God Bless.
Best regards. Master George Kufo

It is important to emphasize that 419 scams are just one of the means by which naïve online users are duped into handing over personal information to the bad guys. Mounting evidence shows that far too many online users have become harmed by identity theft or loss of reputation because they have responded to such online trickery, some of which looks rather convincing and seems to come from a legitimate, trusted source—such as the employer's IT or Finance department. Sometimes the perpetrator who commits a cybercrime that adversely affects others' identities is actually someone from inside an organization—technically referred to as "an insider."

As a case in point of an "insider cybercriminal," in March 2003, a California woman named Charmaine Northern, then age 23, was employed as a member service representative of Schools Federal Credit Union in California. She admitted that between January 22, 2001, and October 2002, she used the credit union computer to obtain customer account information, including names, Social Security and driver's license numbers, and addresses to open accounts in the names of others—thus having them incur unauthorized charges. Some of the credit card accounts were actually opened on the Internet. After the credit cards were established in the names of other customers, Northern used them to make numerous purchases. The estimated amount of fraudulent transactions was more than $53,000. The good news is that no financial institution customers at that time lost any funds as a result of the offense, as they were all federally insured (Schell and Martin 2004).

According to a recent Australian research study conducted by Roberts, Indermaur, and Spiranovic (2013), identity theft and related fraudulent activities reportedly affect approximately 1 in 25 adults each year across Western societies. In fact, according to these authors, recent study findings have suggested that fear of these types of crimes now matches or exceeds the fear of traditional place-based crimes, and has the potential to curtail online activities and hinder the further development of e-commerce applications. This sobering fact helps explain why so many Americans, for example, fear that their personal and financial information may have fallen into criminal hands.

Qualitative research quoted by Roberts, Indermaur, and Spiranovic (2013) in their study findings has suggested that fear of cyber–identity theft incorporates fear of financial losses, damage to reputation, and loss of online privacy. While some researchers have argued that fear of cybercrime in general and identity theft specifically is largely driven by myths perpetuated by the media, their occurrences may or may not be in accurate proportion to the objective reality of these facets of cybercrime, for the "jury's verdict" on actual prevalence rates on these has yet to be determined.

Having said this, however, a 2014 survey of 10,000 consumers undertaken by Microsoft reported that the worldwide annual cost of identity theft and phishing could be as high as $5 billion. Equally alarming is the fact that the cost of repairing damage to one's reputation as a result of these cybercrimes could be even higher—up to $6 billion. In fact, of the 10,000 consumers polled by Microsoft, victims reported losing an average of $632 through various online trickery schemes. Of these 10,000 consumers polled, 15% said that they had been the victim of phishing (losing an average of $158), a further 13% said that their professional reputations had been tarnished (costing, on average, $535 to fix), and about 9% said that they had actually suffered identity theft (costing, on average, $218) (Waugh 2014).

Some Suggestions for Preventing Identity Theft

Generally speaking, experts agree that online users need to become educated about the many forms of Internet fraud and how to better protect themselves when online. Keeping abreast of alerts posted on the IC3 Web site is one sound way of updating one's information regarding known Internet frauds, phishing scams, and attempts at identity theft.

SUMMARY OF U.S. LAWS OFFERING SOME PROTECTIONS REGARDING GOVERNMENT AND CORPORATE HACKING INCIDENTS, INTERNET FRAUD, AND IDENTITY THEFT

18 U.S.C

Newsworthy Internet crimes prosecuted in the United States have generally fallen under the computer crimes statute, 18 U.S.C. Section 1030. In this jurisdiction, the Computer Fraud and Abuse Act (CFAA) has been the primary federal statute criminalizing Internet abuses affecting online users' privacy, security, and trust. A conviction for violating most of the provisions of the CFAA can be up to five years in prison for each count and up to a $500,000 fine for a second offense. Civil action against the perpetrator for damages incurred is also permitted.

To strengthen its powers, the CFAA was modified in 1994 and again in 1996 by the National Information Infrastructure Protection Act and codified at U.S.C. subsection 1030, Fraud and Related Activity in Connection with Computers. The following statutes pertain to specific kinds of Internet crime under 18 U.S.C. (Schell 2014):

- Section 1020: Fraud and related activity regarding access devices
- Section 1030: Fraud and related activity regarding computers
- Section 1362: Communication, lines, or stations
- Section 2510: Wire and electronic communications interception as well as interception of oral communications

- Section 2512: The manufacture, distribution, possession, and advertising of wire, oral, or electronic communication intercepting devices prohibited
- Section 2517: Authorization for disclosure and use of intercepted wire, oral, or electronic communications
- Section 2520: Recovery of civil damages authorized
- Section 2701: Unlawful access to stored communications
- Section 2702: Voluntary disclosure of customers' communications or records
- Section 2703: Required disclosure of customers' communications or records
- Section 3121: Recording of dialing, routing, addressing, and signaling information
- Section 3125: Emergency pen register and trap and trace device installation

Following the 9/11 terrorist attacks on U.S. soil, the U.S. government passed a number of laws to curb Internet crimes. As noted at the start of this chapter, as Internet crimes evolve, so do legislative attempts as a means of staying ahead of the cybercriminal curve.

Health Insurance Portability and Accountability Act of 1996

The Health Insurance Portability and Accountability Act (HIPAA) of 1996 focuses on health protection for U.S. employees in a number of ways, with the Centers for Medicare and Medicaid Services having the responsibility to implement various unrelated provisions of HIPAA. Title 1 of the act maintains that health insurance coverage for individuals and their families continues when they transfer or lose employment, and, important for our discussion here, Title II requires the Department of Health and Human Services to develop and maintain national standards for electronic transactions regarding health care in the United States. Title II also speaks to the security and privacy of online health data—that which can be sent through the Internet. The developers of HIPAA felt that such standards would improve the efficiency and effectiveness of the U.S. health care system by demanding secure and private handling of personal electronic data. From an IT security angle, HIPAA requires a double-entry or double-check of data entered by staff. All U.S. health care organizations had to be compliant with the HIPAA Security Rule by April 21, 2005, which meant taking extra measures to secure online citizens' health information (Schell and Martin 2006).

Digital Millennium Copyright Act (DMCA) of 1998

The protection of intellectual property rights (IPR) from attack by criminals using the Internet is a hugely important concern for many organizations today, as evidenced by the 2014 hack at Sony. The DMCA of 1998 implements certain worldwide copyright laws to cope with emerging technologies by providing protections against the disabling of or bypassing of technical means designed to protect copyright. Thus, the DMCA sanctions apply to anyone attempting to impair or disable an encryption device (Schell and Martin 2006).

Related to the DMCA, on January 26, 2013, a new law went into effect in the United States making it illegal for cell phone users to unlock their cell phones to switch carriers. Anyone who infringes this law can be fined between $2,500 and $500,000, and in some cases, spend time in prison. In essence, the lock feature on mobile devices gives carriers a means to prevent customers from switching to a new plan with another company. Without a carrier's permission to unlock a cell phone, a phone user who unlocks it is committing a crime (Clarke 2013).

Gramm-Leach-Bliley Act (GLBA) (aka Financial Services Modernization Act)

Personal information that many online citizens would consider to be private—such as bank account numbers and bank account balances—is routinely exchanged for a price by banks and credit card companies. The GLBA in 1999 brought in some privacy protections against the sale of U.S. citizens' private information, particularly that of a financial nature. Moreover and important to our discussion here, the GLBA codified protections against "pretexting," defined as the act of getting someone's personal information by a false means. Specifically, the GLBA includes three requirements to protect individuals' online personal data and privacy (Schell 2007):

1. Information of a personal nature has to be securely stored.
2. Institutions, if merged, must notify their clients about their policy of sharing personal financial information with other institutions.
3. The institutions have to give consumers the right to *opt out* of the information-sharing schemes if they want to.

Trademark Law, Patent Law, and the U.S. Anticybersquatting Consumer Protection Act (ACPA) of 1999

Trademark law governs disputes between businesses over the names, logos, and other means used to identify their products and services in both the off-line and online markets. If someone owns a trademark or a service mark (federally registered or not), there could be some domain names on the Internet infringing on that trademark. Although individuals may not realize this, under U.S. trademark law, trademark owners have a duty to police their trademarks and to notify authorities of suspected infringements. If anybody ever receives a letter from an attorney saying that he or she has infringed the ACPA, that individual should hire a lawyer immediately. Once an allegation of infringement lands in court, the damages can skyrocket well above the $100,000 mark (Schell 2007; Schaefer 2012).

Cybersecurity Enhancement Act of 2002 or Homeland Security Act of 2002

In 2002, the U.S. Senate proposed the Cybersecurity Enhancement Act, also known as the Homeland Security Act, establishing in the United States the Department of Homeland Security. This act was meant to keep the networked critical infrastructures in the United States safe from attack or to have a readiness response if they were physically attacked or hacked. The nine subsections of the Homeland Security Act are as follows (Schell 2007):

1. Title I: The Department of Homeland Security (DHS) and its missions and functions
2. Title II: Information analysis and infrastructure protection
3. Title III: Chemical, biological, radiological, and nuclear countermeasures
4. Title IV: Border and transportation security
5. Title V: Emergency preparedness and [disaster recovery] response
6. Title VI: Internal management of the DHS
7. Title VII: General provisions and coordination with nonfederal entities, the inspector general, and the U.S. Secret Service
8. Title VIII: Transitional items
9. Title IX: Conforming and other technical amendments

It is important to emphasize that civil liberties groups objected strongly to the passage of the Homeland Security Act from the very beginning, positing that it is characterized by three trends that can adversely impact U.S. citizens: reduced privacy, increased government secrecy, and increased government powers to protect its own special interests (Schell 2014).

CAN-SPAM Act of 2003

Officially the Controlling the Assault of Non-solicited Pornography and Marketing Act of 2003, the CAN-SPAM Act was passed on November 25, 2003, to regulate interstate commerce by imposing penalties on online users transmitting unsolicited e-mail through the Internet—spam. Penalties included fines as high as $1 million or jail terms for up to five years, or both (Schell and Martin 2006).

A spammer is someone who does any of the following (Schell 2007):

- Gains access to a protected computer without authorization and intentionally initiates the sending of multiple commercial e-mails from or through that computer and a connection to the Internet;
- Uses a protected computer to relay or retransmit multiple commercial e-mails to intentionally either deceive or mislead receivers or any Internet access service as to the origin of such e-mail messages;
- Intentionally falsifies header information in multiple commercial e-mails and intentionally tries sending such e-mails;
- Intentionally falsely represents oneself as a legitimate registrant of five or more Internet protocol (IP) addresses, and then intentionally sends many commercial e-mails from such addresses.

Cybersecurity Enhancement Act of 2002–2005

Though the Cybersecurity Enhancement Act of 2001 was sent to the U.S. House Judiciary Committee by Lamar Smith in December 2001, and later sent to the U.S. Senate in 2002, it was not until April 20, 2005, that the House Committee on Homeland Security, Subcommittee on Cybersecurity, Infrastructure Protection, and Security Technologies passed HR 285: the Cybersecurity Enhancement Act. This act stated that the assistant secretary for cybersecurity would be the head of the Directorate's Office of Cybersecurity and Communications within the National Protection and Programs Directorate (NPPD). The head of the directorate was responsible for enhancing the security, resilience, and reliability of the United States' cyber and communications infrastructure—and creating an effective cyberattack "warning system" for the nation (Schell 2014).

In March 2013, additional changes were proposed to the act, as ordered by the House Committee on Science, Space, and Technology. These included reauthorizing a number of programs under the National Science Foundation (NSF) to enhance cybersecurity by better protecting networks against breaches, requiring the National Institute of Standards and Technology (NIST) to carry on with its cybersecurity awareness program and with the development of standards for better managing personal information being stored on computers, and establishing a task force for recommending appropriate actions to Congress for upgrading research and development activities to improve cybersecurity for the United States and its citizens who enjoy the freedoms provided by the Internet (Schell 2014).

To hear from a cybercrime expert about whether the laws described in this section are providing adequate protections for U.S. citizens against hackers and other kinds of cybercriminals (like identity thieves and spammers), as well as to hear whether a case can be made for even stronger data breach notification legislation in the United States, readers are referred to the interview with Dr. Doug Salane.

INTERVIEW WITH AN EXPERT

Dr. Doug Salane, Director of the Center for Cybercrime Studies at the John Jay College of Criminal Justice

After finishing an undergraduate degree in mathematics, Doug Salane went on to complete his PhD in applied mathematics with a specialization in numerical analysis. Dr. Salane has held positions with Exxon, Sandia National Laboratories, and Argonne National Laboratories. He has been a faculty member at the John Jay College of Criminal Justice, City University of New York, since 1988. For more than 12 years, Dr. Salane served as coordinator of the college's Computer Science and Information Security major. He currently is a member of the graduate faculty in Digital Forensics and Cyber Security and teaches undergraduate and graduate courses in networking and security. In 2006, Dr. Salane became the director of the Center for Cybercrime Studies at the John Jay College of Criminal Justice. The center brings together expertise in law, computing, and the social sciences in an effort to understand and deter computer-related criminal activity. Dr. Salane is a member of the Association for Computing Machinery (ACM), the Institute of Electrical and Electronics Engineers (IEEE), and the Society for Industrial and Applied Mathematics (SIAM). His areas of research interest include cybercrime, data clustering, computer security and forensics, and privacy.

Q With the 2014 hack attacks against corporations like Target, Home Depot, and Sony, on January 12, 2015, President Obama announced that he would call for new U.S. federal legislation to make companies more forthcoming within a 30-day period when consumers' personal data is accessed in an online breach. What other changes in the current breach notification legislation do you think that President Obama will be pushing for and why?

A Recently, the White House offered a draft of privacy legislation known as the Consumer Privacy Bill of Rights, which in addition to setting new requirements for privacy, includes a national data breach notification requirement. Privacy advocates feel the bill puts too much discretion in the hands of companies to determine practices for protecting personal information. Companies would form internal review boards for determining privacy practices, and these boards would be monitored by the FTC. Critics of the draft legislation say the FTC would not have sufficient resources to monitor the review boards. With regard to data breach notification requirements, the draft bill would preempt state breach notification laws now in place in 48 states and limit the ability of state attorney generals to address breach notification violations. Typically, legal firms advise breached companies to respond to breach notification requirements in a way that satisfies the most restrictive requirements in state laws. Although this situation frequently is cumbersome for industry, indirectly, it results in effective breach notification. Critics contend that, although draft national breach legislation would provide uniform reporting requirements and require reporting within 30 days of a breach, the draft bill would be weaker than current state laws and lower the bar for data breach reporting. Data breach legislation and SEC filing requirements are among the few available mechanisms that allow the public to be aware of large-scale breaches of personal information.

Q In this same announcement about much needed legislative amendments, President Obama also called for a new Student Digital Privacy Act and a revised Consumer Privacy Bill of Rights. Could you comment on some particulars that will likely be proposed in these two pieces of legislation—as well as who are likely to be the proponents for or the opponents against such legislation?

A School districts throughout the nation face a difficult situation with the proliferation of educational computing software and, in particular, mobile education apps that are being deployed in the classroom by teachers. Although these technologies offer a range of benefits and are available at little or no cost, school districts can't be sure that student data is not being offered to third parties. Moreover, there is little oversight of the companies providing these services and collecting student data. Also, with the proliferation of student data, many companies are not providing the security needed to protect that data. The proposed Student Digital Privacy Act offered by the administration would prohibit the sale of student data to third parties as well as prohibit targeted advertising directed at students in the educational software. Some privacy advocates, however, are not convinced that the draft legislation would prevent companies from creating student profiles from information gathered and then using these profiles to send students targeted ads or recommendations in other online sites. Recent legislation passed in California, the Student Online Personal Information Protection Act, upon which much of the proposed bill is modeled, prohibits the creation of profiles.

Q What sorts of arguments are commonly made by government agencies and corporations about why these breaches occurred—and are these arguments credible from a consumer and societal vantage point?

A Governments and corporations usually try to release as little information about a breach as possible. Breaches are hard to justify because in hindsight it frequently seems that a breach could have been easily prevented—if only we had a stronger password policy in place or had deployed two-factor authentication sooner. Yet, as is widely acknowledged, hackers have only to find one flaw and an organization has to secure everything. The complexity of modern systems and organizations, which often have to give vendors and partners access to their data and systems, makes it almost impossible to guarantee breaches will not occur. Companies must demonstrate that they are taking all possible measures to protect data and systems. Sensitive data must be encrypted, data should not be held if it is not needed, and reliable response procedures must be in place to mitigate the extent of a breach when one occurs. To maintain consumer confidence, breaches should be addressed immediately. Breaches are indefensible when companies are not in compliance with government or industry security guidelines, as for example, the PCI DSS standards that apply in the card payment industry. When a company is not in compliance with security standards, there are significant liability implications, which often have been the subject of court cases and have resulted in damage awards.

Q Besides the industry best practice standard for safeguarding enterprise networks with network intrusion prevention, network intrusion detection, and network recovery policies and practices, what other solutions might industry consider to make their networks more resilient?

A The business systems that run on these insecure networks must monitor for fraud or misuse. Fraudsters attack the networks, but the target usually is the business systems they support. What is needed is real-time monitoring for anomalous behavior that detects and stops an illicit transaction, much like what occurs in the banking and card payment industries. Of course, the challenge for businesses is to implement these systems in a way that does not lead to customer dissatisfaction. Information sharing within industries is also critical. For example, evidence of malware in a point-of-sale system should be made available to security personnel throughout the industry so all companies can take action if the malware entered through the supply chain.

Q Researchers have commonly argued that Internet fraud and identity theft are, to some extent, preventable. One major problem is that online consumers are too naïve and gullible when it comes to 419 scams and phishing. Are these claims justified and, if so, what are some viable solutions for helping consumers stay safer in the virtual environment?

A Teenagers today, who have grown up with digital technologies, certainly are more aware of online risks than teens of the late 1990s and early 2000s. The classic Nigerian phishing scams are less common, and surveys show that people have become much less trusting on the Internet. In fact, mass phishing e-mails are much less prevalent today due to the very low return on these mailings. Targeted phishing, on the other hand, where fraudsters use a variety of publicly available information to establish trust with a victim, continue to be a growing problem. Even at a top security firm, corporate spies were able to entice selected employees into clicking on an e-mail attachment that downloaded malware by presenting the employees with a bogus announcement of a corporate retirement plan. We all have to constantly remind ourselves not to trust any online communication that we don't solicit, and to look and think before we click.

Q What areas will future research likely focus on regarding better safeguarding of corporate and government networks?

A There are new privacy-enhancing encryption systems, which would keep data to be processed in encrypted form. This is sometimes thought of as the holy grail of security. Most researchers, however, feel these technologies are some years away. In much of the trade security literature, experts advise that breaches are just commonplace, get used to them and be prepared. The focus is turning to response and recovery. For example, in the Target breach, Target had an extensive technical security apparatus in place that allowed its security vendor to monitor in a virtual environment all transactions before they reached the production environment. The security vendor detected fraudulent transactions in the virtual environment, but they reached the production systems nonetheless. Lacking were the policies within the company to ensure the security information was acted on. Technology and policies, however, are only part of the solution. We have to learn how to live in an environment with a global information infrastructure upon which we all rely. If fraudsters can hide in certain areas of this environment and be protected by governments, or if governments use that environment in an adversarial fashion, all bets are off. Intellectual property will continue to be exfiltrated, the costs of cybercrime will continue to increase, and this information system upon which we rely will continue to grow more costly and dangerous. We have to realize our common interests and come up with a system of Internet governance that keeps cybercriminals in check and secures the Internet, while maintaining its openness and power to generate valuable new applications and services.

CONCLUSION

This chapter opened with some extremely costly and harm-producing corporate hacks occurring in 2014, including those at Target, Home Depot, and Sony. Targets of these attacks included the corporations themselves, employees, and their clients—with harms exceeding the $200 million mark for the Sony hack attack alone. But government networks are equally as likely to be targeted as those in industry. At the start of this chapter, we discussed the 2014 hack attack of the Canadian government's academic research network by the Chinese government, which allegedly hired highly skilled hackers to pull off the information heist. We moved on to discuss how hackers generally exploit computer networks and how enterprises are trying to stay ahead of the cybercriminal curve by strategically planning for intrusion prevention, intrusion detection, and disaster recovery. We closed the chapter by focusing on Internet fraud and identity theft and looked more closely at how online citizens can better protect themselves from these virtual-world crimes that far too often have devastating and costly off-line personal outcomes. We also reviewed the many pieces of legislation that the U.S. government has passed over the past decade to safeguard its homeland, its networked critical infrastructures, and its citizens who go online.

Clearly, the battle against the forever-morphing cybercriminals gets increasingly more difficult to fight—and win—with each passing year. For this reason, governments and corporations need to keep investing more money in research and development and resources to strengthen the resilience of their networks against cyberattack. Furthermore, some serious thought needs to be given to how nations can have a more protected Internet, balancing the needs for security and freedom. That's our challenge for this decade. After all, there are laws and enforcement protecting Brinks trucks from robbers on land. Without ramped-up enforcement for online users and the Internet, using this analogy, we will continue to have at least one "virtual Brinks truck" attacked by cyberthieves somewhere around the globe every single day (Dingman, Silcoff, and Greenspan 2014).

REFERENCES

Blackwell, R. (2014, October 20). Firms beef up cybersecurity amid surge in data breaches. *The Globe and Mail*, pp. B1, B4.

Brenner, S. W. (2001). Is there such a thing as "virtual crime"? *Berkeley Journal of Criminal Law, 4.* Retrieved from http://scholarship.law.berkeley.edu/cgi/viewcontent.cgi?article=1077&context=bjcl

Carson, A. (2015). Obama stops by FTC; announces privacy bills on ID theft, student data, consumer privacy. Retrieved from https://privacyassociation.org/news/a/obama-announces-legislation-on-student-id-consumer-privacy/

Chase, S. (2015, January 14). China hack attack: Ottawa sets cost to boost cybersecurity at $100-million. *The Globe and Mail*, pp. A1–A2.

Clarke, J. (2013). Jailbreaking cell phones to become ILLEGAL at midnight: Law makes "unlocking" devices to switch carriers punishable by fines and even prison. Retrieved from http://www.dailymail.co.uk/news/article-2268743/New-law-makes-unlocking-cell-phones-switch-carriers-punishable-fines-prison.html

Copes, H., Kerley, K. R., Huff, R., & Kane, J. (2010). Differentiating identity theft: An exploratory study of victims using a national victimization study. *Journal of Criminal Justice, 38,* 1045–1052.

Dingman, S. (2014, December 9). Sony hack caps "the year of shaken trust." *The Globe and Mail*, p. B5.

Dingman, S., Silcoff, S., & Greenspan, R. (2014, October 25). Hacked a rising threat. *The Globe and Mail*, pp. B8–B9.

Eschelbeck, G. (2012). *Sophos threat report 2012*. Sophos Ltd. Retrieved from http://www.sophos.com/medialibrary/pdfs/other/sophossecuritythreatreport2012.pdf

Fisk, N. (2013). Hacking and criminality. In T. J. Holt & B. H. Schell (Eds.), *Contemporary world issues: Hackers and hacking* (pp. 154–157). Santa Barbara, CA: ABC-CLIO.

Gray, J. (2014, December 24). The link between gift cards and crime. *The Globe and Mail*, p. B3.

Holland, S., & Spetalnick, M. (2014, December 20). Obama to respond to Sony cyberattack. *The Globe and Mail*, p. A15.

Holt, T. J., & Schell, B. (2013). *Contemporary world issues: Hackers and hacking*. Santa Barbara, CA: ABC-CLIO.

Marlow, I. (2015, January 16). Sony shutters Canadian stores. *The Globe and Mail*, p. B4.

Mickelberg, K., Pollard, N., & Schine, L. (2014). *US cybercrime: Rising risks, reduced readiness. Key findings from the 2014 US state of cybercrime survey*. Price Waterhouse Coopers. Retrieved from http://www.pwc.com/us/en/increasing-it-effectiveness/publications/assets/2014-us-state-of-cybercrime.pdf

Newman, J. Q. (1999). *Identity theft: The cybercrime of the millennium.* Port Townsend, WA: Loompanics Unlimited.

Richardson, R. (2012). *2010/2011 CSI computer crime and security survey*. GoCSI.com. Retrieved from http://www.pwc.com/us/en/increasing-it-effectiveness/publications/assets/2014-us-state-of-cybercrime.pdf

Roberts, L. D., Indermaur, D., & Spiranovic, C. (2013). Fear of cyber-identity theft and related fraudulent activity. *Psychiatry, Psychology and Law, 20,* 315–328.

Salane, D. E. (2013). The case for strong data breach notification legislation. In T. J. Holt & B. H. Schell (Eds.), *Contemporary world issues: Hackers and hacking*. Santa Barbara, CA: ABC-CLIO.

Schaefer, E. (2012). How to defend against a claim of cybersquatting: Litigation stories from the jury box. Retrieved from http://tcattorney.typepad.com/domainname dispute/2012/07/how-to-defend-against-a-claim-of-cybersquatting-litigation-stories-from-the-jury-box.html

Schell, B. H. (2007). *Contemporary world issues: The Internet and society*. Santa Barbara, CA: ABC-CLIO.

Schell, B. H. (2011). Female and male hacker conferences attendees. In T. J. Holt & B. H. Schell (Eds.), *Corporate hacking and technology-driven crime: Social dynamics and implications* (pp. 144–168). Hershey, PA: Information Science Reference.

Schell, B. H. (2014). *Contemporary world issues: Internet censorship*. Santa Barbara, CA: ABC-CLIO.

Schell, B. H., Dodge, J. L., & Moutsatsos, S. S. (2002). *The hacking of America: Who's doing it, why, and how*. Westport, CT: Quorum Books.

Schell, B. H., & Martin, C. (2004). *Contemporary world issues: Cybercrime*. Santa Barbara, CA: ABC-CLIO.

Schell, B. H., & Martin, C. (2006). *Webster's new world hacker dictionary*. Indianapolis, IN: Wiley.

Shear, M., & Singer, N. (2015). Obama to call for laws covering data hacking and student privacy. Retrieved from http://www.nytimes.com/2015/01/12/us/politics/obama-to-call-for-laws-covering-data-hacking-and-student-privacy.html?_r=0

Silcoff, S. (2014, December 19). After film is cancelled, controversy erupts. *The Globe and Mail*, pp. A12–A13.

Small, B. (2013). Top complaint to the FTC? ID theft, again. Retrieved from http://www.consumer.ftc.gov/blog/top-complaint-ftc-id-theft-again

Steele, G., Jr., Woods, D. R., Finkel, R. A., Crispin, M. R., Stallman, R. M., & Goodfellow, G. S. (1983). *The hacker's dictionary*. New York, NY: Harper and Row.

Tossell, I. (2012, May). The ABCs of cybersecurity. *The Globe and Mail Report on Business, 28* (10), 55–60.

Wall, D. S. (2001). Cybercrimes and the Internet. In D. S. Wall (Ed.), *Crime and the Internet* (pp. 1–17). New York, NY: Routledge.

Waugh, R. (2014). Identity theft—six tips to help keep you safe. Retrieved from http://www.welivesecurity.com/2014/12/08/identity-theft/

Wente, M. (2014). Who needs nukes when you've got hackers? Retrieved from http://www.theglobeandmail.com/globe-debate/who-needs-nukes-when-youve-got-hackers/article22152089/

Part II

Macro-System Issues Regarding Online Health and Safety

Chapter 5

Technology and Social Behavior: The Rise of Social Media Web Sites

When I thought about writing this post, I was going to use it as a forum to scold those horribly annoying people who can't have lunch with you because they're too busy tweeting about having lunch with you. And then I realized I am one of those people and I grew immensely uncomfortable. I used to be normal. Then I got an iPhone. I used to have this wretched little BlackBerry that did nothing—and even that it does poorly. I would gaze at my husband's iPhone with a longing in my heart: the touch screen, the plethora of apps, Facebook so clear and bright. So when it was finally time for an upgrade, I splurged on my own iPhone. And now it's like crack to me.

—Janelle Hanchett (2015)

OVERVIEW

It is 2015 and social media Web sites—Facebook, YouTube, Twitter, LinkedIn, Instagram, Pinterest, Vine, Snapchat, and Tumblr, to name just a few—are flourishing. Let's look at some recent statistics regarding the most popular social media Web sites. Did you know that in 2014, Twitter had 255 million active users who collectively sent 500 million tweets every day? Or that there were more than 50 million Facebook pages in existence? Or that 20 billion photos were uploaded to Instagram, and that 5% of all "selfies"—pictures taken of oneself, usually with a cell phone camera—were shared on Snapchat (Bennett 2014)?

There is little question that aside from the obvious popularity of social media Web sites with online users worldwide, the entrepreneurial creators of these sites are, indeed, very wealthy billionaires. On Monday, March 2, 2015, *Forbes* released its annual list of the world's richest people, showing an increasing representation of tech-based billionaires. *Forbes* noted that 7 of the world's 15 wealthiest self-made billionaires made their fortunes through tech companies, and the 15 richest people in technology, combined, were worth more than US$426 billion, representing an 11.6% increase in wealth over 2014. Topping the list was Bill Gates of Microsoft (earning $79.2 billion), followed by Larry Ellison of Oracle (earning $54.3 billion), followed by Jeff Bezos of Amazon (earning $34.8 billion), followed by Mark Zuckerberg of Facebook (earning $33.4 billion) (Shufelt 2015).

With this earning, Mr. Zuckerberg is the world's richest person under the age of 40. His wealth is justified, if one considers that Facebook now has 1.4 billion active users worldwide, and this sheer reach on a global basis has given the company bragging rights about its success. This success, in turn, has allowed the company to silence doubts raised in its early days as a public company. Facebook's social media Web site success is reflected, as well, in the increased use of mobile ads, which have pushed the company's revenues by almost 60% since 2014 (Shufelt 2015).

The evolution of social media and social media marketing dates back to the increasing ease of availability of the Internet and the rapid development of Web 2.0. While research has consistently indicated that the Internet is a primary source of information for consumers around the world, the advancement of Web 2.0 has made it possible for consumers to stay connected to the Internet and social media through their mobile devices, just like the woman in the quote at the start of this chapter (Kaplan and Haenlein 2010).

"Social media" is defined as a Web platform enabling an online user to create and maintain a public or semipublic profile. Online users have the ability to selectively connect to other users based on their personal interests. Social media technologies have empowered consumers to share their opinions about brands and products, creating significant online word of mouth. Thus, the rise of social media Web sites and a marked increase in social media marketing over the past five years are intricately connected. By definition, "social media marketing" is a kind of online advertising targeting consumers based on the cultural context of social communities through virtual worlds, social networks, social news sites, and social opinion-sharing sites to meet branding and communication objectives (Tuten 2008).

Social media sites, comparable to virtual communities, are established with the recruitment of friends and family; therefore, online consumers engaging in such environments already have, to a large degree, built-in trust. As a result, online word of mouth generated through these social media platforms is widely and easily accepted by consumers, because it is generally viewed as unbiased, reliable, and trustworthy. Research has shown that online word of mouth has a greater impact on consumer behavior than other traditional marketing means (such as printed advertisements), because word-of-mouth advertising is persuasive and generated from existing relationships (Bélanger, Balib, and Longdenc 2014).

Moreover, as an unconventional marketing channel, opinions and discussions initiated by consumers through social media have a substantial impact on brand image and, therefore, cannot be overlooked by progressive marketing professionals in 2015. This two-way dialogue approach is more likely to be the way of communicating with consumers in the coming years through social media Web sites. Besides governments and corporations, public-sector institutions like universities are increasingly using social media Web sites like Facebook and Twitter to market their strengths to high school students in this very competitive domain (Bélanger, Balib, and Longdenc 2014).

We will focus in this chapter on the rise of social media and social marketing by first looking at some recent statistics, including the Pew Research Center's Social Media Update for 2014. We will then discuss some controversies surrounding social media Web sites, starting with what is known about social media addiction. We will describe what is known about some harms associated with social media Web site usage—particularly sexting—and share some legal, mental health, and policy resolutions for dealing with these harms. We will close the chapter by looking at some recent business challenges to social media Web sites and some recent concerns about criminals lurking in social media Web sites to take advantage of vulnerable users, particularly minors and adolescents.

RECENT 2014 PROFILES OF POPULAR SOCIAL MEDIA WEB SITES

Recent 2014 profiles of the most popular social media Web sites are given below, with statistics on the number of known active members, usage points of interest, the main reason that online users say they visit these social Web sites, and unique features associated with these Web sites (Bennett 2014).

Facebook

Launched on February 2, 2004, by its founder, Mark Zuckerberg, this is a social utility connecting people online with friends, colleagues at work, students at school, or people with common interests. Hugely successful, Facebook as of March 31, 2014, boasted 1.01 billion mobile monthly active users, with 100 million users residing in India alone. More than 70% of online adults admit to visiting the Web site at least once a month, and users can choose to either "like" or "unlike" online posts. Not surprising, the most common reason given by online users for "unliking" some of the more than 50 million Facebook pages available in 2014 was uninteresting posts. About three-quarters of the engagement on a post happens in the first five hours.

Google+

Google executives describe this social Web site, launched June 28, 2011, as a kind of social layer across all of Google's services that allows online users to share their identity and interests. Features include the ability to post photos and status updates to the stream or interest-based communities. Other unique features allow different kinds of relationships (other than friends) to be grouped into "Circles," and a combined text-and-video-chat allows for special interactions called "Hangouts." In April 2014, Vic Gundotra was the executive in charge of Google+, but he left the company and turned the reins over to David Besbris. Adult online users admit to spending about seven minutes a month on this social Web site, with about 22% of online adults admitting to being active here. From a marketing channel perspective, about 53% of the interactions between a Google+ online user and this particular brand are positive.

Twitter

The Twitter social Web site was created on March 21, 2006, and launched that July by founders Jack Dorsey, Noah Glass, Biz Stone, and Evan Williams. Vine is one of Twitter's subsidiaries. Twitter is an online social networking service allowing online users to send and read short 140-character messages called "tweets." In 2014, there were more than 1 billion total users, with about 255 million users admitting to being active monthly. About 500 million tweets are sent per day, with 78% of active "tweeters" saying that they do so using their mobile phones. While 46% of Twitter users admit to tweeting at least once per day, about 44% of Twitter users say that they never tweet others—so they are labeled as "inactive."

Instagram

Instagram is a photo-sharing social Web site launched on October 6, 2010, by founders Kevin Systrom and Mike Krieger. The company grew from just four employees to more than a dozen in just 11 months. By 2014, there were about 200 million monthly active users, with about 23% of online teenagers saying that Instagram is their favorite social Web site. In the last six months of 2014, 50 million users signed up to be active on Instagram, with Thailand alone boasting 1.5 million Instagram users.

LinkedIn

Founded in December 2002, by Reid Hoffman and Jeff Weiner, after recruiting some colleagues from SocialNet and PayPal to work on a new idea, LinkedIn was launched on May 5, 2003. A business-oriented social network, by 2014, LinkedIn had 300 million users, with 187 million being monthly active users. About 72 users sign up to become active on LinkedIn every second. By 2014, there were more than 39 million students and recent undergraduates citing themselves as active in more than 200 countries. About 41% of LinkedIn visits are conducted using a mobile phone, and by 2014, there were about 44,000 daily LinkedIn mobile job applications.

Pinterest

Founded by Paul Sciarra, Evan Sharp, and Ben Silbermann, Pinterest is a Web and mobile application company that is very popular with female online users. Launched in March 2010, this social networking site, oddly enough, has no advertisements displayed on the Web site, but companies can have "pinboards" displaying their products. Competing well against other popular social networking sites like Facebook and Twitter, Pinterest acts like a virtual scrapbook filled with pretty pictures of outfits, recipes, and other goodies appealing to online users. As of 2014, there were 70 million total users and about 40 million monthly active users, with about 80% of users being female. A significant 84% of female Pinterest users say that they are active visitors, while just 50% of the male Pinterest users say that they could classify themselves as such.

Vine

A spinoff of Twitter, Vine was created by Dom Hofmann, Rus Yusupov, and Colin Kroll and launched January 24, 2013. Available in 25 languages, Vine is a video-sharing social network Web site, which has changed the way that marketing teams view videos. By 2014, it boasted more than 40 million total users. In 2014, five "vines" were tweeted every second, with weekends being the most popular vine-sharing days of the week for user activity. Three of five most-retweeted vines are by musicians.

Snapchat

Evan Spiegel, Bobby Murphy, and Reggie Brown created Snapchat and released it in September 2011. A photo-sharing, social networking service, it lets users take photos, record videos, add text or drawings, and send all of these to a controlled list of others online. The sent photographs and videos, called "Snaps," are available to the recipients for a set time limit ranging from 1 second to 10 seconds, after which they will be hidden from the recipient's device and deleted from Snapchat's servers. This social Web site boasted more than 60 million total users by 2014 and 30 million monthly active users. The bulk of Snapchat users—70%—are female. Interestingly, about 5% of overall selfies shared through social media are shared using Snapchat, and about 50% of Norway smartphone users are said to use Snapchat.

YouTube

Founded by Steve Chen, Chad Hurley, and Jawed Karim on Valentine's Day in 2005, this worldwide social network was independent for the first year and then was parented by Google from 2006 to the present. Users can upload videos, view flagged videos, view flagged comments, like videos, and add videos to playlists. An amazing 61 language versions are available to users. With more than 1 billion current users, more than 80% of the traffic is now from outside the United States—where it originated—and 40% of the traffic is from mobile devices. Six billion hours of video are watched by YouTube users per month, and 100 hours of video are uploaded every minute. A whopping one billion is the average number of YouTube mobile video views per day.

Blogs

In 2014, more than 12 million people blogged using social networks, and more than 6.7 million people blogged using blogging Web sites. A significant 77% of Internet users said they read blogs, and 23% of Internet time is spent on blog and social networking Web sites. From an industry perspective, companies having their own blog site have more than 97% more inbound links than companies not having one, and business-to-business marketers using a blog website have more than 67% more leads than those not using one.

THE PEW RESEARCH CENTER'S 2014 SURVEY FINDINGS ON RECENT TRENDS REGARDING AMERICAN ADULTS' SOCIAL MEDIA NETWORK USAGE PATTERNS

The Pew Research Center, a nonpartisan fact tank informing the public about timely issues, attitudes, and trends shaping America and the world, conducted landline and cell phone telephone surveys (in English and in Spanish) in September 2014. In all, 2,003 American adult Internet users aged 18 years or over participated in the survey with the purpose of ascertaining a better understanding of their online social media usage patterns (Duggan et al. 2015).

The percentage of surveyed U.S. adults who were active on the following five social media Web sites were as follows: Facebook (71%), LinkedIn (28%), Pinterest (28%), Instagram (26%), and Twitter (23%). While Facebook has remained the most popular social media site among U.S. adults since 2013, with 71% of American Internet users being active on it (representing about 58% of the entire U.S. adult population), this social media Web site's growth has slowed, though the level of user engagement with the platform has increased. Other platforms like Twitter, Instagram, Pinterest, and LinkedIn saw significant increases over 2013 in the proportion of online adult users visiting there. Other social media network site trends included the following (Duggan et al. 2015):

- Multiplatform usage was on the rise, with 52% of online adults using two or more social media Web sites, an increase from 2013, when just 42% of Internet users followed this pattern.
- For the first time since these surveys were conducted, more than half (56%) of online adults aged 65 or over used Facebook—a number representing 31% of all seniors.
- For the first time since these surveys were conducted, more than half of Internet-active young adults aged 18–29 used Instagram, with about 49% using the Web site daily.
- For the first time since these surveys were conducted, about 50% of Internet users having a college education used LinkedIn.
- Consistent with earlier trends, women continued to dominate visiting Pinterest—with 42% of online women being regular users, but with only 13% of men being regular users.

Given that Facebook users were so prolific in 2014, they were asked additional questions about their friend networks. For 2014, among Facebook users, the median number of Facebook friends was 155, with the respondents admitting that of these, the number of "actual" friends was only about 50—indicating an inflated social media friend count. Other Facebook "friend" statistics were as follows (Duggan et al. 2015):

- About 93% of Facebook users said that they are friends with family members other than parents or children.
- About 91% of Facebook users said that they are friends with current friends.
- About 87% of Facebook users said that they are friends with those from the past, such as high school or college classmates.
- About 58% of Facebook users said that they are friends with coworkers.
- Only about 45% of Facebook users said that they are friends with their parents.

- Only about 43% of Facebook users said that they are friends with their children.
- Only about 39% of Facebook users said they are friends with people they have never met in person.
- Only about 36% of Facebook users said they are friends with their neighbors.

As for the other social network Web sites, Twitter was particularly popular among Internet users younger than age 50 and college-educated users in 2014. Compared with late 2013, the social media service saw significant increases among a number of demographic groups, including men, Caucasian Internet users, those aged 65 and over, those living in households with an annual income of $50,000, and those living in the city. For Instagram users, besides young adults, women were particularly likely to be active on it, along with Hispanics and African Americans, as well as those living in the city or in the suburbs. While Pinterest remained popular among younger adults and women in 2014, there was about an 11-point increase in the proportion of those aged 50 or older who were active on the site; other notable increases in usage included Caucasian adults, those living in the lowest and highest household income levels, those having some college education, and those living in suburbia and rural areas. Finally, college graduates continued to dominate the LinkedIn website in 2014, and it remained the only social media network where online users aged 30–64 were more likely to be active than online users aged 18–29 (Duggan et al. 2015).

Finally, respondents in 2014 were asked how often they engaged with the five social media Web sites—whether on a daily, weekly, or less frequent basis. As in 2013, Facebook users continued to be highly engaged, while the proportion of daily Twitter users decreased. Instagram, Pinterest, and LinkedIn users tended to log on with similar frequency patterns as those noted for 2013 (Duggan et al. 2015).

ATTEMPTS AT DEFINING SOCIAL MEDIA WEB SITE ADDICTION

The concept of cyberaddiction is far from being unanimously accepted by mental health experts and scientists (Ko et al. 2012; Pezoa-Jares, Espinoza-Luna, and Vasquez-Medina 2012). The same statement is true about Internet users' addiction to video games (Hellman et al. 2013) or to social media Web sites like Facebook (Andreassen et al. 2012; Levard and Soulas, 2010).

The concept of Internet or cyber addiction was originally proposed satirically by Ivan Goldberg in 1995 on a chat forum used mainly by psychiatrists. In 1996, Kimberly Young suggested considering Internet addiction as an actual new clinical pathology. Based on pathological gambling criteria present in the *DSM-IV*, Young created a 20-item test to measure how seriously the Internet adversely affects a person's social life (Young 1996).

Today, Facebook's milestone of one billion users has been exceeded, and on a per capita basis, Canadians are actually the greatest Facebook users in the world; on average, the typical social media user has 225 "friends." But is this number of online "friends" healthy—or indicative of cyberaddiction? Several scientific studies have attempted in recent years to determine whether and to what extent overuse of Facebook can constitute cyberaddiction (Suissa 2015).

Experts exploring why people act against their own better judgment and intentions when they go online to communicate with others have suggested that addiction to social media networks is primarily caused by a lack of constraints imposed by this social medium, compared to, say, those imposed when one tries to obtain psychoactive substances in the nonvirtual world. Although controlled substances like alcohol and tobacco are known for their addictive properties, they generate much lower levels of desire and need in users than the urge to consult social networks. Thus, affirm mental health experts, addiction to social media is more difficult to treat than addiction to alcohol or cigarettes, primarily because this kind of desire is more difficult to resist in view of its greater availability and lower cost (Suissa 2015).

A doctoral thesis completed in 2012 by Couderc, a French psychiatrist, tried to answer the question of why people are so infatuated with Facebook and other social media. This scholar found that young "addicts" spend three times as much time on Facebook as the average social media user: 191 minutes per day. The intense need to connect with social media sites and the concurrent postponement of real-life obligations—school, work, administrative, or household duties—ensure that the monomaniacal, exclusive investment in Facebook or other social media overtakes other sources of interest and pleasure, creating in the addicted individual what has become known as "social media anxiety disorder, or SMAD" (Suissa 2015).

Another study conducted by Andreassen, a Norwegian psychologist, and his research team (2012) led to the creation of an empirical tool called the Bergen Facebook Addiction Scale, based on a study sample of 423 students. This research team's findings were similar to those of Couderc; namely, that addiction is more likely to occur among young users who are anxious and who live in precarious social situations in which virtual communication is less anxiety-provoking than face-to-face communications with others in the high-stress real world (Suissa 2015).

Thus, Facebook or other social media addiction can probably best be defined as "occurring when people are afraid to disconnect from Facebook or some other social media site, because they think they are going to miss something important." In short, some social media users develop an abusive relationship with Facebook or other social media connections. Therefore, an Internet site that was designed to facilitate social ties may, in some cases, actually culminate in strongly harming the online users (Suissa 2015).

Suissa (2015) suggests that social media addiction builds over time and comprises the following five phases:

1. An individual feels alone, uncomfortable, and not accepted by his or her identifying group. Thus, the individual experiences low self-esteem, feeling as though he or she is living in a crisis, and fixating on a perceived reality that things are not going well at home or at work.
2. Consequently, there develops an intoxication with interacting on social media or other preferred Web sites, such as a gambling site; thus, the pain seems to be gone temporarily, as involvement in social media or online gambling increases.
3. There emerges an artificial feeling of well-being, filling the emptiness of phase one but only temporarily soothing one's negative emotions without dealing with root causes of underlying intrapersonal and interpersonal issues.
4. With addiction to social Web site interactions or gambling, the online user eventually experiences a "down" feeling mixed with guilt and low self-esteem.
5. Finally, the addicted individual may seek assistance from a mental health expert to explore more healthful opportunities and regimes for breaking the addiction to social media Web sites and the vulnerability and potential harm that such addiction causes.

A Closer Look at Why Users Get "Hooked" on Facebook and Other Social Media Web Sites

One reason that Facebook is the most popular social networking site is the scope of affordances it provides for users. These include the ability to connect with one's landline network online and to easily form new connections online by posting and sharing functions or social information. For Facebook, in particular, online users can provide feedback to this shared information in the form of comments and "likes." Besides offering the convenience of network-wide, group, and private communication channels through one interface, Facebook has marketed well the "be anywhere" mobile application, ensuring that users can access the social networking Web site at any time and at any place from their cellular devices. Collectively, these pluses help explain why Facebook has grown in immense popularity among online users and maintained a diverse and very devoted user base globally (Fox & Moreland 2015).

Although considerable marketing and social research has focused on the benefits of using and becoming involved with social media networks—such as increased social capital, social support, and relationship maintenance (see, for example, McEwan 2013; Nabi, Prestin, and So 2013)—fewer studies have recently examined the nature of negative outcomes for adult users. Given that social media users expect positive outcomes and often initially visit these Web sites for relaxation, entertainment, or social connections (Ku, Chu, and Tseng 2013; Park, Kee, and Valenzuela 2009), users may not initially anticipate experiencing the negative events or interactions over time that eventually make these online experiences more potent and hurtful.

In an effort to get a clearer understanding of the dark side of Facebook engagement, two U.S. researchers, Fox and Moreland (2015), conducted interviews with focus groups of adult Facebook users ($N = 44$). This pair of researchers uncovered narratives surrounding online users' negative psychological and relational experiences related to this particular social networking site and its known affordances: connectivity, visibility, accessibility, persistence, and ease of social feedback. The researchers then conducted a thematic analysis, resulting in the following five key themes regarding Facebook stressors:

1. *Managing inappropriate or annoying content in posts, photos, or comments.* Because Facebook does post rules regarding obscene content, it does not afford selective filtering. As one male study participant noted, "There aren't obviously clear-cut boundaries as established by, like, Mark Zuckerberg as to what you should be doing on Facebook. . . . I just feel there are natural boundaries that exist on how much you should be sharing."
2. *Being tethered to the social networking site.* Most participants lamented spending too much time on Facebook, as it often detracted from face-to-face interpersonal interaction, work, studies, or sleep. One male participant disclosed that he often would be late to class and work because of his need to check Facebook before he left his home. Another female participant confessed that her schoolwork suffered because she could not control her time on Facebook, noting that "The paper took me twice as long as it should have. . . . I told myself it would be 15 minutes. . . . It's kind of a problem." The latter participant demonstrated what mental health experts refer to as a "distraction addiction."
3. *A lack of privacy and control when engaging in the Web site.* First, because of the affordances of sharing, replicability, and connectivity online, Facebook users must cope with the inability to hide things from their network. Second, because Facebook controls users' privacy, participants complain often about their inability to hide things from others coexisting in the virtual world. Facebook unilaterally determines how it shares information with others, even making

material on Facebook searchable on the Internet. In fact, members outside of one's established network can gain access to a user's Facebook profile.

A middle-aged male study participant experienced a surprise on Facebook after a teenage girl contacted him and claimed he was her father, a chronological impossibility, he said, though he knew her mother at one time. He felt compelled to maintain contact, he admitted, but he began to feel very uncomfortable with the situation. After the girl got in trouble, her mother contacted the man via Facebook asking what they should do with "their" daughter. At that point, the man could no longer manage the stress of the Facebook connection, so he blocked the teen and her mother. The man became very stressed, he shared, after his wife saw the communication on Facebook and then she got really mad. In the end, the man strengthened his privacy management on Facebook because, he affirmed, "You just never know what's going to jump up out of the past."

4. *Intense social comparison and jealousy formation with others online*. For participants who started Facebook as a young teen, the first basis of comparison and competition is often the number of "friends" one has on the social media network—a notably quantifiable kind of popularity contest. As one female study participant said, "[Getting Facebook friends] seems like such an arms race." Although study participants generally indicated that their "friend count" did not matter when they matured, others said that the "friend" measure may still serve as a heuristic cue, particularly for outliers (i.e., judging "friend sluts" with thousands of friends). Study participants also reported comparing their lives to those of their Facebook friends, which often resulted in feelings of jealousy or dissatisfaction. One female participant said that she became preoccupied with others' posts, affirming, "I feel like it consumes you . . . to the point that you can't live your normal life because you see everyone else's. . . . I think it makes you think your life is not as fun or as exciting or interesting than other people's, which is sad because it's not true." Other participants complained that their real-world friends became so preoccupied with constantly documenting and uploading every moment on Facebook that they didn't even want to get together anymore.
5. *Relationship tension and conflict*. Given that Facebook networks typically mimic off-line networks, it is not surprising that landline interactions may carry over into the Facebook virtual world. Often, study participants suggested that Facebook could both exacerbate existing off-line conflicts as well as create new sources of conflict. As one female study participant noted, "Facebook definitely causes drama." One often-cited area for drama was romantic relationships, given that Facebook's affordances allow relationship partners to link their profiles (i.e., go "Facebook official"). One male study participant noted Facebook as a frequent source of interpersonal conflict, saying, "It's kind of

stressful sometimes because it becomes drama, it becomes conflict. The stupid little fights, and it comes up bigger and bigger and bigger, just for these little reasons—'oh, you didn't comment me back, or oh you didn't post this picture up.' I think every relationship is like that—my past two girlfriends were like that the same way."

Fox and Moreland (2015) concluded their study by saying that although Facebook users often experience negative emotions, they feel pressured to access the social networking site frequently, primarily caused by a fear of missing out and to fulfill relationship maintenance demands. Study participants reported a number of personal harms caused by engagement on Facebook, such as privacy violations due to Facebook's visibility, connectivity, and persistence; a constant social comparison with other network members; and relational turbulence in online interactions because of the public nature of conflict on Facebook. Finally, many study participants talked about overarching contradictions with Facebook engagement; though initially they claimed that Facebook was inconsequential, they later recounted significant stressful or hurtful events associated with intense engagement on Facebook.

Psychopathological Profiles of Very Engaged Facebook Users

Because of the dramatic increase in the use of Facebook and other social media sites in recent years, there is a recognized problematic usage issue seen by an increasing number of mental health experts. Therefore, the objective of a recent published study by Moreau and colleagues was to explore the psychopathological profiles of Facebook users in particular (Moreau et al. 2015).

The study sample consisted of 456 French adolescents and young adults aged from 12 to 25 years having a Facebook account. The study participants answered an online self-questionnaire assessing Facebook use, motives for Facebook use, depressive symptoms experienced and social anxiety experienced, sensation seeking, borderline personality traits, parental bonding and attachment, and peer attachment. The results of this study, noted the research team, suggest that three clusters can be identified for avid Facebook users who may or may not exhibit a constellation of pathological traits (Moreau et al. 2015).

The first cluster, called "borderline" personality features (defined by mental health experts to include a pervasive pattern of instability in interpersonal relationships, self-image, and emotions), was well above the normative population mean on the constellation including borderline traits, depressive symptoms, social anxiety, and sensation-seeking. A second cluster, labeled by the researchers as "sensation seeking," was distinguished by high levels of sensation-seeking and low levels of other psychopathological variable presence. The third cluster, called "low traits," was well below the mean on all of the psychopathological symptoms assessed for this study group (Moreau et al. 2015).

According to the authors, this was the first comprehensive study examining mental health associations between problematic Facebook usage, motives, attachment, and psychopathological symptoms in a sizable sample of adolescents and young adults. With the growing global popularity of the Facebook social network, the authors posited that the first two clusters containing many or a few psychopathological features could become increasingly evident in young adults actively engaged in social media networks.

Additionally, these study results showed that the borderline cluster reported more dysfunctional relationships (i.e., a lower degree of attachment to peers and parents and a higher degree of need to have control over others) than the other two clusters. These study findings tend to be consistent with previous ones suggesting that children with borderline traits tend to perceive their relationship with their mother, in particular, as an affectionless control relationship having more parent-child aggression and neglect than what other children experience in the mentally healthier control groups. This finding also helps explain the adverse relationship seen between a nonoptimal parental attachment and problematic Facebook use. Therefore, virtual relationships are engaged in by the borderline personality child or young adult to avoid hurtful face-to-face interactions occurring in the real world. Ironically, while adolescence arouses in most young people the need for a healthy separation from parents, Facebook likely represents a viable means by which troubled young adults can maintain a compensatory level of emotional involvement with their peers (Moreau et al. 2015).

Consistent with the mental health literature, this study also confirmed that the three principal motives for Facebook use involved "relationship maintenance," "entertainment," and "passing time." Using social media Web sites for relationship maintenance appeared to be the most important motive. These study results suggest that the latter motive is an indicator only of Facebook use in general. None of the three motives was specific to problematic Facebook use or of prevailing psychopathological symptoms in young adults (e.g., depression, social anxiety, or borderline traits in particular) (Moreau et al. 2015).

Social Media Network Addiction and Poor Emotional Regulation

Another recent study conducted by Hormes, Kearnes, and Timbko (2014) assessed disordered online social networking use in 253 undergraduate students in the northeastern United States, along with substance dependence and difficulties with emotional regulation. Measurements included disordered online social networking use (using the Young Internet Addiction Test), alcohol abuse and dependence (using the *DSM-IV-TR* diagnostic criteria for alcohol dependence, the Penn Alcohol Craving Scale, and the Cut-down, Annoyed, Guilt, Eye-opener [CAGE] screen, along with other tools), and emotional regulation issues (using the White Bear Suppression Inventory and the Difficulties in Emotion Regulation Scale). The study findings indicated that disordered online social networking use was present in 9.7% of the sample surveyed, and that this problem was significantly and positively associated with higher scores on the Young Internet Addiction Test, greater difficulties with emotional regulation, and problems with alcohol abuse (Hormes, Kearnes, and Timbko 2014).

Given these findings, the authors concluded that very active use of online social networking sites is potentially addictive for young adults, particularly for those having underlying addiction and emotional issues. Thus, available reliable measures of substance abuse and dependence seem to be suitable predictors for also assessing potential disordered online social networking use in clients. Disordered online social networking use also seems to arise as part of a cluster of symptoms related to poor emotion regulation skills, which may require mental health interventions to help reduce clients' addiction susceptibilities.

Online Users' Need for Autonomy, Need for Competence, and Need for Relatedness and the Propensity for Social Media Addiction

Self-determination theory posits that people have inherent growth tendencies and innate psychological needs, which form a critical basis for their motivations, behaviors, and psychological well-being over the longer term. According to this theory, people generally seek to satisfy three intrinsic needs: the need for autonomy (defined as a feeling of having self-will and the absence of external pressures), the need for competence (defined as having the capacity to act effectively and to develop generally positive feelings by pursuing something meaningful in one's life), and the need for relatedness (defined as having a feeling of closeness and connectedness with others in the world).

In the mental health literature, high satisfaction of these three intrinsic needs is strongly correlated with psychological health and well-being and the long-term fostering of effective self-regulation. Thus, thwarted intrinsic needs can be satisfied through habituated media use, such that social media can provide users with specific gratifications that may compensate for lower need satisfaction. The important question was then asked by the German research team of Masur, Reinecke, Ziegele, and Quiring (2014) if there is an interplay between intrinsic need satisfaction and Facebook-specific motives in explaining some online users' addictive behaviors to this site (like the woman in the quote at the start of this chapter).

The research team, therefore, conducted an online survey among 581 social network Web site users in Germany, hypothesizing that motives mediate the influence of thwarted intrinsic need satisfaction on addictive behavior. The researchers assumed that (1) a lack of autonomy leads to a higher motivation to use social network Web sites for self-presentation and escapism, (2) a lack of competence predicts the motive to use social network Web sites for getting important information and for self-presentation, and (3) a lack of relatedness fosters users' motives to use social network Web sites for self-presentation and meeting new people. These motives, in turn, were predicted to be strongly correlated with higher levels of social media Web site addiction when the individual felt that his or her motives could not be fully realized just through interactions with others in the real world. The research team's study findings indicated that, in the end, all of these assumptions were supported by the study data (Masur et al. 2014).

Treatment Interventions for Social Media Addiction

As with other types of Internet addictions, mental health experts generally agree that until more is known about the cycle of social media Web site addiction per se, cognitive behavioral therapy (CBT) is the preferred treatment intervention for this affliction. CBT has been shown to be an effective treatment for compulsive disorders, such as pathological gambling, as well as for substance abuse, emotional disorders, and eating disorders (Hucker 2004; Beck et al. 1993). In CBT, clients are taught not only to monitor their thoughts in order to identify those provoking addictive feelings and actions, but to hone new coping skills and other means to prevent relapses from occurring. The typical range for CBT is from three to four months, or about 12 weekly sessions with a mental health professional.

At the early stages of CBT, the therapy is behavioral in nature, with a focus on specific behaviors or life situations where a client's impulse control disorder causes the greatest difficulty. As the CBT sessions evolve, the focus tends to move to the cognitive assumptions and distortions that have become ingrained in the user, triggering the compulsive behavior and various adverse effects. For social media addiction in particular, the therapist will advocate moderated and controlled use of the Internet by the user, with the primary goal of abstaining from problematic applications of Internet behavior (such as going on the social media Web site to "like" posts or to communicate with others), while retaining controlled use of the computer for legitimate employment or educational purposes (Orzack 1999; Greenfield 1999).

BULLYING AND SEXTING IN SOCIAL MEDIA NETWORKS

The availability and use of social networking sites creates both opportunities and risks for young Internet users. We will now discuss the concerns in North America and Europe about most appropriately dealing with both cyberbullying and sexting. The ultimate goal, of course, is to identify a number of elements for a comprehensive strategy to ensure that the known risks of cyberbullying and sexting are dealt with in a useful way that empowers young users to enjoy the opportunities afforded by social media network communications without being unnecessarily harmed by them.

Over the past 10 years, the popularity of social network sites (SNS) has increased dramatically, attracting an extraordinary number of new Internet users, of which a significant proportion are teenagers. The recent EU Kids Online study showed that in Europe, 77% of 13–16-year-olds are active on SNS (Livingstone et al. 2012). Even though most SNS stipulate that the minimum age required for creating a profile is 13, this 2012 study found that 38% of 9–12-year-olds have created a profile on SNS, despite their being below the stipulated age limit. According to recent statistics from the United States, about 73% of 12–17-year-olds are active on Facebook alone, reinforcing the observation that social media use has a wide appeal for young adolescents and teens (Pew Research Center 2014).

Social science research has increasingly shown that smartphones with social networking capabilities are, indeed, hugely popular with children and young adults, suggesting that many in this age group would "die" without their phones, that phones and social networks play a "massive part" in their relationships, and that they are shaping most aspects of young people's daily lives. In May 2013, 47% of U.S. teenagers reportedly owned a smartphone. In short, the availability of and the use of SNS and smartphones bring both opportunities and risks to young social media users. As the Council of Europe put it in their 2012 recommendation on the protection of human rights regarding SNS, while the latter have great potential to promote the exercise and enjoyment of human rights and fundamental freedoms (in particular, the freedoms to express, to create, to exchange content and ideas, and the freedom of assembly), the fact that SNS allow users to share status changes (through status updates, messages on "walls," or instant messaging), to share photos or video snippets, and to communicate in real time with new or established friends creates a number of risks. Whereas in recent years discourse related to child safety online has tended to focus on child predation and grooming, social scientists have increasingly begun to posit that the resultant success of e-safety campaigns is evident in teenagers' awareness of advised practices to reduce risk brought about by online strangers. Now it is time to shift the focus, they say, toward reducing risk from known peers who may resort to bullying and/or sexting in SNS (Lievens 2014).

Although it is often mistakenly assumed that the Internet in general and social networks in particular function within a sort of legal vacuum, in reality, a spectrum of different legal options and mental health interventions are applicable to users experiencing SNS risks. However, there remains a lack of clarity about these risks and how to carefully and appropriately attend to them by young adults, parents, teachers, and policymakers (Lievens 2014).

Bullying and Sexting Defined

Whereas bullying has been broadly defined as "negative, aggressive behavior that is intentional, involves an imbalance of power, and is, most often, repeated over time," cyberbullying, in particular, has been characterized as "being cruel to others by sending or posting harmful material or engaging in other forms of social cruelty using the Internet or other digital technologies." SNS provide a virtual environment allowing both types of these harmful behaviors to flourish (Lievens 2014).

Interesting recent research has drawn attention to the fact that adults and teenagers may have very different conceptions of bullying; as compared to adults, teens may discuss their bullying experiences merely as "drama" rather than as "bullying" or "cyberbullying." This difference in characterization may, therefore, have a significant impact on accurate projections regarding the frequency of such behaviors in SNS (Lievens 2014).

Sexting has been defined as "youth writing sexually explicit messages, taking sexually explicit photos of themselves or others in their peer groups, and transmitting those photos and/or messages to their peers." Sexting thus refers to sexually explicit content communicated via text messages, smartphones, or visual and Web 2.0. forums, such as SNS (Lievens 2014).

The practice of sending sexually suggestive images is not limited to the younger online population, for the reality is that adults also engage in this type of behavior as part of the dating or partnership cycle. Our focus here, however, is on the younger adult.

It is also important to note that sexting may be a normal part of young adults' expressing their sexuality. Accepting that there is a normal expression of sexting that is possible, recent social science research has tended to focus on the coercive sides of both bullying and sexting. Therefore, a distinction should be made between primary and secondary sexting, with the former meaning that minors or young adults take pictures of themselves and share these with peers online, and with the latter meaning that another party online forwards or further shares a picture that was sent to him or her by a person that took the picture of himself or herself (Lievens 2014).

From a legal perspective, whereas primary sexting can be consensual (unless it is the result of coercion), secondary sexting is likely not to be consensual but rather part of revengeful actions (by, say, a previous partner) or bullying behavior—both of which have criminal sanctions associated with them in various jurisdictions worldwide (Lievens 2014).

Prevalence Statistics on Bullying and Sexting

According to the recent EU Kids Online study, only about 6% of 9–16-year-olds have received hurtful messages online, but despite this relatively low percentage, 80% of those who received such messages were fairly upset or very upset. When openly asked, about 3% of 9–16-year-olds in the EU Kids Online study admitted to having bullied others. Thus, when comparing bullying risks with other online risks like child predation, it seems that while bullying is among the least common risks, it is the obvious online risk upsetting children the most. With regard to sexting, the EU Kids Online study found that 15% of 11–16-year-olds received sexual messages on the Internet, and about 25% of them who received these were very bothered or upset. Only about 3% of 11–16-year-olds in the EU Kids Online study said that they had posted or sent sexual messages online in the past year (Lievens 2014).

A U.S. study completed in 2011 by the Pew Research Center found similar trends—with 8% of teens aged 12–17 years voicing that they had experienced some form of online bullying, and with 67% of the respondents saying that they had witnessed online cruelty to others. Only 2% of the young U.S. respondents said that they had sent sexually suggestive images or videos to others online, but about 1 in 6 respondents admitted that they had received them and were quite disturbed by them (Lievens 2014).

A Closer Look at the Role of Planned Behavior in Young Users Who Sext

One of the possible consequences of young teens' sharing self-generated sexually explicit material is an association with cyberbullying or harassment incidents. A number of recent highly publicized cases involving adolescents sharing nude pictures online have prompted sexting lawsuits in various jurisdictions around the globe, especially following profound teenage harassment or suicide—such as that experienced by Amanda Todd in Canada. It is, therefore, not surprising that a significant portion of the academic interest to date has been devoted to the legal side of sexting.

Besides a recent increase in a quantitative focusing on the prevalence of sexting and its correlates (see, for example, Livingstone and Görzig 2012), a number of qualitative studies have yielded additional insights into the motives behind adolescent sexting (see, for example, Lippman and Campbell 2012). Accepting the valuable contributions made by these studies, questions remain about sexting and its predictors. A study revealing the determinants of adolescents' motivation to engage in sexting could provide policymakers, mental health experts, and educators with more information about the profiles of sexting adolescents and, thereby, suggest potential points of intervention for tackling the undesirable consequences of adolescent sexting. A 2014 study conducted by Walrave, Heirman, and Hallam built on the scarce research currently available on sexting by examining predictors of this activity among adolescents.

Here, a paper-and-pencil questionnaire was completed by 498 students aged between 15 and 18 years (54% females; *n* = 270) from two Belgian secondary schools. The survey's purpose and procedures were explained to students and teachers, and the research team assured participants that their responses would remain anonymous and confidential; no data would be given to teachers, parents, or fellow students. The study was completed in two phases. In the first phase, a qualitative prestudy was conducted to inform the development of the questionnaire and to elicit respondents' most salient beliefs on sexting. This phase resulted in the following:

- A list of six behavioral beliefs, that is, sexting leads to (1) getting more attention, (2) increasing opportunities to find a romantic partner, (3) a lower likelihood of getting an STD, (4) a higher likelihood of being blackmailed, (5) getting a bad reputation, and (6) being misrepresented by the person to whom you sent the sext
- A list of five normative beliefs, that is, the referent was (1) siblings, (2) a romantic partner, (3) friends, (4) parents, and (5) teacher
- A list of five control beliefs, that is, (1) more sexting when sender is in a romantic partnership, (2) more sexting when the other person can be trusted completely, (3) less sexting when the parents monitor the contents of the mobile phone, (4) less sexting when the conversation partner is someone not well known from previous off-line encounters, and (5) less sexting when the sender thinks that the conversation partner will show the content of the message to others

In the second phase, the beliefs yielded during the in-depth interviews were integrated into a close-ended questionnaire using reliable scales previously validated in research studies related to the context of adolescents' involvement in sexting. Engaging in sexting was measured with one item: "Have you sent sexts in the last two months?" Answers ranged from never (= 1) to daily (= 5). This definition was provided to the study respondents: "Sexting encompasses sending naked or semi-naked pictures of yourself or sending a sexually-exciting text message with your mobile phone or smartphone" (Walrave, Heirman, and Hallam 2014).

The study results showed that 26% of the teens surveyed had engaged in sexting in the two months preceding the survey. Most had done so once or only a few times (21%; *n* = 104). After calculating the sum scores for the items designed to measure attitude toward sexting, a score reflecting teenagers' general attitude was found, ranging from 3 (an extremely negative attitude) to 21 (an extremely positive attitude). In the study sample, the average sum score on attitude towards sexting tended to be slightly negative ($M = 10.1$; $SD = 5.3$).

According to this study's authors, the importance of perceived social pressure outweighs the relative importance of adolescents' attitude and perceived control in predicting the involvement of young adults in sexting. Rather than adapting their motivations to sext to their own subjective evaluations, adolescents seem to be influenced more by the social pressure that they anticipate receiving from significant others. The study results suggest that to reduce sexting among adolescents, preventive initiatives should allude to what significant others in teenagers' lives think about them partaking in sexting—a view that tends to be negative (Walrave, Heirman, and Hallam 2014).

Furthermore, to provide policymakers and educators with more specific ideas about effective targets and points of intervention, the researchers conducted additional analyses to assess the importance of the sources of social pressure. This analysis revealed that teens are mainly influenced by social pressure from peers, as no significant independent predictive value was found for the influence of adults in their lives (i.e., teachers and parents). These results are consistent with other study findings showing the importance of peer influence during adolescence in general, and particularly regarding risky sexual behaviors. In short, peer pressure and the acceptability of sexting should be the focus of interest in awareness-raising initiatives. The importance of parents' and teachers' voices in sexting could be increased by integrating the topic of sexting in adolescents' sexual education. Furthermore, teaching adolescents how to better cope with the pressure of romantic partners and peers is important, as is emphasizing the point that sexting is not the norm among all adolescents. This is a key message that needs to be transmitted: Contrary to popular belief in this age group, not everybody is sexting (Walrave, Heirman, and Hallam 2014).

The second most important predictor of adolescents' motivation to sext was their attitude toward sexting. Additional statistical analysis of sexting intention on the various behavioral beliefs assessed produced the key finding that only those behavioral beliefs that expect positive outcomes of sexting behavior had a statistically significant predictive value; no significant influence was detected regarding any of the beliefs expressing a negative outcome of sexting. This result is consistent with other research findings that adolescents in the virtual world often make decisions based on the perceived benefits of their intended behavior, as opposed to the perceived risks involved (Walrave, Heirman, and Hallam 2014).

Finally, regarding gender differences, the present study found that females have a more negative attitude toward sexting and a more negative perceived social influence than males do. This result is consistent with qualitative research into females' assessment of sexting and how those who send sexts are perceived by their peer group (Lippman and Campbell 2012). Despite this result on gender differences, previous studies have shown that some females are often pressured by their partners or potential partners to send sexts. This close interpersonal influence, therefore, could prevail over the broader social disapproval factor, thereby inducing some females to engage in sexting, despite the risks it entails for their own well-being and reputation (Walrave, Heirman, and Hallam 2014).

A Closer Look at Laws Aimed at Combating Sexting in the United States and Australia

Laws Aimed at Combating Sexting in the United States

In some U.S. states, laws created to prevent and sanction child abuse images are being used by prosecutors to prosecute teenagers who send or possess sexting images (Lippman and Campbell 2012). This heavy-handed legal approach, regardless of the age of the young adults being examined, has been criticized widely by scholars in a number of jurisdictions (Stone 2011; Williams 2012).

Critics argue that legislators' broad-brush approach fails to recognize young adults' sexual agency and their ability to consent to sexting when they are over the legal age of consent. Stated bluntly, young adults' potential for sexual agency needs to be acknowledged, rather than casting them solely as victims or perpetrators (Albury and Crawford 2012).

The results of the Walrave, Heirman, and Hallam (2014) study provide support for a call for a more educational approach rather than a strictly legal approach for dealing with this modern-day issue in social media networks. Scholars posit that educational programs need to be developed focusing on helping teenagers make informed decisions, develop a greater capacity for coping with peer pressure, and recognize both the benefits and the undesirable consequences of sexting.

In several countries, sexting has already been addressed by the courts as a criminal activity. In the United States, the application of child pornography legislation to sexting activities in social media networks has resulted in the conviction of minors who took pictures of themselves or of their boyfriends/girlfriends and shared them using their cell phones. The individuals who were convicted are often subjected to prison sentences and, over the longer term, are required to register as sex offenders (Haynes 2012).

In the summer of 2014, a 17-year-old Virginia teen named Trey Sims was charged with manufacturing and distributing child pornography while exchanging texts with his then-girlfriend, who was 15 at the time. His iPhone and iPad were seized by police, and he was taken into custody. Sims feared that if convicted, he would be sent to prison and be required to register as a sex offender on his release. However, in

August 2014, Sims was given a one-year probation period, and the judge's ruling put off for one year any declaration of his guilt or innocence. The probation came with several stipulations; Sims was prohibited from texting, using social media, or using the Internet for the year. He also was required to complete 100 hours of community service and not to contact the victim or the victim's family. Sims will not be placed on the sex registry or on the sex offender list, and if by August 2015, he has abided by all the stipulations, all charges could be dismissed (Culver 2014).

By 2013, prompted by a growing number of high-profile teen sexting cases in the courts, some U.S. state legislatures realized that existing child pornography laws were poorly equipped to handle cases of teen sexting. Consequently, 32 states have enacted or proposed statutes specifically aimed at teen sexting that would otherwise have qualified as child pornography. These statutes provide for reduced penalties for teenagers who sext, relative to sentences declared under child pornography laws. However, these new statutes also preserve the possibility of prosecution for minors who engage in sexting, either in the juvenile justice system or in adult criminal court (Lampe 2013).

The criminal offense level of teen sexting varies from state to state. New laws enacted in Florida and Nevada and a law proposed in South Dakota treat the first instance of sexting by a minor as a noncriminal offense but subject a reoffending minor to criminal prosecution. Five states have reduced teen sexting to a misdemeanor, and seven others intend to follow suit. Three states encourage the referral of teen sexting cases to juvenile proceedings or to family court, and four states allow teenagers who sext to enter diversionary programs instead of facing criminal sanctions. These reforms generally suggest an emerging trend away from criminal punishment for sexting (Lampe 2013).

Most U.S. states have provided for lesser penalties for teen sexting by leaving adult child pornography laws unchanged and creating new offenses with less severe penalties for minors who sext. Nebraska's legislature has gone one step further; by maintaining its existing child pornography law, it has also created an affirmative defense that entirely immunizes private, consensual sexting between minors over the age of 15 and defendants under the age of 19 from criminal liability (Lampe 2013).

Laws Aimed at Combating Sexting in Australia

Moreover, in Australia, the courts have convicted minors who have sexted based on existing child pornography legislation in that jurisdiction. The rationale behind using child pornography legislation has typically been to punish adults who sexually abuse and exploit children, so it seems to be uncomfortably disproportionate to apply legislation with such heavy sanctions to minors sexting one another, thus potentially ruining their lives. Indeed, this policy of applying child pornography legislation to minors who sext images has been questioned by scholars in multiple jurisdictions, who have posited that sexted images should be protected by the right to freedom of expression—thus placing them, for example, within the protections of the First Amendment in the United States and similar protections elsewhere (Haynes 2012).

Some scholars in Australia and elsewhere have also posited that child pornography per se should be redefined to exclude sexting images, or that legislation should be amended to include an affirmative defense in child pornography statutes for minors who voluntarily self-produce and transmit such images to other minors. In Europe, the debate on the legal consequences of sexting is much less active than in the United States or Australia, perhaps because few, if any, high-profile cases have yet been brought before a court (Lievens 2014).

Closing Thoughts

Technology use is, without question, an area in which teenagers need guidance concerning safe and appropriate behavior, and it seems both fair and prudent to subject teenagers using cell phones and the Internet to adult-set limits. However, the legislation in some U.S. states and in other jurisdictions globally attempting to deter consensual teen sexting through criminal or juvenile prosecutions does not appear to be the proper or sound response to this problem existing within social media networks (Lampe 2013). Clearly, there are other solutions that seem patently more reasonable. For an expert's opinion on this complex area, the reader is referred to the Interview with an Expert with U.S. criminologist Dr. Tom Holt.

INTERVIEW WITH AN EXPERT

Dr. Tom Holt, Associate Professor of Criminology and Criminal Justice

Dr. Tom Holt is an associate professor in the School of Criminal Justice at Michigan State University, specializing in criminology and criminal justice. He has published extensively on hackers, malware, privacy, and various forms of cybercrime, including more than 35 peer-reviewed articles in journals such as *Crime and Delinquency*, *International Journal of Cyber Criminology*, and *Social Science Computer Review*. Dr. Holt has written a number of books, including *Crime On-Line: Correlates, Causes and Context* (2010) and *Hackers and Hacking* (2013). He has received grants from the

National Institute of Justice to examine the social and technical drivers of Russian malware writers, data thieves, and hackers using online data. Dr. Holt presents regularly at DefCon and other academic venues.

Q With the magnificent rise of social media Web site popularity among young adults in recent years, sites like Facebook have become known for providing the venue for serious harmful activities like cyberbullying and sexting. What factors do you believe make social media such a hotbed for these kinds of activities?

A Social media sites allow youth to send text, images, and video in near real time to others in their immediate peer group and the world as a whole. Thus, posting comments or images makes sense for youth in order for their friends to see what they are doing. The social rewards that can accrue through social media, such as someone liking a pic, retweeting a message, or commenting can also be important for young people, which may make this a more enticing environment to engage in certain activities.

Q Despite the fact that adolescent females seem to hold negative views about sexting, the reality is that they often succumb to doing it on social media Web sites. What factors do you believe lower females' resilience, and why do you think that females are more apt to sext than males their age?

A Girls may be requested to send nude pictures by boys, and do so either as a joke, to maintain an intimate relationship, or see it as an extension of flirting and dating norms among others in their peer groups. Thus, sexting may be viewed by some as a normal part of romantic life, and others may do it out of a sense of social pressure. Boys do send nude or seminude images of themselves, so it may be that they are socialized to believe that this is an acceptable request and be willing to reciprocate an image if necessary.

Q In some U.S. states, existing child pornography laws are being used to prevent and sanction sexting. Do you believe, as a criminologist, that this is sound? Why or why not?

A This is not necessarily a sound strategy, as many sexting incidents involve youth of similar ages. Child pornography laws are extremely serious and may involve too harsh a punishment for an individual if the exchange of content was initially consensual. This highlights the need for improved legislation dealing with the misuse of technology. If laws do not exist (as in the case of sexting in 2009 and 2010), then prosecutors must attempt to find laws that may be applied to a specific activity. Child pornography laws may appear sufficient to use to prosecute sexting cases, but they may be too punitive and inappropriately applied relative to the letter of the actual law.

Q Since 2013, approximately 32 U.S. states have enacted or proposed statutes specifically aimed at teen sexting that would otherwise have qualified as child pornography. Can you comment on the content of these statutes and how they are improvements over legislation drafted specifically for child pornography?

A Some states have improved on existing laws by establishing less severe penalties and requiring educational campaigns regarding the harm that may result from engaging in sexting. This is a positive step as it attempts to adjust attitudes toward sexting through social change and promotion of acceptable behavior rather than simply criminalizing a behavior for all youth.

Q Media reports have recently announced that police are trying to crack down on E-Crime 2.0 activities like child pornography transmission or child predation on new media messaging services such as Kik and Snapchat. Why are child predators drawn to these two particular social media sites, and what measures do you think may be helpful in deterring and sanctioning them?

A These sites have a lower adoption rate among adults and provide greater short-term protection of information than sites like Facebook, which archive exchanges. Thus, offenders may view these sites as a more effective venue to target youth without any increase in the risk of detection. Increasing awareness of the use of these applications among parents and educators may be an important first step in increasing the risk for offender detection. Open dialogues between parents and youth about the risk of victimization in these environments are also essential to ensure kids recognize when and how they may be targeted.

Q What new areas regarding social media Web sites do you think that criminology scholars will focus their research energy on in the near future and why?

A Criminologists are increasingly focusing on the ways that social networks on social media influence behavior on and off-line and the extent to which individuals' social connections actually communicate beliefs that encourage or espouse criminal activity. Such knowledge is extremely important to improve our knowledge of the ways that social media sites directly affect the activities of youth.

ANOTHER DETERRENT TO BULLYING AND SEXTING: TERMS OF SERVICE OF SOCIAL MEDIA WEB SITES LIKE FACEBOOK

In addition to the existing legislative provisions outlined for various jurisdictions around cyberbullying or sexting, the Terms of Service (ToS) of various social media network providers often contain stipulations regarding these activities and the consequences resulting from them.

As a case in point, the Statement of Rights and Responsibilities section of Facebook's ToS clearly stipulates: "You will not bully, intimidate, or harass any user. You will not post content that is hate speech, threatening, or pornographic; incites violence; or contains nudity or graphic or gratuitous violence. You will not use Facebook to do anything unlawful, misleading, malicious, or discriminatory."

Furthermore, the Protecting Other People's Rights section of Facebook's ToS clearly affirms: "We respect other people's rights, and expect you to do the same. You will not post content or take any action on Facebook that infringes or violates someone else's rights or otherwise violates the law. We can remove any content or information you post on Facebook if we believe that it violates this Statement or our policies."

Finally, Facebook's Community Standards section of Facebook's ToS clearly states:

> Facebook does not tolerate bullying or harassment. We allow users to speak freely on matters and people of public interest, but take action on all reports of abusive behavior directed at private individuals. Repeatedly targeting other users with unwanted friend requests or messages is a form of harassment. Facebook does not permit hate speech, but distinguishes between serious and humorous speech. While we encourage you to challenge ideas, institutions, events, and practices, we do not permit individuals or groups to attack others based on their race, ethnicity, national origin, religion, sex, gender, sexual orientation, disability or medical condition. Facebook has a strict policy against the sharing of pornographic

Group-level analysis showed significant improvements regarding males' reports of having been bullied or socially isolated, but these same positive results were not found for females. Also, the positive outcomes did not remain for males in the second year of the study. The authors, therefore, suggested that the absence of a positive outcome in the second year might be due to the lack of continuous support of the program. There was also a decrease in incidents of bullying reported to parents, in the number of students who intervened in known bullying episodes, and in the number of adults who addressed students who were bullying or being victimized. Finally, females were found to be more tolerant toward bullying in the second year of the study, attributed to the perceived short-term commitment of the schools toward the program in the second year (Van Ouytsel, Walrave, and Van Gool 2014).

While both the KiVa Antibullying Program and the Olweus Bullying Prevention Program can inspire the implementation of an effective sexting-prevention strategy at schools, key to both approaches is schoolwide training about the issue under discussion. By offering proper training about sexting, the entire school should learn what sexting entails, why adolescents engage in it, and how it is related to other forms of high-risk behavior. Furthermore, the program should address how sexting messages can easily be shared and made public to unintended audiences, thus increasing harm to innocent parties. Moreover, the role of bystanders should be discussed, since bystanders often either choose to support the victim or, conversely, support the dissemination of the sexting message (Van Ouytsel, Walrave, and Van Gool 2014).

Prevention programs should involve the following critical components (Van Ouytsel, Walrave, and Van Gool 2014):

- Although the thought of discussing sexual topics with their students could be embarrassing for some teachers, such obstacles can be overcome; thus, teachers should learn how to cope with these emotions and how to talk about sexuality in a professional manner during classes that provide a good climate for discussing such sensitive issues.
- Educators should try to master the jargon of online and mobile communication, they should keep themselves updated on the latest applications adolescents use, and they should discuss with their students safe and unsafe social media use. Familiarity with the students' various motives for and possible consequences of sexting behavior could facilitate an open dialogue and improve the credibility of teachers among their students.
- Before introducing the concept of sexting in the classroom, teachers should describe it as the practice of exchanging sexually explicit written and visual messages by cell phone or on the Internet. This description could be used in

school policy documents and prevention materials, as well as during classroom discussions.

- Teachers should integrate sexting prevention into other online safety lessons, such as cyberbullying. These subjects could include the role of electronic communication in romantic or other relationships. Educators could also review the social, emotional, legal, and other relevant risks of sexting behavior with their students, emphasizing that any form of intimate online communication could be captured (e.g., by taking a screenshot) and forwarded to a wider audience. This activity, unfortunately, could lead to bullying and reputational damage.
- Teachers should use current educational materials about sexting with realistic and recognizable sexting scenarios. Some educational materials might create the impression that the producers of sexts (in most cases, females) are to be blamed for anything that might happen to them. Such materials should be avoided or used to criticize the "blame the victim" mentality that victims of sexting often face.
- The school may adopt an antisexting policy wherein sending and possessing images that are sexually explicit are prohibited. In the United States, state laws can form the basis of an internal policy, how sexting incidents will be dealt with, and which sanctions may apply to perpetrators forwarding messages and to bystanders who retext sexting images. This policy, along with the antibullying policy of the school, should be further communicated to pupils and parents.
- In class, teachers should tell students which people they can turn to for advice when sexting incidents occur, as well as where they can report other problematic behaviors like cyberbullying. Teachers should know which members of staff will likely become involved when they are aware of sexting incidents.

Finally, intervention strategies when sexting incidents are known could include the following (Van Ouytsel, Walrave, and Van Gool 2014):

- School administrators should create a contingency plan including a script to follow when sexting victims are known. It is important that school administrators seek appropriate legal guidance that is consistent with local and state laws and that includes remedies for legal liabilities that may be involved. It needs to be underscored that when confronted with sexting, the victim should never be blamed; thus school counselors and other health professionals involved in resolving such incidents should work from this foundation.
- A script for sexting incidents might contain the following types of questions: Who was involved in the production and distribution of the sexting message, and how many people received it? What kind of sexting message was sent

(e.g., a text message, a partially nude photo, a fully nude photo, and/or a depiction of sexual intercourse or screenshots of such activities)? Why was the sext sent? What was the context of the sexting message (e.g., as a form of flirtation, as part of an intimate relationship, to extort another, to bully another, or as an act of voyeurism)? Was the message forwarded to friends or posted on a specific Web site?

- With the student(s) involved, strategies can be created to deal with the immediate harms, to stop the spread of the sexting message to others, and to collect and keep evidence if the courts become involved and criminal charges are eventually filed.
- School officials should determine whether students involved in sexting are also involved in other risk behaviors or have psychosocial problems that need to be addressed by a mental health professional.

MEDIA REPORTS OF BUSINESS GROWTH AND CRIMINAL ACTIVITY GROWTH THROUGH SOCIAL MEDIA NETWORKS

In recent years, online citizens and businesses alike have enjoyed the opportunities afforded them through social media networks. However, besides this bright side, recent media reports have indicated a dark side to social media networks, with harm-producing criminal activity occurring in this lucrative venue.

Media Reports of Business Growth Through Social Media Networks

Let's turn our attention to how businesses are capitalizing on social media networks and look more carefully at some of the challenges that businesses face as a result of their success. At the start of this chapter, we talked about the growth of social media networks as a result of successful marketing campaigns with advertisers who "connect well" with particular networks.

In 2015, social media giant Facebook continued to dominate in this sector, trumping Google. In the first quarter of 2015, for example, Facebook's daily active user tally was 890 million, an increase of 18% over the last quarter of 2014. Moreover, for Facebook in the first quarter of 2015, the number of mobile-only users grew by more than 100%, its revenue grew by about 49%, and its earnings per share were up 69% over 2014 (Umiastowski 2015).

What factors might account for Facebook's marketing success with advertisers and users? Some business analysts maintain that the growth of digital advertising is not simply a zero-sum game; dollars are not simply moving from "old media" like print or television to new digital platforms. But while this movement from one platform to another one was a definite trend in 2015, there are currently millions of small business owners in the United States and globally who are admitting that they are now able to enter the highly competitive world of entrepreneurship because of Internet-based advertising, the growth of social media, and innovative marketing automation tools associated with the latter. The modern-day reality is that without these marketing automation tools, many startup and small business owners just would not be able to efficiently and effectively attract a customer base (Umiastowski 2015).

For example, at a recent business conference in California, one entrepreneur talked with enthusiasm about how his survival gear company was growing through engagement in social media networks. If online users visit his company blog, a tracking pixel remembers the users' interest in the page. The next time users go to the Facebook page, a promotion ad appears suggesting that consumers can buy a special kind of survival product for a terrific price. The business advertising campaign is created on the concept of acquiring a solid customer relation at nearly zero net cost, he affirmed. From a business angle, he added, the gross margin from a low-price offer is enough to offset his online advertising costs (Umiastowski 2015).

As Wall Street will no doubt continue to keep a keen eye on social media network growth, there is little doubt in anyone's mind that successful social media giants like Facebook, Google, Twitter, and LinkedIn will continue to innovate and give advertisers of both small and large firms some amazing tools to target the right audience, thereby continuing to successfully whet social media consumers' appetites.

But as companies utilizing these unique automated marketing tools have recently recognized, with successful product or service launches come some rather unique user challenges. The one sure-fire way to bolster business revenues is to let consumers post messages on Facebook or Twitter. The idea behind such campaigns is one that in recent years has become widespread in social media ad land; namely, among the most valuable things that brands can do to gain influence is to get "regular people"—consumers—to do the advertising for them. Consumers, as noted earlier in this chapter, always trust word of mouth from friends and family members more than they trust paid messages from companies. For digitally savvy young consumers, excited by new ways of communicating with one another in the virtual world, getting their personal endorsements is becoming increasingly important to business maintenance and growth (Krashinsky 2015).

A study from the analytics firm Chartbeat in 2014 found that consumers were much more likely to pay attention to tweets written by third parties—regular people—than by brands promoting themselves. Another 2014 study by Veritas Communications and Northstar found that brand endorsements from friends and family have doubled the influence on Canadians' decisions (Krashinsky 2015).

But, unfortunately, consumer posts affiliated with a particular brand are not always generously positive. In March 2015, Canadian media reports emerged of corporations advertising on social media like Facebook asking the latter to shut down image-tarnishing posts by dissatisfied consumers. In 2013 and 2014, Lululemon Athletica and Target's Canadian division's business missteps caused a blast of consumer wrath in comments posted on Facebook. In 2013, Lululemon, in particular, was hit with a ton of complaints on its Facebook page when its products suffered noticeable quality issues—and consumers took notice and then talked openly about it in the virtual environment (Strauss and Dingman 2015).

For example, a revamping by the social media giant during March 2015 quietly changed the posting of the negative comments game so that the nasty consumer posts would no longer be readily available on corporate pages. Rather, users would have to click an icon to view them or view the left-hand side of the page. This revamping would provide some relief to companies like Lululemon Athletica and Target. However, with this revamping comes additional negative feedback. Critics like the president of the Canadian retail consultancy Shikatani Lacroix Design charged that Facebook's 2015 revamping was detrimental, primarily because it defeats the whole purpose of Facebook—which is to engage the online audience. In short, this revamping incident underscores the present-day challenges companies face in grappling with harsh consumer feedback about their initiatives or products posted on social media (Strauss and Dingman 2015).

It is little wonder, then, that as social media giant Facebook continues to court companies to advertise with them to vastly increase revenues, it is making visible moves that could minimize public criticism of fee-paying companies. We can expect that these efforts may threaten to dissuade online consumers from heading to their pages. Facebook spokeswoman Meg Sinclair proclaimed that Facebook collapsed the comment posts because it created a better experience for users, and not that the revamping change was made in response to requests from brands advertising on the site who faced the wrath of dissatisfied consumers (Strauss and Dingman 2015).

Media Reports of Criminal Growth Through Social Media Networks

Besides startup businesses, criminals have also made their way into social media networks in recent times to commit their acts of harm in a large-payback fashion. The profound impact of the Internet in reshaping forms and patterns of crime is now a phenomenon that is widely accepted. Real-world problems like the exponential growth of computer viruses and malicious software, hacking, fraud, copyright piracy, and the online dissemination of obscene and hateful representations are nowadays discussed by academics, lawyers, the police, and the mass media on a regular basis.

In recent years, careful scholarly attention has been given to the multitude of ways that emerging communication technologies have enabled the emergence of such offenses, generating new forms of computer-focused crime and transforming preexisting types of offenses. Within the past three years, in particular, scholars' attention has turned to criminal activities lurking in social media networks. Yar (2012), for example, coined the term "E-Crime 2.0" to comprise offenses exploiting online users engaged in emerging communication technologies such as social media.

Yar (2012) maintains that if we understand the Internet not as a technology per se, but as a shifting set of technologically enabled social practices, we can begin to see how changes to the online environment (i.e., how it works and how people habitually use it to engage with others) can reshape patterns of crime and victimization. Thus, this scholar refers to the emergence of the "social web" or Web 2.0 and how it contributes to the creation of new forms of vulnerability, such as spamming and child predation, thus reconstituting the prevalent patterns of online crime.

Yar (2012) describes the predecessor of E-Crime 2.0 as E-Crime 1.0. In the latter, he notes that the dominance of one-to-many and one-way communication was exploited in a variety of ways, including online users' disseminating online prohibited obscene, hateful, and libelous content; committing fraud through the online sale of stolen, counterfeit, defective, or otherwise misrepresented goods; and downloading content like music and software breaching legal protections on copyright—all of these reflecting the dominant structure of communication that configured the media themselves. For example, given a media experience that habituated users to receiving and accepting communication from just a few senders, cybercriminals were earlier able to reproduce this one-way structure. Thus, they could rather easily present themselves as purveyors of content that was in some sense "authorized, reliable, or trustworthy." Consequently, cybercriminals could spoof the official Web sites of banks, online stores, and news channels to deceive online users.

When online communications became two-way and more personalized, forms of criminal predation developed in tandem with this phenomenon. Thus, in the more advanced online environment, we saw the explosion of spam circulation, phishing e-mails, stalking, and hate message e-mails. With the emergence of E-Crime 2.0, the development of new, interactive Web capacities has brought in new vectors of crime and victimization exploiting the distinctive properties of the changed and even more impressive media environment (Yar 2012).

In short, maintains Yar (2012), the explosion of social networking platforms has enabled E-Crime 2.0. Social media network platforms utilize Internet-based applications enabling online users to present themselves and share details of their lives, activities, interests, and viewpoints with others online anywhere in the world—through Facebook, MySpace, and Bebo, as well as through micro-blogging platforms like Twitter, Tumblr, and LinkedIn. All of these new media spaces enable users to present themselves in a quasi-public arena, narrating and displaying their identities for others to see, comment on, and interact with.

These platforms are also increasingly integrated with a range of impressive technological devices like smartphones, which, in turn, enable instantaneous capturing and real-time sharing of images, videos, and text by mobile phone users. Essentially, mobile phones can be classified as social-sharing devices connecting millions of users around the globe (Yar 2012).

Crucially important to the logic of these media is the increased visibility of any user's self in an extended space and the means to display one's formerly "private self" in a very public forum. Without question, this ability to display, share, and narrate one's self for the global online world defines the main appeal of social media networks. Utilizing various social media sites, users have a global community of correspondents. They, in turn, can in real-time gain a vast array of intimate knowledge about other people's lives and activities. With these positives associated with two-way and many-to-many communications come significant implications for users' vulnerability to predation and other forms of online exploitation (Yar 2012).

Of particular concern is that young people may become increasingly vulnerable to criminal victimization arising from their extensive use of new social media. The statistics alone tell the opportunity story for child predators wanting to lure young people engaged on these sites. In 2009, about 73% of 12- to 17-year-olds in the United States were regular users of social networking sites. In 2015, many minors younger than this age were active. In the United States in particular, there are about 7.5 million children younger than 12 years of age who are avid users of Facebook. Count in other fast-growing applications like Kik and Snapchat, and the number of potential young victims exceeds 8 million easily. Furthermore, about 44% of 12-year-olds in the United States report placing profiles on social networking sites, though they admit that they are aware they are breaching the network's age restrictions by doing so. Similar patterns of usage have been found among European minors—with 31% of 10-year-olds, 44% of 11-year-olds, and 55% of 12-year-olds posting and viewing information on social media sites (Yar 2012).

Furthermore, there have been worries among mental health experts and the authorities that social network sites provide child sex offenders with an easy way to target children for abuse. Such abuse can include opportunities in which an online user targets sexual communications at a minor, describes explicit sexual scenarios with minors, asks questions of a sexual nature of minors, and incites minors to engage in sexual behaviors like undressing or self-touching and then sending photos to the requester via social media. These communications may also serve as preparation for subsequent acts of off-line contact abuse by adults, such as "grooming" minors by gaining their trust so as to arrange for subsequent land-based meetings at which physical abuse can take place (Yar 2012).

Recent media reports have also discussed other kinds of nefarious activities taking place in social media venues. For example, in 2012, Pinterest became a notable venue. Because of its rapidly growing popularity, Pinterest had a problem at that time with fake users spamming the site to make money from its advertising potential. Picture this: As an unsuspecting consumer, you go to the Pinterest Web site, and a friendly-looking woman tells you that she loves a particular dress because the fabric is soft. Interestingly, you observe, the woman has no hands. Why is that, you wonder? Answer: Pinterest is really an e-commerce and marketing platform linking to other Web sites where the coveted items can be purchased. There is no real woman speaking to you.

Fast forward to 2015. Fake accounts created by spammers, formulated to push out content and drive links to illegitimate advertised products, increase daily on social media outlets. A tech-blog called "The Daily Dot" revealed that one Pinterest spammer in 2012 created multiple fake accounts to manipulate the algorithm tracking a post's popularity. In other words, the more consumers "repinned" an advertised item, the more popular the item appeared to be—which was important intelligence for this particular spammer. In retaliation, Pinterest took on a vigilante role, deleting some of the spammer's fake accounts (Krashinsky 2012).

In March 2015, Canadian media reports announced that police were trying to crack down on E-Crime 2.0 acts like child pornography on new media messaging services such as Kik and Snapchat. The police affirmed that these two social media sites are popular among teens, in particular, and thus a popular target for online predators. Kik Messenger launched four years ago and already has 200 million registered teens, drawn to the social media site primarily by anonymity. Kik users can sign up anonymously without requiring or sharing a functioning mobile phone number—an entry requirement of, say, messaging service provider WhatsApp. Because of this anonymity feature of Kik, a subculture of so-called bad actors is also drawn here, primarily to avoid detection or tracking by the authorities (Dingman 2015).

Earlier, in the fall of 2014, a court in Texas sentenced former schoolteacher Gregory Bogomol to 60 years behind prison bars for preying on dozens of young adults who visited social media sites—including Kik. Another New York ex-teacher was accused in 2014 of using Kik to groom at least four male teens and bribe them to send photos to him. Also in 2014, a Canadian man named Robert Alexander Kowalk was convicted, sent to prison, and placed on Canada's national sex offender registry for luring young people and transmitting to them through Kik pictures of his genitals (Dingman 2015).

Meanwhile, with all of this negative press, Kik executives insist that they are doing their best to fight the cybercriminal threat. Rod McLeod, a public relations spokesman for Kik, posited that child exploitation is an industrywide problem that has been lurking on social media Web sites like Facebook, Twitter, Reddit, and Snapchat for years. Having said this, however, he said that the company recently announced plans to use Microsoft's PhotoDNA software to prevent such abuses. Essentially this software "premoderates" images that users share inside the service and blocks attempts to share child pornography, in particular. Moreover, known offenders can be turned in to the authorities by this social media site. Kik's spokesman said that it will also join the Virtual Global Taskforce to combat these bad actors. This taskforce is a partnership involving businesses, child protection agencies, and global police services (Dingman 2015).

Snapchat, another social media industry leader among young adults, allows them to share "ephemeral" disappearing messages with others that last just 10 seconds before being deleted. Critics have charged that this application is a sort of "blessing" for child predators, and, sadly, a number of cases in recent years have found this to be the harsh reality.

For example, in 2013, 10 young males in Quebec, Canada, used the Snapchat application to share images of female minors with their smartphones. After being caught by a teacher, the males were consequently charged by the authorities with distributing child pornography. In 2014, a Canadian youth protection organization named Cybertip observed a 117% increase in reports that people were sharing child pornography via mobile applications, including Kik and Snapchat (Dingman 2015).

Though many technology companies grow so fast these days that they may not plan for illegal content exchanges, Microsoft says that as of March 2015, more than 55 organizations are using PhotoDNA technology, available for free as a cloud service to companies and the police, to hone in on the bad actors. There are, however, still exceptions to this fight-back-against-the-bad-guys rule by social media companies around the globe. Japan's Line, for example, a social media competitor to Kik and Facebook, has more than 500 million registered users. However, this messenger app does not apply any such filters to content being exchanged, so vulnerable minors remain at the mercy of online predators electing to capitalize on this reality (Dingman 2015).

CONCLUSION

This chapter focused on the amazing rise of social media Web sites in recent years. We heard about the lure of these Web sites to consumers and businesses alike, because of all of the positives that social media Web sites bring to the Web 2.0 environment. The chapter opened with an overview of the most popular social media Web sites and then described the 2014 Pew Research Center's trend report on American adult social media usage patterns.

Then the chapter looked more closely at some of the health and safety issues concerning scholars and the authorities regarding social media Web sites—including user addiction, bullying and sexting, spamming, and online predation. The chapter closed with a discussion of why a kind of "love relationship" exists between social media Web sites, small businesses wanting to expand, and cyber-criminals wanting to capitalize on their prey.

Because of the many benefits accorded by social media Web sites—and despite the challenges that success breeds—this chapter closed on the optimistic news that these communication channels will, no doubt, continue to innovate and flourish. In this hugely revenue-generating social media space, successful companies like Facebook are constantly on the lookout for application innovations that they can bring to market.

For example, in March 2015, Twitter paid almost $100 million for Periscope, a live-video streaming application that is in beta-testing. During this same time period, Facebook's Mr. Zuckerberg said that his company drove 3.5 billion application installations in 2014 alone, and has shared more than $8.5 billion in revenue with innovative mobile phone application makers in recent years. We can expect to hear more in the coming years about social media companies' willingness to innovate and thus reap the harvests of this much-needed innovation (Shufelt and Dingman 2015).

REFERENCES

Albury, K., & Crawford, K. (2012). Sexting, consent and young people's ethics: Beyond Megan's story. *Continuum*, *26*, 463–473.

Andreassen, C. S., Torsheim, T., Brunborg, G. S., & Pallesen, S. (2012). Development of a Facebook addiction scale. *Psychological Reports*, *110*, 501–517.

Beck, A. T., Wright, F. D., Newman, C. F., & Liese, B. S. (1993). *Cognitive therapy of substance abuse*. New York, NY: Guilford.

Bélanger, C. H., Balib, S., & Longdenc, B. (2014). How Canadian universities use social media to brand themselves. *Tertiary Education and Management*, *20*, 14–29.

Bennett, S. (2014). Facebook, Twitter, Instagram, Pinterest, Vine, Snapchat—Social Media Stats 2014 [INFOGRAPHIC]. Retrieved from http://www.adweek.com/socialtimes/social-media-statistics-2014/499230

Culver, D. (2014). "Sexting" teen given one year probation; no declaration of guilt or innocence. Retrieved from http://www.nbcwashington.com/news/local/Trial-for-Teen-Accused-of-Sexting-Begins-Friday-269521611.html

Dingman, S. (2015, March 17). For fast-growing chat apps, a pervasive threat. *The Globe and Mail*, pp. B1, B6.

Duggan, M., Ellison, N. B., Lampe, C., Lenhart, A., & Madden, M. (2015). Social media update 2014: Pew Research Center. Retrieved from http://www.pewinternet.org/2015/01/09/social-media-update-2014/NUMBERS,FACTSANDTRENDS SHAPINGTHEWORLD

Fox, J., & Moreland, J. J. (2015). The dark side of social networking sites: An exploration of the relational and psychological stressors associated with Facebook use and affordances. *Computers in Human Behavior*, *45*, 168–176.

Frans, E., & Bruycker, A. D. (2012). *Raamwerk seksualiteit en beleid. Kwaliteit, preventie enreactive in jouw organisatie* [Framework sexuality and policy: Quality, prevention and reaction in your organization]. Brussels: Sensoa and Child Focus.

Greenfield, D. (1999). *Virtual addiction: Help for netheads, cyberfreaks, and those who love them.* Oakland, CA: New Harbinger.

Hanchett, J. (2015). Confessions of a social media addict. Retrieved from http://www.parenting.com/blogs/true-mom-confessions/janelle-hanchett/social-media

Haynes, A. M. (2012). The age of consent: When is sexting no longer "speech integral to criminal conduct"? *Cornell Law Review*, *97*, 369–404.

Hellman, M., Schoenmakers, T. M., Nordstrom, B. R., & Van Holst, R. J. (2013). Is there such a thing as online video game addiction? A cross-disciplinary review. *Addiction Research & Theory*, *21*, 102–112.

Hormes, J. M., Kearnes, B., & Timbko, C. A. (2014). Craving Facebook? Behavioral addiction to online social networking and its association with emotion regulation deficits. *Addiction*, *109*, 2079–2088.

Hucker, S. J. (2004). Disorders of impulse control. In W. O'Donohue & E. Levensky (Eds.), *Forensic psychology*. New York, NY: Academic Press.

Kaplan, A. M., & Haenlein, M. (2010). Users of the world, unite! The challenges and opportunities of social media. *Business Horizons*, *53* 59–68.

Ko, C.-H., Yen, J.-Y., Yen, C.-F., Chen, C.-S., & Chen, C.-C. (2012). The association between Internet addiction and psychiatric disorder: A review of the literature. *European Psychiatry*, *27*, 1–8.

Krashinsky, S. (2012, March 29). Neworking site Pinterest in battle against spammers. *The Globe and Mail*, p. B6.

Krashinsky, S. (2015, March 27). Samsung lets your avatar do the waiting. *The Globe and Mail*, p. B5.

Ku, Y. C., Chu, T. H., & Tseng, C. H. (2013). Gratifications for using CMC technologies: A comparison among SNS, IM, and e-mail. *Computers in Human Behavior*, *29*, 226–234.

Lampe, J. R. (2013). A victimless sex crime: The case for decriminalizing consensual teen sexting. *University of Michigan Journal of Law*, *26*, 703–736.

Levard, O., & Soulas, D. (2010). *Facebook: Mes amis, mes amours . . . des emmerdes!* Paris: Michalon Éditions.

Lievens, E. (2014). Bullying and sexting in social networks: Protecting minors from criminal acts or empowering minors to cope with risky behaviour? *International Journal of Law, Crime and Justice*, *42*, 251–270.

Lippman, J. R., & Campbell, S. W. (2012, May 24–28). *Teenagers and sexting: Perceived norms and sexual double standard.* ICA Conference, Phoenix, AZ.

Livingstone, S., & Görzig, A. (2012). "Sexting": The exchange of sexual messages online among European youth. In S. Livingstone, L. Haddon, & A. Görzig (Eds.), *Children, risk and safety on the Internet* (pp. 151–164). Bristol: Policy Press.

Livingstone, S., Olafsson, K., O'Neill, B., & Donoso, V. (2012). Towards a better Internet for children. EU kids online. Retrieved from http://www2.lse.ac.uk/media@lse/research/EUKidsOnline/EU%20Kids%20III/Reports/EUKidsOnlinereportfortheCEOCoalition.pdf

Masur, P. K., Reinecke, L., Ziegele, M., & Quiring, O. (2014). The interplay of intrinsic need satisfaction and Facebook specific motives in explaining addictive behavior on Facebook. *Computers in Human Behavior*, *39*, 376–386.

McEwan, B. (2013). Sharing, caring, and surveilling: An actor–partner interdependence model examination of Facebook relational maintenance strategies. *Cyberpsychology, Behavior, and Social Networking*, *16*, 863–869.

Moreau, A., Laconi, S., Delfour, M., & Chabrol, H. (2015). Psychopathological profiles of adolescent and young adult problematic Facebook users. *Computers in Human Behavior*, *44*, 64–69.

Nabi, R. L., Prestin, A., & So, J. (2013). Facebook friends with (health) benefits? Exploring social network site use and perceptions of social support, stress, and well-being. *Cyberpsychology, Behavior, and Social Networking*, *16*, 721–727.

Orzack, M. (1999). (1999). Computer addiction: Is it real or is it virtual? *Harvard Mental Health Letter*, *15*, 8.

Park, N., Kee, K. F., & Valenzuela, S. (2009). Being immersed in social networking environment: Facebook groups, uses and gratifications, and social outcomes. *Cyberpsychology and Behavior*, *12*, 729–733.

Pew Research Center. (2014). 6 new facts about Facebook. Retrieved from http://www.pewresearch.org/fact-tank/2014/02/03/6-newfacts-about-facebook/

Pezoa-Jares, R. E., Espinoza-Luna, I. L., & Vasquez-Medina, J. A. (2012). Internet addiction: A review. *Journal of Addiction Research and Therapy*, *6*, 2.

Shufelt, T. (2015, March 3). Rise of the tech titans. *The Globe and Mail*, pp. B1, B6.

Shufelt, T., & Dingman, S. (2015, March 26). Facebook recruits Canadian app makers. *The Globe and Mail*, p. B3.

Stone, N. (2011). The "sexting" quagmire: Criminal justice responses to adolescents' electronic transmission of indecent images in the UK and the USA. *Youth Justice*, *11*, 266–281.

Strauss, M., & Dingman, S. (2015, March 23). Social media: Sour comments harder to find on Facebook's corporate pages. *The Globe and Mail*, pp. B1, B7.

Suissa, A. J. (2015). Cyber addictions: Toward a psychosocial perspective. *Addictive Behaviors*, *43*, 28–32.

Tuten, L. T. (2008). *Advertising 2.0: Social media marketing in a Web 2.0 world*. Westport, CT: Praeger.

Umiastowski, C. (2015, February 26). My social media strategy: Buy the giants. *The Globe and Mail*, p. B15.

Van Ouytsel, J., Walrave, M., & Van Gool, E. (2014). Sexting: Between thrill and fear—how schools can respond. *The Clearing House*, *87*, 204–212.

Walrave, M., Heirman, W, & Hallam, L. (2014). Under pressure to sext? Applying the theory of planned behaviour to adolescent sexting. *Behaviour & Information Technology*, *33*, 86–98.

Williams, J. L. (2012). Teens, sexts, & cyberspace: The constitutional implications of current sexting & cyberbullying laws. *William & Mary Bill of Rights Journal*, *20*, 1017–1050.

Yar, M. (2012). E-Crime 2.0: The criminological landscape of new social media. *Information & Communications Technology Law*, *21*, 207–219.

Young, K. (1996). Internet addiction: The emergence of a new clinical disorder. Paper presented at the 104th Annual Meeting of the American Psychological Association, Toronto.

Chapter 6

Copyright Infringement, File Sharing, and Peer-to-Peer (P2P) Networks

According to an oft-cited report by the Institute for Policy Innovation, every year, illegal downloading causes the U.S. economy to lose $58 billion in total output. Other losses include 373,375 jobs and $2.6 billion in annual tax revenue.

—Institute for Policy Innovation (2013)

OVERVIEW

The protection of intellectual property rights (IPR) from attack by online users or cybercriminals has been a major concern for many corporations for more than 15 years, because taking the creative works of someone else without paying a legitimate fee costs industry billions of dollars annually—in lost revenues and in jobs. It is for this reason that in 1998 the Digital Millennium Copyright Act (DMCA) was passed in the United States, implementing certain worldwide copyright laws to cope with emerging technologies by providing protections against the disabling of or bypassing of technical measures designed to protect copyright. At the time of its passage, the DMCA sanctions applied to anyone attempting to impair or disable an encryption device (Schell and Martin 2006).

It is important to emphasize that intellectual property law is fairly consistent in jurisdictions around the world, but the ethical lines are often blurred on what's owed to the originators of the design. Part of the reason for this blurred reality is that every category and field of created work—including music, fine art, fashion, and books—has different standards, tests, and intellectual property (IP) laws. Infringement of these IP laws, consequently, has made some lawyers quite wealthy and some infringers quite poor. For example, musician Robin Thicke was found guilty of IP law infringement and is now paying Marvin Gaye's estate more than US$7 million in damages after a court ruled that he used Gaye's groove in a hit song (Atkinson 2015).

Furthermore, according to a recent report in *The Guardian*, "The prospect of the return of *Game of Thrones* has prompted a surge in Internet piracy, with fans making more than 100,000 illegal downloads per day of episodes of the show" (Doyle 2015, L2). For readers who don't know this fine fact, *Game of Thrones* is the most pirated (defined as copying or downloading a creative work without authorization; Schell 2014) show in the world, with more than seven million episodes downloaded in just four months at the start of 2015. The countries where the illegal downloading takes place are as follows (Doyle 2015): in first place, Brazil; followed by France; followed by the United States; followed by Canada; followed by Britain. What is noteworthy is that apart from Brazil, illegal downloading is a "First World phenomenon" because of legislation put in place in these jurisdictions like the DMCA to combat piracy. But online citizens are not the only ones engaging in piracy.

According to a recent BBC report (Doyle 2015, L2), "Media piracy has even become fertile new territory for organized crime rings that previously dealt in drugs and prostitution." So, readers, according to television journalist John Doyle (2015 L2), "you with your software allowing you to watch or download some show you won't pay to see, you are part of a criminal element you should be embarrassed to be associated with."

According to Doyle (2015), three reasons are generally given as a rationale for piracy: first, it is allowed by "social justice," because cable companies charge too much to watch good shows—and if you're poor, you are doing your part to fight against the 1% of wealth by doing illegal downloading; second, piracy would be a nonissue if the best television series were more broadly available to the population, who are tired of paying for the branding of channels like HBO; and third, there is no excuse for piracy because in some jurisdictions, like Canada, the existence of broadcasters like shomi and CraveTV has illustrated that shows not previously available can be accessed online—as long as clients pay a reasonable fee.

An interesting alleged infringement of the DMCA making Canadian media headlines began in 2011 and 2012 and ended in 2015. The case began after U.S.-based Voltage (creator of the film *The Hurt Locker*) made court filings demanding that the Canadian courts order its telecommunication companies—including Bell Canada, Cogeco Cable, Videotron, and TekSavvy—to provide the personal information related to about 2,000 "John and Jane Doe" accounts suspected of allegedly illegally downloading copyright-protected movies. This request for users' personal information was one of the largest in Canadian history. In response to this request, TekSavvy and some of the other telecommunication companies took steps to ensure their users' privacy rights were protected, including providing notice to subscribers of the filings, assuring them that they would have ongoing support, and ensuring that they would have an opportunity to be represented in court (TekSavvy 2015).

On March 19, 2015, a Federal Court decision was rendered, with a narrowly read decision resting on a 2014 ruling that recognized the important consumer privacy rights issue being called into question—a ruling that at that time was created to discourage "copyright trolling" in Canada. "Copyright troll" is a derogatory term implying that a large company has built a business model by threatening to sue small-time downloaders (read: online citizens) to extort settlements from them. Companies like Voltage tend to argue that they are only trying to enforce copyright under the DMCA—which they cannot do without getting the subscribers' personal data. In the end, TekSavvy officials said that they could recover only $21,500 (less than 6%) of the costs incurred in defending its subscribers and protecting their privacy. The TekSavvy CEO posited that for online consumers concerned about their privacy, this narrow reading by the Canadian Federal Court was sending the wrong kind of signal. It basically tells copyright claimants that protecting the end users' privacy is someone else's problem, not theirs. TekSavvy officials further posited that they would notify clients of the next steps in this ruling and that the company would not disclose any client personal information until all of the conditions of the 2014 and 2015 rulings were met (TekSavvy 2015).

This chapter looks at the fascinating controversies surrounding copyright infringement, peer-to-peer networks, and file sharing in the United States and elsewhere. The chapter opens by defining these terms and then discusses recent file-sharing trends in various jurisdictions. The next focus is on legislation aimed at curbing copyright infringements and illegal file sharing through peer-to-peer networks, followed by a section on understanding the intentions behind illegal downloading. Next, the chapter looks at how the criminal arm uses peer-to-peer networks to share illegal files, including child pornography. The chapter closes with policy implications of technology for detecting peer-to-peer and copyright violations.

COPYRIGHT INFRINGEMENT, ILLEGAL FILE SHARING, AND PEER-TO-PEER NETWORKS DEFINED

Copyright Infringement Defined

Because colleges and universities perceive that a major part of their role is to inculcate ethical values in their students, it is common for segments of these educational institutions' Web sites to include definitions of copyright infringement, peer-to-peer, and illegal file sharing.

For example, the University of Tennessee Knoxville's Office of Information Technology has defined copyright infringement as "the act of violating the exclusive rights of a copyright owner." Examples cited include copying or performing a work without the copyright owner's permission or creating a work of one's own that derives from a copyrighted work (University of Tennessee Knoxville 2015).

Stanford University's Academic Computing Web site notes that copyright law protects creative original expressions—including songs, movies, television shows, Web sites, and students' papers written for class—for a certain period of time (generally the lifetime of the author, plus 70 years). Furthermore, though it has not always been the case, today copyright law applies automatically to works upon their creation; although it is not necessary to register the copyright (though there are good reasons to do so), such original expression works are afforded copyright protections. The copyright of a work gives the holder a limited monopoly on reproduction, distribution, and display of that work, so when a consumer purchases a copyrighted work, she or he gets limited use of it, but not the right to distribute it (Stanford University 2015).

So, affirms Stanford University, the consumer can listen to a purchased CD or read a purchased book, but cannot give a copy to a friend without permission from and generally payment to the copyright holder. In the Internet environment, it is within a legal reading to make a copy of a purchased CD to be able to listen to it on the iPod, say, but it is not within a legal reading to give that song to a friend without permission from the copyright owner. Also, it is not within a legal reading to share the song on a peer-to-peer (P2P) system, thus giving others access to the song without paying for it. Finally, it is not permissible to download copyrighted songs, movies, or books for one's personal enjoyment without paying for them (again, unless one has express permission from the copyright owner) (Stanford University 2015).

The Stanford University Web site goes on to explain that there are some limitations to copyright, known as "fair use," allowing individuals to use a small portion of a work in an academic setting. Through fair use application, students can legally quote a copyrighted work in papers written for class as long as they credit the source—which itself needs to be legitimate. So, in a class presentation, students can show fellow classmates an excerpt from a show or a movie on a legal DVD but not from a pirated DVD or a video file downloaded from the Internet without obtaining permission from the source. The Stanford University Web site issues this stern warning: "Copyright owners get to call the shots about whether their material is shared online, and the downloader is left to bear the responsibility for not respecting the copyright owners' decisions" (Stanford University 2015).

File Sharing and Peer-to-Peer (P2P) Networks Defined, with Consequences for Alleged Copyright Violation

According to the University of Tennessee Knoxville Web site, by definition, "file sharing" is a term for sharing digital files electronically—whether these files are music, audio recordings, movies, television shows, games, computer software, or any form of digital files. Criminal acts—involving criminal sanctions—include sharing files with others of works not created by oneself as an original, work that is not in the legitimate public domain (such as legal cases placed for the public to visit on government Web sites), or files that one does not have permission to share with others. When the University of Tennessee gets information to track an alleged copyright offender (e.g., locating the IP address and date/time of the incident), the following procedure is set in motion (University of Tennessee Knoxville 2015):

1. *First Offense*: The student is contacted by the Office of Information Technology and it is explained why the alleged behavior is illegal and in contravention of university policy. The office instructs the student to clear the illegal content from his or her computer and advises the student of future consequences if the offense is repeated.
2. *Second Offense*: The university disables the student's network connection, the student is required to take his or her computer to the Office of Information Technology to show that the protected copyrighted materials have been removed, and the student is reminded of the seriousness of future consequences, should the offense reoccur.
3. *Third Offense*: The infringing computer is disabled immediately from the university's network, the incident is reported to Student Judicial Affairs—which may impose additional sanctions—and the student will be told to take the computer to the Office of Information Technology to show that the copyrighted material has been removed.

The Stanford University Web site provides more details on how file sharing is typically completed. Besides defining "file sharing as the process of exchanging files over the Internet," it goes on to say that the most common forms include running an FTP server or using an FTP program, Internet relay chat (IRC), or peer-to-peer (P2P) programs like KaZaA, LimeWire, or BitTorrent, which commonly share files by default, allowing the maximum amount of sharing across the given network (Stanford University 2015).

What is at issue is that the bulk of P2P usage is illegal because it involves sharing copyrighted materials without permission from the copyright owner. Most complaints are from the Recording Industry Association of America (RIAA), the Motion Picture Association of America (MPAA), and firms belonging to those organizations—such as record companies and movie studios. Year after year, complaints are increasingly filed by television producers, digital book publishers, and software vendors (Stanford University 2015).

Essentially, posits the Stanford University Web site, U.S. law stipulates that students cannot have anything on their computers that they do not own, and they cannot share files that they are not legally entitled to. Copyright violations can result in significant civil penalties of up to $150,000 per violation—which is considerably more than those imposed in Canada. So, if students illegally share files with 10 other people, they could be facing statutory damages of $1.5 million. In addition to civil liabilities, there is potential criminal liability in copyright cases, with penalties depending on the number of and value of products exchanged. Furthermore, downloading (i.e., taking) and uploading (i.e., sharing) content are both risky (Stanford University 2015).

For example, in a "John Doe" action involving a Stanford University online user, the defendant argued that he had purchased most of the music, which was then shared with others on KaZaA. The defendant did not think that his actions were culpable because he had paid for the music in question. The plaintiffs in the lawsuit disagreed. Moreover, on the downloading front, another Stanford University student with multiple copyright infraction complaints raised the point that she only downloaded television shows, which she could have legally recorded on a VCR or DVR (digital video recorder) when they aired, so where was the harm? The bottom line is this: the "harm" question is not the downloaders' question to ask, because, again by law, copyright owners are in control about whether their material is shared online. Consequently, the downloader is left to bear the responsibility for not respecting the copyright owners' decisions (Stanford University 2015).

Handling DMCA Complaints

The Stanford University Web site notes that the DMCA, passed in 1998, provides limitations for liability relating to material online and, specifically, contains a section stipulating a university's responsibilities as an Internet service provider (ISP). In other words, the DMCA tells Stanford University what it can and cannot do with respect to facilitating the transfer of files. As a service provider, the university can give its users the online connections they need to transfer files, but if any illegal activity is detected, the university must guarantee that the transfers have ceased. The DMCA holds the university liable if illegal file transfers persist, but limits the university's liability if it cooperates fully with every aspect of the law (Stanford University 2015).

The Stanford University Web site emphasizes that the DMCA provides a mechanism for copyright owners or their agents to complain to Internet service providers (ISPs) about illegal file sharing. Consequently, the university is then obligated to respond to the "DMCA Complaint." In fact, copyright owners often hire companies to monitor file-sharing networks to find the IP addresses (identifiers for computers or devices on a network) of computers sharing illegal files. Once an IP address has been logged, the ISP can be tracked and notified that the computer (and presumably the computer's owner/user) is sharing an illegal file (Stanford University 2015).

P2P GROWTH TRENDS GLOBALLY—AND RAISED LEGAL CONCERNS

The Fung and Lakhani (2013) Assertions

In 2007, the Hong Kong Court of Final Appeal's decision in *Chan Nai Ming v. HKSAR* upheld that the use of the BitTorrent P2P software constituted an active, intentional step toward copying and distributing copyrighted material, thereby violating Hong Kong's copyright laws. For the first time in its history, Hong Kong convicted a private citizen for publicly sharing copyrighted material over the Internet using P2P software. This landmark case was not only a driving force behind Hong Kong's efforts to increase protections against digital content piracy, but also coincided with a growing international interest in legal issues involving the digital content market (Fung and Lakhani 2013).

P2P file sharing, as noted, is an Internet-based technology allowing computer users having the software to connect with each other to share digital media; it was originally used in its earlier form in 1999 under the name Napster. Napster consisted of a remote central server facilitating the searching of users' files and establishing a connection between online users wanting the file and those having it available for download. The most recent version of BitTorrent allows online users to create "torrent files" to establish a connection to a specific file on their computers; so, rather than having to search for digital media through this software, users can simply look for the torrent files online—which themselves can be created and distributed anywhere on the Internet. The torrent files are, in essence, a downloadable "roadmap" to the shared material. The impact of this file-sharing process is that thousands of files protected under a jurisdiction's copyright laws are being shared online without recognition of, payment to, or protection for the copyright owner under various copyright laws (Fung and Lakhani 2013).

With BitTorrent, each online user is assigned an IP address, a digital footprint of users' online activities. The IP address is, therefore, the most direct way to trace and identify anyone involved in file transfers. One critical point to raise, however, is that Internet service providers (ISPs) typically reuse and randomly assign a limited number of IP addresses to users every day, further complicating the tracing process. Furthermore, in the end, if it is possible to identify the alleged perpetrators, there is the usual hassle of getting the ISP's cooperation in identifying the users of interest, because ISPs try to maintain the trust of their clients in order to secure their business contracts (Fung and Lakhani 2013).

Today, P2P file sharing (often using BitTorrent) constitutes a significant portion of all global Internet traffic. A 2010 study by the networking company Sandvine found that on fixed networks, P2P file sharing accounted for 11.0% of all Internet traffic in Europe, 19.2% of all Internet traffic in North America, 25.7% of all network traffic in the Asia-Pacific region, and 36.7% of all network traffic in Latin America. While estimates of trends in this traffic change from study to study, the Sandvine report indicated that from 2009 to 2010, the percentage of P2P file-sharing traffic increased in all areas except for Europe, where Web-browsing traffic grew the fastest (Sandvine 2010).

P2P file sharing is likely to remain a significant percentage of Internet traffic in all four geographic regions cited, because P2P file-sharing applications like BitTorrent continue to evolve from new business models and because of online users' strong preferences for files that they can download and keep rather than having to access files displayed over streaming media that they cannot download. A recent 2009 study found that more than three-quarters of online users would be willing to pay for files shared legally on P2P networks (Peoples 2009), suggesting that the trend to share files online with others will continue to morph well into the future. If the segment of "legitimate" users is so willing to pay a fee for this service, how large is the criminal arm that also seeks this service for nefarious means? Whether by sharing files on P2P networks is deemed to be legal or illegal is a growing concern of legislators in these four geographic locations.

The Sung and Huang (2014) Assertions

P2P file-sharing networks originally arose after the legal shutdown of server-based Napster in 2002, following a 2001 U.S. court ruling. The rather frightening statistic shared at that time was that one-quarter of Americans, or 75 million people, were partaking in illegal copyright infringement activities by exchanging MP3 format music files through the Napster P2P platform.

As a single point of distribution, server-based networks like Napster were vulnerable to failure and detection, and to the extent they were at times used for sharing files illegally, they were rather easily identified. Using more recent decentralized catalogues and files that are transmitted directly between users, P2P networks nowadays avoid reliance on a central server—which is why P2P file sharing grew so quickly from 2005 through 2010 after Napster was brought down. In fact, even in 2005, there were 8.9 million estimated average monthly P2P users in the United States alone (Peoples 2009). The popularity of P2P file-sharing networks has continued to balloon over the past decade.

P2P multimedia transmissions as multimedia works are increasingly generating copyright disputes worldwide. The reason that P2P networks conflict with the regulations of copyright law is quite straightforward: current copyright law evaluates infringement responsibilities via a simple copyrighted works distribution and usage dichotomy classification; however, the application of P2P networks exceeds this narrowly defined classification. Simply stated, the copyright law was written during the analog era; consequently, the interpretations of infringement were designed to target individuals making copies of cassettes and compact disks. By 2005, jurisdictions around the globe began to realize that a new regulation concerning digital file transactions was required, for without it, because of the vagueness of the copyright law, more and more so-called "innocent infringers" would become snared in the pitfall called copyright protection. Industries applying P2P network operations were directly threatened by trends of copyright infringement jitters.

A major reason for the current popularity of P2P systems is that they are multimedia access, application-friendly. Besides file downloads, multicast streaming through P2P networks is hugely popular, including video distributions like Video on Demand and live streaming, as well as audio distributions—such as Voice over IP (VOIP) and music streaming. P2P networks provide a well-designed media-sharing platform, where technically speaking, the files and information are exchanged in a logical network formed by logical links and nodes.

Therefore, the three major benefits of P2P networks to multimedia processing and communications have been cited by Sung and Huang (2014) to be as follows:

1. Because P2P networks provide for real-time and redundant networks between communicating online users, the resources and contents can be easily shared and stored, unlike the more conventional server-client architecture—where the server controls all the contents and the resources, and a server breakdown often results in the loss and damage of contents.
2. Because P2P networks enable an all-time process for users relative to the more conventional server-client network, there is no need to employ a system administrator. For this reason, the ongoing operations of P2P networks are not fatally doomed by either a server failure or the failure of any peer.
3. P2P networks are in every aspect imaginable consumer-centric media, whereby each online user becomes the administrator of his or her node and is thus able to determine which resources to share and how best to regulate the operation schedule.

With regard to these three benefits, every online user in the P2P network is a "creator" as well as a potential "infringer." The network can be used to share any type of digitized media, but any user may employ these benefits to share copyrighted music and video files without proper authorization. To this point, the distribution of any unauthorized copyrighted multimedia file would result in P2P users in the network committing so-called "collective infringements." In short, while accepting the social benefits of P2Ps, the conveniences offered by this communications technology have also stirred considerable hostility from the copyright law regimes.

The inherent legal problem with P2P software as viewed from copyright holders, note this research team, is that the operations of the network destroy the copyright holders' most important mechanism for copyright enforcement: copying and distribution control—the major source of the copyright holders' profits. Another major concern is that the P2P networks permit the direct transmission of files among users; each user's computer, then, can be regarded as both a server and a client. The "many-to-many" transactions that occur on these networks include both file uploads and downloads, which designate every computer on the network with the functions of both file distributor and file receiver.

Far too often, it seems, copyright infringement and the laws guarding against it gets confused with the benefits associated with emerging technologies. As clarified by the Napster decision in 2002—after which it was shut down—copyright law sets out rules regarding direct infringement and indirect infringement (also known as secondary liabilities). However, it must be noted that P2P platforms were not invented to facilitate copyright infringement; these platforms were technological advancements made in response to bottlenecks in the computer network architecture.

LAWS PROPOSED AND PASSED FOR COMBATING COPYRIGHT INFRINGEMENT AND ILLEGAL P2P FILE SHARING

The Stop Online Piracy Act (SOPA)

In January 2012, digital rights activists, online citizens, and a number of high-profile technology companies collaborated on an Internet blackout to protest against two U.S. congressional bills: the Stop Online Piracy Act (SOPA) and the Protect IP Act (PIPA). The high-tech companies included the popular news-sharing Web site Reddit, the browser pioneer Mozilla, Google, and the photo-sharing Web site Twitpic. All expressed solidarity with the protest by putting anti-SOPA material on their home pages. Furthermore, these online protests were accompanied by on-land protests in New York City, where thousands of the city's technology industry participants demonstrated outside the offices of U.S. senators Chuck Schumer (D-NY) and Kirsten Gillibrand (D-NY) (Schell 2014).

Both of these bills had the objective of combating piracy on non-U.S. Web sites hosting content allegedly infringing on U.S. copyrights. If passed, they would have allowed the U.S. attorney general to order that ISPs had to block any Web site containing so-called infringing material. However, both bills were withdrawn after the online blackout and public outrage.

Following the failure of SOPA to pass as law, the U.S. government authorities decided to use other means to bring down groups they believed were dissident and a menace to society. For example, the micro-blogging Web site Twitter received a number of subpoenas from the U.S. government asking for information on so-called antisecrecy organizations like WikiLeaks (run by Julian Assante) and the Occupy Wall Street movement (a leaderless hacktivist movement whose Web site says that members are opposed to the greed and corruption "of the 1%" and will use tactics of the revolutionary Arab Spring to achieve their ends). However, rather than giving the U.S. government the information being subpoenaed, Twitter challenged these requests in court—and was successful (Schell 2014; Ruth and Stone 2012).

The Copyright Act of 1976 and P2P Copyright Infringement

The reason why most P2P networks are regarded as defying the regulations of copyright law is relatively simple: though current copyright law evaluates infringement responsibilities through a simple copyrighted work distribution, the application of P2Ps defies this simple classification. In addition, in 2015, copyright regulations still referred to the Copyright Act 1976, as Amended, which was passed long before the proliferation of personal computers. Prior to digitalization technology, copyrighted works were generally regarded as physical goods. For example, music venues like cassettes had to be put in players to be listened to. So, cassettes became the equivalent of copyrighted works, and a notice of copyright infringement was visibly displayed on such tangible goods. Now fast forward to 2015. The same logic or manifest warning is not applicable when one downloads intangible/digitized property. Therefore, many users on the Internet can be defined as "innocent infringers" on digitized copyrighted works (Sung and Huang 2014).

However, the most important aspect of copyright infringement is the purpose of copy and usage; that is, whether the works are used for commercial means or whether their usage can be regarded as "fair use," as earlier described. Furthermore, even though P2P users can be regarded as "innocent infringers," they might be responsible for so-called "contributory and vicarious" liability in the infringement. In the passage of the U.S. copyright law, the courts made certain unfavorable judgments regarding new technologies, based on the premise that these technologies could facilitate massive copyright infringement (Sung and Huang 2014).

The users of P2Ps include downloaders (i.e., clients), uploaders (i.e., clients/servers), and distributors (i.e., servers). Since the activities of downloaders differ from those of distributors, the legal consequences for each are different. For example, in the case of users who download and distribute, both sets of consequences would refer to "direct" and "indirect" infringement to the copyrighted works. For the P2P users, several activities could possibly involve copyright infringement following from this act, including the following four types (Sung and Huang 2014):

1. *Search and explore*: Here, users may have searched the links and the files for the desired information.
2. *Download*: Here, users may download the files through searched links.
3. *Upload*: Here, a key feature of P2Ps is that the network programs organize download and upload activities simultaneously. The exception is the group known as the "network free-riders"—those who selfishly download files without caching and sharing any files.
4. *Distribution*: Here, compared to merely sharing files, P2Ps require certain users to provide the original file in particular forms (such as torrent files).

In conclusion, a P2P network is only a protocol for information-sharing among online users. Though the tool is intrinsically innocent, it cannot prevent online users from utilizing it for illegal means. As for the difficulties of P2Ps, the current copyright law encompassing both the Copyright Act of 1976 (and its amendments) and the DMCA are offering increasingly less space for the operation of P2Ps. Furthermore, while the broader goal of the communication industry is to eliminate barriers to information sharing among online users, barriers to the freedom to do so include the rights of copyright holders regarding distribution control (their major profit source). Because of the recognized benefits to both copyright holders and the communication industry, it becomes difficult, note Sung and Huang (2014, 39) to "strike a balance between a copyright holder's legitimate demand for effective—not merely symbolic—protection of the statutory monopoly, and the rights of others freely to engage in substantially unrelated areas of commerce."

Furthermore, accepting the example of SOPA, it is clear to see that multimedia industries in the United States have both the strong political and financial power to continue to profit in the name of copyright protection. Should this power bring down P2P technology—just as it did for Napster—online users will sacrifice technological progress all in the name of so-called copyright protection (Sung and Huang 2014, 39).

THE IMPORTANCE OF BALANCING COMPETING INTERESTS OF COPYRIGHT HOLDERS AND THE RIGHTS OF OTHERS: *MGM STUDIOS, INC. V. GROKSTER*, 125 S. CT. 2764 (2005)

In 2005, an important legal case dealing with the balance of interests between the creation of emerging technology and the difficulty of asserting intellectual property rights with P2P file-sharing software was the *MGM Studios, Inc. v. Grokster* case. Here, the U.S. Supreme Court set out the rules for P2P distributors. MGM Studios confronted Grokster and StreamCast Networks, the defendants, for illegally distributing decentralized P2P software connecting online users, thereby giving them the indexing capacity to search files without going through a central server. The defendant companies were taken to court for infringing copyright by the copyright owner, MGM, who asserted that the defendants "knowingly and intentionally distributed their software to enable users to reproduce and distribute copyrighted works in violation of the Copyright Act." The statistics showed, argued the lawyer for MGM, that nearly 90% of the files shared using the software were copyrighted works—even though it was not known whether the download had been authorized or not (Cheng and Lai 2010).

The U.S. Supreme Court found that the defendants never engaged in any preventive measures to mitigate copyright infringement by their clients. The way that the Supreme Court "balanced" the interests of protecting copyrights and promoting technological innovation was to draw a definite line between "actively fostering" copyright infringement and a "nonfostering" online environment. The distinction on which side of the line the evidence fell was based on whether there was in existence "the object of promoting its use to infringe copyright, as shown by clear expression or other affirmative steps taken to foster infringement" (Cheng and Lai 2010).

Cheng and Lai (2010) maintained that, primarily because of the alleged widespread copyright infringement by online users utilizing P2P software and the real-world difficulty in tracing and investigating claims by the copyright holders to provide concrete evidence in court of copyright violation, the U.S. Supreme Court seemed willing to assign the secondary liability to the software distributor as a means of placating the copyright owner and as a means of "safe harboring" the P2P software distributor. Finally, it is worth noting that even if secondary liability (also known in legal jargon as contributory infringement liability or inducing infringement liability) could rightly be imposed on the P2P software distributor because of its promoting commercial free speech, it would be very difficult to impose the same kind of liability on a private individual because of the possibility of violating freedom of speech rights (Cheng and Lai 2010).

The basic argument used against P2P software distributors' liability is the "neutrality" of technology—meaning that simply inventing a new technology without an intention to break the law will not be impugned into liability when someone else misuses it. Therefore, the question in court proceedings moving into the future will inevitably become how to strike a balance between promoting the invention of new technologies and asserting intellectual property rights, given the prolific use of such technologies by online users—who may or may not be copyright-respectful (Cheng and Lai 2010).

UNDERSTANDING THE INTENTIONS OF ILLEGAL DOWNLOADING: A COMPARATIVE VIEW OF AMERICAN AND KOREAN COLLEGE STUDENTS: THE SANG, LEE, KIM, AND WOO (2015) STUDY

For the past decade or so, more and more people—usually young adults, particularly college and university students—have used P2P Web sites to download or distribute copyrighted material illegally. A 2013 report by Columbia University's American Assembly, a public policy institute, reported that 13% of U.S. Internet users have used P2P file-sharing sites, and among the under-age-30 group, the percentage was a much larger 20% (Karaganis and Renkema 2013). Moreover, as the quote at the start of this chapter suggests, every year, illegal downloading results in the U.S. economy's losing a projected $58 billion. Yet, it is an individual online user's attitude about the legitimacy of certain file-sharing behaviors that determines whether she or he will violate copyright legal provisions. In short, it is a person's perceived attitude about the legitimacy of certain behaviors that will determine whether she or he engages in that behavior. Having internalized the norms, rules, and core values of his or her society, the person may or may not engage in that behavior.

According to Hofstede (1984), having internalized the norms, rules, and values of a society, people from one culture are likely to share similar perceptions of their social environments. These shared perceptions—the cultural factors, so to speak—are then likely to influence people's thoughts about what behaviors are socially acceptable or not. This reality leads to the question, "Does a certain culture tend to produce a permissive attitude about illegal file downloads?"

Study Objectives

Because not much is known about the level of cultural differences on such behaviors—that is, whether people from one culture are more inclined to use unauthorized P2P file-sharing sites than those from other cultures—the study by

Sang, Lee, Kim, and Woo (2015) aimed to fill this gap by comparing American and Korean college students' attitudes and intentions regarding illegal digital downloading. This study applied the theory of planned behavior to the context of illegal downloading, with variables affecting people's intention to use unauthorized P2P Web sites, including level of morality, perception of copyright importance, and group and moral norms.

The theory of planned behavior (TPB) argues that an individual's intentional behavior is shaped, to a large degree, by his or her attitude toward the behavior, perceived level of control, and subjective norms. An attitude is generally viewed as a person's positive or negative feelings about performing a given behavior; control refers to a person's perception of the ease or difficulty of performing the given behavior; and subjective norms refers to a person's perception about how others important to him or her think about performing a given behavior. TPB is a well-established behavioral intention model that has been shown to be useful in predicting and explaining the behavioral intention of individuals—particularly with regard to P2P file-sharing sites, including digital music piracy, digital piracy of movies, the illegal downloading of online games, and software piracy. A number of studies over the last 10 years have demonstrated that the TPB variables are significant predictors of individuals partaking in digital piracy. For example, Morton and Koufteros (2008) found that respondents' attitudes toward online music piracy, subjective norms, and perceived behavioral control were significant predictors of their intention regarding illegal music downloading.

Description of the Study Survey

In the current self-report survey study by Sang, Lee, Kim, and Woo (2015), TPB components and other variables were measured using a number of items scored on a 5-point Likert scale, ranging from strongly disagree to strongly agree. These measurements were adopted from previous studies, including Wang and McClung (2011), Lee (2009), and Chang and Woo (2010). The measurements were for the following key variables: (1) intention to download digital content through unauthorized P2P file-sharing sites (e.g., "I am likely to download digital content through unauthorized peer-to-peer file-sharing sites, without special consideration of copyright"); (2) subjective norms (e.g., "Most people whose opinion I value would think it is OK if I download digital content from unauthorized peer-to-peer file sharing sites"); (3) behavioral control (e.g., "If I want, I am likely to download digital content from unauthorized peer-to-peer file-sharing sites"); and (4) attitude toward illegal downloading—such as utilitarian function-cost and availability (e.g., "Using unauthorized peer-to-peer file-sharing sites to download digital content would help me save money").

Additional variables were measured, including the following: (1) level of perception of copyright protection (e.g., "Movies should be protected by copyright"), (2) level of morality (e.g., "When things [go] wrong, I try not to blame others"), (3) value-expressive function—illegal and morally wrong (e.g., "Downloading songs/movies without paying for them should be banned by laws"), (4) utilitarian function/illegality concern (e.g., "There is a chance I would be caught if I download many songs/movies through unauthorized peer-to-peer file-sharing sites"), (5) ego-defensive function—afraid of risk (e.g., "Not downloading digital content from peer-to-peer file-sharing sites shows that you are lagging behind the online trend"), (6) ego-defensive function-overpriced (e.g., "Digital content on the Internet/through peer-to-peer file-sharing sites is meant to be freely shared"), (7) group norm (e.g., "Most of the students attending my university prefer illegal downloading than buying the digital content since it is free"), and (8) moral norm (e.g., "I personally think that downloading digital content through unauthorized peer-to-peer file-sharing sites is ethically undesirable").

The self-administered online survey was created in English and was distributed to American participants recruited by their instructors through e-mail. The survey was translated into Korean and distributed to Korean student participants, with special efforts made to provide equivalent instruments in this cross-national survey design.

Sampling Method and Sample Characteristics

The current study focused on college students, primarily because a number of previous studies have demonstrated that college-age students are the most likely to engage in online piracy compared to other age groups. The main purpose of this research was not to draw generalizations about the broader public but to develop a better understanding of college students' intentions to download digital content through P2P networks from a comparative perspective of American students and Korean students. A convenience sampling method was adopted, and respondents were asked to voluntarily participate in the study. Because of the sensitive nature of the study query, respondents' anonymity was guaranteed.

The sample consisted of 262 American undergraduate students enrolled in campuswide introductory media studies classes at a large southern university in the United States, and 270 Korean undergraduate students enrolled in campuswide communication classes at a South Korean university with two campuses in Seoul. After adjusting for some data completion issues, the adjusted sample size was 507 students (250 American respondents and 257 Korean respondents).

The average age of American respondents was 19.7 years (*SD* = 1.70), and 46.4% of the respondents were female. Regarding Internet use, the American student respondents spent an average of 219 minutes each day (*SD* = 121.73) online. A breakdown of the grade level for the American student respondents included the following: 35.2% freshmen, 36.4% sophomores, 17.2% juniors, and 11.2% seniors. In all, 8.4% of the American student participants admitted to having experience with uploading digital content to unauthorized P2P sites. Less than half of the respondents (46%) had downloaded digital content from unauthorized P2P sites within the past month.

The average age of the Korean student respondents was 21.51 years (*SD* = 2.36), and 58.8% of the respondents were female. Korean student respondents spent an average of 195.01 minutes each day (*SD* = 78.07) online. A breakdown of the grade level for the Korean student respondents included the following: 24.5% freshmen, 31.9% sophomores, 12.5% juniors, 29.2% seniors, and 1.9% were "other." In all, 20.6% of Korean respondents said that they had experience with uploading digital content to unauthorized P2P sites, and a significant 94.2% of the participants had downloaded digital content from unauthorized P2P sites within the past month.

Study Findings

Key study findings were as follows:

1. First, the study results indicated that a much higher number of Korean students get involved in illegal downloading compared to their American peers, resulting from differences in respondents' motivations and intentions. American and Korean respondents' intentions to download were positively predicted by utilitarian motivations associated with cost and availability. This finding was consistent with that reported by Wang and McClung (2011).
2. The present study also had findings different from those of Wang and McClung (2011) with regard to respondents' value-expressive motivations, as assessed by this item: "believing that illegal downloading is a violation of laws and moral standards." In the current study, value-expressive motivation not only failed to significantly predict either American or Korean student respondents' intentions, but this factor also was not a consistent predictor across the two geographic locations. It is also interesting to note that the level of morality variable showed a significant negative relationship with American student participants' intentions to download but showed no significant statistical relationship to Korean student participants' intentions. For both groups, however, the perception of copyright protection consistently produced a statistically negative relationship with intentions to engage in illegal downloading.
3. Third, Wang and McClung's (2011) study findings showed that American college students who had concerns about being regarded as "afraid of the risk of

being caught" were more likely to engage in illegal digital downloading. Consistent with their study findings, the current study results indicated that American participants' ego-defensive motivation (i.e., being afraid of risk) also predicted students' intentions to illegally download. Earlier, Wang and McClung (2011) adopted a psychological reactance thesis to explain the minimal effects of high-profile lawsuits imposing heavy fines on illegal downloaders. However, in the current study, and particularly with the Korean student sample, there was no significant statistical relationship found between ego-defensive motivation (i.e., being afraid of risk) and intention to illegally download. These mixed study findings suggest that caution should be used in adopting psychological reactance theory within the context of illegal downloading. Moreover, another ego-defensive function (i.e., "digital content is overpriced") was a significant predictor for the Korean student participants' intentions to illegally download, but not for the American students. The magnitude of the positive influence of the utilitarian function (i.e., cost and availability) as predicting intentions to illegally download within the Korean sample was much stronger statistically than it was for the American students. It is possible that Korean participants are more concerned about practical considerations regarding illegal downloading, compared to American students.

4. Fourth, group norm was not a significant factor in predicting American respondents' intentions to illegally download, whereas it was a positive predictor for the Korean student respondents to do so. In contrast, moral norm was not a significant factor in predicting Korean respondents' intentions to illegally download, but this predictor was significantly negatively related to the intentions of the American student participants. It can likely be posited that if the industry wants to discourage illegal digital downloading, then given these study findings, it should tailor its message for cultural differences. To this point, American college students seem more likely to consider moral or ethical dimensions in deciding whether to download content illegally, whereas Korean college students seem more likely to consider the amount of support from their reference group. This difference in study findings may be explained, in part, by the difference between individualistic cultures and collectivistic cultures, as suggested by Hofstede (1984). Applying Hofstede's distinction between individualism and collectivism to the current study findings, the United States can be considered to be an "individualistic society" but Korea can be considered to be a "collectivistic society." Therefore, when breaking societal rules, individuals raised in an individualist society would tend to feel guilt based on their own ethical decision, whereas individuals raised in a collectivist society would tend to feel shame based on a collective obligation.

The research team of Sang, Lee, Kim, and Woo (2015) concluded that those industry marketers who design, develop, and distribute campaign messages to discourage citizens from illegally downloading files need to consider the cultural differences of their target audiences. In the current study findings, there was some variation in the predictive variables between the two student groups, with the results showing that cultural differences may play an important role with regard to people's intentions to engage in illegal downloading. To better understand the relationships between cultural factors and factors predicting individuals' intentions to download digital content illegally, more research is needed. Perhaps an attitude functional theory and social norms approach, combined, would yield some interesting and important outcomes.

HOW THE CRIMINAL ARM USES P2P NETWORKS TO SHARE ILLEGAL FILES—AND HOW TO INVESTIGATE THESE NETWORKS: THE LIBERATORE, ERDELY, KERLE, LEVINE, AND SHIELDS (2010) STUDY

The investigation of P2P file-sharing networks is currently of critical interest to law enforcement, because they are extensively used by criminals for sharing and distributing contraband, particularly child pornography files. The use of Gnutella and BitTorrent are especially popular among cybercriminals. This section looks at some of the salient technical and legal issues inherent in forensic investigations of P2P systems, because poorly executed investigative techniques provide erroneous evidence for court. Such mistakes can not only be costly in terms of resources and the erosion of public trust, particularly in the context of criminal law, but they are often the product of insufficient understanding of the information being provided by the P2P system.

To prevent such mistakes, the U.S. research team of Liberatore, Erdely, Kerle, Levine, and Shields (2010) maintains that investigators need to understand these systems at an appropriate level to realistically and professionally relate to the technical and legal issues of investigating the systems correctly. To meet this goal, their study objective was to enable accurate online investigations of P2P, where investigators could adequately say from where and how various forms of evidence were acquired; could fully understand the importance of credible evidence gathering; and could validate that evidence from search warrants. To accomplish this goal, the researchers described and analyzed the functionality of two heavy-use P2P systems by criminals: Gnutella and BitTorrent.

Second, the study team designed RoundUp, a tool to facilitate investigations of the Gnutella P2P system. This tool, when utilized by law enforcement, allows them to perform forensically sound investigations in both a localized and a loosely coordinated fashion; the tool has been effective in generating both leads and sound evidence. Since October 2009, more than 300,000 unique installations of Gnutella have been observed sharing known child pornography files in the United States; using leads and evidence from the RoundUp tool, at least 558 search warrants have been issued and executed.

The remainder of this section will discuss a technical description of Gnutella and BitTorrent, move on to discuss the steps of a sound investigative process, cover the legal issues in P2P investigations, and close with a brief description of the RoundUp tool.

Technical Description of Gnutella and BitTorrent

When investigating a P2P system, as noted, an investigator must be aware of related legal and technical issues. P2P networks allow Internet peers to communicate and share files through a specific protocol. Furthermore, particular applications may support multiple protocols and thus multiple P2P networks. Of course, while the main objective of P2Ps is to support efficient distribution of content shared among the peers, many P2Ps also directly support content searches by peers, and some allow direct browsing of the files made available by a remote peer.

Technical Aspects of Gnutella

Gnutella is a completely decentralized protocol. Because of this feature, peers bootstrap the process of joining the network by, first, contacting a known Web site server that provides a partial list of current peers (called "a GWebCache"), or by using a list of known peers distributed with the Gnutella application. The joining host creates TCP connections to some of the peers on the list, becoming their neighbor on the network. (During a connection via TCP/IP to a host, the host produces an initial TCP sequence number, known as an ISN. This sequence number is then used in the conversation occurring between itself and the host to assist in keeping track of each data packet. This sequence number is also helpful in ensuring that the conversation continues in an adequate fashion. Both the host and the client produce and use these sequence numbers in TCP connections; Schell and Martin 2006.)

Because more peers can be "learned" from the initial neighbors, the peer topology is considered by technical experts to be unstructured and fairly random. Peers are uniquely identified by a self-assigned, randomly chosen 16-byte ID called a globally unique ID (or GUID). The GUID is consistent across changes to the computer's IP address, but it can be changed at will by the user. Users search for shared files by issuing queries to neighbors. Queries broadcast on the Gnutella network are text strings, and remote peers match the text in these strings to file names. Any peer with content matching the query's text replies with a response that is usually routed back along the path the query traveled along. Remote peers respond with their IP address and port, GUID, and information about matching files—including names, sizes, and hash values. According to the Gnutella specification, queries can also be for a specific hash value; however, this feature is deliberately not fully supported in many clients. Gnutella allows for both search support and browse support.

Technical Aspects of BitTorrent

BitTorrent, unlike Gnutella, needs ancillary support to search for files and to find peers with those files. Users start by locating a torrent file describing content they want to download. It is important to emphasize that any user may create a torrent, whereby the latter describes a set of files that can be obtained through the BitTorrent protocol, giving enough information to allow this process. Minimally, this information includes file names, sizes, SHA-1 hash values (commonly used to verify the integrity of digital media and to ensure that secure e-mail has not been altered during transmission; Schell and Martin 2006), and the URLs, or uniform resource locators, of one or more trackers. (A URL is a specially formatted sequence of characters representing a location on the Internet. The URL contains three parts: the network protocol, the host name or address, and the file location; Schell and Martin 2006.)

Some torrents contain additional optional information, such as per-file hashes. If the per-file hashes are omitted, it becomes less straightforward when investigators try to determine if content is known contraband, as the pieces will not align with complete files. To overcome this dilemma, investigators can determine the hash values of the corresponding piecewise subset of each file, but this operation must be performed *after* the torrent is observed. Torrents usually also contain an extensive comment field. Along with file names described by the torrent, this comment field is typically used by Web-based torrent aggregation and search sites (such as thepiratebay.org) to allow online users to rapidly discover torrents of interest by using a simple text search.

To find peers sharing files described by a specific torrent, a peer next queries one of the trackers listed in the torrent file. The tracker identifies whether it manages a matching torrent by its infohash—the SHA-1 hash of fixed fields within the torrent identifying the files being distributed (i.e., the file names, sizes, and piece sizes and hashes). The tracker then responds with a peer list having a recent interest in this torrent, created by keeping track of previous queries and peers. (The latter are described by their IP address and port, and sometimes by their peer ID.) Peers contact trackers from time to time to update each other's peer list and to keep trackers informed of their download progress and ongoing interest.

To download files, a peer either directly connects to a remote peer at an IP address and port provided by the tracker, or it is contacted by a remote peer. It needs to be emphasized that the BitTorrent protocol does not distinguish between inbound and outbound connections; it just assumes that the goal of all peers interested in a torrent is to upload and download as much of the file as possible to and from any interested peers. The peers exchange a list of the "pieces" that they own, and then request "pieces" from one another. Periodically, the peers may update one another when they have "new pieces" from other peers. Because bandwidth is limited, the BitTorrent protocol has a mechanism known as "tit-for-tat" to encourage peers to upload and to download.

The Investigative Process

The research team emphasized that the legal issues that they discussed in this study involved the criminal arm specifically dealing with child pornography file distribution—and not the legal issues involved in copyright infringement per se. Knowingly possessing or distributing contraband is a felony offense in most U.S. states.

An investigator's end goal is to obtain credible evidence by observing data from the Internet. Whenever an investigator collects such evidence, it is either "direct" or "hearsay." The former is when an investigator has a direct connection; that is, a TCP connection to a process on a remote computer and, consequently, she or he receives information about that specific computer. The latter is when a process on one remote machine relays information for or about another machine; for example, a peer in a P2P may claim that another peer has a specific file. Depending upon the purpose of the evidence sought, hearsay may be less useful in court than direct evidence.

In a typical criminal investigation, the investigator performs the following eight steps:

1. One or more files of interest (FOIs) are identified. The latter may be actual contraband (that is, child pornography), or it could be material indicative of a user's sexual interest in children. These files are acquired through Internet searches, P2P downloads, and from seized media. Because FOIs are uniquely identified by hash values, investigators only need to have access to these hash values to identify FOIs.
2. The P2P is used to locate a set of candidates, or IP addresses corresponding to potential possessors and distributors of FOIs. At the early stages, these investigations typically do not require a search warrant, since they are similar to a police officer's "walking the beat" to look for signs of criminal activity. So,

only information that is accessible publicly (i.e., in "plain view")—like keyword searches conforming to P2P protocols—is collected. Since the main goal of P2Ps is broad dissemination of files, investigators tend to connect to the system as "a user" to get information on other system users. The controlling case law in this area suggests that law enforcement officers need to be "legally present" (as are millions of other online users) and that evidence collected has been in "plain view." At this early stage, the investigator must understand the types of evidence being collected—both hearsay and direct. At this early stage, since the investigator is collecting leads, both kinds of evidence are valid.

3. Of these candidates, some are chosen for more intense investigation. This decision to dig deeper could be influenced by factors such as an investigator's jurisdiction, the type and quantity of files of interest that are owned by the candidate, and the known history of the candidate.
4. The investigator then tries to verify a candidate's ownership of or distribution of contraband. When practical, the investigator will rely on direct communications —like browsing and downloads—to create a credible case and to gather credible evidence for legal processes, including charging candidates and obtaining search warrants. Hearsay evidence should be used as a last resort at this middle stage, and if it is used, it should include evidence over a period of time and from various sources. Ideally, the investigator connects directly with the candidate and notes the files that the candidate freely claims to own. Sometimes, the investigator may download the entire file from just the candidate in question and not from other peers; the latter is called "a single-source download." Single-source downloads are commonly seen by the courts to be sound evidence.
5. As part of steps 3 and 4, each candidate's IP address and other P2P identifying information is logged. Because most P2Ps assign a unique identifier to each installation, while these GUIDs exist to aid routing in the P2P network, they are generally seen in court as providing strong evidence. Any other potential corroborating evidence (like application-version information) is also collected at this time.
6. On the basis of this evidence, a subpoena to the Internet service provider affiliated with the candidate's IP address is obtained to ascertain the person responsible and to get a land-based location associated with the observed behavior. The exact evidence the subpoena yields will vary, in large part, based on the ISP's record-keeping policies.
7. On the basis of the evidence of contraband and the subpoenaed information, a search warrant is issued in search of the computer and the contraband associated with the investigation. IP addresses corresponding to mobile devices may introduce additional difficulties in determining the physical location of the device and the materials sought.

8. At this late stage, an investigator typically has a warrant for a location, but the computers and individuals involved in the alleged crime are typically unknown. A search is then conducted, and if relevant evidence is obtained, it may be used as the basis for an arrest and further legal action, provided it can be linked to a particular individual. Investigators will locate the computers used by verifying the link between observed P2P behavior and the discovered evidence. Usually this process includes examining the media for known contraband and correlating GUIDs of P2P clients installed on local machines with GUIDs observed during the P2P investigation. Once the computer and the account are identified, a concrete link to the responsible person can be ascertained.

Legal Constraints and Issues

The following six legal constraints and issues will now be discussed, for it is important to emphasize that at each step of the aforementioned eight steps in an investigation, the investigator's behavior is bound by law. Investigators who gather evidence illegally will likely find that their evidence is inadmissible in court under the so-called "fruit of the poisonous tree doctrine." Some U.S. states do have a "good faith" exception. As a result of this reality, the investigator must be aware of the specifics of the protocol used by the P2P under investigation and must understand how his or her tools interact with the system. The following six legal constraints and issues have been identified:

1. *Searches*: The Fourth Amendment to the U.S. Constitution has severe warnings about illegal searches of citizens, since it is their right to be secure in their persons, houses, papers, and effects. Law enforcement personnel are strictly bound by this principle, and therefore are cautious about when to get a search warrant. P2P investigations are enabled by the so-called "promiscuous nature" of the protocols themselves. By freely advertising content, by responding to search queries, and by handling download requests, P2Ps are, in essence, acting "in public" rather than under the protection of the Fourth Amendment. Thus, no warrant is required for issuing keyword queries or download requests to a peer under these circumstances.
2. *Encryption*: P2Ps may support end-to-end encryption between peers. It is important to note that this feature was not intentionally developed to deter investigations but was put in place to prevent ISPs from "throttling" P2P traffic. It is also important to note that an investigator running his or her own P2P client will not be adversely impacted by this encryption, for it presents an obstacle only to a third-party packet sniffer (e.g., one operated by the ISP). If encryption is used within the protocol, the "key" is negotiated between the investigator and

the peer being investigated, precluding any requirement for a search warrant. In current P2P implementations, an anonymous Diffie-Hellman key exchange takes place, meaning that the keys are generated as needed and used just one time. (The latter algorithm upon which a number of secure connectivity protocols on the Internet are built was developed in 1976 by Whitfield Diffie and Martin Hellman; Schell and Martin 2006.) Thus, no public-key infrastructure is leveraged.

3. *Technology*: In a U.S. Supreme Court ruling in *Kyllo v. United States,* 533 U.S. 27 (2001), direction was given regarding the use of technology in conducting surveillance or searches. In general terms, the outcome of this case was that the U.S. government is not permitted to conduct searches using devices not in general public use to explore details of the home that would previously have been unknown without physical intrusion. Investigators tend to view this ruling as saying that tool builders must stay within the bounds of a protocol's specification; thus, investigators can use only evidence provided by the protocol when conducting investigations.
4. *Uploads and Downloads*: Though by law distributing contraband is illegal, it is important to emphasize that most P2P applications default to allowing uploads. BitTorrent applications may even punish nonuploaders by limiting their download bandwidth, and attempts to circumvent these punishments by uploading junk data are detected by hash trees. Accepting this reality, investigators cannot let their tools perform uploads of contraband. P2P systems attempt to perform downloads from many peers simultaneously; consequently, when an investigator is trying a single-source download, multipeer downloads must be disabled.
5. *Record Keeping*: Investigators must keep careful track of all relevant evidence recovered during the investigation. It is important to underscore that the provenance of evidence is critical when obtaining subpoenas and warrants, as well as when entering evidence into a criminal proceeding. Times and dates, methods, search terms, hash values, IP addresses, and GUIDs are among the important data typically required. Good tools will record all of these information items, and, again, the investigator needs to make the distinction between direct and hearsay evidence at every step of the way.
6. *Validation*: When a search warrant is executed, the investigator should link his or her observations through the P2P to evidence obtained under the warrant, meaning that the investigator should conduct an on-site triage-style investigation of seized machines and media, or complete a more comprehensive forensic investigation in a lab. The goal, in the end, is to find evidence of earlier observed P2P identifiers like GUIDs and contraband. It is important to emphasize that the range of evidence that can be legally searched for is very dependent on

> the language found in the search warrant. To this point, search warrants are usually written to search the premises for any collection of child pornography (thus, searching all digital media found on the premises) or for evidence that the alleged perpetrator intended to possess or distribute contraband. The latter evidence often includes, but is not limited to, stored keyword searches, carefully organized and sorted child pornography collections, and backups of contraband to fixed media. In other words, there does not have to be a strict link, but the evidence gathered from the online investigation can serve as "probable cause" justifying a search warrant. If a different GUID and different contraband are found when the search warrant is executed, the owner of the content would likely be charged with a criminal offense.

All of the evidence collected is circumstantial, because the investigator is inferring that a computer (and ultimately, the person) behind an IP address is responsible for possessing or distributing contraband. The first step in resolving an IP address into a land-based person is to determine the location of the machine responsible for traffic on that IP address. With enough direct evidence, the investigator can get a subpoena from a magistrate asking that an ISP return account information for that given IP address at a given time.

ISPs in the United States generally assign IP addresses and usually keep logs of these assignments for about six months. Relevant U.S. federal law, such as the Communications Assistance for Law Enforcement Act (CALEA), does not, however, mandate the retention of these records. If this street address is within the investigator's jurisdiction, he or she may get a search warrant from a magistrate, again on the basis of directly observed evidence. This search warrant specifies an address and targets, but typically the targets are broadly defined as "any electronic devices or media capable of storing or transmitting digital contraband, or evidence of intent." Protocols vary by locale, but investigators will typically perform an onsite investigation of any computers on the site—with the primary goal of corroborating evidence observed through network connections with data on the computer in question.

In the case of Gnutella, for example, the investigator's finding a matching GUID is considered extremely strong evidence that ties the computer in question to network traffic.

The RoundUp Tool

The RoundUp tool was developed, as noted, for forensically valid investigations of the Gnutella network. RoundUp is a Java-based tool allowing for both local and collaborative investigations of the Gnutella network and for implementing the important principles and techniques just described. This investigative tool was developed through a close collaboration between law enforcement and computer science experts. The research team believes the success of RoundUp, to date, suggests the way toward the future for similar scientifically based investigative tools for Internet crime detection and sound evidence collection. Readers wanting a fuller technical description of the tool are advised to obtain the full study details (Liberatore et al. 2010).

POLICY IMPLICATIONS OF TECHNOLOGY FOR DETECTING P2P AND COPYRIGHT VIOLATIONS: THE PEHA AND MATEUS (2014) STUDY

The effectiveness of many proposed policies regarding both online copyright protection and "network neutrality" depends on the degree to which it is technically possible to detect P2Ps, the transfer of copyrighted files, or both. "Net neutrality," by definition, refers to a so-called level playing ground where Internet service providers (ISPs) allow access to all content without favoring any particular Web site (Schell 2014).

There is little question that P2P traffic has consisted of almost one-third of the world's Internet traffic for the last few years (Cisco 2012). When demand on limited network resources from all network traffic (including P2P) becomes excessive, the quality of service (QOS) is degraded for some or all Internet traffic. This degradation has led some ISPs and enterprise networks to use a variety of technical means to identify P2P traffic and to reduce its consumption of network resources, thereby improving QOS for applications other than P2P. One high-impact example occurred several years ago when a U.S. ISP began identifying and terminating P2P transfers (Peha and Mateus 2014). This case led the U.S. Federal Communications Commission (FCC) to hold "network neutrality" hearings and, in the end, to produce the "Open Internet"—prohibiting some forms of discrimination based on application (e.g., P2P) or content.

The other reason that P2P is so controversial is that a huge amount of the content transferred in P2P networks globally and in some local environments—like university networks—consists of copyrighted material being distributed through the Internet without the authorization of copyright holders. Globally, far more copies of copyrighted music and movies are illegally transmitted through P2Ps than are legally distributed through the fee-based, legitimate sale of media devices like CDs and DVDs or through legal download sites like iTunes (Peha and Mateus 2014). What is more, accurately calculating the economic impact of these illegal P2P transfers is notoriously difficult and estimates differ greatly, but as the quote at the start of this chapter suggests, the costs are in the billions of dollars per year—and growing.

There are many rather complex network detection approaches used to ascertain illegal downloading and piracy, some of these conducted by specially trained network operators and some of these conducted by application-layer agents. The 2014 paper by Peha and Mateus describes the technical capabilities, the technical limitations, key privacy issues causing concern, and policy implications of detection technologies and their countermeasures. However, a considerable portion of this excellent paper is outside the scope of this book and this chapter because of the technical expertise required to have a full understanding of the remedies being suggested. Therefore, we will now focus on some of the broader and relevant notions that were discussed.

Different approaches for detecting and combating piracy are better for different purposes. For example, network operators are well positioned to estimate how widespread copyright violations are, but application-layer detection from outside entities has important advantages when the purpose for detection is punishment of the guilty parties. Furthermore, because detection is imperfect, policies put in place should require transparency regarding how it is done. Sadly, this transparency is sorely lacking in today's Internet-connected world. Although network operators may not detect every illegal transfer, and they typically miss more video than audio illegal transfers, they can identify most individuals sharing copyrighted files through P2P after several weeks of monitoring network traffic—as long as it is unencrypted (Peha and Mateus 2014) . (Encryption, by definition, is the mathematical conversion of information into a form using algorithms from which the original information cannot be restored without using a special "key"; Schell and Martin 2006).

However, if encryption is already in use, it effectively prevents network operators from detecting transfers of copyrighted content; so if network operators are held responsible for monitoring illegal file sharing, there is an obvious tension between using detection to identify violators of copyright law for punishment—which is likely to result in even greater use of encryption—and using detection for other purposes, such as creating fair revenue-generating schemes for works' copyright-holders. Copyright-holders typically warn users that they may be violating copyright law if they try to "break" or "crack" encryption put in place.

Alternatively, posit Peha and Mateus (2014), there are forms of detection that are not evaded through encryption; consequently, application-layer agents rather than network operators are primarily responsible for these. These copyright policy issues are often tied into network neutrality policy in very subtle ways. Simply stated, network neutrality rules do not protect illegal transfers of copyrighted content, but if network operators are responsible for enforcement, then regulators must ascertain when it is reasonable to terminate or degrade service based on allegations of copyright violation, given the limitations of detection technology to "prove" those allegations 100% of the time. Without question and consistent with the previous chapter discussion, allegations of copyright violation should be considered invalid unless they are accompanied with information about how the detection was performed—along with a chance for rebuttal. Unfortunately, such transparency has been routinely lacking in both laws and industry agreements.

Because of the complexity of many of the topics in this chapter, readers are referred to the Interview with an Expert, Dr. Michael Bachmann, who serves as USAID consultant to help combat the rampant crime of extortion in developing countries.

INTERVIEW WITH AN EXPERT

Dr. Michael Bachmann, Editor-in-Chief of *Journal of Technology and Crime*

Dr. Michael Bachmann is an associate professor of criminal justice at Texas Christian University and the editor-in-chief of the *Journal of Technology and Crime*. His research spans all facets of the intersection of high technology and the law, ranging from computer hacker subcultures and ethics to the facilitation of crime investigations through geospatial mapping applications. In short, his research generally focuses on the social dimensions behind technology-driven crimes. Specifically, Dr. Bachmann's research covers the facets of high-tech and the law, including Internet piracy, fraud, espionage, malicious code releases, and the use of Internet technology by human trafficking and terrorist organizations. He is the author of several book chapters and articles on cybercrimes.

Aside from working on several federally funded research projects with a volume of currently over $3 million, Dr. Bachmann serves as USAID consultant to help combat the rampant crime of extortion in developing countries by advising on issues pertaining to cybercrimes and cyber-investigations, cyber-forensics, and electronic search and seizure procedures, as well as cell phone interception, surveillance, and tracking techniques. He also trains investigators in developing and crime-ridden countries in digital forensics and electronic investigations.

Dr. Bachmann supports efforts by the Cook Children's Health Foundation's Center for Prevention of Child Maltreatment as a consultant for geospatial and statistical analyses. An expert witness for the courts, Dr. Bachmann provides written reports, oral depositions, and testimony on questions of foreseeable crime, reasonable standards of care, and adequate security in liability cases.

Q The countries where the illegal downloading of copyrighted works occurs most frequently are Brazil, France, the United States, Canada, and Britain. Could you comment on why, apart from Brazil, illegal downloading is a "First World phenomenon," despite laws such as the Digital Millennium Copyright Act (DMCA) passed to combat piracy?

A Quantifying any illicit activity online, especially on a global scale, is an extremely difficult undertaking, and the resulting estimates are often so far apart that they seem to tell the public more about the interests and motives of the collecting organization than to contribute concretely to solutions related to the actual underlying problem. This phenomenon of lack of useful information for crime prevention is especially true for estimates of illegal downloading activity. In fact, the evidence has shown that the numbers vary greatly between film, music, and software industries. Too, the estimates vary when one adds to the mix torrents, live streams, or cyberlockers.

The software industry, for instance, estimates that software piracy rates are the highest at over 90% in many emerging countries such as Armenia, Bangladesh, Moldova, and Zimbabwe, and that the biggest annual loss due to piracy is incurred in the Asia-Pacific region. I guess the film and music piracy phenomenon you are describing has both a technological and a cultural component to it. The reasonably fast streaming or torrenting of often large movie files requires a high-speed broadband connection most commonly found in Western countries, and the music and movies protected under the DMCA are produced primarily in English and with Western consumers in mind, so there might be a culture-centric interest component to it, too.

Q An interesting alleged infringement of the DMCA making Canadian media headlines began after U.S.-based Voltage (creator of the film *The Hurt Locker*) made filings in 2011 and 2012 in Canadian courts to order telecom companies like Bell Canada, Cogeco Cable, Videotron, and TekSavvy to provide the personal information on about 2,000 "John and Jane Doe" accounts for allegedly downloading copyright-protected movies. In your view, what key strategies should these telecom companies follow to comply more effectively with copyright laws? Furthermore, what do you think will be the likely outcome of this court case should it come to termination, and what impact will it likely have for Internet service providers (ISPs), in general?

A What concerns me most about this particular legal case is the expansion of warrantless personal information disclosure that might become more commonplace globally, as well as the implications of such practices for consumers. Legislative acts such as the pertinent digital privacy act have to strike a balance between assisting investigations into criminal activities and protecting consumer rights online. In cases where connection records are solicited by non–law enforcement agencies, ISPs should not have to carry the cost burden for inquiries, and they should, at a minimum, have to notify consumers of the accusations and the actions sought against them. Looking at this legal case in a broader context, I think that it is merely one of many instances where ISPs have been bullied by "copyright trolls" to be complicit in their attempt to scare masses of Internet users into costly settlements. Unfortunately for Canadian consumers, Voltage's success in this case will render them a more attractive target for other copyright enforcement companies. Such practices are, in my opinion, a questionable, dangerous, and obsolete tactic for the movie industry to pursue, because they have repeatedly been shown to fail to deter crime. Yet, for the most part, these practices criminalize and alienate consumers.

Furthermore, I believe that the problem is at least partially self-created by an industry that insists on antiquated "movie theater first" release tactics instead of adopting more contemporary simultaneous release cycles that would render new releases immediately available via theater, disc, and streaming. Such a switch to more open distribution would be a much more lucrative and effective strategy to curb illegal movie downloads than pursuing remedies through the courts.

Q Colleges and universities nowadays post illegal file-sharing policies on their Web sites for undergraduates, in particular, as a means of deterring such behavior. On the whole, do you think that these policies have been effective in meeting their goals? Why or why not?

A It's not so much the posting of policies that is effective, but the active monitoring and sometimes even throttling or blocking of typical torrent ports and protocols that is practiced on most campuses where deterrent strategies have been deemed to be effective. For the universities involved in such proactive measures, the benefits are manifold. Through the monitoring and revocation of access for repeat offenders, these measures significantly decrease the total traffic volume generated on campus, lower their connection costs, and increase their bandwidth for faster speeds of other important traffic. By exercising proactive due diligence, universities further put themselves in a favorable position in case of any potential future litigation. For the students, such proactive policies are a mixed blessing. On the one hand, they ensure reasonably fast connection speeds for everybody, and on the other hand, they might prohibit access to perfectly legal downloads such as, for instance, several Linux distributions that are distributed via torrent networks to save costs.

Q Today, peer-to-peer (P2P) file sharing (often using BitTorrent and Gnutella) constitutes a significant portion of all global Internet traffic. Particularly in Europe, North America, Asia-Pacific, and Latin America, concerns have been raised about this phenomenon. Can you comment on the main concerns in these jurisdictions and if these concerns are justified?

A Internet traffic, as a whole, seems to be following an exponential growth curve and is expected to continue to do so well beyond the year 2020. Consider, for example, that the total traffic online in the year 2011 was about 1 zettabyte (1 billion terabytes) and that, according to some estimates, about 20 broadband-connected households consumed more traffic during that year than that circulated on the entire Internet in 2008. According to Sandvine Research, the torrent share of all Internet traffic has sharply declined from 31% in 2008 to merely 6% in 2014. Netflix alone seems to consume, by far, the most online traffic and has done so since 2011. Furthermore, YouTube and even iTunes now generate more traffic than torrents. This sharp decrease is not solely a comparative phenomenon, but could, at least in the United States, also be at least partially attributable to Comcast's admitted throttling of torrent traffic. In any case, I think that the generated traffic volume is a favorite argument of antipiracy advocates, but overall a much smaller concern today than it was in recent years, according to the evidence that I just cited.

Q The investigation of P2P file-sharing networks is currently of critical interest to law enforcement, because they seem to be extensively used by criminals for sharing and distributing contraband, and child pornography files in particular. Since this is a major area of research for you, can you please summarize some of your findings in this regard?

A Thankfully, the mechanisms to detect child pornography have become much more effective in recent years. Many tech, hosting, and cloud services already employ comprehensive databases of hashes of known child porn pictures, movies, or archives to automatically flag any such material and notify the appropriate law enforcement agencies. Even though law enforcement still finds a wide range of obscene to illegal pornography being shared via torrent networks, the fact that such networks provide only very limited options to masquerade real IP addresses has rendered them increasingly risky and unattractive for the exchange of highly illegal materials. TOR, I2P, and other anonymizing networks provide much higher levels of anonymity, especially for distributors. Moreover, they offer the ability to charge consumers anonymously in bitcoins or other cryptocurrencies; thus, because of these features, they are rapidly becoming the first choice not just for illegal black market sites but also for distributors of child pornography.

CONCLUSION

Illegal downloading causes economies worldwide billions of dollars each year. This chapter opened with a discussion of the U.S. Digital Millennium Copyright Act (DMCA) and then detailed some of the interesting legal cases arising from alleged violations of copyright protections afforded creative works. One such legal case was recently launched by U.S.-based Voltage against Canadian telecommunication companies. Voltage requested the personal user information from these telecoms related to about 2,000 "John and Jane Doe" alleged infringers who downloaded copyright-protected movies. Inevitably, we noted, because of a combination of wealth and power, the large companies—often the multimedia ones—win their copyright violation cases in the courts.

We looked at how some universities set copyright usage policies not only to educate undergraduate students about copyright law but to encourage them to respect copyright mandates as they continue into adulthood. We then looked more closely at the motivations of college and university students for illegally downloading or transmitting copy-protected files—a segment of the population where violations of copyright law has been more widespread than in other segments. We noted, too, that culture plays an important role in such motivations.

We then discussed the challenges of law enforcement in nabbing cybercriminals who share contraband and child pornography files through P2P networks—and the importance of collecting credible evidence in order to effectively prove the case in criminal court. The chapter closed with policy implications of technology for detecting P2P and copyright violations—a complex and technically sophisticated topic area. While, we noted, calculating the economic impact of illegal P2P transfers is notoriously difficult and such estimates differ greatly, as the quote at the start of the chapter suggests, the costs are in the billions of dollars per year—and growing. Why? Because of the ease with which online users can seamlessly upload and download files and share them with online peers having common interests.

REFERENCES

Atkinson, N. (2015, April 2). Spot the difference. *The Globe and Mail*, pp. L1, L4.

Chang, M., & Woo, H. (2010). A comparative study between Korean and Chinese college students on behavioral intention of the illegal contents download. *Korean Journal of Journalism Communication Studies, 54,* 54–76.

Cheng, F.-C., & Lai, W.-H. (2010). An overview of VOIP and P2P copyright and lawful interception issues in the US and Taiwan. *Digital Investigation, 7,* 81–89.

Cisco. (2012). Cisco visual networking index: Forecast and methodology, 2011–2016. Retrieved from http:/www.cisco.com/en/US/solutions/collateral/ns341/ns525/ns537/ns705/ns827/white_paper_c11-481360.pdf

Doyle, J. (2015, April 14). You want *Game of Thrones*? Pay for it. *The Globe and Mail*, p. L2.

Fung, W. M. J., & Lakhani, A. (2013). Combatting peer-to-peer file sharing of copyrighted material via anti-piracy laws: Issues, trends, and solutions. *Computer Law and Security Review, 29*, 382–402.

Hofstede, G. (1984). *Culture's consequences: International differences in work-related values.* Newbury Park, CA: Sage.

Institute for Policy Innovation. (2013). IPI policy report no. 189: The true cost of copyright industry piracy to the U.S. economy. Retrieved from http://www.ipi.org

Karaganis, J., & Renkema, L. (2013). Copy culture in the US and Germany. Retrieved from http://piracy.americanassembly.org/wp-content/uploads/2013/01/Copy-Culture.pdf

Lee, H. (2009). The effect of cyber-harmfulness upon juvenile cyber delinquency: An analysis through structural equation model (SEM). *Journal of Cybercommunications Academic Sociology, 26,* 163–198.

Liberatore, M., Erdely, R., Kerle, T., Levine, B. N., & Shields, C. (2010). Forensic investigation of peer-to-peer file sharing networks. *Digital Investigation, 7,* S95–S103.

Morton, N., & Koufteros, X. (2008). Intention to commit online music piracy and its antecedents: An empirical investigation. *Structural Equation Model: A Multidisciplinary Journal, 15,* 491–512.

Peha, J. M., & Mateus, A. M. (2014). Policy implications of technology for detecting P2P and copyright violations. *Telecommunication Policy*, *38,* 66–85.

Peoples, G. (2009). Study: 86% would pay for legal P2P. Retrieved from http://www.billboard.biz/bbbiz/content_display/industry/e3i4fc650632bff09ac1c703fa11ae848c8

Ruth, S., & Stone, S. (2012). A legislator's dilemma. *IEEE Internet Computing*, *16,* 78–81.

Sandvine Inc. (2010). Global broadband phenomena 2010. Sandvine intelligent broadband networks report. Retrieved from http://www.sandvine.com/downloads/documents/2010%20Global%20Internet%20Phenomena%20Report.pdf

Sang, Y., Lee, J.-K., Kim, Y., & Woo, H.-J. (2015). Understanding the intentions behind illegal downloading: A comparative study. *Telematics and Informatics*, *32,* 333–343.

Schell, B. H. (2014). *Contemporary world issues: Internet censorship*. Santa Barbara, CA: ABC-CLIO.

Schell, B. H., & Martin, C. (2006). *Webster's new world hacker dictionary*. Indianapolis, IN: Wiley.

Stanford University. (2015). File-sharing and copyright law: How it affects you. Retrieved from https://acomp.stanford.edu/info/dmca

Sung, C., & Huang, P.-H. (2014). Copyright infringement and users of P2P networks in multimedia applications: The case of the U.S. copyright regime. *Peer-to-Peer Network Applications*, *7,* 31–40.

TekSavvy. (2015). TekSavvy disappointed by narrow Federal Court copyright decision. Retrieved from http://teksavvy.com/en/why-teksavvy/in-the-news/press-releases/2015-press-releases/March-19th-2015-TekSavvy-disappointed-by-narrow-Federal-Court-copyright-decision

University of Tennessee Knoxville. (2015). Copyright infringement, peer-to-peer, and file sharing. Retrieved from https://oit.utk.edu/policies/copyright/Pages/default.aspx

Wang, X., & McClung, S. R. (2011). Toward a detailed understanding of illegal digital downloading intentions: An extended theory of planned behavior approach. *New Media Sociology*, *13,* 663–677.

Chapter 7

Obscene and Offensive Content and Online Censorship

Badawi, 31, was sentenced last May [2014] to 10 years' imprisonment and 1,000 lashes—50 at a time over 20 weeks—and fined 1m Saudi riyals (£175,000). He has been held since mid-2012, and his Free Saudi Liberals website, established to encourage debate on religious and political matters in Saudi Arabia, is closed. He received his first 50 lashes on 9 January [2015], but the punishment was not carried out a week later.

—Ian Black (2015b)

OVERVIEW

The quote above speaks clearly to the notion of what can happen in some countries when an online user says something using Internet access that the government, a strong religious or political element, or the courts deem to contain "obscene" and "offensive" content. In some countries, an online perpetrator may have his or her online content censored by filters that have been put in place. Or the Web site where such information exists might be closed. Or, as was the case with Raif Badawi, the online user may be jailed for committing some alleged heinous "cybercrime" in that jurisdiction.

So what was it that Raif Badawi did that caused him to be sentenced to 10 years in prison, fined the equivalent of about $319,000 in Canadian currency, and receive 1,000 lashes—50 lashes by cane every Friday for 20 weeks, if his health allowed it (Galloway 2015a)?

Raif Badawi's crime was, in part, that he created a Web site that championed free speech in the autocratic kingdom of Saudi Arabia. His blog, known as "the Saudi Free Liberals Forum," was shut down after his arrest in 2012. His crime was also, in part, that he criticized clerics and insulted Islam through the content of his blogs. Mr. Badawi received his first caning and survived but was deemed by a group of physicians in Saudi Arabia as not able to receive his second and third canings, since his body had not yet healed from the first episode.

While this 31-year-old, slightly built prisoner awaits the cane piercing his back and legs week after week as he sits in prison in Jeddah, his wife, Ensaf Haidar, and the couple's three young children sought and were given political refuge in Canada, nearly 10,000 miles away. Representatives of all political parties in Canada said that they stood united in "common cause" with Mr. Badawi, and they asked politicians from other countries believing in free speech to help press the Saudis to end the "cruel and inhuman" floggings. Canadian representatives also encouraged politicians in other countries to raise their voices for the release of both Mr. Badawi and his lawyer, who was imprisoned for acting on Raif Badawi's behalf. Among other interventions, the Canadian foreign affairs minister raised Badawi's case with a member of the Saudi royal family at a meeting in Switzerland in late January 2015, and the Canadian prime minister's spokesman said publicly that the punishment given to Raif Badawi "is a gross violation of human dignity." Canadian officials vowed to continue openly raising concerns about this case until the day that he is set free (Galloway 2015a).

So, what exactly did Mr. Badawi say on his blog that was deemed to be so obscene and offensive? First, on his views regarding clerics. In his earlier writings on August 12, 2010, Raif Badawi blogged about the stifling of creativity when he said, "As soon as a thinker starts to reveal his ideas, you will find hundreds of fatwas that accused him of being an infidel just because he had the courage to discuss some *sacred topics*. I'm really worried that Arab thinkers will migrate in search of fresh air and to escape the sword of the religious authorities." Second, on September 28, 2010, after clerics urged citizens not to attend "heretical" celebrations marking Saudi National Day, Mr. Badawi blogged that he was in favor of "secularism [as] the most important refuge for citizens of a country." He went on to say that secularism is the practical solution to lift countries (including Saudi Arabia) out of the Third World and into the First World. Secularism, he posited, respects everyone and does not offend anyone (Black 2015a).

Third, in May 2012, shortly before he was arrested, Mr. Badawi blogged about the importance of liberalism. He took full ownership of his thoughts by saying: "For me, liberalism simply means, live and let live. This is a splendid slogan. However, the nature of liberalism—particularly the Saudi version—needs to be clarified. It is even more important to sketch the features and parameters of liberalism, to which the other faction, controlling and *claiming exclusive monopoly of the truth*, is so hostile that they are driven to discredit it without discussion or fully understanding what the word actually means. They have succeeded in planting hostility to liberalism in the minds of the public and turning people against it, lest the carpet be pulled out from under their feet. But their hold over people's minds and society shall vanish like dust carried off in the wind." His final blog remark that day included a quote from Albert Camus: "The only way to deal with an unfree world is to become so absolutely free that your very existence is an act of rebellion."

Around the world, in recent times there have been other notables who have argued for free speech and, as a result, have been imprisoned. One such case was that of Chinese professor Liu Xiabo, a prominent democracy activist since the 1989 demonstrations at Tiananmen Square. In December 2010, he was imprisoned for 11 years on the grounds that he had "incited subversion" in China, a charge stemming from a pro-democracy manifesto known as Charter 08 that Professor Liu helped to write and disseminate online. At the government's command, police were deployed around the apartment building where he and his wife lived in west Beijing just hours before Liu's Nobel Peace Prize win was formally announced (MacKinnon 2012).

The Charter 08 manifesto appealed in all media for freedom of expression—including freedom on the Internet, democratic elections in China, and respect for human rights. In court, Liu was allowed to make a public statement. That speech, entitled "I have no enemies," was perhaps the finest articulation of the struggle for information and free speech in modern China, illustrating why this esteemed professor was so deserving of the Nobel Prize. In place of an acceptance speech in Oslo, Liu's "I have no enemies" speech was read by Norwegian film artist Liv Ullmann (Halvorssen 2012).

Liu's wife is also a victim. While Liu spends his life in a Chinese prison, his wife has been cut off by Chinese authorities from the world outside her apartment. She is not allowed guests, she cannot make telephone calls to the outside world, and she cannot use the Internet to communicate with anyone else online. Though she has not been charged with any crime in this jurisdiction, she is being punished for being the wife of China's most famous political dissident. His wife told the press in December 2012: "I felt I was a person emotionally prepared to respond to the consequences of Liu Xiabo winning the prize. But after he won the prize, I really never imagined that after he won, I would not be able to leave my home. This is too absurd. I think Kafka could not have written anything more absurd and unbelievable than this" (MacKinnon 2012, A20).

Consequently, Chinese author Mo Yan went to Stockholm to collect his Nobel Prize in literature—the first Chinese national not in jail or in exile who was allowed to win and also collect a Nobel Prize. While announcements of Liu's Nobel Prize win was effectively squelched by the Chinese authorities to the point that most Chinese citizens never even heard about his good news story, Mo, a writer with strong ties to the Communist Party in China, has been touted as a hero by that country's state-controlled media (MacKinnon 2012).

This chapter will define what is meant by obscene content (including pornography and child pornography), offensive content/hate speech, and online censorship. We will then explore why—even in jurisdictions like the United States that support freedom of speech and internet openness—there will never be total freedom of the press or a lack of press and Internet censorship, with the media headline cases of Assange, Manning, and Snowden serving as illustrations of key points. Then we will look at the methods used by governments to censor content on the Internet, and close with the results of the *Freedom on the Net 2014* findings.

THE GRAY AREAS OF OBSCENE CONTENT (INCLUDING PORNOGRAPHY AND CHILD PORNOGRAPHY), OFFENSIVE CONTENT, AND HATE SPEECH—AND HOW THE UNITED STATES HAS DEALT WITH THEM THROUGH LEGISLATION

Web 2.0 enables people from all over the world to not only connect online through Internet service providers (ISPs) but to contribute content to various Web sites. Although technology is rapidly advancing and old online platforms are constantly being replaced by new ones, online users can (1) ask questions or provide answers at online forums; (2) write blogs or make comments on others' blog posts; (3) publish reviews of travel-related services (such as at TripAdvisor.com) or of books (such as at Amazon.com); (4) participate in multiuser discussions on social networking services (such as through Facebook, Twitter, or LinkedIn); (5) share photos and videos or make comments on others' photos (such as on Instagram or Flickr); and (6) participate in collaborative online writing meta-projects (such as Wikipedia). Some of these user contributions may be perceived by others online as defamatory, thus placing them in the category of "obscene content," "offensive content," or "hate content." Let us look more closely at how these terms have been viewed by the courts in various jurisdictions by discussing some real-world examples (Perry and Zarsky 2014).

Since Web 2.0 has turned every online user into a potential public speaker with a global audience, it has also dramatically increased the group of potential "wrongdoers." Depending on the jurisdiction where the harm is assessed, a variety of options are available to those who want others to pay for the harm incurred (Perry and Zarsky 2014).

Offensive Content, Obscene Content, and Hate Speech: The Role of the U.S. First Amendment

In the United States, under the First Amendment to the Constitution, offensive content and online hate speech have the same protections as any other form of speech, and it is safe to say that these speech protections are more robust than those found in other countries. Thus, some experts would posit that hate organizations in the

United States are relatively protected when they launch their hate messages online. Moreover, because the First Amendment guarantees freedom of speech broadly, the U.S. government is quite limited in its ability to regulate online speech through existing civil and criminal laws. The principle underlying free speech is a "marketplace of ideas," in which distasteful or offensive speech is answered by more speech (see, for example, *Abrams v. United States*, 1919). Within this so-called marketplace of ideas, citizens typically work through posted beliefs and ideals that best resonate with them and avoid those Web sites having content that does not resonate well. Once "hate speech"—usually aimed at a particular gender, sexual orientation, or religion—is displayed publically or in an online forum, it can be answered by speech that reveals its falsity and offensiveness and also by counter-postings advocating for more positive and enlightened values (Henry 2009).

Some online vigilantes feel that hate speech needs to be taken to task, regardless of the laws in place in any given jurisdiction. One such individual is a Canadian self-proclaimed Craigslist crusader who hunts down individuals on the Internet whom he believes cite offensive and racist comments on the Craigslist site, a classified ad site offering a variety of items and services. The man's name is Cran Campbell, and he has been flagging postings under a heading called "rants and raves" in the personal section of the company's Vancouver, British Columbia, Web site. By calling on police, human rights tribunals, and politicians across Canada to take action, Campbell has asked authorities to force companies maintaining Internet servers outside the country but using the .ca domain name to comply with Canada's hate speech laws. But Campbell has a huge fight ahead, for the individuals behind Web sites with .ca domain names are not required to live in Canada or to operate their Internet servers there (Drews 2013).

What is even more important is that the organizations managing those Web sites do not mandate what laws the operators must follow—not to mention the reality that Canada's hate speech laws are complex and broad. While Campbell says that he has reported his concerns to Craigslist officials through e-mail, he never received a response. The Canadian authorities say that for a message to be deemed as "hate propaganda" under Canada's Criminal Code, the message has to be made publicly and it must target one of five identifiable protected groups based on race, color, religion, ethnic origin, or sexual orientation. The authorities must also determine whether someone online or on land is attempting to incite disdain or hatred toward a protected group (Drews 2013).

The complexity of hate speech laws regardless of jurisdiction is, without question, perplexing and quite difficult to manage. In recent years, the U.S. government's attempts at passing new content-based laws regulating speech have been declared to be unconstitutional. Although hate speech in particular is largely protected from governmental regulation, it can be creatively and effectively responded to by nongovernmental organizations (NGOs), such as the Southern Poverty Law Center (SPLC) and the Anti-Defamation League (ADL), both U.S.-based. The SPLC tends to use the Internet as a weapon in the battle against hate and hate groups, while the ADL tends to cooperate with Internet service providers (ISPs) to identify hate speech, first, and to encourage enforcement of Terms of Service contracts, second, with the goal of removing hateful content from the Internet. While identifying originating ISPs is not an easy task, ISPs may voluntarily stop providing Internet access to Web sites after they are made aware of offensive or hate content (Henry 2009).

There is little question that U.S. jurisprudence leans heavily on the side of public discourse and away from speech regulation—whether such offensive or hateful messaging occurs on land or online. In fact, in 1997, the U.S. Supreme Court ruled that the First Amendment applies in full measure to speech on the Internet as well as on land (see, for example, *Reno v. ACLU*, 1997). Consequently, the government cannot restrict online speech unless that speech falls within an unprotected category—such as speech deemed to be "obscene" or speech representing a "true threat" to citizens. The bottom line is this: the U.S. government can only regulate speech based on content *where it can show that the regulation is necessary to serve a compelling state interest, and where it is narrowly drawn to achieve that end.* Besides the 1997 case just cited, other cases heard by U.S. courts have ruled that the judges hearing the case should exercise extreme caution before silencing viewpoints with which they disagree (Henry 2009).

Now let's look at the special case of content deemed to be "obscene." By definition, "obscenity" is a legal term that applies to anything deemed to be offensive to the morals of citizens or that has the potential to corrupt the public morals by its indecency or lewdness. Thus, "obscenity" and "obscene content" have often been equated with the terms "pornography" and "child pornography" (Henry 2009).

Pornography—which is commonly viewed as content including, more or less, consenting adults engaging in sexual acts—is a term with legal limits and subject to any given community's standard for tolerance of such materials. Today, the term "pornography" is often used to refer to erotic content found in books, magazines, films, and recordings—whether these vehicles are found on land or online. In the United States in recent years, there have been some interesting court challenges regarding the interpretations of "obscene content" and "pornography"—and the harms that they cause to members of society. While obscenity and obscene content both include pornography, it has been argued that these terms also include the less offensive acts of nude dancing, sexually oriented commercial messages, and distasteful comedy routines. Thus, content in earlier times labeled as "pornographic" may, in many recent cases, be more properly labeled as "erotic" (Henry 2009).

An interesting court case in the United States in this regard occurred in 1989 (*Sable Communications of California, Inc. v. Federal Communications Commission*);

here, the Supreme Court unanimously held that the First Amendment's guarantee of free speech protected indecent, sexually explicit telephone messages known as "Dial-a-Porn." The Court found that though a federal law tried to ban "Dial-a-Porn" commercial services over interstate telephone lines to protect minors from hearing obscene or pornographic content, banning it altogether was unconstitutional. In short, the First Amendment rules applied to "indecent" as well as to "obscene" speech. The Court concluded that if the content of the phone conversations *did not* exceed the community standard of tolerance, erotic content phone calls were protected. However, the Court found that telephone messages containing "obscene" or "non–consenting party" sexual content were prohibited by the First Amendment (thefreedictionary.com 2015).

To summarize, in recent years, there is little question that the U.S. courts as well as those in other jurisdictions worldwide have had a difficult time determining what is "obscene" in the virtual environment. It is important to underscore that this labeling problem has had serious legal implications, because if an online message is deemed to be "obscene," it is not protected by the First Amendment. It then places the perpetrator in the cybercriminal category and, if convicted, facing stiff penalties.

The Critical Role of the Communications Decency Act (CDA) and Content Providers' Liability

Some scholars have called for a unified discussion of content providers' liability for inappropriate online speech or activities involving informational nontruths—including defamation; copyright violations; misrepresentation of products on sales platforms; speech crimes like incitement and creating or selling hate speech or obscene content; and, perhaps, disseminating computer viruses. In the context discussed in this chapter, it is quite safe to say that U.S. legislation tends to block lawsuits against online content providers, particularly section 230 of the federal Communications Decency Act (CDA).

Having said this, U.S. law offers some redress against anonymous online speakers who have posted offensive or hateful things. For example, it allows plaintiffs to bring actions against intermediaries, requiring them to disclose information regarding potential defendants. In turn, this information might enable the lifting of the "veil of anonymity," resulting in direct legal action being taken by the victims against the anonymous speakers (Perry and Zarsky 2014).

The enactment of section 230 of the CDA responded to several earlier court cases addressing platform liability under common law, which differentiates between various types of intermediaries. First, common carriers such as telephone companies, noted the courts, only transmit information and are not liable for offensive content or defamation. Second, distributors of published offensive material—such as bookstore owners—distribute content but do not control the content; therefore, they are liable only when they have actual knowledge of the offensive or defaming nature of the publication, or had reason to know. Third, publishers such as newspapers exercise significant control over published content and are, therefore, subject to stricter liability measures (Perry and Zarsky 2014).

The 1991 legal case of *Cubby v. CompuServe* serves as a good illustration of the court's rulings in this regard. Here, the U.S. court found that CompuServe, which operated online special-interest forums, should not be liable for content posted as part of a nonmoderated discussion. The company provided online users with access to a daily newsletter about broadcast journalism and journalists. Lawyers representing the company said that CompuServe just uploaded information but did not review its contents. The plaintiffs argued, on the other hand, that the daily newsletter included false and defamatory statements about a competing newsletter that they published. In the end, the court held that CompuServe was the distributor of the information rather than the publisher of such, and therefore was not liable (Perry and Zarsky 2014).

The balance struck by the CDA's section 230 and the broad immunity arising from it have certainly not been without criticism. In view of the law's broad interpretation by the courts, some legal experts in the United States have argued for its amendment and limitation, positing that although this section has proven to be valuable in terms of upholding free speech, in an Internet context, in particular, it might be unfair toward targets whose reputations have been tarnished by defaming statements made in an anonymous fashion online. Moreover, CDA section 230 enables harassment that is not only problematic but is personally harm-inducing, particularly when online anonymous comments are directed toward women, those in the LGBT (i.e., lesbian, gay, bi, or transsexual) community, and visible minorities. Though viewed in this light, given the CDA and section 230's key role in the regulation of U.S. platforms and its possible contribution to economic success, legal experts have generally concluded that there is relatively little chance of any considerable amendments being made in this regard to this act in the near future (Perry and Zarsky 2014).

The Role of the Communications Decency Act (CDA), the Child Online Protection Act (COPA), and the PROTECT Act Regarding Child Pornography

A number of attempts by the U.S. government to regulate child pornographic content both on land and online have met with limited success in the past 20 years. U.S. congressional attempts to prevent the Internet from being used to distribute obscene material, in particular, have been blocked by a number of Supreme Court decisions. As noted, the Communications Decency Act (CDA), enacted in 1996, was designed to outlaw obscene and indecent sexual content in cyberspace. Regarding child pornography, the CDA made it a crime to use telecommunications to transmit any comment, request, suggestion, proposal, image, or other communication deemed to be "obscene" or "indecent"—knowing that the receiver of the communication was underage and regardless of whether the creator of the message placed the call or initiated the online communication.

In 1997, one year after the CDA's passage, the American Civil Liberties Union (ACLU) and 20 other plaintiffs filed a lawsuit questioning the constitutionality of the CDA, particularly the section regarding indecent material. Thus, in the 1997 *Reno v. American Civil Liberties Union* case, the Supreme Court recognized the legitimacy of the U.S. government in protecting minors from harmful materials but ruled that the CDA abridged freedom of speech and was therefore unconstitutional. Of particular concern was that the act's undefined terms of "indecent" and "patently" raised ambiguities about how these two "standards" were defined and how they meaningfully related to each other. In the end, the Supreme Court concluded that the CDA could have a "chilling effect" on free speech (thefreedictionary.com 2015).

In 1998, the U.S. Congress tried to address these shortcomings in the CDA when it passed the Child Online Protection Act (COPA). COPA tried to restrict limitations on materials deemed to be "pornographic" on the grounds that such communications were made for commercial purposes. This time around, the ACLU and a number of online Web site operators challenged the constitutionality of COPA, arguing that it was overly broad. They also argued that the proper use of the community standards test of tolerance should allow any community in the United States to file civil and criminal lawsuits under COPA. Several years later in the 2002 case of *Ashcroft v. the American Civil Liberties Union*, the Supreme Court decided that COPA, like the CDA, might be overly broad. So it referred the case back to the district court for a full hearing on the merits of the case (thefreedictionary.com 2015).

Another important piece of legislation in the United States intended to fight Internet-based child pornography was the PROTECT Act—the Prosecutorial Remedies and Tools against the Exploitation of Children Today Act. Despite the previous controversy surrounding the CDA and COPA regarding their application to child pornography, the PROTECT Act was passed in February 2003 with an extraordinary vote of 84 senators in favor and 0 senators opposed. The objective of this piece of legislation was to assist law enforcement in their attempts not only to identify but also to track online predators using the Internet to seduce minors. Besides strengthening the government's ability to prosecute crimes involving child pornography, it also attempted to extend prosecutorial power beyond U.S. jurisdictions (Schell 2007).

The PROTECT Act remains enforceable to this day because of its many positive outcomes. This act implemented the credible Amber Alert communication system, allowing for nationwide alerts when children go missing or are kidnapped, and redefined "child pornography" to include not only images of real children engaging in sexually explicit conduct but also computer-generated depictions indistinguishable from real children engaging in such acts. "Indistinguishable" was further defined as that which an ordinary person viewing the image would conclude is a real child engaging in sexually explicit acts. However, cartoons, drawings, paintings, and sculptures depicting minors or adults engaging in sexually explicit acts, as well as depictions of actual adults looking like minors engaging in sexually explicit acts, were excluded from the definition of child pornography (Schell 2007).

DEFINING INTERNET CENSORSHIP AT THE MACRO LEVEL AND A BRIEF COMMENT ON RECENT GLOBAL TRENDS

At a basic level, online content can be censored by individuals (like Canadian Cran Campbell) or by governments. Generally speaking, self-censorers tend not to be active in politics because they think that their views will not matter. Significantly, individuals living in censorious jurisdictions often say that they must adopt this mode of behavior if they want to avoid imprisonment or endure violence for saying "the wrong thing"—either on land or online. Self-censorers tend to be shy, socially anxious, low in self-esteem, and worried about what others think of them (Hayes, Glynn, and Shanahan 2005).

At a macro level, "Internet censorship" occurs when governments try to control citizens' online activities, restrict the free flow of information, and/or infringe on the rights of online users. Since about 2005, the battle over governments maintaining "Internet freedom" versus "censorship" of perceived offensive online content has been heating up around the globe.

With every passing year, various governments' attempts to control Internet content have increased, and this trend has been seen even in jurisdictions that have been strongly opposed to curtailing free speech, including the United States. Whether for internal political reasons, for religious reasons, or to justify an intensive war against terrorists, governments' needs to control content on the Internet and the means employed to do so—including greater Internet surveillance—are becoming more intense and more sophisticated. Some of the more aggressive means used by governments have included causing planned Internet connection disruptions or giving sizable amounts of money to professional commentators to sway discussions in particular directions in targeted online chat rooms (Freedom House 2012).

ONLINE CENSORSHIP VERSUS NATIONAL SECURITY—AND WHY THERE WILL NEVER BE TOTAL FREEDOM OF THE PRESS, EVEN IN JURISDICTIONS LIKE THE UNITED STATES

In the developed nations over the years, there has been an ongoing tug-of-war between a government's allowing for censorship in the media when concerns arise about national security and giving journalists full freedoms to publish either online or in print what they deem fit for public consumption without having recognizable censorship rules put in place. In the U.S. First Amendment, a number of freedoms are cited—most notably, freedom of the press.

In an effort for the founders of the United States to distinguish their new government from that of England—where there had been a long history of censorship of the press in order to safeguard national security—the First Amendment in the U.S. Constitution has often been referred to as the creation of the "fourth institution" outside the government as an additional check on the three official branches—the executive, the legislature, and the judiciary. The latter was created to maintain checks and balances between those advocating for more freedoms compared to those who saw threats to national security, particularly in times of war—when this freedom is often set aside for what governments claim is a means of defending national security (Goodale 1997).

Until the Korean War and later (including the war in Iraq), the media and journalists were perceived to be helpful in educating citizens in the United States and elsewhere to better understand the issues in conflict between warring nations. Recently, however, scholars have raised a key question about what is "appropriate" information sharing with the public; namely, how much censorship is deemed to be appropriate in defending national security, while still permitting adequate freedom to reporters in support of the First Amendment (Schell 2014)?

For example, Doris Graber (2003) noted that justifying press censorship can be quite difficult, and she labeled it "the high-stakes dilemma." She maintained that in one sense, press freedom is particularly important in times of national crisis like a war or terrorist attacks, but that risks to security can result when and if there is a "leak" of information that was intended to be strictly confidential. Consequently, restrictions on what journalists can share with the public have developed over time, and more so in recent times with advancements in technology—such as mobile phones and the Internet.

There is little question that in recent times, technology has advanced world culture and narrowed the gap between the so-called "haves" and the "have-nots" along a digital divide. To this point, Graber maintains that in today's networked world, the reality is that there is someone—a journalist, hacker or hacker group, or some business—that will go against the moral grain, depart from established military protocols, and share sensitive information either in print or over the Internet for the whole world to see.

A historic case of this nature occurred in March 2003, when Geraldo Rivera allegedly engaged in rogue reporting, thus endangering U.S. soldiers in Iraq. Apparently, he told his photographer to tilt his camera downward in the sand so that he could draw a map of both Iraqi and U.S. military movements. Rivera took the confidential information he was privy to and intentionally tried transmitting it to Fox News in the United States. Unfortunately, he carelessly shared it with the rest of the world because of technology advancements at that time. The U.S. government took a hard line on Rivera's action, maintaining that what he did could have caused immense harm to the fighting troops. So he was escorted out of Iraq; what's more, he immediately lost contact with the 101st Airborne Division to which he was assigned in trust (Schell 2014).

"Rational" censorship was targeted not just at journalists during the Iraq war but at U.S. troops who were under tight disclosure rules in the field. Apparently, Internet "kill switches" (i.e., mechanisms used to shut down or disable machinery, programs, or devices to, say, protect data on a mobile device from being altered or stolen) were used on U.S. military information networks in Iraq so that if there were an attack on the forces there, or if there were a number of casualties or some other newsworthy event, a senior military officer had the right to literally "pull the plug" on the communications networks so that soldiers and journalists could not transmit confidential information outside of the zone. However, military officers soon realized that cell phones in the field were very difficult to control, because they sent out signals through local Iraqi networks—which placed them outside the domain of kill switches (Wielawski 2005).

Just imagine for a moment the horror if the very personal information about a killed soldier was shared with the world before it was shared with the deceased's family members. It is for this reason, in part, why there continues to be an ongoing tug-of-war between online censorship versus national security—and why there will never be total freedom of the press during times of national security crisis, even in freedom-loving jurisdictions like the United States.

ADEQUATE INFORMATION RELEASE VERSUS INTERNET CENSORSHIP: THE U.S. GOVERNMENT'S RECENT REACTIONS TO THE ASSANGE, MANNING, AND SNOWDEN ONLINE INFORMATION "LEAKS"

Besides grappling with, at times, competing agendas of journalists and soldiers in order to safeguard against critical data "leaks" during periods of national security concerns, the U.S. government recently has had to deal with "insider" and "outsider" hackers and hacker groups intent on sharing confidential information with the global online community. For example, recently mainstream media outlets began featuring "headliner" names like those of Julian Assange, Private Bradley Manning, and Edward Snowden and their real-life information leak stories. Let's now take a closer look at why these incidents were so critical to the issue of confidential information release and Internet censorship for the U.S. government, in particular.

On one side of the coin is the reasonableness of governments being able to restrict some content from the public during periods of national security concerns or war, and on the other side of the coin are those who see themselves as information freedom fighters. By definition, information freedom fighters feel that all information should be free and accessible; thus, individuals holding this view resist any kind of control by governments, particularly that limiting information access to citizens—online or on land.

To this point, the U.S. government has stated openly that it intends to be fair and reasonable to, say, reporters embedded with soldiers in the field during times of war so that they can maintain an open communication channel with the public. Having said this, however, necessary precautions need to be taken before any information is allowed to be released. The reality is that business press releases are written ahead of the time that they are actually transmitted to the public, and a similar protocol exists in the battle zone.

As a case in point, in the Iraq War, a military officer could share with reporters planned attacks in any given region—but it was stipulated conclusively by the U.S. government that the information could be released to the public only at a stipulated time, such as after the said crisis or battle had transpired. Sometimes, this directive could be especially challenging, given increased access by many to the Internet—including reporters in the field. Consequently, rules for censorship and disclosure that may have been constructed within the past five years must be continually revised in the United States and elsewhere to reflect emerging developments in global military confrontations on land and through the Internet (known nowadays as cyberwars). To be sure, censorship on land and online is a subject that whenever addressed in any public debate will have clear supporters as well as clear opponents (Schell 2014).

The Challenge of WikiLeaks and Outsider Hacker Julian Assange to the U.S. Government

As the Internet continues to evolve and as military conflicts continue to emerge in various parts of the world, the debate between the freedom fighters and the degree of appropriate censorship of harm-inducing secret information rages on. Over the past seven years, such a debate has been fueled around concerns over the leaking of secret U.S. military documents by the hacktivist group WikiLeaks. Julian Assange created this hacker group in 2006 to provide an outlet to cause regime change and open information sharing to expose injustice and abuses of power (Greenberg 2010).

The WikiLeaks Web site has published materials related to the Church of Scientology, Guantanamo Bay, military strikes, and classified documents from around the world. WikiLeaks is probably most famous, however, for its acquisition and publication of 251,000 American diplomatic cables ranging from unclassified documents to secret documents (Greenberg 2010).

In 2010, a U.S. Army soldier named Bradley Manning downloaded these diplomatic cables while stationed in Iraq. He then shared the content over two years with Julian Assange, who then leaked the news to outlets like the *New York Times* and *Der Spiege*l (Harrell 2010).

There is no question that the release of these cables caused massive controversy and embarrassment for the U.S. government because of the sensitive nature of the content. In fact, a distributed denial of service (DDoS) hack attack was launched against WikiLeaks shortly after the first information release, taking it offline. Subsequently, the companies that provided funding and infrastructure for WikiLeaks, such as PayPal, pulled their financial support. As a consequence, hacker cells worldwide began similar DDoS hack attacks against the financial service providers to punish them for their actions. The controversy over these documents led some in the United States to call for the arrest of Assange as the alleged head of "a terrorist group"—and even called for his execution in some cases, though he was an Australian and not an American (O'Brien 2010).

Since 2012, Julian Assange has been "on the lam." As of October 13, 2015, he remains there (Bilefsky 2015). However, citing the strain on resources, London police said that they were ending their round-the-clock monitoring of the embassy where he had been "holed up." Though the police were intent on arresting Assange should he try to leave the building, the costs for the surveillance were becoming excessive; as of the end of April 2015, the cost to British taxpayers was estimated to be a staggering $22.1 million. The costs prompted public outcry from local politicians, citing misuse of public resources for this purpose (Bilefsky 2015).

In June 2012, Assange took refuge in the Ecuadorian embassy in Britain to avoid extradition to Sweden, where he was wanted not for hacking-related exploits but for questioning by authorities about sexual assault allegations. His real fears, it seems, stemmed from the fact that he believed Sweden would extradite him to the United States to face charges related to WikiLeaks' disclosure of the huge treasure of classified U.S. military and diplomatic documents associated with Bradley

Manning. Despite these fears and his being in hiding in the embassy, Assange decided that he would run for a Senate seat in Australia in September 2013; he lost by 3,000+ primary votes, after he poked fun at Australian politicians by releasing a video of them on the Internet. In response, Ecuadorian president Rafael Correa chastised Assange, telling him that as a matter of courtesy, Ecuador would not bar him from exercising his rights and freedoms by running for a seat in his homeland, but he needed to stop using the Internet to make light of people he didn't agree with (Paramaribo 2013).

The controversy around Julian Assange and his online exploits continued into 2015, with some bystanders viewing him as an information freedom fighter hero and others seeing him as a traitor. There was even a pocket of journalists from around the world who identified with him as "an online journalist."

Many bystanders were wondering what moves the U.S. government was planning against this cyberperpetrator. Then, on January 25, 2015, some light was shed on this mystery. The British newspaper *The Guardian* reported that the U.S. Justice Department got a warrant in 2012 to seize the contents—plus the metadata on e-mails received, sent, drafted, and deleted—of three WikiLeaks' staffers' personal Gmail accounts. This move by the U.S. government apparently was kept secret even from the staffers for almost two and a half years. The reporter said in the article that it is likely that this warrant for the staffers' e-mail was connected to the grand jury that the U.S. government convened in 2010 to look into WikiLeaks' publication of the leaked State Department cables, along with Afghan and Iraq war logs. The reporter also noted that the warrants were issued by a federal judge in the Eastern District of Virginia, the same jurisdiction in which the grand jury was created. Moreover, it is likely that the investigation was ongoing as late as May 2014. The warrant apparently specifically indicated that the Justice Department is investigating WikiLeaks for "conspiracy to commit espionage" (Timm 2015).

Trevor Timm, the author of the *Guardian* piece, underscored in his article that though WikiLeaks' legal troubles have been largely ignored by journalists around the globe, they shouldn't be. The U.S. Justice Department has continued to treat the Web site's staffers with contempt and has ignored its own guidelines for issuing warrants and subpoenas to journalists publishing leaked materials. In essence, the FBI and the U.S. government have pressed ahead with all-out surveillance of (in Timm's words) "a news publisher." Just imagine, noted Timm (2015), that if the FBI were to place a paid informant inside the *New York Times*, there would be protests on the steps of the Justice Department within 24 hours.

Despite the ongoing legal pressure by the U.S. government, WikiLeaks has continued to publish important documents in the so-called public interest using the Internet. For example, in 2014, the Web site published draft texts of the Trans-Pacific Partnership, a trade agreement that was openly opposed by public interest groups because of the extreme secrecy around the treaty's global negotiations. Furthermore, in December 2014, WikiLeaks published online a secret CIA study showing the negative effects of the U.S. government's policy of targeted killing in Afghanistan. Trevor Timm (2015) concluded his piece by saying that it should not be the U.S. government's role to decide who is enough of a journalist in its view to qualify for the constitutional and legal protections that can be and should be afforded to all journalists. Timm affirmed that it is clear that almost nobody qualifies—not reporters at the *New York Times*, not Julian Assange, and not the staffers at WikiLeaks. Despite this flurry of media activity around the Assange case, as of the end of February 2015, neither Julian Assange nor any of his staffers had been charged with any particular online crime.

The Challenge of Information Freedom Fighter and Insider Hacker U.S. Private Bradley Manning to the U.S. Government

The recent case of U.S. soldier Bradley Manning illustrates the delicate relationship between the government's maintaining national security during war and the role of "insider" hackers in overriding established rules of information disclosure to the public. On day one of Private Manning's trial, which began in the United States on June 4, 2013, and involved a number of criminal charges, the accused confessed to being the sole source for the vast archives of secret military and diplomatic documents made public by WikiLeaks. An official with the military argued on that day that Manning systematically harvested hundreds of thousands of classified documents and then dumped them onto the Internet—into the eyes of not only the public but also the enemy—material that Private Manning knew would put the lives of his fellow soldiers at risk (Savage 2013).

Manning's defense lawyer countered that Private Manning had, in fact, tried to ensure that the several hundred thousand documents that he released would not cause harm; he was, after all, selective about what he gave to Julian Assange and WikiLeaks. The lawyer went on to argue that the soldier's motivation for engaging in this particular online activity was to make the world a better place (Savage 2013).

Then on Manning's second day of trial, the link between the soldier's relationship with a known hacker was made explicit. Military prosecutors called to the witness stand a computer hacker named Adrian Lamo, who had befriended Manning online and then turned him in to army investigators. Lamo, who in 2004, at age 22, was charged in a Manhattan federal court with cracking into the computer network of the *New York Times*, said that Manning had contacted him online in May 2010 from his base in Iraq and asked for guidance on encrypted online chats. Lamo noted in his testimony that in his view, Manning saw him as a kindred "idealist" who believed in freedom of information and free speech. According to Lamo, Manning apparently wanted to show the American public the harsh reality of war in Afghanistan and Iraq. During these early days of the trial, the prosecution posited that there apparently was nothing on Manning's seized laptop indicating that he had in any way a hatred for America or American values (Simpson 2013).

These disparate views at both ends of the freedom fighter and the need for censorship continuum underscore the conflict at the heart of Manning's trial. Early in the trial, the press noted that if found guilty of violating the U.S. Espionage Act and aiding the enemy, Manning could serve a life sentence behind prison bars (Savage 2013).

Later in the trial, U.S. First Amendment lawyer James Goodale noted that a Manning conviction on any one of the eight espionage counts he was facing, or on a federal computer fraud charge, would in many ways enable the U.S. government to go after and charge other information freedom fighters residing in other jurisdictions—Julian Assange in particular (Dishneau 2013).

In mid-August 2013, Private Manning took the stand. He began with an apology to the American people, noting (Dishneau and Jelinek 2013, A14): "I'm sorry that my actions hurt people. I'm sorry that it hurt the United States." While he admitted that he understood what he was doing and the decisions that he made, he affirmed that he did not believe at the time that his actions would cause harm.

In his defense, an Army psychologist noted that Manning's private struggle with gender identity in a hostile workplace put incredible mental pressure on the soldier. Consequently, Private Manning's gender identity disorder, along with narcissistic personality traits, his postadolescent idealism, and his lack of friends in Iraq caused him to "reasonably conclude" that he could change the world—for the better—by leaking classified documents over the Internet (Dishneau and Jelinek 2013).

On Wednesday, August 21, 2013, a military judge sentenced Private First Class Manning to 35 years in prison, the longest sentence handed down in a case involving a leak of U.S. government information released to the public. Although he could be eligible for parole in as little as eight years, as Manning stood in the courtroom, dazed on hearing the verdict, a handful of supporters in the room labeled Manning "a hero" in the war for information freedom fighting (Savage and Huetteman 2013).

The Challenge of U.S. Information Freedom Fighter and NSA Contractor Edward Snowden to the U.S. Government

On June 9, 2013, a 29-year-old undercover CIA employee named Edward Snowden announced that he was the main source of recent disclosures in the United

States about top-secret National Security Agency (NSA) surveillance programs that tracked telephone and Internet messages around the globe with the U.S. government's alleged objective of thwarting terrorist threats. Snowden, a tech specialist who was under contract with the NSA and was also employed by the U.S. consulting firm Booz Allen Hamilton, affirmed to the press that he disclosed secret documents in the *Washington Post* and the *Guardian* because of the unfairness of the systematic surveillance of innocent citizens by the U.S. government (Blake, Gellman, and Miller 2013).

Fearing that he would face the same prison fate as Private Manning, Snowden fled from the United States and took initial refuge in Hong Kong in June 2013. Snowden argued on his safe landing in Hong Kong that allowing the U.S. government to intimidate its people with threats of retaliation for revealing wrongdoing was clearly contrary to the public interest. He publicly announced that he would seek asylum from any country that believed in free speech and was opposed to victimizing citizens' global privacy (Blake, Gellman, and Miller 2013).

Within 24 hours of Snowden's public confession, Senator Dianne Feinstein of California, who headed the State Intelligence Committee and supported the notion of Internet surveillance as a means of keeping U.S. citizens safe, accused U.S. citizen Edward Snowden of committing "an act of treason" and argued that he should be treated accordingly (Jakes 2013).

On June 23, 2013, a global cat-and-mouse game involving Snowden and the U.S. authorities ensued, as the latter tried to catch "the leaker" before he reached what many thought would be his longer-tem safe haven: Ecuador. It was on this day that Snowden unexpectedly left Hong Kong and took a flight to Moscow, Russia (Barrett and Chen 2013).

Shortly thereafter, in July 2013, Ecuadorian president Rafael Correa said that even if Snowden wanted to seek asylum in Ecuador, he was at that time still under the care of the Russian authorities, positing that the fugitive could not leave the Russian airport without the consent of the Russian government (Weissenstein 2013).

Then on August 13, 2013, Edward Snowden thanked the Russian government for giving him temporary asylum for a one-year period. Snowden was pleased that he had been able to work in Russia during this time period and, importantly, was safely out of the reach of U.S. prosecutors. Immediately, some U.S. lawmakers called for some form of tough retaliation against Russia for harboring Snowden, suggesting, perhaps, a boycott of the Winter Olympic Games that were scheduled to be held in Sochi, Russia. Other politicians in the United States held firm to the belief that Snowden should immediately be tried on espionage charges (Myers and Kramer 2013).

By October 2013, the alleged Snowden connection brought into the international fray new government players in the cyberspace field. The president of Brazil, for example, accused Canada of cyberwar after allegations that Canadian hackers hired by their government tried to steal state secrets from the South American country's mining and energy ministry in 2012—a disclosure that threatened to create a lasting rift between Canada and Brazil, now the world's sixth-largest economy and a crucial bilateral partner for Canada (Nolen, Freeze, and Chase 2013).

But where was the link between this alleged government hacking event and Edward Snowden? Actually, the link was brought to light by Glenn Greenwald, an American journalist based in Brazil. During the early fall of 2013, Greenwald publicized over the Internet and through the media leaked documents regarding the extent of an elaborate electronic eavesdropping campaign generated by the U.S. government under the code name "Prism." Specifically, Prism was conducted by the U.S. National Security Agency (NSA) as a means of snooping on U.S. citizens suspected of engaging in terrorist activities (Nolen, Freeze, and Chase 2013).

Apparently, the bulk of the top-secret documents given to this journalist and to filmmaker Laura Poitras in Hong Kong (who later produced the film *Citizenfour*, the Edward Snowden documentary about mass illegitimate government surveillance) were provided by Edward Snowden. Interestingly, this international case brought to the surface earlier voiced concerns by many IT security and legal experts regarding the overlapping nature of the critical online aspects of security, trust, privacy, and censorship in our networked world. Given the reality of Prism, experts say that in the heavyweight fight between privacy and security, it looks as if citizens' mobile phone privacy is "on the ropes"—given that the U.S. government feels that it is entitled to listen in on citizens' conversations if they are, for any reason, suspected terrorists (Nolen, Freeze, and Chase 2013; Renzetti 2015).

In the midst of the controversy over Prism, Snowden's original Russian one-year asylum term expired in August 2014, reopening media discussions that he might be returned to the United States to face a hearing on three charges brought by federal prosecutors in the United States (Renzetti 2015). However, in January 2015, Snowden's Russian lawyer, Anatoly Kucherena, publicly announced that a residential term was set for another three years so that he could remain relatively unscathed in Russia (Circa 2015).

And on a lighter note, while journalists from around the world would be thrilled to have an interview with Edward Snowden about his views on why he is so divisive (he apparently gets about 50 requests per day for an interview), an 18-year-old Toronto, Ontario, Canada, high school student from Upper Canada College named Conor Healy was able to snag a 40-minute interview with Snowden the first week of February 2015—the contents of which he then shared with his fellow high school students (Bradshaw 2015).

Conor Healy said that he communicated with Edward Snowden through a lawyer at the American Civil Liberties Union (ACLU) named Jameel Jaffer, adding that his communications with the lawyer was the easy part of the interview ordeal. The harder part, he shared, was getting the school's approval to share the contents of his interview, since the principal wanted to avoid any legal trouble or undue criticism (Bradshaw 2015).

So what did Edward Snowden focus on during his interview with the high school students? Most of what he spoke about was his concern about a new bill tabled by the Canadian government in the first week of February 2015, known as Bill C-51; its stated purpose was to prevent terrorism on Canadian soil. Designed to stop any activity that undermines the sovereignty, security, or territorial integrity of Canada, the bill, if eventually passed, would give the Canadian Security Intelligence Service (CSIS) new powers to actively disrupt terrorist threats, not just collect information about them or their perpetrators (Crawley and Walmsley 2015a)

During the interview, Snowden told the students that citizens in any country should be very wary when their government tries to pass new laws under the guise of an increased threat of terrorism. These were Snowden's words: "I would say we should always be extraordinarily cautious when we see governments trying to set up a new secret police within their own countries," noting further that intelligence powers used by governments in ways related to political ideologies, radicalization, and the influence of governments and how people develop their politics are a definite cause for concern (Miller 2015).

Snowden further affirmed in his talk: "We need to be very careful about this [new bill proliferation] because this is a process that is very, very easy to begin. It always happens in time of fear and panic—emergency legislation—they say we're facing extraordinary threats and again if you look at the statistics while the threats are there, they're typically not as significant as presented. . . . Once we let these powers get rolling, it's very difficult to stop that pull though. So I would say that we need to use extraordinary scrutiny in every society, in every country, in every city, in every state to make sure that the laws we live under are the ones we truly want and truly need" (Miller 2015).

The bottom-line statement that Snowden made to the students was this: The nature of surveillance has changed from tracking the so-called bad guys to tracking everyone. "When this happens in secret, outside the context of public laws, public debate, and public consent, not only does this change the nature of democracy, it changes our ability to control the government" (Renzetti 2015).

A document that surfaced in Canada in March 2015 indicated that the U.S. NSA has been infiltrating and trying to map the communications traffic of key corporations around the world. These corporations included Canada's largest bank, Royal

Bank of Canada, and Canada's largest wireless carrier, Rogers Communications. Other firms targeted by the NSA included U.K.-headquartered Rolls Royce Marine and Rio Tinto and U.S.-based RigNet (Freeze and Dobby 2015).

The fact that *Citizenfour* won the best documentary Oscar at the end of February 2015 indicates that Snowden's message has resonated with a very broad audience (Renzetti 2015). However, with the harsh 2015 reality that there was a surge of the Islamic State (IS) along with the terrorist attacks in Canada and Europe, that the caliphate was sawing people's heads off in the desert on a so-called justified mission, and that the Canadian government had already spent more than $120 million waging a war on IS, February 2015 Canadian polls indicated that Snowden's message was falling on predominantly deaf ears. A significant 76% of Canadians approved of their involvement in fighting IS in Iraq and supported the new antiterror legislation known as Bill C-51 in early February 2015, and by the end of the month, 82% of Canadians said that they supported the new law in particular (Wente 2015; Southey 2015).

HOW OFFENSIVE ONLINE ACTIVITIES MAY BE RELATED TO ECONOMIC SANCTIONS AGAINST COUNTRIES OR CRIMINAL SANCTIONS FOR ONLINE CITIZENS

Beyond the anxieties around cyberwars and threats to national security as voiced by governments around the globe, and as alluded to by Edward Snowden in his interview with Conor Healy, might there somehow be a link between hacking, criminal sanctions placed on citizens by the courts in certain jurisdictions because of some perceived online wrongdoings, and economic sanctions placed against countries at times of cyberwars and targeted network hacks?

Offensive Online Activities and Economic Sanctions Against Countries

Let's start with economic sanctions against countries at times of cyberwars and targeted network hacks. We need to acknowledge that from a macro-system perspective, all countries, not just, say, China, are engaged in hacking and cyberespionage activities—either to gain military advantage over another nation or to steal some proprietary information belonging to a particular industrial sector (such as the mining sector).

In China, in particular, government agencies and industry networks have been reported to have been hacked by mal-inclined perpetrators bent on spreading malware to try to steal identity numbers and virtual money from various targeted online venues. In February 2015, China announced that it had dropped some of the world's leading technology brands from its approved state purchase lists, while approving thousands of locally created products. The reason for this change? Some experts say that this was China's response to revelations of widespread Western cybersurveillance and hacking of its networks, while others suggest that this was China's protectionist reaction to shield its domestic technology industry from competition—with, perhaps, the largest North American casualty being U.S. network equipment maker Cisco Systems. In 2012, Cisco still had 60 technology products on China's Central Government Procurement Center's (CGPC) list but by late 2014, the company had none (Carsten 2015).

Interestingly, China's change in approach coincided with leaks by former U.S. NSA contractor Edward Snowden in mid-2013 that exposed several global surveillance programs, many of them operationalized by the NSA with cooperation from telecom companies and European governments. Tu Xinquan, associate director of the China Institute of WTO Studies at the University of International Business and Economics in Beijing, said that not only had the Snowden incident become a real concern, especially for top leaders, but that in some sense, the American government had some responsibility for that—adding that China's concerns had been legitimate (Carsten 2015).

Furthermore, because of China's dependency on Microsoft products (i.e., about 90% of the Chinese government offices use Windows), and given that a lot of software in China is pirated so that software vulnerabilities cannot be fixed with known patches, Chinese government networks are, indeed, vulnerable to hack attacks by insiders and outsiders. These hack attacks could even be funded by other governments. Furthermore, despite what the North American media has suggested about the prevalence of hack attacks paid for by the Chinese government aimed at particular government and industrial networks in the United States and Canada, the fact is that like the United States and Canada, China, too, has its own antihacking laws aimed at deterring its citizens from engaging in such acts. In China, it is not uncommon for hackers to spend three years in prison and be fined tens of thousands of dollars if convicted of a cybercrime (Lynch 2010).

The reality of today's virtual world is that networks all over the world are being hacked by insiders and outsiders alike, even if legislation is in place to act as a deterrent at all levels. From a global perspective, when one country becomes angered at another because of some acts of network hacking, cyberespionage, or asylum granting, a common way for countries to deal with such perceived wrongdoings is to issue various forms of economic sanctions against the "offensive actor." We saw this kind of reaction from the United States, for example, when Russia agreed to grant asylum to Edward Snowden.

Offensive Online Activities and Criminal Sanctions Against Citizens in a Given Jurisdiction

From a pragmatic and theoretical point of view, clearly defining a macro-system link between Internet censorship and criminal sanctions imposed on online citizens is very challenging, indeed, because usually the wrongdoings are assessed by the courts on a case-by-case basis. Maybe the logical way to approach this challenge is to accept that what in one jurisdiction (say, in China or in Saudi Arabia or in Egypt) may be perceived by the courts to be a criminal offense for an online wrongdoing may in another jurisdiction (say, in the United States or Canada) be seen by the courts as merely some hacktivistic act—a combination of hacking and activism and technically a criminal nonoffense.

In any given jurisdiction where an act is perceived to be "criminal," perpetrators are subject to criminal sanctions. The three discussed cases of journalist Badawi in Saudi Arabia, Professor Liu in China, and Private Manning in the United States illustrate how online citizens in each of the aforementioned jurisdictions were handed severe criminal sanctions because of their online wrongdoings, as deliberated by the courts. Regardless of how innocent these individuals believed they were in pursuing certain online activities—such as Private Manning in the United States, who professed to putting confidential government information on the Internet because he was in favor of freedom of information and was opposed to Internet censorship and the ugliness of war—they all eventually have their day in court. Sometimes they fight the law and win, but many times they fight the law and lose. Of the three cases we looked at—journalist Badawi, Professor Liu, and Private Manning—all had their day in court and all lost in the jurisdictions in which they were tried.

Offensive Online Activities and Criminal Sanctions Against Individuals Involving Multiple Jurisdictions or "Outside" Citizenship

Though the U.S. jurisdictional case of Bradley Manning had its challenges from both the prosecution's and the defense's perspectives, offensive online activities involving cross-border jurisdictions make for much more difficult prosecution than singular jurisdiction cases, and often competing rulings and remedies are made by the courts.

Let's look more closely at the case of Julian Assange. Is he guilty of a cybercrime relative to his involvement with Private Manning, and in which jurisdiction should he be tried? Also, what law, if any, did he violate in the United States?

First, let's consider some salient background information on him. Julian Paul Assange is the editor-in-chief and founder of the whistle-blowing Web site WikiLeaks.

During his youth in Australia, he was involved with the hacker group known as the International Subversives, where he used the online name "Mendax." In 1991, he was caught by the Australian police after hacking systems of the communications company Nortel. He was also affiliated with various hack attacks against universities (including in Australia), as well as against targeted U.S. government systems, and for these exploits, he was charged with 31 counts of hacking and related cybercrimes in Australia, his homeland.

In 1995, Assange pleaded guilty to 25 of the 31 counts but was released from prison by the Melbourne courts and issued a small fine and no additional time behind bars. In fact, the judge for this case indicated that Assange's hack attacks were not malicious but rather a consequence of his intelligence and tech-savvy curiosity. Thus, the Australian judge ruled that Assange did not merit more substantive punitive sanctions (Schell 2014).

Though in 2006 Assange founded WikiLeaks to provide, according to the Web site, a means of causing regime change and to advocate for open information sharing to expose injustices and abuses of power, perhaps Assange's and his Web site's biggest call to universal fame came with the publication of the American diplomatic cables on the Internet that were forwarded to him by Bradley Manning in 2010.

In December 2011, news broke that military investigators had uncovered evidence of what appeared to be a direct link between Manning and Assange after a U.S. digital forensic expert examined Manning's computer and retrieved communications between the two men. Although Assange has always denied having direct contact with Manning—though he never revealed how the materials that Manning stole happened to come into the possession of WikiLeaks—a file included in the computer investigation contained this line: "You can currently contact our investigations editor directly in Iceland at 354.862.3841: 24 hour service: ask for Julian Assange" (Schell 2014, 79).

Though these revelations seem to provide some evidence suggesting that Assange had lied about his contact with Manning while he was in Iraq, the bigger questions for the U.S. courts, if they were ever to try him in that jurisdiction, is whether this fact strengthens any potential American legal charges against Assange. Until this time, it seemed as though Assange would remain relatively untouchable, because there was no direct evidence that he had been in contact with Manning prior to, or subsequent to, the data theft. Going by the evidence just cited, there is a strong suggestion that Assange was likely affiliated with Manning prior to the data theft, perhaps even coaching him about what to look for in the confidential files of interest (Schell 2014).

Taking a closer look at Assange's guilt prospects, there is quite a difference between a case where Assange was just the recipient of documents from some anonymous third party who had gotten the secret documents from Manning and a case where Assange was actively in contact with Manning before, during, and after the theft of the said classified documents. In the first case, the defense could argue that Assange was merely acting as a journalist and was not guilty of any crime. In the second case, Assange would have some legal liability to contend with, for his guilt would be that he was aiding and abetting an act of espionage. That said, lawyers maintain that U.S. authorities could face tremendous legal hurdles if they tried bringing criminal charges against Assange, assuming in the first place that they could get Assange out from his current hideaway in the Ecuadorian embassy. Three specialists in espionage law have argued that prosecuting someone like Assange on espionage charges in the United States would require evidence that the defendant was not just in contact with representatives from some foreign power but that he also intended to provide them with secrets. This would be rather far-fetched since no such evidence has surfaced in the case of this Australian-born former hacker who is now an international celebrity (Schell 2014).

Further to this point, Mark Stephens, a London lawyer retained by Assange to represent him should a trial on U.S. soil be put in motion, responded, "Until I see a specific allegation, then it is difficult for me to respond." Stephens also remarked that given that Manning made unauthorized disclosures of secret documents while employed for the U.S. government, there is on its face a much stronger legal foundation of a criminal case against him than one that could be made against Assange (Reuters 2010).

Apart from the legal debate just outlined, other experts believe that the argument against an Espionage Act prosecution of Assange should not be built upon a denial on his part that he spoke with Manning. Rather, the fact that Assange communicated with Manning—directly or indirectly, through an intermediary, or both—should be embraced and protected, because the pair's ability to communicate is the tenet that deserves protecting in a free society, whether that communication occurred in person or through the Internet (Khatchadourian 2011).

As for an espionage case being brought forward by the U.S. government against NSA contractor and U.S. citizen Edward Snowden if he is ever released from Russia and extradited to the United States, it is likely that any lawyer retained by him would be much more worried. He was both officially hired as a contractor with the U.S. government, and he is a U.S. citizen.

To give readers additional insights about relevant legal arguments regarding the case of Edward Snowden and some of the other information freedom "leakers," an interview with Canadian barrister David Butt is included as the Interview with an Expert. A former Harvard teaching fellow, Mr. Butt has designed and delivered many different professional education programs for lawyers and other professionals.

INTERVIEW WITH AN EXPERT

Mr. David Butt, Lawyer

David Butt is a trial and appellate lawyer in Toronto, Ontario, Canada, with a wide-ranging practice. He graduated from Queen's Law School in Kingston, Ontario, Canada, and earned his LLM at Harvard Law School, which he attended as Canada's 1988 Viscount Bennett Scholar. He clerked for both the Court of Appeal for Ontario and the Supreme Court of Canada, the first Canadian to have completed such a double clerkship. Called to the Bar of Ontario in 1989, he has served as the lead counsel more than 24 times in the Supreme Court of Canada and hundreds of times in the Court of Appeal for Ontario, dealing with a broad range of issues involving criminal law, privacy law, and the Canadian Charter of Rights and Freedoms.

A former Harvard University teaching fellow, Mr. Butt has designed and delivered many different professional education programs for lawyers and other professionals across Canada. He is a frequent speaker on a variety of legal topics and a regular commentator on Canadian national and local news outlets, including the *Globe and Mail.* He currently serves as counsel to KINSA, a Canadian charity working closely with law enforcement to rescue children whose images of abuse are circulated online.

Q Since Web 2.0 has turned every online user into a potential public speaker with a global audience, it has also dramatically increased the group of potential "wrongdoers." Depending on the jurisdiction, a variety of options are available to those who want others to pay for the harm incurred. Can you please describe some of these options and their relevance to obscene and offensive online content?

A Those victimized by obscene and/or offensive content online do have an increasing variety of legal options. These options increase as lawmakers come to understand how online victimization is a pressing social problem. The options available to victims fall into two categories: criminal remedies and civil remedies. If the online content is so bad that it violates an applicable criminal law, the victim can report his or her victimization to the police. The police will then take over the investigation, and if there is enough evidence, arrest the alleged perpetrator, charge him or her with the various applicable crimes, and put the case before the courts. If there is a conviction, the courts can put the offender in jail and order compensation for the victim.

A person suffering from online victimization can also sue the perpetrator civilly. This involves hiring a lawyer who carries forward the lawsuit on behalf of the victim. In civil proceedings, the perpetrator will not be convicted of a criminal offense and will not go to jail. However, the perpetrator can be ordered to pay money or "damages" to the victim to compensate him or her for the harm suffered. The perpetrator can also be ordered by the court to stop any victimizing behavior. Violating a court order to stop such victimizing behavior can land the perpetrator in jail.

A victim usually need not choose between pursuing civil and criminal remedies. Usually a victim can pursue both.

Q By definition, "obscenity" is a legal term applying to anything deemed to be offensive to the morals of citizens or that has the potential to corrupt the public morals by its indecency or lewdness. Thus, "obscenity" and "obscene content" have often been equated with the terms "pornography" and "child pornography." Can you please describe some court cases in the United States and Canada deemed to be landmarks in this regard and why?

A Obscenity law is constantly evolving. What was considered shocking and offensive 50, 20, or even 10 years ago may not be shocking today. So the courts must constantly revisit obscenity laws to ensure they keep pace with modern standards. That is why most contemporary obscenity laws in North America use a standard known as the "community standard of tolerance." In applying this standard, judges look to the prevailing values of a community, and in light of those prevailing values, assess what sort of materials are so bad as to be not just distasteful, but intolerable. This standard naturally evolves as the community standard evolves. And by criminalizing only "intolerable" material, it limits the reach of obscenity law to the worst of the worst. Criminalizing only "intolerable" material also has the effect of preserving as much as possible a broad freedom of expression that can be enjoyed by everyone, even if the subject matter of the expression is controversial or distasteful.

Q In 2013, the case of soldier Bradley Manning made media headlines after he was found guilty of violating the U.S. Espionage Act and aiding the enemy. He is now behind bars. In 2013, Edward Snowden announced that he made recent disclosures about top-secret NSA surveillance programs tracking telephone and Internet messages. Fearing the same fate as

Manning, he fled to Hong Kong and Russia. Some accused Snowden of treason and posited he should be imprisoned. Others labeled him an information freedom fighter hero. Can you summarize legal arguments for both sides of this equation?

A If Edward Snowden ever faced prosecution in the United States, it is highly likely that he would be convicted. The applicable law prohibits the kind of disclosure of information he made on such a grand scale. The more interesting question is whether this form of lawbreaking serves a greater good. That is the most interesting debate in the Snowden case.

Those in favor of penalizing Snowden heavily argue that he was a rogue actor, entrusted with confidential information but who breached that trust. He was deceptive, knew he was breaking the law, but went ahead anyway. His leaks endangered many innocent people carrying out sensitive intelligence operations of the kind that most governments routinely carry out. So, the argument goes, his crimes had serious consequences for innocent people and undermined legitimate government activity.

Those on the other side of the debate take a broader view of the situation. They look beyond the technical legalities to the bigger moral questions in play. They say that Edward Snowden was acting in the finest traditions of civil disobedience by refusing to stand idly by when the government itself was engaged in lawless behavior. They say Edward Snowden was a brave whistle-blower who made government more honest and accountable by exposing widespread misdeeds. They say history will judge Edward Snowden favorably.

The debate about Edward Snowden's actions is one of the most important debates we can have about proper governance in the electronic age.

Q During the first week of February 2015, Snowden was interviewed by Canadian high school students. He focused on Bill C-51, stating its purpose was to prevent terrorism on Canadian soil. Snowden affirmed that the nature of surveillance has now changed from tracking the bad guys to tracking everyone. He added that when this happens in secret, outside the context of public laws, public debate, and public consent, not only does this change the nature of democracy, but it changes our ability to control the government. Can you comment on this?

A Snowden makes some very important points. But there are points against him that must receive equally careful consideration. First, he is right to say that citizens everywhere deserve government that is open, transparent, and accountable. And he is right to say that without openness about what the government is up to, there cannot be accountability, and there cannot be informed debate about whether the government is on the right track—or whether the government should continue to enjoy the democratic support of voters.

On the other hand, it can be problematic to simply assume that openness and transparency must prevail in every situation. Covert operations of many kinds are essential to maintaining public safety and security for a simple reason. There are many different kinds of threats to our safety and security, perpetrated by many different kinds of offenders. And if we cannot in some circumstances both gather intelligence and investigate in secret, intelligence gathering will fail. Offenders will see investigations coming from a long way off, avoid detection, mock us for our incompetence, and continue to perpetrate their harmful acts. So secrecy will always be an important part of maintaining public safety, because secrecy is essential to effective intelligence gathering, effective investigation of wrongdoing, and successful apprehension of wrongdoers.

The very tricky challenge that every society and every government must wrestle with is one of balance. Both openness and secrecy are essential. But how much of each strikes the optimal balance? And what types of activities can and cannot be carried out in secret? Maintaining the optimal balance requires constant vigilance.

One important way to advance the needs for both openness and secrecy is through oversight. Oversight means that there are people appointed who are totally independent of the police or intelligence-gathering services to examine how those services operate. Oversight bodies do not reveal everything they know to the public, because that would compromise sensitive and important intelligence gathering and investigations. However, oversight bodies do make public any problems they see in the behavior of police and intelligence-gathering services. Effective oversight bodies can ensure that maintaining necessary secrecy does not mean giving police and intelligence-gathering services unlimited powers to behave however they wish.

Q Globally, governments order brutal attacks or imprisonment of bloggers, surveillance of online content, manipulation of Web content, and restrictive laws to regulate free speech online. These restrict information freedom. Pushback by civil society, journalists, technology companies, and the courts fighting against Internet censorship are prevalent. Please comment on notable victories in jurisdictions.

A The fight to preserve a vibrant freedom of expression globally is a fight that will never end. Why? Because no government is perfect, and governments are naturally interested in seeking to extend their rule. To extend the rule of an imperfect government, it will always be tempting to try to limit the dissemination of information about a government's mistakes or misdeeds that could make it unpopular. We see this phenomenon of government trying to "control the message" taking place in the worst dictatorships and also in the most open of democracies. No doubt, some governments are more repressive than others, but in every country the people governed have a deep interest in ensuring that there is a vibrant and independent journalism profession to maintain the free flow of information and to call out those in both business and government trying to control the flow of information for self-serving reasons.

A CLOSER LOOK AT THE DEFINITIONS OF FREEDOM OF INFORMATION, INTERNET FREEDOM, AND INTERNET CENSORSHIP ON A GLOBAL SCALE—AND THE METHODS USED BY COUNTRIES TO CENSOR INTERNET CONTENT

On a global basis, brutal attacks on or imprisonment of bloggers (like Badawi) in some Internet-connected nations, politically motivated surveillance of online content (such as what occurred with Professor Liu), proactive manipulation of Web content by some governments, and emerging restrictive laws aimed at regulating free speech online are just some of the diverse threats against information and Internet freedom that have emerged since 2010. But the story is not all bleak, for increased pushback by civil society and journalists, technology companies, and independent courts—all believing in defending information freedom and fighting against Internet censorship or unfair imprisonment of citizens for online "misdemeanors"—have resulted in some notable victories.

A Closer Look at the Mohamed Fahmy Case in Egypt

A 2015 legal case in Egypt making international media headlines and resulting in a partial victory involved three men who said that they believe in the important role of information freedom: a Canadian journalist named Mohamed Fahmy (who also held Egyptian citizenship); an Egyptian producer, Baher Mohamed; and an Australian reporter, Peter Greste. All three were convicted in 2014 on charges that they communicated with and funded the banned Muslim Brotherhood, a political party overthrown in a military coup in 2013. All three sat in an Egyptian prison from December 29, 2013, until February 1, 2015, when the Australian reporter was released and deported back to his homeland—after the head of Australia intervened on his behalf (Galloway 2015b).

Egyptian president Abdel Fattah el-Sissi said that he could expel foreign nationals who had been convicted in Egypt and were being held in an Egyptian prison. Given Peter Greste's prison release on February 1, 2015, the same positive fate was expected immediately for Mohamed Fahmy, who renounced his Egyptian citizenship in 2014 and welcomed positive interventions by Canada's foreign minister, John Baird, to get his rapid release from prison and his return to Canada—where his fiancé was waiting for him. There was considerably less hope for the freedom of the Egyptian producer (Galloway 2015b).

In a surprise turn of events, though, after spending more than 14 months behind bars for the crime of being a journalist in postrevolutionary Egypt, Mr. Fahmy thought that he was on his way home to Canada in the second week of February—but was informed that on January 1, 2015, his conviction had been stayed by an appeals court and a new trial was ordered. Upon hearing this negative news, there were renewed calls from journalists to have Canadian prime minister Steven Harper intervene on the journalist's behalf (Crawley and Walmsley 2015b).

Though the appeal trial was scheduled to begin on February 12, 2015, on February 11, 2015, Egypt's president said that he was considering amnesty for Fahmy and his Egyptian colleague. The president noted that the case of the three Al Jazeera journalists, the focus of an international campaign for press freedom, had become a headache for him; he would like to convince the Western world that he was a sensible leader dedicated to democracy and human rights. "I never wished these problems on myself. They harm Egypt's reputation," he affirmed. Though the three journalists were convicted of conspiring with the banned Muslim Brotherhood to spread false news online, there was no consistency in their sentencing. Mr. Greste and Mr. Fahmy were sentenced to 7 years in jail, while Mr. Mohamed was given 10 years. The retrial was to take place because the deputy head of Egypt's highest court of appeal cited a lack of evidence at the original trial. He said that the violence requirement for the terrorism charge was not met, and that the defendants were under pressure to confess (Galloway 2015c, A3).

On the morning of February 12, 2015, following ongoing interventions by the Canadian government, the trial for Mr. Fahmy began in Egypt. Mr. Fahmy's brother Adel said that when Canada's former foreign minister was in Cairo, he made an unacceptable diplomatic error in proclaiming publically that Mr. Fahmy would not be retried in Canada if he were deported. He went on to say (Mackrael and Stevenson 2015, A10): "This is not just about Mohamed, it's about all innocent Canadians who could find themselves in prison in the Middle East or elsewhere. . . . All we've seen is mistakes and mild rhetoric—this does not portray the government as one that stands for free expression. . . . A conservative approach by the government at a time of such urgency has failed us and left Mohamed behind bars for perhaps another year as this retrial continues."

As the trial opened for Mr. Fahmy on February, 12, 2015, he got some partially good news. Though he had to withstand a rehearing, he could be put on bail until the next court hearing if his family paid about $40,000—which his brother Adel did on hearing this request. If there were any hope at this point, it was that although the Egyptian government still had the authority to deport Mr. Fahmy, it might wait for his hearing to resume on February 23, 2015, or later. Unfortunately, the retrial that was to resume in February was delayed until March 8, 2015, and delayed again after that when key prosecution witnesses failed to appear at the scheduled March court session where they had been slated for cross-examination (Galloway, Mackrael, and Stevenson 2015; Stevenson and Mackrael 2015; Malsin and Mackrael 2015).

After several more distressing legal twists and turns for Mr. Fahmy, in September 2015, Mr. Fahmy and his Egyptian co-defendant, Baher Mohamed, received an Egyptian presidential pardon. On October 11, 2015—one day before Canadian Thanksgiving—Mr. Fahmy returned home to Canada with his wife. "This is what I've been waiting for," Mr. Fahmy said while landing in Toronto. "I felt humbled and safe seeing the kind and heartfelt vibes from the police officers and security at the airport who were extremely hospitable and recognized my face despite my attempts to keep my arrival quiet. It was mind-boggling that the cab driver, passengers on the flight, and strangers recognized me in the airport and knew the details of my story. I felt lots of warmth and love" (The Canadian Press 2015, A8).

Generally speaking, from a global perspective, where there are low tolerance levels for information freedom and Internet freedom, there is a greater degree of Internet censorship. "Freedom of information is the foundation of any democracy. Yet almost half of the world's population is still denied it" (Reporters Without Borders 2012). Let's look at how these three terms are defined and implemented from a macro-system perspective.

Freedom of Information Defined

Freedom of information generally refers to a citizen's right to access information held by the government. In many developed countries such as the United States and Canada, this freedom is supported as a constitutional right. In the United

States, for example, the Freedom of Information Act (FOIA), Title 5, U.S. Code, Section 552, was signed into law on July 4, 1966, by President Lyndon B. Johnson. Afterward, the FOIA was amended a number of times—in 1974, 1986, and in 1996 with the enactment of the Electronic Freedom of Information Act Amendment of 1996. The FOIA requires U.S. federal agencies to make public records available to citizens both electronically and through public reading rooms.

Though the FOIA applies to records created and kept by agencies in the executive branch of the federal government, such as the Department of Energy, it does not apply to Congress, the judicial branch of the federal government, or to state or local governments. Nevertheless, many state governments in the United States have enacted open records laws to support the Freedom of Information Act (U.S. Department of Energy 2013).

Cleary, the FOIA in the United States was created to broaden access to government information to citizens, regardless of whether the venue is online or on land. The Freedom of Information law in the United States and similar laws in other countries were established to have transparency, government accountability, public protection against mismanagement or corruption, and general education for citizens. In the United States and elsewhere, related human rights include such protections as freedom of expression, data protection privacy, and the freedom of association. It is important to emphasize that more than 70 countries with government representation have approved similar freedom of information legislation. For example, in China, the Freedom of Government Information Act has been in effect since December 28, 2005 (Janssen 2013).

Internet Freedom Defined

To show that they support, in varying degrees, Internet freedom, around the globe, governments have adopted diverse legal and policy decisions as a response to increased access to Internet-based communication technologies for their citizens. Sometimes the motives for endorsing Internet-based technologies includes emphasizing cultural norms or transmitting to the masses key political objectives. One rather convenient way to profess some degree of Internet freedom is to set up a series of Internet cafes so that citizens in more urban areas, at least, can have Internet access. Speaking in January 2010, then–U.S. secretary of state Hillary Clinton compared the spread of Internet-driven information networks to "a new nervous system for our planet." She said, "[I]n many respects, information has never been so free. [But also] we've seen a spike in threats to the free flow of information" (U.S. Department of State 2010, 1).

As for defining what "Internet freedom" is on a macro-system basis, that is a more difficult problem. From a rhetorical point of view, most global citizens and their government leaders will espouse support for the concept of Internet freedom. But what "freedom" is, per se, means many different things to various citizens and governments, primarily because culture plays such a huge factor in defining life and one's priorities in life. This normative divergence plays out in debates over access to information and education, threats to freedom, online content controls, and Internet governance in general. In short, the concept of "Internet freedom" holds within it a series of conflicts about how the Internet should function. Consequently, accepting these tensions appears to be a sound approach in defining the term *Internet freedom* (Bambauer 2010).

From this angle, several realistic statements about the premises underlying Internet freedom can be made (Bambauer 2010):

- First, in order to enjoy the wide range of content available on the Internet 24/7, citizens need to have access to the Internet. Countries and nation-states vary in their access policies for citizens. For example, in the United States, the ability to "go online" is treated more like a market access privilege issue than as an entitlement. Simply stated, if citizens can afford to pay for access to the Internet, they are welcome to do so, but if they cannot afford to have a private account, they are dependent on Web sites available to the public—such as those found at libraries or in schools. In contrast, Finland has a policy whereby having a 1 MB connection to high-speed broadband is a basic right for all citizens. Also, France's Constitutional Council has declared that high-speed broadband access is a legal right for all citizens.
- Second, countries and nation-states vary on the question, "Free *from whom* or *from what*?" One threat in some countries is that the nation-state can actually impinge online liberties in a myriad of ways, ranging from criminalizing online speech or conduct, to monitoring messages communicated over the Internet, or blocking material on the Internet altogether. While Americans tend to be focused on preventing unchecked governmental powers, other countries such as those in Europe are concerned about the vast amounts of personal information about online users that corporations have accumulated—and may misuse. Over the past several years, the latter fear seems to have been substantiated to some degree—accepting, for example, the controversy generated over Google's video service in Italy and Google's Street View geo-mapping projects in numerous jurisdictions that raised concerns about adequate privacy protections for citizens.
- Third, liability for "inappropriate" Web site content varies from country to country. In some countries, for example, there is a need to prevent impingements on one's freedom generated by other users, such as concerns about the harm that may be done to one's reputation should someone decide to place false and highly

defamatory content on Web pages. For this reason, some governments have a policy requiring Internet service providers and social networking Web sites to police questionable content so as to avoid liability suits, while other countries have policies that provide immunity for anyone but the author of such content.

- Fourth, there is little question that different countries and nation-states "balance" in a variety of ways "freedom of expression" and "access to information" against "concerns about the harm caused by perceived 'offensive content.'" Generally, there is concern about *harm* done to individual citizens (such as online defamation of someone's character), religious or ethnic minorities, or common and prioritized societal values. For example, the United States views the free exchange of information as "weighty enough" to displace concerns of a competing nature—which helps to explain why so-called "offensive" materials like hate speech and pornography are protected by the U.S. Constitution. Having said this, however, the U.S. Constitution does prohibit certain online threats like child pornography and obscene materials—those perceived to surpass established community standards of tolerance. In contrast, while European countries like France and Germany adhere to and strongly protect "open expression" online, both countries ban online pornographic content. Finally, in Saudi Arabia, where the bulk of citizens are followers of the Sunni segment of Islam, Web sites featuring tenets of the Baha'i faith or the Shia teachings of Islam have their content blocked by government authorities.

Thus, given these four factors, if one were to view "Internet freedom" as protecting unfettered expression online, this liberty is counterbalanced in various degrees by competing concerns even within countries and jurisdictions. As stated, this counterbalancing of competing factors occurs even in countries having a history of strongly protecting citizens' free speech (Bambauer 2010).

Finally, countries vary in their perception of *who should actually govern Internet freedom and how this process should occur*. Clearly, this debate has been ongoing since the Internet "went commercial." Given that the U.S. government created the Internet's initial architecture during its early stages when it was known as ARPAnet, to this day the United States maintains some degree of control over the workings of the Internet because of the strong connection between the U.S. Department of Commerce and ICANN (the Internet Corporation for Assigned Names and Numbers), which is primarily responsible for overseeing the Domain Name System (Schell 2007).

While the United States has strongly protested against the transfer of ICANN's functions to other entities because of its strong belief that putting the Internet under international control would weaken freedom of expression, in particular, other countries have argued vehemently that moving forward, there needs to be a larger voice in decision making about the Internet's underlying protocols and standards. Many countries believe that the Internet is currently overrun by America's fixation to properly balance privacy, security, trust, and Internet censorship (PSTC) issues. This debate has reared its controversial head in a number of venues, such as in the World Summit on the Information Society (WSIS).

While the Australian government argued for mandatory Internet filtering, other government officials argued that such filtering is too broad. In closing, countries having access to the Internet tend to not only hold different views about what constitutes "Internet freedom," but they also have vastly different views on how the latter can actually be achieved—and by whom. Perhaps, notes Bambauer (2010), "Internet freedom" is a term that should be abandoned for now, because in a real-world sense, it is too general to be useful.

Internet Censorship Defined

When governments try to control citizens' online activities, restrict the free flow of information, and infringe on the rights of online users, all of these actions are called "Internet censorship." Since about 2005, attempts to maintain Internet freedom and openness have been challenged in a number of countries. Moreover, the methods used to control content on the Internet by governments are also becoming increasingly sophisticated, whether in developed or in developing nations.

The Role of Web Filters and Firewalls Aimed at Internet Censorship

Now we will discuss how various countries and jurisdictions around the globe use Web filters and firewalls to censor content on the Internet.

Based on the types and numbers of controls implemented to engage in Internet censorship, the editors of *Freedom on the Net 2012* classified countries in one of three content-censoring categories (Kelly, Cook, and Truong 2012, 3–4):

1. **Blockers**: Here, the government blocks a large number of politically relevant Web sites and certain social media platforms. The government also places considerable resources into hiring people with the right kind of talent and technical capacities to identify "offensive" content that should be blocked. In 2012, countries considered to be "blockers" included Bahrain, China, Ethiopia, Iran, Saudi Arabia, Vietnam, Syria, Thailand, and Uzbekistan. Blocking and filtering have been the key tools for implementing Internet censorship in these jurisdictions, but the authorities have also used intense pressure on bloggers and Internet service providers, hired progovernment commentators to advance their

positions, and arrested online users posting comments deemed to be critical of the authorities.

2. **Nonblockers:** Here, the government is not yet at the stage of systematically blocking politically relevant Web sites, although the authorities may have restricted online content, especially after noticing the critical role that online tools can play in overturning the political "status quo." Typically, the authorities like to show that they respect Internet freedom and openness, so they tend to use less visible or less traceable censorship tactics. They may engage in, for example, "anonymous" cyberattacks targeting influential news sites at the "right" political moment. Moreover, these jurisdictions may adopt a harsh legal framework around free speech; it is not unlikely, in fact, that online users who post information critical of the government will find themselves charged, detained, or arrested—as a number of cases in this chapter have shown. Countries in this category in 2012 included Azerbaijan, Egypt, Jordan, Malaysia, Venezuela, and Zimbabwe.
3. **Nascent blockers**: Here, the governments appear to be at a crossroad; though the authorities impose politically motivated blocks, the blocks tend to be sporadic, and the blocking system is far from being institutionalized. Countries in this category in 2012 included Belarus, Sri Lanka, Pakistan, and Russia. In Russia, for example, government authorities officially block content considered to promote "extremism" but because of the range attributable to this term, political Web sites tend to be blocked as well.

It is quite clear that the motivations for Internet censorship vary from country to country, ranging from the blocking of, say, unsuitable content that should not be seen by minors (which is what parents also commonly do to prevent their children from viewing Web sites with pornography, gambling, hate speech, or chat rooms) to completely controlling a nation's access to information. There are several software products on the market that can limit or block access to specific Web sites and are known as "Web filters."

Most Web filters use two main techniques to block content (Strickland 2013):

1. **Blacklists**: Lists of websites that the Web filter's creators have designated as undesirable. These tend to change over time, so most companies marketing this software offer updated lists for free. The bottom line is that once this software is installed, any attempt to visit a blocked site fails.
2. **Keyword Blocking**: With keyword blocking, the software actually scans a Web page as the user tries to visit it. The program quickly analyzes the Web page to determine if certain keywords exist, and if the program determines that the Web page is "inappropriate," it blocks users' access to the page.

Another common option for blocking content is by installing a firewall. In essence, a computer firewall provides protection from dangerous or undesirable content. Firewalls can be either software or hardware; their purpose is to act as a barrier between the Internet and the computer network. Firewalls are designed to allow only safe content through and to prevent everything else from entering the network. Firewalls tend to require considerable IT skill for implementation and maintenance, and for this reason, businesses and government agencies employ network administrators. In short, firewalls contain rule sets that either grant or deny traffic flowing into or out of a network; simply put, firewalls are to the perimeter of a network what a moat and wall are to a castle (Schell and Martin 2006).

Business-Government Policies and Laws for Internet Censorship

There is no question that if companies want to do business in various countries and jurisdictions worldwide, they have to be careful to abide by national policies and laws pertaining to Internet freedom, openness, and censorship. Let's face it: Businesses and government agencies, alike, rely on firewalls as well as Web filtering software. Thus, by using firewalls, both can literally "pick and choose" which Web pages or even entire domains to block. This way, companies and government agencies can avoid blocking Web sites that employees or citizens need to access legitimately. Even in countries deemed to be "free," when an online user tries to access a restricted Web site, he or she will see a message that typically includes the option of petitioning the network administrator to unblock access if he or she feels that the Web site is wrongfully blocked. Afterward, the network administrator can adjust which Web sites are restricted through firewall settings. (Strickland 2013).

Further, in blocking various Web sites, government agencies rely on cooperation from businesses like telecom and cable companies, for they play a critical role in determining what content customers or citizens can access on the Internet—which is, by the way, an ongoing debate in jurisdictions worldwide.

For example, in the United States, there is an ongoing debate over a concept called "Net neutrality," which refers to a so-called level playing ground where Internet service providers (ISPs) allow access to all content without favoring any particular Web site. There are, of course, opponents of this concept, and in the United States, telecom and cable companies have successfully petitioned the Supreme Court to dismiss it. Without Net neutrality, ISPs can charge content providers a fee for bandwidth usage such that the content providers paying the fee will have greater broadband access. With more broadband access, there is a faster loading of Web sites compared to the competitors who choose not to pay the fee.

So, let's say that Yahoo paid the fee to an ISP but Google chose not to; consequently, the ISP's clients would find that Yahoo's search engine loads much more quickly than Google's. Proponents of "Net neutrality" maintain that such preferential treatment is simply Internet censorship. Recently, search engine companies like Yahoo and Google have been criticized by censorship opponents for helping restrictive countries like China to maintain control of the Internet. Though the companies may have their headquarters in the United States, they still need to obey local government restrictions if they want to do business in any jurisdiction (Strickland 2013).

Moreover, one would be naïve to think that any country is totally "free" from Internet censorship, for even democratic countries restrict access to content on the Internet at some level. Though labeled "free," even the United States has laws (such as the Children's Internet Protection Act) that impact the kind of information that citizens can access on the Internet, even in public spaces like schools or public libraries.

The OpenNet Initiative (ONI), an organization dedicated to letting the public know about Web filtering and surveillance policies globally, tends to classify Web filtering into four purposes consistent with the tenets of prevailing laws in any given jurisdiction (Strickland 2013):

1. **Political**: Content belonging to Web sites that include views counter to the respective countries' policies regarding the Internet and allowable content. This category also includes Web site content related to human rights, religious movements, and other causes of a social nature.
2. **Social**: Content belonging to Web sites that focus on sexuality, gambling, drugs, and other social-cultural issues that a country's authorities may find offensive.
3. **Conflict/Security**: Content belonging to Web sites relating to wars, skirmishes, overt dissent, and other conflicts occurring either within a nation or in some other nation.
4. **Internet Tools**: Content belonging to Web sites offering tools like e-mail, instant messaging, language translation applications, and those aimed at circumventing censorship.

Some democratic countries like Australia and the United Kingdom—deemed by Freedom House to be "free" in 2012—are fairly liberal with their government-business policies and laws restricting a minimum of Web pages. Yet other countries, such as China and Iran, have more restrictive government-business policies and laws and were deemed by Freedom House in 2012 to be "not free." China's advanced filtering system, known internationally as "the Great Firewall of China," is intensely restrictive, and it can actually search new Web pages and restrict access in real time. This advanced filtering system can also search blogs for subversive content and block Internet users from visiting them (Kelly, Cook, and Truong 2012).

Alternative Tactics for Restricting Free Speech and Encouraging Internet Censorship

While, as noted, blocking and filtering the content of Web sites are two of the preferred methods of restricting citizens' access to online content, other countries are increasingly using four main tools to "put the lid" on political and social speech deemed by the authorities to be offensive, in excess of established community standards, or a means of intentionally offending the existing authority structure or its preaching. These alternative tactics include the following four major actions (Kelly, Cook, and Truong 2012):

1. Governments introduce vague laws prohibiting certain types of online content.
2. Governments proactively manipulate Internet discussions so as to reflect their followings.
3. Governments arrange for actual physical attacks to occur against bloggers and other Internet users whose speech is deemed to be "offensive" and "inappropriate."
4. Governments arrange for increased surveillance of citizens' online activities.

VERY RECENT TRENDS IN INTERNET CENSORSHIP ACCORDING TO *FREEDOM ON THE NET 2014*

Threat Findings from *Freedom on the Net 2014*

According to a study entitled *Freedom on the Net 2014: Tightening the Net: Governments Expand Online Controls*, some very recent trends on Internet censorship support the concerns of online citizens—who have voiced openly that we now live in a world of ubiquitous Internet censorship and surveillance (Kelly et al. 2015). These 2014 trends cited by the editors are as follows:

- Internet freedom globally has dropped for the fourth consecutive year, with an increase in countries introducing online censorship and monitoring practices that are more aggressive and more sophisticated in targeting individual online users.
- Before, censorious governments tended to adhere to more covert approaches to Internet control through blocking and filtering (which are still widely used),

but now the trend is to quickly adopt new laws legitimizing repression and criminalizing online dissent. Consequently, more online users are being imprisoned for their Internet activities, online media outlets are being pressured to censor or to face stiff legal sanctions, and private companies are being told bluntly to comply with government requests for data on online users (who may prove to be an assumed terrorist threat) or for immediate deletions of certain content. The good news is that since 2013, less physical violence is being used on online citizens by governments.

- Some countries used the news of widespread Internet surveillance by the U.S. National Security Agency (NSA), spread by Edward Snowden, to augment their own monitoring capabilities of online users, frequently with little or no oversight and often aimed at online political opposition leaders and human rights activists (i.e., hacktivists).
- Syria was the most dangerous country in the world for journalists, with dozens killed in 2014, while progovernment hackers reportedly infected 10,000 computers with malware disguised as warnings against potential cyberattacks. Also in 2014, Iran held the position of the worst country for advancing Internet freedom.
- Of the 65 countries assessed by Freedom House in 2014 for various degrees of Internet freedom, 36 experienced a negative trajectory since May 2013, with the greatest declines occurring in Russia, Turkey, and Ukraine. The Russian government increased control over the Internet, particularly before the Sochi Olympic Games and during the ongoing crisis in Ukraine. In Turkey, the government blocked social media, paid for cyberattacks against opposition news sites, and assaulted online journalists during 2014. Ukraine decreased its score in Internet freedom in 2014, because the government targeted social-media users and online journalists during the Euromaidan protests, the government paid for many cyberattacks against targets, and ousted president Viktor Yanukovych conducted online surveillance of hacktivists, journalists, and opposition leaders.
- In 2014, the greatest increases in Internet freedom occurred in India and Brazil. In India, authorities relaxed restrictions on Internet access, and in Brazil, following years of debates and amendments, lawmakers approved a bill known as "the Marco Civil da Internet," containing important provisions governing Net neutrality and ensuring strong privacy protections for online citizens.
- The bottom line for 2014 was that Iran, Syria, and China were the world's worst abusers of Internet freedom of all 65 nations assessed by Freedom House. Online users in China were intimidated and arrested during crackdowns regarding online "rumors" as President Xi Jinping consolidated rigid control over social media.

- From May 2013 to May 2014, 41 of the 65 countries assessed by Freedom House passed or proposed legislation to penalize legitimate forms of online speech, to increase the government's right to more forcefully control online content, and to expand the government's online surveillance capabilities.
- In 2014, worldwide, more people were detained or prosecuted for their digital activities than ever before. Even more alarming is that in some jurisdictions, Internet users were in some cases tried in court for not only what they posted online but for content they might post. For example, in Thailand, a man was given a prison sentence of seven years after police confiscated his computer and found pictures deemed to be insulting to the king. He was convicted of attempting to commit lèse-majesté (a charge with no legal basis), as investigators argued that he intended to later upload the material to the Internet.

Emerging Threats According to Freedom House

Besides the clear infringements on Internet freedom resulting from the growth in restrictive laws and the arrests of online users and journalists globally in 2014, Freedom House identified three emerging threats that will further put the rights of Internet users at increased risk. These emerging threats include the following (Kelly et al. 2015):

1. There will be more data storage localization, as private companies will be required to keep data storage centers within a given country to maintain greater government control over confidential information being stored there.
2. There will be an even harsher online environment for women and members of the LGBTI (lesbian, gay, bisexual, transgender, and intersex) community—who are currently underrepresented in the virtual world relative to members in mainstream society and who have been consistently and disproportionately harassed for their online activities.
3. There will continue to be a lack of cybersecurity for hacktivists and political opposition members in various jurisdictions worldwide; these individuals have become increasingly targeted for technical attacks and spying by repressive governments.

CONCLUSION

This chapter looked at the complex and increasingly tangled legal environment in various jurisdictions around the globe regarding online offensive and obscene content, as well as Internet censorship. We reviewed the individual cases of imprisoned online citizens in some jurisdictions (such as Mohamed Fahmy) and heard about media headline makers and self-proclaimed Information freedom fighters like Julian Assange, Bradley Manning, and Edward Snowden. We observed some disturbing trends noted by the authors of *Freedom of the Net 2014*, seeing a rather dramatic growth in numerous jurisdictions of governments passing in a rapid fashion surveillance measures aimed at so-called terrorists and politically active online citizens.

We closed the chapter by looking at three emerging threats: (1) an increase in the localizations of data and data centers to enable governments to have greater control over confidential information stored within their boundaries, (2) an increase in threats to online members of the LGBTI protected classes, and (3) increased surveillance by governments regarding political opponents and hacktivists.

But the reality is that we should all worry about cell phone and computer searches, not just the hacktivists among us. Sadly, even in jurisdictions like the United States and Canada, which have deemed themselves supporters of Internet and information freedom, legislation is being rapidly passed to give police access to citizens' communications, private pictures, telephone call logs, records of places the citizens have been, and other private details of their lives. For example, on December 11, 2014, the Supreme Court of Canada effectively made this kind of information available when it ruled that police can, without a warrant, search the cell phones of citizens under arrest for certain conditions. Surely, this decision is a major step backward in the ongoing struggle to protect citizens' digital privacy (Kowalski 2015).

Furthermore, though laws have been and could be passed to keep a closer eye on citizens' digital particulars, there is little surprise to discover that industry is creating its own unique technological solutions to provide added information security protection to critical data. In March 2015, for example, BlackBerry introduced a tablet computer aimed at government and corporate customers that it claims can let users access consumer applications like YouTube and WhatsApp while keeping confidential work-related information from worrisome spies or cybercrooks. The SecuTABLET, shown at the CeBIT conference in Hanover, Germany, in the spring of 2015, utilizes special software to wrap applications holding secrets into a virtual container where they cannot be harmed by malware. Interestingly, Germany's computer security watchdog has begun a process to certify the device for classified government and corporate communications (Rahn 2015).

REFERENCES

Bambauer, D. (2010). The enigma of Internet freedom. Retrieved from http://infousa.state.gov/media/internet/docs/defining-internet-freedom.pdf

Barrett, D., & Chen, T.-P. (2013, June 24). U.S. scrambles to snare Snowden as he flees Hong Kong. *The Globe and Mail*, pp. A1, A11.

Bilefsky, D. (2015, October 13). Scotland Yard ends 24-hour watch on Assange. *The Globe and Mail*, p. A2.

Black, I. (2015a). A look at the writings of Saudi blogger Raif Badawi—sentenced to 1,000 lashes. Retrieved from http://www.theguardian.com/world/2015/jan/14/-sp-saudi-blogger-extracts-raif-badawi

Black, I. (2015b). Planned flogging of Saudi blogger Raif Badawi postponed again. Retrieved from http://www.theguardian.com/world/2015/jan/22/flogging-saudi-blogger-raif-badawi-postponed

Blake, A., Gellman, B., & Miller, G. (2013, June 10). NSA secrets leaker revealed. *Las Vegas Review-Journal*, pp. A1, A4.

Bradshaw, J. (2015, January 31). Securing Snowden. *The Globe and Mail*, p. A13.

The Canadian Press. (2015, October 15). Journalist Fahmy back in Canada. *The Globe and Mail*, p. A8.

Carsten, P. (2015, February 16). China drops U.S. brands for state technology purposes. *The Globe and Mail*, p. B14.

Circa. (2015). Russian intelligence sought to recruit Snowden. Retrieved from http://cir.ca/news/edward-snowden-nsa-leaker

Crawley, P., & Walmsley, D. (2015a, February 6). An anti-terrorism bill that's anti-everything. *The Globe and Mail*, p. A10.

Crawley, P., & Walmsley, D. (2015b, February 10). Mohamed Fahmy: Mr. Harper, please pick up the phone. *The Globe and Mail*, p. A12.

Dishneau, D. (2013, June 12). Leaks revealed tactics, evidence suggests. *Las Vegas Review-Journal*, p. A8.

Dishneau, D., & Jelinek, P. (2013, August 15). WikiLeaker sorry "actions hurt people." *The Globe and Mail*, p. A14.

Drews, K. (2013, February 19). Craigslist crusader hunts Internet haters. *The Globe and Mail*, p. A8.

Freedom House. (2012). New report: Governments grow increasingly repressive online, activists fight back. Retrieved from https://freedomhouse.org/article/new-report-governments-grow-increasingly-repressive-online-activists-fight-back

Freeze, C., & Dobby, C. (2015, March 17). RBC, Rogers named in NSA papers. *The Globe and Mail*, pp. A1, A9.

Galloway, G. (2015a, January 30). Wife of Saudi blogger seeks Harper's help. *The Globe and Mail*, p. A9.

Galloway, G. (2015b, February 3). Fahmy's release imminent, Baird says. *The Globe and Mail*, p. A3.

Galloway, G. (2015c, February 11). President el-Sissi gives hope for Fahmy's release. *The Globe and Mail*, p. A3.

Galloway, G., Mackrael, K., & Stevenson, T. (2015, February 13). Fahmy gets bail as Cairo signals it will let court decide his fate. *The Globe and Mail*, pp. A1, A7.

Goodale, J. C. (1997). The First Amendment and freedom of the press. *Issues of Democracy, 2,* 4.

Graber, D. A. (2003). Styles of image management during crises: Justifying press censorship. *Discourse & Society, 14,* 539–557.

Greenberg, A. (2010). An interview with WikiLeaks' Julian Assange. Retrieved from http://www.forbes.com/sites/andygreenberg/2010/11/29/an-interview-with-wikileaks-julian-assange/

Halvorssen, T. (2012). Nobel laureate Liu Xiabo's imprisonment a painful reminder of China's dictatorship. Retrieved from http://www.huffingtonpost.com/thor-halvorssen/nobel-laureate-liu-xiaobo_b_1166012.html

Harrell, E. (2010). Defending the leaks: A & A with WikiLeaks' Julian Assange. Retrieved from http://content.time.com/time/world/article/0,8599,2006789,00.html

Hayes, A. F., Glynn, C. J., & Shanahan, J. (2005). Willingness to self-censor: A construct and measurement tool for public opinion research. *International Journal of Public Opinion Research, 17,* 298–323.

Henry, J. S. (2009). Beyond free speech: Novel approaches to hate on the Internet in the United States. *Information and Communications Technology Law, 18,* 235–251.

Jakes, L. (2013, June 11). US spying raises fresh anger. *Las Vegas Review-Journal*, pp. A1, A6.

Janssen, C. (2013). Technopedia explains freedom of information. Retrieved from http://www.techopedia.com/definition/24976/freedom-of-information

Kelly, S., Cook, S., & Truong, M. (2012). *Freedom on the Net 2012: A global assessment of Internet and digital media*. New York, NY: Freedom House.

Kelly, S., Earp, M., Reed, L., Shahbaz, A., & Truong, M. (2015). Freedom on the Net 2014: Tightening the Net: Governments expand online controls. Retrieved from https://www.freedomhouse.org/sites/default/files/resources/FOTN%202014%20Summary%20of%20Findings.pdf

Khatchadourian, R. (2011). Manning, Assange, and the Espionage Act. Retrieved from http://www.newyorker.com/news/news-desk/manning-assange-and-the-espionage-act

Kowalski, W. (2015, March 16). Supreme Court: We all should worry about phone searchers. *The Globe and Mail*, p. A11.

Lynch, E. M. (2010). Adam Segal discusses US-China relations in a cyber world. Retrieved from http://chinalawandpolicy.com/2010/04/14/adam-segal-discusses-u-s-china-relations-in-a-cyber-world/

MacKinnon, M. (2012, December 7). Nobel laureate's wife a prisoner in her home. *The Globe and Mail*, p. A20.

Mackrael, K., & Stevenson, T. (2015, February 12). Ottawa makes last-minute diplomatic efforts ahead of Fahmy trial. *The Globe and Mail*, pp. A1, A10.

Malsin, J., & Mackrael, K. (2015, March 9). Fahmy in legal limbo after retrial postponed. *The Globe and Mail*, p. S4.

Miller, A. (2015). Edward Snowden speaks to Toronto students, urges caution on new terror bill. Retrieved from https://ca.news.yahoo.com/edward-snowden-speaks-toronto-students-urges-caution-terror-013631537.html

Myers, S., & Kramer, A. (2013, August 2). Snowden thanks Russia after being granted temporary asylum for a year. *The Globe and Mail*, p. A3.

Nolen, S., Freeze, C., & Chase, S. (2013, October 9). Cyberwar threatens Brazil rift. *The Globe and Mail*, pp. A1, A16.

O'Brien, M. (2010). Republican wants WikiLeaks labelled as a terrorist group. Retrieved from http://thehill.com/blogs/blog-briefing-room/news/130863-top-republican-designate-wikileaks-as-a-terrorist-org

Paramaribo, S. (2013, August 31). Ecuador rebukes Assange for mocking Australian politicians in video. *The Globe and Mail*, p. A20.

Perry, R., & Zarsky, T. Z. (2014). Liability for online anonymous speech: Comparative and economic analyses. *Journal of European Tort Law*, *5*, 205–256.

Rahn, C. (2015, March 16). Technology: BlackBerry boosts security to woo corporate users. *The Globe and Mail*, p. B3.

Renzetti, E. (2015, February 21). Snowden's message to citizens: Democracy itself is threatened. *The Globe and Mail*, p. A2.

Reporters Without Borders. (2012). Who we are? Retrieved from http://en.rsf.org/who-we-are-12-09-2012,32617.html

Reuters. (2010). Hard case for US against Wikileak's Assange: Lawyers. Retrieved from http://www.reuters.com/article/2010/12/01/us-wikileaks-legal-idUSTRE6B00F020101201

Savage, C. (2013, June 4). Leaker portrayed as "good-intentioned" and a traitor. *The Globe and Mail*, p. A3.

Savage, C., & Huetteman, E. (2013, August 22). Manning's 35-year sentence "the longest in a leak case." *The Globe and Mail*, p. A3.

Schell, B. H. (2007). *Contemporary world issues: The Internet and society*. Santa Barbara, CA: ABC-CLIO.

Schell, B. H. (2014). *Contemporary world issues: Internet censorship*. Santa Barbara, CA: ABC-CLIO.

Schell, B., & Martin, C. (2006). *Webster's new world hacker dictionary*. Indianapolis, IN: Wiley.

Simpson, I. (2013, June 5). Witness at Manning trial focuses on motives. *The Globe and Mail*, p. A11.

Southey, T. (2015, February 28). Bill C-51: The Nickelback of legislation. *The Globe and Mail*, p. F3.

Stevenson, T., & Mackrael, K. (2015, February 24). Fahmy retrial begins with a misfire. *The Globe and Mail*, p. A12.

Strickland, J. (2013). How Internet censorship works. Retrieved from http://computer.howstuffworks.com/internet-censorship.htm

Thefreedictionary.com. (2015). Obscenity. Retrieved from http://legaldictionary.thefreedictionary.com/obscenity

Timm, T. (2015). The war on leaks has gone way too far when journalists' emails are under surveillance. Retrieved from http://www.theguardian.com/commentisfree/2015/jan/25/war-on-leaks-gone-way-too-far-journalist-emails-are-under-surveillance

U.S. Department of Energy. (2013). What is the Freedom of Information Act (FOIA)? Retrieved from http://www.wipp.energy.gov/library/foia/foiadefined.htm

U.S. Department of State. (2010). e journal: Defining Internet freedom. Retrieved from http://infousa.state.gov/media/internet/docs/defining-internet-freedom.pdf

Weissenstein, M. (2013, July 1). Ecuador president says Snowden can't leave Moscow. *The Globe and Mail*, p. A7.

Wente, M. (2015, February 21). Freedom of religion: Why Mr. Harper is playing niqab politics. *The Globe and Mail*, p. F2.

Wielawski, I. M. (2005). For troops, home can be too close. Retrieved from http://www.nytimes.com/2005/03/15/health/psychology/15fami.html?pagewanted=print&position=&_r=0

Chapter 8

Online Personal Health Records and Health Services

The person with the least access to data in the system is the patient. You can get it, but the burden is always on the patient. And it is scattered across many different silos of patient data.

—Steven Keating, doctoral student at the Massachusetts Institute of Technology's Media Lab (Lohr 2015)

OVERVIEW

The Internet is quickly becoming a widely used resource for health information by online users around the globe, with 2011 estimates suggesting that as many as 71% of U.K. citizens used it at least once to find health information, compared to just 37% in 2005 (Dutton and Blank 2011). Similar trends have been reported elsewhere, particularly where citizens have ready access to information on the Internet. For example, in the United States, 72% of American adult Internet users say they looked online for health information in 2014 (Pew Research Center 2015).

THE U.S. HITECH ACT

On February 17, 2009, U.S. President Obama signed into law the Health Information Technology for Economic and Clinical Health (HITECH) Act as a means of stimulating in the United States the adoption of electronic health records (EHRs) rather than continued reliance on paper records (often called PHRs or patient health records). Besides supporting the development and application of secure emerging technologies built to withstand hackers' exploits, the HITECH Act was considered to be part of the economic stimulus bill known as the American Recovery and Reinvestment Act (ARRA) of 2009. Similar acts have been passed in other jurisdictions, including the European Union, Australia, and Japan (Rouse 2009).

The HITECH Act stipulated that, starting in 2011, health care providers in the United States would be offered incentives for demonstrating the meaningful use of EHRs, with incentives for usage being given out until 2015. After this date, penalties would be levied on government agencies and businesses not demonstrating such uses. The HITECH Act also established grants to train the personnel required to support a health IT infrastructure (Rouse 2009).

MEDICAL RECORD LEGAL ACCESS DENIED: THE CASE OF AMERICAN STEVEN KEATING

But while the United States and other jurisdictions have recently passed legislation to move patient health records and health services online, pragmatically speaking, patients wanting access to their own medical records may not find it so easy to get. American Steven Keating is a real-world case in point. His doctors and medical experts view him as somewhat of a citizen of the future. Eight years ago, a brain scan showed that he had a slight abnormality but it was not worth worrying about, the medical doctors advised. During the eight years, Steven studied brain structure, its function, and the possible arrival of troublesome cells. In 2010, Steven had another brain scan, which again, the medical doctors advised, indicated no need to worry. As a result of his research over the years, Steven came to realize that his so-called brain abnormality was near the brain's olfactory center, so when he began experiencing whiffs of vinegar in the summer of 2014, he self-diagnosed himself as having "smell seizures." But Steven didn't stop there. He urged doctors to complete an MRI on his brain, and three weeks later, surgeons in Boston removed a cancerous tumor the size of a tennis ball from his brain (Lohr 2015).

At every stage of educating himself (and his physicians), the 26-year-old doctoral student at MIT's Media Lab pushed and prodded, he admits, to get his own medical information, plus he collected about 70 gigabytes of information on his own. Still, Steven says that he encountered a medical culture even in the progressive United States that was strongly resistant to sharing his own medical data with him—owing to tradition, conservative business practices, and legal concerns on behalf of the medical institutions. Yet, Steven's case illustrates what medical experts say could be gained if patients had full and easier access to their medical records. Better-informed patients are more likely to take better care of their health, comply with prescription drug routines, and even detect early warning signs—which is what Steven did. Dr. David Bates, the chief innovation officer at Brigham and Women's Hospital in the United States (where Steven Keating had his surgery), shared with the media (Lohr 2015, L7): "Today he is a big exception, but he is also a glimpse of what people will want: more and more information."

That said, some of the most advanced hospitals in the United States and elsewhere around the globe are just beginning to make patients' health records available to them. For example, Brigham and Women's Hospital as of April 2015 had 500,000 patients with Internet access to some of the information in their health records, including known medical conditions, prescribed medications, and test results. "This is what the next generation, which lives on data, is going to want," Keating maintains. "The person with the least access to data in the system is the patient. You can get it, but the burden is always on the patient. And it [the information] is scattered across many different silos of patient data" (Lohr 2015, L7). Because patient information is highly personal, even when the patients' names and other key identifiers are protected, health care providers and legal professionals raise major privacy concerns. While Keating admits that he is a strong believer in privacy, he believes that the benefits of giving patients access to their own medical information far outweigh the risks. Steven notes that younger people who have been reared using social networks and smartphones will not only want access to their own medial information but they will want to be able to share it with other people of their choosing.

MEDICAL RECORD ILLEGAL ACCESS: COMMUNITY HEALTH SYSTEMS HACKED

To say that patients, physicians, and health systems have major concerns about medical records being accessed illegally by hackers is real and serious, for patients' medical information is worth 10 times more than individuals' credit card numbers on the global black market. In August 2014, the FBI warned health care providers in the United States to guard against hack attacks after one of the largest U.S. hospital operators, Community Health Systems, said that Chinese hackers had illegally accessed its computer network and stolen the personal medical information of 4.5 million patients. Security experts maintain that mal-inclined hackers are increasingly targeting the $3 trillion U.S. health care industry, because many institutions continue to rely on outdated computer systems lacking the latest security features—which may have their own vulnerabilities. "As attackers discover new methods to make money, the health care industry is becoming a much riper target because of the ability to sell large batches of personal data for profit," said Dave Kennedy, an expert on health care security and CEO of TrustedSEC LLC. "Hospitals have low security," he adds, "so it's relatively easy for these hackers to get a large amount of personal data for medical fraud" (Humer and Finkle 2014).

While a number of online citizens have major concerns about cybercriminals stealing their credit card information to use it to buy things or to steal their identities and then commit crimes, few online citizens give careful thought to how medical identity theft may be even more lucrative. The medical data for sale on the black market include names, birthdates, policy numbers, diagnosis codes, and billing information for patients—information that patients believe health care providers will safeguard to maintain their clients' privacy, security, and trust.

"Privacy," by definition, is the state of being free from unauthorized access. "Security," by definition, is a sense of being protected from adversaries, particularly from those who do harm—unintentionally or otherwise—to property or to a person. IT Security issues include but are not limited to authentication, disaster recovery, intrusion detection and network management, malicious code software protection, physical security of networks, security policies, and wireless security. "Trust" is a complex concept studied by scholars from a number of disciplines. It is defined to be present in a business relationship when one partner willingly depends on an exchanging partner in whom one has confidence. The term "trust" can take on a number of different meanings, including the willingness of one partner to be vulnerable to the actions of the other, or the expectation that one partner will receive ethically bound behaviors from the other partner. IT security issues, in particular, center on maintaining trust in online or e-commerce transactions (Schell 2014).

Despite privacy, security, and trust principles, once fraudsters get access to medical information as a result of networks being hacked, they can use this data to create fake IDs to buy medical equipment or drugs that can be resold, or they can piece together a patient number with a false provider number and then file falsified claims with insurers (Humer and Finkle 2014).

So, how much would stolen medical record information cost the average black market criminal? According to Don Jackson, director of threat intelligence at PhishLabs, stolen health credentials can go for $10 each, which is about 10 or 20 times the value of a U.S. credit card number. Equally upsetting is the fact that the percentage of U.S. health care organizations reporting a network breach rose to 40% in 2013 from 20% in 2009, according to an annual survey by the Ponemon Institute (Humer and Finkle 2014).

In the United States, health care providers and insurers must publicly disclose data breaches affecting more than 500 people, but there are no laws in that jurisdiction requiring criminal prosecution. Consequently, the total cost of hack attacks on the health care system is difficult to ascertain. Insurance industry experts posit that hacking-related costs are ultimately passed on to Americans as part of rising health insurance premiums. Sometimes the health care provider doesn't disclose the breach in a timely fashion, and the consumer discovers that his or her credentials have been stolen only after someone tries to use his or her medical identity to get health services. Then, when unpaid bills are forwarded to debt collectors, the latter will search for the fraud victims and seek payment. There was a 2013 case in the United States where a patient learned that his medical records at a major hospital chain were compromised after he started receiving bills related to a heart procedure that he did not have. The patient's credentials were also used to buy a mobility scooter and several pieces of medical equipment, amounting to tens of thousands of dollars in fraud (Humer and Finkle 2014).

KPMG partner Michael Ebert said that network security has been an afterthought for many medical providers, whether it is building encryption into software used to create electronic patient records or setting medical institutional budgets. Stated bluntly, Ebert said this about how many hospital administrators think, "Are you going to put money into a brand-new MRI machine or laser surgery or are you going to put money into a new firewall?" The answer is likely going to be the former over the latter (Humer and Finkle 2014).

This chapter looks closely at the benefits and controversies surrounding online health records and online health services, primarily by disclosing key research study findings in the United States, the European Union, and Japan. The chapter opens with definitions of online health records and online health services and then discusses the opportunities and concerns of online citizens and health care professionals regarding these concepts. Particular concerns from legal, privacy, security, and trust perspectives are detailed for particular patient groups, including adolescents, those seeking mental health assistance, and the elderly. Suggested institutional remedies for dealing with these concerns are then outlined, along with the relevance of the U.S. legislation known as HIPAA, or the Health Insurance Portability and Accountability Act of 1996. The chapter closes by discussing policy issues regarding online health records and online health services, and how lessons learned from Japan might be applied to other jurisdictions, including the United States.

PERSONAL HEALTH RECORDS AND ONLINE HEALTH SERVICES DEFINED

Personal Health Records Defined

Development of a national health information technology (HIT) infrastructure in the United States, in general, as advocated by the Institute of Medicine (IoM) in 2001 and more recently by the HITECH Act in 2009, includes the following key elements: personal health records (PHRs), electronic medical records (EMRs), and medical record interoperability—being able to obtain medical records online from various sites. All of these elements have the potential to increase system efficiency, decrease medical errors, and improve health care quality. PHRs, when used in conjunction with EMRs, may change how patients interact with the health care system and, consequently, help advance the U.S. online health care system toward the prescribed goals of an increase in safety, effectiveness, timeliness, efficiency, and patient-centeredness (Witry et al. 2010).

A PHR has traditionally been defined as "any paper-based health record maintained on a patient by a health care provider or a paper-based record prepared by the patient." PHRs have nowadays evolved to include Internet-based sets of tools allowing professionals to access and coordinate lifelong health information on patients and to make appropriate parts of the patient'srecord available to those who require it. PHR components are constantly expanding; they now include patient-friendly disease-state management tools, Web-based decision support, provider communication tools, health information resources, and patient annotation capabilities (Witry et al. 2010).

Through these features and emerging others, electronic PHRs have the potential to advance personal patient engagement in health care, resulting in a more positive and hugely improved transformation of the patient-provider relationship. PHRs also can coordinate currently existing fragmented health information—like test results and medical records from different health care providers—and incorporate new data sources—such as the nonprescription or over-the-counter medicines a patient may take, patient-reported blood pressure readings or glucose readings, information from allied health professionals, and contributions from other health wellness providers like fitness coaches and nutritionists (Witry et al. 2010).

Online Health Services Defined

In 2001, the Institute of Medicine (IoM) identified the use of information technology (IT) as one of four critical forces necessary to improve the quality of health care in the United States (Medicine Io 2003). Since then, a vast number of health care institutions have implemented Web sites providing online health services (Corrigan, Donaldson, and Kohn 2001).

By definition, "online health services," or OHS, generally include two key features (Moreno, Ralston, and Grossman 2009): (1) online patient–provider communications, and (2) readily available online access to medical records. In recent years, the IoM has maintained not only that electronic patient–provider communications should be a core functionality of online health services but that the online communications occurring through e-mail or text messaging need to occur within a secure server environment to ensure that patients' records are safe from interference or alteration by insider or outsider hackers.

Surveys undertaken in recent years have shown that adult patients report great interest in e-mail communications with their providers, with some studies indicating that electronic communication is actually preferred by both providers and adult patients, primarily because it requires fewer telephone calls, fewer office visits, and fewer other types of communication burdens for both parties. Two advantages often cited have been an increased level of health provider productivity and greater patient convenience. Adult patients have shown a keen interest in not only having access to their own electronic medical records but in being able to access electronically their children's medical records. The noteworthy bottom line is that with online communications and with more readily available information access by both health care providers and patients, patient care has improved dramatically. Two main reasons given are that online health services have become more widely available to adults, and that some health institutions have allowed proxy information access for parents of young children (Moreno, Ralston, and Grossman 2009).

PERCEIVED BENEFITS AND CONCERNS OF HEALTH PROFESSIONALS AND OF PATIENTS REGARDING ONLINE PHRs IN THE UNITED STATES

While the potential for electronic PHRs to improve health care is significant, there have been documented barriers to a widespread adoption of them. The U.S. public seems to be relatively unfamiliar with and inexperienced in using electronic PHRs, although 60% of Americans responded favorably in a survey toward the idea of an online PHR service (Markle Foundation 2008). Consequently, the probability of individuals' considering PHRs as a sound method to manage their own personal health information appeared to be quite low in 2015—especially for seniors, who tend not to be tech-savvy. Americans are also reportedly concerned about the privacy, security, and trust of their personal health data, as noted, including concerns about inappropriate use by employers and insurers. Let us now review some key study results focusing on these perceived opportunities and barriers.

The Fuji, Galt, and Serocca (2008) Study Results

An important barrier to widespread PHR implementation has been the integration of PHRs into medical practice. For example, a 2008 survey of U.S. ambulatory care physicians conducted by the study team of Fuji, Galt, and Serocca found that 25% of the respondents were unfamiliar with PHRs, and a significant 60% of them were unaware of whether any of their patients even kept PHRs. These study results also indicated that paper-based PHRs were the most popular among patients during this time frame. Very few physicians in the survey reported an ability to integrate PHR information into their EMRs.

The Witry, Doucette, Daly, Levy, and Chrischilies (2010) Study Results

Physicians are instrumental stakeholders in the successful use of interactive PHRs, and although some literature reporting physician attitudes toward electronic communication exists, it is quite dated. Therefore, in 2010, the research team of Witry, Doucette, Daly, Levy, and Chrischilies conducted a study investigating PHRs, especially in the areas of their integration into physician workflow and provider and patient acceptance. In short, the objective of this study was to explore physicians' and medical staff's views on the benefits of, the barriers to, and the use of PHRs. Four focus groups were conducted at four family medicine practices in Iowa and included a total of 28 health care providers.

Transcripts from the focus groups were analyzed using a multiple-step process identifying core themes representative of the participants' views. The research team, including a nurse, a physician, and two pharmacists, reviewed the transcripts to arrive at a set of common themes and to compile quotations that represented these themes. The latter were then used to guide the summary and interpretation of the results. The authors agreed upon the following five main themes from the focus groups relating to PHRs:

1. *PHR benefits*: Participants identified patient groups they felt could especially benefit from using PHRs; these included mobile populations, such as truckers, snowbirds (retirees who travel south for the winter months), or anyone spending considerable time away from home. There were also medical reasons for using a PHR—including pregnancy, complex medical conditions, and the patient's taking many medications. The respondents said that PHRs could also be very valuable for patients visiting emergency rooms. Overall, the health care providers felt that PHRs could increase efficiency and decrease health care costs. Representative quote: "I'll visit with a patient and their children will hand me a piece of paper that has all the meds, allergies, past medical history, what surgeries they have had before, and that's awesome. It doesn't negate me talking to them, but just to have that makes life easier at 2 in the morning when you are trying to find out what's wrong with a patient."
2. *Concerns with PHRs*: Providers voiced two main concerns: accuracy and privacy. The bulk of providers were concerned about the validity of information contained in PHRs and the resulting negative implications of using inaccurate information for treatment protocols. Their main privacy concern entailed inappropriate and unauthorized access to sensitive patient medical information contained in PHRs. Some providers expressed the concern that patients might not know what is appropriate to put in their health record, or that they might

input information that had not been verified by a health care professional. Some providers were less concerned about possible inaccuracies, stating that PHRs should be treated no differently than other forms of patient self-reports. One physician expressed concern that some patients might withhold some important information due to possible insurance ramifications, and other providers were concerned that some patients might try to use PHRs to inappropriately elicit prescriptions for narcotics from physicians. Representative quote: "It's only as good as what goes in. If there is an error, that goes in everyone's system."

3. *How PHRs might be used by providers*: Some providers said that they already had exposure to paper-based or online PHRs, while others had not. Participants identified several positive aspects of PHRs, including providing an up-to-date list of medications, allergies, past medical history, diagnoses, surgeries, and a list of other health care providers consulted. Providers also speculated about how they might incorporate PHRs into their existing workflow and existing medical records—with most settling on scanning documents and manual data entry. Another physician suggested that PHRs could serve as a check for the official medical record kept by the physician's office. Still other physicians felt that they didn't have the time to let patients, say, log onto Google to try to locate the PHR document. Some study providers admitted to not being all that tech-savvy themselves—thus preferring the paper document provided by the patient rather than some online version. Finally, other providers perceived the usefulness of PHRs and the likelihood of emerging interoperabilities, particularly given that the U.S. government was advocating movement toward the possibility of universal medical records. Representative quote: "Why are we adding more layers of complexity that will just add more errors? Why don't we just make the layers we do have talk with each other?"
4. *PHR maintenance*: Concerns over accuracy seemed to contribute to providers wanting control over data input into the PHRs; consequently, they advocated for providers being in control of information regarding health issues and pharmacists being in control of information regarding, say, prescriptions on file. Participants were also adamant that insurers not be involved with PHRs, and that claims data should not be used to populate PHRs. Representative quote: "I think patients should have total control of who gets access, but the information put in there should be from professionals like pharmac[ists] or doctors. Patients should not be able to enter any information without the doctor or someone else validating it. Otherwise that information is just subjective."
5. *Perceptions about how patients might use and interact with PHRs*: Overall, providers seemed to doubt that patients would want to take the necessary responsibility for creating a PHR and for updating it regularly. Furthermore,

> providers in two of the focus groups suggested that patients may not see the need for PHRs, because they just assume that providers have more information on patients and access to more information than patients themselves have. Finally, consistent with the notion that PHRs may be too demanding for most patients, several physicians stated that simpler personal records, such as medication lists, may be sufficient. Representative quote: "I think it's the patient's responsibility to keep track of what's going on. If they don't want to keep track of what's going on, it's really difficult for [the] physician to keep track of everything because they're the ones that actually go to the visit. You have to rely on the patient to do it, but 70 percent of people won't."

The study team concluded that their focus group findings helped to expand on previous survey research on physicians' attitudes toward PHRs and addressed several assumptions made by early PHR innovators and researchers. First, comments regarding the benefits and potential uses of PHRs (online or otherwise) suggest that the participants viewed PHRs primarily as a resource for physicians rather than as a useful tool for patients. Second, the information that providers wanted in a PHR was that which they already were getting from some patients through patients' oral reports or through paper-based PHRs. While a few physicians had patients who maintained a PHR using a spreadsheet or word-processing document, few had experience viewing a patient's PHR in an electronic format. Thus, these study findings triangulated with previous survey research concluding that providers are relatively unfamiliar with electronic PHRs and their potential benefit as a tool for patients. Consequently, this unfamiliarity appears to have created negative preconceptions about the use of online PHRs that may slow PHR adoption on a broader basis.

Finally, the study participants echoed some common concerns about accuracy and privacy; in particular, they were concerned that patient-entered data would not be correct, that existing medical information on patients should not be reentered into a PHR, and that medical records should be shared directly between medical providers (either online or off-line)—who should maintain control of patients' medical histories.

BENEFITS AND CONCERNS OF EHRs VOICED BY PATIENTS IN EUROPE

Initiatives in the United Kingdom to enable patients to access their electronic health records (EHRs), the online version of PHRs, have been gathering momentum in recent years, just as in the United States. All citizens of the European Union should have access to their electronic health records by 2015, a target that the

United Kingdom has endorsed. In England, patients' access to their health records is guaranteed under the National Health Service (NHS) constitution for England; so by 2015, patients should enjoy online access to their PHRs held by general practitioners (GPs) in the NHS.

The direction and intended speed of adoption of EHRs, as described in the information strategy, have as a major goal putting citizens in control of their own health and health care information. The strategy also described the process that would be required to make patients' health information both accessible and transparent. In short, the needs of patients and their caregivers were to drive local innovation, thereby enabling and encouraging access to personalized information. From this angle, the online patient health record is the cornerstone of the EHR system, beginning with transactions like booking appointments to ordering repeat prescriptions. Over the longer term, patients should be able to access letters from caregivers, test results, and personal care plans—thus promoting patients' participation in their health and wellness decision making. This comprehensive online health management process was to lead to an improvement in good lifestyle choices—resulting in improved health outcomes and lower health care costs for the U.K. population (Department of Health 2012). Record access has been endorsed by a number of professional organizations of health care providers in the United Kingdom, including GPs; however, just as in the United States, some reservations have also been expressed—including the high cost of implementing such a system (Royal College of General Practitioners 2010; Cross 2011).

Earlier work in the context of the National Programme for Information Technology focused on summary care records, the portion of the PHR intended to be accessible to patients (Pagliari, Detmer, and Singleton 2007). Furthermore, while in principle, patients seemed positive about having PHRs available online, their attitudes were strongly linked to their previous access experiences (Greenhalgh et al. 2008). Other research on record access has more broadly reported concerns about data sharing and the confidentiality of PHR information.

There is little question that while the potential for U.K. primary care practices to provide patients with online access to EHRs is increasing, realistically, in practice, being able to effectively do so remains somewhat limited. In 2012, for example, the Royal College of General Practitioners reported that only 25% of general medical practices allowed patients to book and cancel appointments online, even though 73% of the practices had the systems in place to enable this opportunity for patients. Moreover, while 53% of the general medical practices could provide access to records and letters in 2012, fewer than 1% actually did so (Royal College of General Practitioners 2012).

To date, there have been limited research studies conducted in the United Kingdom that effectively evaluate the success of online PHR records. Though an earlier 2004 study with U.K. patients indicated considerable reservations about confidentiality and data accuracy of online PHRs—though patients generally saw online PHRs as being useful in helping them to personally manage their health—more recent 2009 research in U.K. primary care has indicated that online PHR access is very well received by regular users, who see it as beneficial. The primary asset cited was that online access enabled them to prepare for their physician consultations more effectively. Patients also appreciated the opportunity to compare their recollection of the consultation with their GP's record of it—thus reassuring them that no critical health information was being hidden from them. Patients also reported that their online PHR access had improved their knowledge of their health state and its clinical management, and they generally noted the positive potential of further online developments in better enabling personal and system efficiency gains and cost savings (Fisher, Bhavnani, and Winfield 2009).

The Shah, Fitton, Hannan, Fisher, Young, and Barnett (2015) U.K. Study Results

To identify the ways in which U.K. patients have in more recent years used their access to their increasingly online PHRs, what they sought to achieve, and the extent to which PHR access was related to the concept of ensuring savings, the research team of Shah, Fitton, Hannan, Fisher, Young, and Barnett (2015) conducted an audit of patients' online access to medical records in July and August 2011, using a survey questionnaire. In total, 226 patients who were registered with two general practices in the NHS and who had accessed their online PHRs at least twice in the preceding 12 months (i.e., from July 2010 to July 2011) were invited to complete the questionnaire. Data analysis was then completed along thematic lines regarding the patients' comments to the open-ended questions presented.

Overall, the study results indicated that U.K. patients' evaluations of their online PHR access were positive. Four main themes relating to the ways in which patients accessed their records were identified; these are shown below, along with the percentage of respondents who identified each theme:

1. *Making savings (27.2% of the respondents):* The greatest savings, as reported by patients, related to calls to the practice and appointments with their doctors. Thirty participants (about 13%) thought that they had made extra appointments with their doctor as a result of online record access. Patients reported saving themselves time (e.g., less need to take time off from work for appointments) and money (e.g., purchased less gasoline to make office visits or made fewer phone calls). Patients also discussed the likelihood of savings in terms of

doctors' time being freed-up because of fewer appointments being scheduled. Other patients explicitly said that they had no significant cost savings, but they drew attention to their having PHR access as being indicative of better quality health care.

2. *Checking past activity (33.5% of the respondents):* Patients discussed a range of checking activities online either as part of, or in response to, previous interactions with health professionals, particularly surgeons. The opportunity to obtain test results online rather than having to phone the surgeon was welcomed. It was also obvious that providing test results online was a valued facility by patients, with the process itself being considered by the majority of patients to be trusted and to provide reassurance.
3. *Preparing for future action (22.5% of the respondents)*: Information in health records about a particular condition sometimes stimulated further information-seeking activities by patients; for example, patients would say that to find out more about a particular condition, they would either do a general Internet search (say, through Google) or consult the link provided. The proactive ways in which patients used their access to their EHRs was evident in the way that they prepared themselves for a visit with their GP or another health care professional. This preparation enabled them to be clear about the issues that would be discussed in the appointment and to consider what kinds of questions to ask. It was clear that online health record access was not an end in itself, but that patients used it to support their decision making and to determine what action to take. One action often considered was whether to make an appointment or to decide that an appointment was not necessary. If there was a problem with accessing a result in the EHR, due to technical problems or because the result was not in the EHR, patients would then contact the physician's office for clarification. Monitoring the course of a patient's condition over time was clearly important to some patients, and here, EHR access provided evidence to them of stability or change.
4. *Setting new expectations (8.7% of the respondents)*: For some patients, the process of accessing EHRs created a new set of expectations around what was possible in managing their own health. The process also brought some frustrations. Some of these frustrations were related to technical issues in easily accessing the system or having the information that one was seeking be temporarily unavailable. Other frustrations centered on perceived limitations in the content (e.g., wanting to know more about one's test results or wanting more details on GP-hospital interactions).

The research team concluded that their audit study found that EHRs were very useful to patients for the following important reasons:

- U.K. patients actively used online patient record access to more fully comprehend their health status and the health care processes within which their health status was managed. Although they tended to appreciate that access to their records could save them time and money and provide increased efficiencies for health care providers, it is important to underscore that within the context of an audit focusing on assessing savings, there were many other benefits of EHRs cited by patients. EHRs were actively used for a range of purposes, including monitoring and tracking health states, comparing test results over time, establishing what is "normal," and ascertaining acceptable degrees of variation in test results. Furthermore, access to personal medical records gave patients the opportunity to identify and communicate errors or omissions in the records to their GPs.
- The use of EHRs by patients was linked to a range of health information–seeking activities either prior to or following face-to-face consultations with health professionals. Accepting that the Internet is the most prevalently relied upon resource for health information by patients (71% used it at least once to find health information in 2011, compared to 37% in 2005), this kind of activity is not always warmly welcomed by health professionals because of wrong information available on the Internet or patients' erroneous interpretations of the information. Nonetheless, Internet information-seeking is a strong sign that patients are desiring to play an active role in managing their health. EHRs can capitalize on this reality by providing links to relevant, credible, and authoritative sources—thus positively contributing to patients' health literacy.
- Patients reported time and money savings for themselves and clearly anticipated that EHRs could have a role in streamlining their timely access to GPs. There was no evidence of patients' access to EHRs generating excessive queries or their seeking additional or unreasonable contact with health care professionals.
- It is noteworthy that the trust regularly accorded GPs seems to have become extended to include an online manifestation of that specialist-patient relationship. The veracity of the information provided in the EHR was accepted by the bulk of patients, and in many cases provided reassurance.
- It is also notable that while those who took part in the study had used EHRs, there was almost no mention of concerns regarding privacy, security, or confidentiality —factors reported in many other studies of a similar nature. The reason for this is quite unclear. It may well be that it is the tech-savvy patients who perceive few issues with online security and who have a more trusting stance that are the early adopters of EHR access. It may also be that initial concerns centered on privacy, security, trust, and confidentiality are quickly outweighed by the benefits of using EHRs—such as enhanced trust in the health professional–client relationship. Further research is needed to understand this process more clearly, thus assisting with the promotion of confident EHR use in a broader patient population.

- Overall, and consistent with previous literature reports, it was found that patients generally evaluated access to EHRs positively. Patients saw the main attributes as being convenience, usefulness, usability, and flexibility. However, not all evaluations by patients were glowing; negativity was generally associated with patients' reports of EHR access being limited. This limitation was linked either to an assessment that there was little to no real access to the EHRs or, in some instances, that there was an inability to access more EHRs frequently because of technical problems.

The Hoerbst, Kohl, Knaup, and Ammenwerth (2010) Study Results

Other European studies conducted within the last five years have found that citizens' reports of major concerns about EHRs were related to privacy and confidentiality issues. One such study was conducted by the research team of Hoerbst, Kohl, Knaup, and Ammenwerth, who utilized standardized interviews on a convenience sample of 203 Austrian and 293 German citizens recruited in two metropolitan cities. Because acceptance by citizens seemed to be crucial for the future success of an electronic health record (EHR) systemic process in Germany and Austria, these researchers analyzed citizens' knowledge and expectations about the concept and contents of an EHR. They also addressed possible fears and barriers and investigated desired EHR functionalities relevant to citizens in this jurisdiction.

Almost 75% of the interviewed citizens said that they already collected and stored medical documents at home, but, significantly, mostly in paper-based form. No respondents admitted to already using an Internet-based personal health record. Accepting this reality, 80% to 90% of the respondents were supportive of the notion of an electronic exchange of health-related data among health care providers as a core functionality of an EHR. However, many respondents voiced concerns with regard to data protection and data security within an EHR. The EHR functionalities most supported by respondents included the electronic vaccination record, online information regarding doctors and hospitals, and the administration of appointments and reminders with family physicians.

BENEFITS AND CONCERNS ABOUT ONLINE HEALTH SERVICES FOR U.S. ADOLESCENTS: THE LANDRO (2005) AND THE MORENO, RALSTON, AND GROSSMAN (2009) STUDY RESULTS

Since discussions by health care professionals and patients on the benefits and concerns of online health services have become more open and frequent in the United

States, some health institutions there have allowed proxy access for parents having very young children. However, providing proxy access for parents of adolescent children had not yet become the standard in the United States even by 2005 (Landro 2005).

In fact, in 2005, a *Wall Street Journal* article published an interesting media piece on this dilemma. The article began with the real-life case of Ursula Scott. Using her health plan's Web site, this woman, who lived in Washington, said that she could view the medical records of her two-year-old and five-year-old daughters, check their immunization schedules, review test results, exchange e-mails with their pediatrician, and make appointments for their next office visit. However, when it came to Ursula's 16-year-old stepson, neither she nor anyone else in the family could gain access to any aspect of his electronic medical records—not even the teen himself. While an increasing number of health plans, doctors' offices, and hospitals have been making the switch to electronic medical record systems in response to President Bush's and President Obama's push to make online records available to all Americans by 2015, in the long-running effort to "balance the rights" of parents and adolescents in making decisions about medical care, technology has resulted in new legal and technical challenges. The outcome seems to be that teens and their parents have often been barred from accessing adolescents' online health records or services (Landro 2005).

Generally, efforts to gain such medical information access have often run afoul of the federal and state legal complexities allowing adolescents to seek confidential family-planning and mental health services without their parents' consent. Furthermore, because certain U.S. laws make some aspects of teens' health records off-limits to their parents, electronic medical records systems have not yet developed—as of 2015—a foolproof way to flag confidential material, thereby hiding it from teens' parents. With paper records, such a feat is possible.

Moreover, teens cannot on their own enter into the security agreements required to grant access to their online records, because they are considered to be "minors." The bottom line is that until health care providers can ascertain how to give parents access to basic health care information for a teen without breaking confidentiality or online accessibility rules, many health institutions will continue to omit adolescents from the full privileges allowed through electronic health systems. This problem is further exacerbated by the fact that parental access to their children's records is usually revoked once the children turn 13 years of age in the United States (Landro 2005).

From 2005 through 2009, a number of studies on adults described the expectations and experiences of adults using online health services, but during this period, little was known about the benefits and barriers associated with providing these services to adolescents. Through findings from a series of semistructured expert interviews and a thorough literature review, the U.S. research team of Moreno,

Ralston, and Grossman (2009) investigated the potential benefits and barriers associated with providing adolescents access to online health services. A total of 18 interviews with experts were conducted, with the study group including 11 physicians (three family practitioners, three pediatricians, four adolescent medicine specialists, and one internist), three administrators who directed clinical information systems, three attorneys, and one health policy legislative expert. Ten institutions were represented in total.

The main study findings were as follows:

1. *The benefits*: There was little question that by 2009, U.S. adolescents were avid Internet users, with more than 90% of teens having Internet access and most reporting daily online use. By 2009, many adolescents accessed health care information via the Internet. Two common themes emerged from the interview data regarding how adolescents' facility with the Internet may allow new opportunities to participate in health care. First, health care systems that provide online health information allow teens to access more accurate information than may be obtained through generic Internet search engines like Google, as well as a greater potential for individualized information. Second, providing opportunities for adolescents to exercise increased responsibility over their own health care may help them independently manage their own health care as adults. Furthermore, giving teens the responsibility for making appointments using online health systems provides them an active role in their own health care management at an earlier age and promotes health literacy over the longer term. One senior health plan employee noted the irony that "just at the age at which many teens are becoming very computer literate, around age 13, is the age at which most health care systems revoke online access for both parents and teens."
2. *The benefits*: Although the literature on adolescent access to online health services has not fully addressed the impact on the patient–provider relationship, developing rapport with an adolescent patient in any health care environment is considered to be both a challenge and a key aspect to providing quality care. Several study interviewees expressed the belief that allowing adolescents access to online communications with their health care providers would enhance the physician–patient relationship and improve rapport.
3. *The benefits*: Although adolescents generally receive appropriate preventive care regarding immunization status and blood pressure screening, not all teens are screened for sexual activity or substance use, despite the availability of clinical screens designed to identify these health risk behaviors. Health risk behaviors are also associated with the leading causes of adolescent death, including injuries, homicide, and suicide. Accepting that studies have not yet identified

the role of preventive screening for adolescents in the online health care environment, several study interviewees conjectured that an area of great promise in improving adolescent preventive care would be the systematic use of an online health risk assessment (HRA), especially if linked to follow-up discussion and guidance with a health practitioner. Studies have shown that adolescents prefer computerized over traditional questionnaires, and that the prevalence of reported risk behaviors such as substance use is higher in computerized questionnaires than in face-to-face interviews, implying that the former seem to promote more accurate reporting of stigmatizing behaviors in teens.

4. *The benefits:* Though adult studies have consistently shown the value of promoting patient review of the medical record as part of multifaceted interventions in chronic disease management, giving patient access to electronic medical records and a more continuous model of health care through effective online communication has the huge potential to shift the U.S. health care system from the acute visit–based model to a model that better meets the needs of patients with chronic conditions. Although similar studies on adolescents having chronic medical conditions are sorely lacking, the study experts noted that online health system access may be even more paramount for adolescents living with chronic conditions than for those without such conditions.
5. *The barriers:* A major concern expressed by the study interviewees when considering access to medical records for adolescents or the parents of adolescents was the complexity of health information. Providing online medical record access to teens or their parents was not an all-or-nothing phenomenon; furthermore, there was no consensus regarding which medical record elements should be available and to whom. Distinguishing "standard" from "protected or confidential" adolescent health information was the crux of the challenge.
6. *The barriers:* Confidential adolescent health information like sexual health or substance use information tends to be legally protected from parental access in the majority of U.S. states. In contrast, standard health information like an ankle sprain can be accessed by parents. Moreover, there are areas of overlap between these two categories. Nearly all study interviewees agreed that the granularity of adolescent medical record information contributes unique challenges to the creation of comprehensive online health services. Because adolescent privacy laws vary by state, health care organizations providing coverage to multiple states using a single electronic medical record must seek creative ways to address this challenge. In 2009, there was no widely available technology that could distinguish between confidential and standard medical record information.
7. *The barriers:* Even if electronic medical records were able to make the distinction between confidential and standard medical record information, health care

providers would have to consistently label chart information in a way that flagged confidential information to ensure its protection. Accepting that an adolescent's preventive care visit may involve considerable amounts of confidential and standard information, health care providers may not be able or willing to consistently make this distinction during documentation. Also, when health records are obtained from outside health care organizations attended by adolescents (like Planned Parenthood), these would need to be reliably assessed by health care providers to protect confidential information contained therein. One option in addressing this complexity, noted the study interviewees, would be to allow adolescent patients to review their online medical information and to choose to sequester any information that should be legally protected as confidential. This review could be completed in the medical clinic or from a home computer.

8. *The barriers:* Legal issues affecting adolescent health care are well known obstacles to allowing adolescents online access to health services. Two major considerations expressed by the interviewees were (1) adolescents' ability to consent to care, and (2) adolescents' access to medical records. Adolescents who are legally minors may consent to their own health care only in certain circumstances. When a minor can consent to his or her own health care, then under the HIPAA (Health Insurance Portability and Accountability Act of 1996) Privacy Rule, the adolescent can access medical records regarding that care. It is important to point out that the HIPAA Privacy Rule defers to state or other applicable laws when determining whether a parent can access records when an adolescent has consented to care or when there is an agreement of confidentiality. These other laws may forbid access, require access, or allow health care providers to have discretion in the matter.
9. *The barriers:* Whether a teen has access to nonconfidential medical records is frequently unclear from a legal perspective, as the teen is not the individual consenting to care. Although the HIPAA Privacy Rule states that a teen's parent or guardian may generally access medical information about health services when the minor has not given consent or there is no agreement of confidentiality, the rule does not explicitly forbid teens from also having access to their own health care records. It is important to note that by 2009, some U.S. states adopted health privacy laws explicitly specifying the life circumstances under which minors would have authority over their own medical records. Without question, these complex legal issues complicate the notion of teens having legal access to even their own standard health care records or of parents' access to their confidential health care records. In some cases, teens may access confidential medical records, but their parents may not, and in some cases, parents may access standard medical records, but their teens may not. Overcoming

these barriers, noted the study interviewees, will involve an ongoing careful review of all relevant federal and state laws and continual development of policies and implementation strategies consistent with these laws.

10. *The barriers:* Several study interviewees expressed their concerns that some teens may not be developmentally able to understand the information contained in their medical records. Some study interviewees further said that they had concerns that some teens may be unable to comprehend this reality: that any online communication with health care providers becomes a permanent part of the medical record, and that verbal disclosures made during clinic visits may also become part of that patient's permanent medical record.
11. *The barriers:* Because teens do not typically advocate on behalf of their own health care needs and because they are not the primary subscribers on any given health insurance plan, teen online service needs may not be among a health care organization's priorities. Furthermore, given that providing online health care services to teens also includes financial, legal, and other risks to health care organizations, coupled with the fact that teens may not overtly request this innovation, the reality is that health care organizations tend to not be inclined to prioritize online services to teens. One exception by 2009 was the Palo Alto Medical Foundation Adolescent Interest Group, which invited health care providers from various disciplines to work toward improving adolescent health care and online service provision. Another notable exception by 2009 was the Kaiser Permanente system in Colorado, which sponsored a teen advisory council.
12. *The barriers:* Some study interviewees stated that another concern they observed was the pressure placed by some parents on their teens to release their online service passwords. To address these concerns, one health care system implemented a means by which any report of a parent's demanding inappropriate access to the teen's online information would result in revocation of online access for both the parent and the teen. Another health care system's solution was to allow the teen to reset his or her individual access password at any time; thus, if a parent obtained access to the health record using the teen's password, the teen could then reset the password.
13. *The barriers:* Some study interviewees raised concerns about the ability of teens to appropriately use online patient–provider communications, as the asynchronous nature of Internet communications is not appropriate for highly urgent patient concerns like suicidal ideation. Despite these concerns, most providers that were interviewed currently used e-mail communications with teen patients and/or their parents, adhering to the guidelines for online provider communications with patients available from the American Medical Informatics Association.

The Moreno, Ralston, and Grossman study team had a number of conclusions. First, they recommended prioritizing teen access both to online patient–provider communications and to online medical records, to give teens a secure environment for electronic communication with their health care providers that would increase teens' access to health care in an online medium that most in this age group have comfort with and considerable skill in. These experts also believed that the perceived developmental concerns regarding online communications becoming part of a teen's medical record are no greater than the risks associated with any other kind of medical encounter, such as a health clinic visit. Providing teens access to their own electronic medical records not only promotes ownership and responsibility for this personal information but may hone critical health literacy skills for navigating today's adult health care systems. For example, transferring the responsibility to teens for managing medication refills or appointment scheduling may seem like an unrealistic goal to some, but today's technology-savvy teens already possess the skills to navigate these systems.

Furthermore, while making online access to teens a system priority may cause some parents to feel alarm at being left out of their teens' health information, providing parental education regarding the benefits of shifting health information responsibility from parents to teens and promoting health literacy among teens will alleviate many of these somewhat unfounded concerns. Reassuring parents that they will retain medical record access when needed for all appropriate health information for their teen may also be of benefit in reducing parental concerns.

Finally, increasing teens' access to online health services will require a high level of involvement by health care systems at many levels, particularly when trying to overcome the financial and legal barriers that will appear when trying to implement these much-needed system improvements.

ONLINE HEALTH SERVICES IN MENTAL HEALTH: THE JONES AND ASHURST (2013) STUDY RESULTS

Though planned electronic health innovations in the United States and in the United Kingdom have often been found to be effective in trials, like other health service innovations, implementation of these innovations on a broader scale has not always proven to be totally effective or without client or health service provider resistance. The implementation of online health services in mental health, in particular, requires careful consideration because of its highly sensitive nature.

In 2012–2013, the U.K. research team of Jones and Ashurst sought to ascertain stakeholder concerns in using e-health services in mental health, first, by conducting a thorough literature review on this topic, and then presenting thematic transcripts to 31 U.K. participants: 19 mental health professionals, or MHPs, and 12 mental health service users, or MHSUs. They were told the purpose of the study was for discussion and insights on 12 topics through online focus groups. The research team identified (1) areas that should be first implemented, (2) areas where further education and engagement are necessary before e-health methods can be used, and (3) areas needing further research.

The study research design was completed with these four stages: (1) development of the 12 topics for discussion, (2) recruiting stakeholders and creating three one-week courses in which participants could discuss the 12 topics online, (3) completion of a thematic analysis of the discussion transcripts, and (4) a comparative analysis of the study findings with existing literature.

The 12 topics for anonymous online discussion included the following, along with some key study findings for each of these mental health topics:

- *Computerized Cognitive Behavioral Therapy (CCBT) for depression*: E-health research has tended to focus on CCBT, or computerized cognitive behavioral therapy (described more fully in chapter 1). CCBT was introduced in the context of Web sites like Moodgym and Living Life to the Full, shown to be effective for people experiencing depression or anxiety. These six themes developed from the online discussion: (1) *lack of support*: concerns were expressed about CCBT usage without adequate professional support and guidance; (2) *online therapy range*: concerns were expressed regarding the need for choice of online therapy types, not just online cognitive behavioral therapy (CBT); (3) *individual differences*: concerns were expressed in the literature and in the online forums that there exists no clear guidance on which patients CCBT might benefit the most; (4) *severity*: concerns were expressed that CCBT should be aimed at mild to moderate severity levels of depression and anxiety but not at high severity levels; (5) *usability*: concerns were expressed about the need for more user-friendly CCBT websites; and (6) *access*: concerns were expressed about the exclusion of patients without Internet access.
- *Discussion forums*: Numerous discussion forums for mental health exist, and most of the study MHSUs and some MHPs reported prior use. The study findings showed that views on discussion forums were mixed, with benefits and disadvantages raised under eight themes: (1) *support*: the respondents felt that discussion forums may provide mutual support or add to feelings of loneliness and lack of support to those experiencing mental health issues; (2) *social contact*: the respondents felt that discussion forums may provide or reduce social contact and inclusion for those experiencing mental health issues; (3) *timing*: the respondents felt that discussion forums may be useful at certain stages of treatment and conditions for mental health clients but not at others; (4) *size*: the respondents felt that discussion forums may be easier to find and get responses

to if large but be more personal if small; (5) *anonymity*: the respondents felt that discussion forums would make it easier to share information with others because of anonymity but may lead to disinhibited, irresponsible, and nonhelpful posts by participants; (6) *moderation*: the respondents felt that discussion forums would need to be moderated; (7) *recommendation*: the respondents felt that discussion forums could be recommended by MHPs, but there were mixed views about MHPs' involvement in these discussions; and (8) *style of communication*: the respondents felt that discussion forums may be useful for MHSUs preferring written communications over verbal communications.

- *Lifestyle change intervention Web sites*: There are many lifestyle change Web sites aimed at helping clients reduce alcohol intake, increase exercise, lose weight, and quit smoking. There is evidence in the mental health literature that these may result in improved short-term understanding for clients along any of these dimensions, but most studies are on too short a time scale to show improved mental health outcomes for clients over the longer term. The study respondents focused on five themes: (1) *motivation*: the respondents generally felt that such Web sites are useful only for self-motivated patients; (2) *lack of human contact*: the respondents felt that the overall effectiveness of these Web sites is probably limited because of the absence of important nonverbal communication cues and a lack of social inclusion compared to other effective face-to-face methods; (3) *professional role*: the respondents felt that professionals needed to be involved in reviewing and recommending particular Web sites for clients; (4) *self-assessment*: the respondents felt that these Web sites could be useful as a self-assessment tool, but that as in any self-report test, some patients may not be truthful in answering the items; and (5) *concern about cost cutting*: the respondents saw some potential benefits in recommending moderated Web sites in addition to established mental health treatments but were concerned if the intention was to replace face-to-face methods with Web site interventions.
- *Webcast group therapy*: The literature indicates little to no discussion on webcast group therapy. Four themes emerged from the study discussion: (1) *dislike of group therapy*: some participants said that they would be willing to try webcasts but some MHSUs, in particular, did not like group therapy, whether face-to-face or online; (2) *online skills*: some MHPs had concerns about their ability to manage a therapy group online; (3) *relationships*: the study respondents had rather contrasting views on relationships, with some MHPs concerned about the online distance between the mental health professional and the patient and the loss of nonverbal communications—both factors probably curtailing online relationship development; and (4) *therapy or education*: the study respondents suggested that rather than focusing on Web site therapy,

it may be more appropriate to focus on online education or follow-up for clients.

- *Videophone*: The discussion focused on videophone use, say, Skype. In this study, a few MHSUs and some MHPs indicated having prior Skype experience with friends and family, but only one MHP used Skype with patients. Though some MHPs and MHSUs expressed an interest in using Skype for mental health care, other MHSUs did not express such an interest. Seven themes arose from the discussion: (1) *robustness of technology*: although some MHPs thought that there was potential in using videophone, a number of concerns focused on the fact that the technology was not yet sufficiently reliable, it suffered from insufficient bandwidth, and there were connection disruptions—with restrictions placed by some mental health care settings; (2) *more choice for MHSUs*: some respondents felt that video consultations could offer an additional choice of contact; (3) *comparison with telephone*: most MHPs preferred telephone to Skype for ease of use, and while some thought that the addition of a picture of the patient would be useful, others disagreed; (4) *need for prior contact*: some MHPs thought Skype should not be used without prior face-to-face communication with the client, and some felt that Skype lost valuable face-to-face information; (5) *benefit of the event*: one MHSU, in particular, reported seeing greater benefits from the experience of attending an appointment with the mental health practitioner than in communicating with him or her from home; (6) *cost and practical benefits*: both MHPs and a MHSU saw the potential of using Skype in geographically remote areas and for immobile patients; and (7) *patient state*: mental health practitioner respondents had concerns that if patients were ill at ease with how the therapy discussion was going, they could just walk away from their computer screens.
- *E-mail*: There appears to be relatively little research published on the routine use of e-mail between patients and their mental health providers, though a U.S. article suggested that in 2005, few actually used e-mail for this purpose, because there were concerns such as the potential for an increased workload for clinicians and privacy issues for patients. Six themes arose from the study discussion: (1) *convenience*: some MHSUs saw e-mail as convenient for anytime access for nonintrusive communications, and one MHP saw e-mails as more likely to be replied to than missed telephone calls; (2) *timing*: there was a voiced concern that e-mail is not a fast response method for patients in mental health crisis and should not be used as such; (3) *disinhibition*: two MHSUs viewed e-mail as more effective for emotional expression and revelation than face-to-face communications; (4) *trust*: some respondents thought e-mail was helpful when combined with face-to-face care, and that prior face-to-face contact was needed to develop trust with the health care provider before e-mail

could be effective; (5) *printed record*: some MHPs reported potential benefits of e-mail in terms of patients' recorded information for reflection, but they expressed concerns about misinterpretations and the effects of written text; and (6) *security*: two MHPs reported that they were personally prohibited from e-mail communications with patients by health care trust rules, and one MHSU saw mail as not being secure and would not personally correspond by e-mail, even for appointments.

- *Computer–patient interviews*: Computer–patient interviewing (CPI) has been used for patient history-taking in mental health since 1966. Four themes arose from the study discussion: (1) *quantity of questions*: some respondents thought that patients might lose motivation or feel overwhelmed by the number of questions issued in computer–patient interviews; (2) *impersonal method*: some respondents had concerns that the method of questioning might be impersonal, exacerbated by use of clinical language, thus restricting possible responses from patients; (3) *support*: though some respondents saw the benefits of allowing patients to answer questions in their own time, there was a concern that MHSUs would dislike completing questions without health practitioner support or the opportunity to discuss potentially upsetting questions with mental health professionals; and (4) *screening and outcome measures*: some respondents thought that CPI could provide useful information for population screening.
- *Map of Medicine*: Map of Medicine is an evidence-based online clinical knowledge resource, using a pathway approach to provide visual representations of evidence-based practice. Because only two MHPs had prior experience with these, and accepting that they commented briefly on its helpfulness as a diagnostic tool, two other respondents commented that they had only minimal knowledge of this tool.
- *Patient access to their online medical records*: While patients in the United Kingdom can apply to access their online medical records for a possible fee, and given that some clinicians give their patients routine access to these records, particularly in general practice, diabetes management, and renal disease, no study participants had experience with online medical records. Six themes emerged from the discussion: (1) *security/privacy*: MHSUs thought that security and privacy were critical, giving rise to concerns about patients' capabilities to implement Internet security measures; (2) *reflection*: some MHPs suggested that online notes could be beneficial for mental health patients to reflect on their treatment, but some MHSUs thought personal reflection would lead to rumination on problems and possible distress production in the clients; (3) *support*: some respondents thought that records should only be viewed with mental health professional support to avoid upset,

disappointment, and potential mistrust by patients; (4) *empowerment*: if access to records improved patient–professional communications, then it was welcomed, because it should encourage patients to become active partners in their mental health care; (5) *accessibility*: there was some agreement that online records would improve patient accessibility to their notes, but one MHSU was concerned about reading too much into them; and (6) *unnecessary*: some MHSUs preferred face-to-face medical health methods or the copying of letters, so they did not see the need for online medical methods. Respondents' wariness about patient online access to their records was at odds with the positive research evidence found in the literature.

- *Barriers to greater use of the Internet in mental health*: The following five themes arose from the study discussion: (1) *access*: respondents had concerns about patients who were not confident computer users or who had no Internet connection, with some noting that though patients could get public access (e.g., from libraries), this venue would be unsuitable for mental health use; (2) *organizational support*: MHPs said that while there was a need for the National Health Service (NHS) to support Internet use in mental health practice, the reality was that professionals' ability to use technology varied greatly; (3) *security*: for many respondents, concern for security was seen as a major barrier to Internet use, including NHS trust restrictions; (4) *awareness*: MHSUs saw the lack of awareness of Internet resources and lack of such provision as main barriers; and (5) *personal choice and ability*: respondents noted that some mental health patients may prefer face-to-face methods and will resist using the Internet, particularly older patients who may not have the ability or the confidence to use new technology. These barriers have been identified in the literature and policy—including access issues, the need for organizational support and for training, security concerns, lack of awareness of Internet resources, and personal preferences.
- *Groups who would benefit from the Internet*: Five themes emerged from the discussion: (1) *generalization*: some respondents thought that there were too many individual factors to be able to generalize about the groups most likely to gain from the Internet; (2) *physical restrictions to health care*: respondents generally thought that those with physical and psychological restrictions to health care access, including those in rural communities, the disabled, and those working antisocial hours may benefit the most from Internet use; (3) *professionals*: two reasons were cited why mental health professionals may benefit from a greater reliance on the Internet—reduced costs and being able to seek personal help anonymously (e.g., the mental health practitioners who themselves were suffering from burnout and who, therefore, felt concerned about risking their jobs); (4) *computer users*: groups inclined to turn to online

resources for help were viewed as benefiting the most from the Internet, but there were concerns voiced by the respondents that some groups of clients may need face-to-face contact with other clients and their mental health professionals, so they would tend to not appreciate having to use the Internet; and (5) *initial stages*: different Internet uses at different stages of therapy were recognized by the respondents; it was thought that those in the initial stages of seeking help might benefit the most from Internet use.

- *Implementation and requirements for supporting the Internet uses*: Respondents discussed how they would like to see the Internet used in mental health services and what would be needed to support these uses. Six themes evolved from the discussion: (1) *supplement*: some responded that they wanted e-health services as additional resources, to complement but not replace face-to-face therapy; (2) *individual differences*: respondents voiced the need to tailor services to patients and therefore voiced concerns that e-health methods might not be suitable for all MHSUs, but that, for example, younger people would likely be okay since they expect up-to-date use of technology; (3) *ideas for particular implementation*: respondents had specific ideas about how the Internet could be used in mental health interventions, including NHS-run discussion forums, peer support e-mails, computerized therapies other than CBT, and the use of text reminders; (4) *research evidence*: respondents voiced the need for more evidence regarding comparisons between the effectiveness of the Internet and more conventional face-to-face methods of therapy provision; (5) *training and guidelines*: respondents generally agreed that training and guidelines were needed for implementing e-health methods; and (6) rationale: respondents confirmed that how the use of e-health was presented by mental health practitioners—in other words, its underlying rationale—was critically important; there might be opposition if its usage was presented simply as a cost-cutting strategy rather than as a means of improving patient health care quality.

Jones and Ashurst (2013) concluded that their study findings illustrated that giving both patients and mental health professionals more choice in the methods of communication used in mental health practice was important—not only in using different online methods for therapy development but in deciding whether to use or not use online interventions as part of the therapy regimen. The use of online methods will largely depend on the type and stage of treatment process. For example, discussion forums were considered by some respondents to be good for initial patient–practitioner exploration; e-mail and Skype were considered to be useful when there was an existing real-world relationship between the mental health professional and the client; and CCBT and lifestyle change Web sites were considered to be useful primarily for after-care (i.e., following land-based treatment interventions).

A CLOSER LOOK AT THE HEALTH INSURANCE PORTABILITY AND ACCOUNTABILITY ACT (HIPAA) OF 1996

The Health Insurance Portability and Accountability Act (HIPAA) of 1996, alluded to in earlier chapter sections, focuses on health protection for U.S. employees in a number of ways, with the Centers for Medicare and Medicaid Services having the responsibility to implement various unrelated provisions of HIPAA. Title I of the act maintains that health insurance coverage for individuals and their families continues when they transfer or lose employment, and Title II requires the Department of Health and Human Services to develop and maintain national standards for electronic transactions regarding health care in the United States. As well, Title II speaks to the security and privacy of online health data—that which can be sent through the Internet. The developers of HIPAA felt that such standards would improve the efficiency and effectiveness of the U.S. health care system by demanding secure and private handling of electronic data. From an IT security angle, HIPAA requires a double-entry or double-check of data entered by staff. All U.S. health care organizations had to be compliant with the HIPAA Security Rule by April 21, 2005—which meant taking extra measures to secure online citizens' health information, including their online medical records (Schell and Martin 2006).

A summary of the key elements of the HIPAA Security Rule, including who is covered, what information is protected, and what safeguards must be in place to ensure appropriate protections can be found at the following Web site: http://www.hhs.gov/ocr/privacy/hipaa/understanding/srsummary.html.

In 2009, the U.S. Department of Health and Human Services Office for Civil Rights announced a final rule that implemented a number of provisions of the Health Information Technology for Economic and Clinical Health Act—enacted as part of the American Recovery and Reinvestment Act of 2009—to increase the privacy and security provisions for health information set out in HIPAA. The latter rule was designed to strike a balance between permitting important uses of health information for patients and protecting their privacy rights. Given the diversity of the health care market in the United States, the rule was designed to be flexible and comprehensive to effectively cover the variety of uses and disclosures that needed to be addressed. HIPAA-covered health plans are now required to use standardized HIPAA electronic transactions (Schell 2014).

In January 2012, an interesting *California Watch* media story focused on questionable Medicare billing practices at the Prime Healthcare Services hospital chain in the United States. The FBI was apparently investigating the hospital chain after some questionable information surfaced. Furthermore, over an 18-month period beginning in July 2010, three California congressmen asked Medicare to investigate the Prime Healthcare Services chain for a type of Medicare fraud known as up-coding, whereby a health care provider files false claims via computerized billing codes to receive enhanced reimbursements. Former employees of the hospital chain claimed that the chain's owner, Dr. Prem Reddy, encouraged physicians and coders to log conditions paying a premium when treating elderly Medicare patients. The hospital chain initially denied any wrongdoing, saying its Medicare billings were legal and proper (Schell 2014).

In 2013, the controversy continued to grow. In an effort to rebut the initial media story, the hospital chain apparently shared through e-mail a certain patient's medical files with local newspapers and 900 of their own employees—causing California regulators to fine the hospital chain $95,000 for violating state confidentiality laws and the HIPAA federal law. The lawyer representing the hospital chain insisted that the company was not guilty of any wrongdoing. Then in June 2013, Prime Healthcare Services agreed to pay $275,000 to the Department of Health and Human Services to settle alleged HIPAA violations (McCann 2013).

THE 2011 STUDY OF CHON, NISHIHARAB, AND AKIYAMAC: POLICY SPECIFICATION LESSONS LEARNED FROM JAPAN AND APPLIED TO THE UNITED STATES

Transforming health care with IT requires committed governmental policy, a willingness of both providers and patients to adopt the technology, and the promotion of progress toward meeting societal challenges in health care delivery. The EU and the U.S. studies discussed so far in this chapter underscore this point. Now we will add Japan to the geographical mix. In recent years, the Japanese government has also been keenly focusing on increasing their health care information technology (HIT) footprint.

Despite Japan's having nearly the healthiest population in the world at a comparatively lower cost than other countries, the government believed that advancing HIT would boost significantly a reform of its national health care. The need to reform was caused by a number of factors challenging Japanese society, including, foremost, caring for an increasingly senior population—and the medical costs that come with that care. There were also increasing risks associated with being able to sustain the insurance foundation and with appropriately dealing with strained medical resources within hospitals.

The overarching goals of the Japanese government regarding HIT were outlined first in "E-Japan Strategy" in 2001, followed by "E-Japan Strategy II" in 2003, the "New IT Reform Strategy" in 2006, "i-Japan Strategy 2015" in 2009, and "A New Strategy in Information and Communications Technology" in early 2010. All of the policy documents were developed under the direction of Japan's IT Strategic Headquarters, the primary area of the Japanese government responsible for developing and establishing IT strategy and resulting policies, led by the prime minister. The premise of the strategy was that by increasing the capabilities of information sharing across the broad range of health care, there would be a significant reduction in costs and a significant improvement in patient service quality.

The main goals of the health care reform strategy, which were to be met by 2015, addressed a number of Japan's societal challenges, including the following: patient-centric regional networks of medical institutions with electronic medical record systems; a nationwide online insurance claim system, to be used with anonymized health data to support evidence-based medicine and important epidemiological analyses; a patient-controlled medical record database for lifelong health care; the promotion of rural and distance medicine; and the integration of patient and administrative information available across medical services, elderly care, and health and welfare services.

The Objectives of the 2011 Study

The 2011 study focused on the impressive HIT efforts already implemented in Japan during the period from 2002 through 2010. The study's purpose was to provide details on effective policy aimed at promoting HIT adoption to provide effective and efficient online health care services to Japanese citizens and to governments wanting to adopt a similar HIT effort. A case study of HIT use in the Kyoto Yamashina area of Japan was the main focus, with a key objective of the research team to discuss issues for the refinement of HIT adoption policy that could be used in other jurisdictions, such as in the United States. The study data collection techniques included interviews of individuals involved in policymaking for HIT in Japan, such as health care professionals, government officials, and academics involved in this line of research.

Specifically, the study explored HIT adoption in Japan mainly from the national level. Insights were gained from archived Japanese government policy documents; more than 50 hours of interview data of ministry personnel, consortium personnel, and academics whose area of expertise was in HIT adoption and health care reform; expert and firsthand knowledge of policy development from the research team member who served as the special advisor to the prime minister of the IT Policy Office and the chair of the Japanese Association of Healthcare Information

Systems Industry (JAHIS) at the time of the study; and more than 20 hours of interview and archival data regarding the Kyoto Yamashina area HIT initiative. The research team synthesized their study data with existing literature on the topic. The bulk of the research effort took place from November 2008 to July 2009, with follow-up interviews of government officials completed through December 2010.

Context for the 2011 Study: IT Innovation at the Otowa Hospital

The Problem

The health care system in the geographic location under study consisted of a main acute and emergency care hospital (i.e., Otowa Hospital), government-run facilities, and private ambulatory clinics located throughout the local community. The system serviced about 137,000 people, provided comprehensive care in a multifaceted health care environment, and was affiliated with 45 other health care facilities. Accepting that the hospital's specialization was actually in complex and critical medical conditions, hospital physicians spent an inordinate amount of their time caring for the large senior population in this location. To complicate matters, seniors often inundated the hospital emergency rooms with nonemergency issues, thereby consuming unnecessary medical resources. In fact, with the large number of seniors being seen for outpatient services in the emergency room, there was a six-hour-plus wait-time for registered patients, forcing overwhelmed doctors to first see patients needing critical care and then to see patients doing the six-hour wait. Because of this severe patient bottleneck in the emergency room, the hospital administration considered at one point turning away seniors wanting to be seen for chronic but manageable diseases typically associated with aging—such as congestive heart failure, high blood pressure, and diabetes.

The hospital administration decided not to go with this initial plan for resource reallocation, because the majority of seniors heading to the emergency room had limited mobility; thus, they were unable to go elsewhere for medical treatment. Additionally, from a strictly revenue-generating angle, the hospital received 33% of its earnings from servicing these elderly patients.

A Proposed Solution

In 2000, the hospital director decided to separate functions and convert some hospital property to diagnosis and treatment rooms. The director also felt that staffing needed to be more efficiently matched to support either inpatient or outpatient functions. At about this time, the medical IT director also realized that there had to be a better way to integrate the hospital with associated clinics. The medical IT director suggested using HIT to better utilize an already heavily taxed medical staff and to more appropriately align the service environment with the medical needs of the patients and the doctors' skill levels.

In short, the hospital director and the medical IT director decided jointly that hospital-wide use of HIT would facilitate a more efficient care process. Therefore, patients could be assessed in the emergency department, an electronic medical record system (EMR) could be generated and viewed by the physician on duty, and the patient could be scheduled immediately for a clinical visit if deemed necessary by the physician. An EMR could enable access to patient information from multiple sites—including the clinic, the hospital, the nursing home, and rehabilitation facilities, thereby streamlining the process for more efficiently deploying medical personnel for elder care. This increased efficiency would alleviate capacity issues in the main hospital and elsewhere, and emergency staff could be focused once again on emergency care for patients who needed it.

Obtaining Initial Funding for the Proposed HIT Solution

In 2003–2004, the hospital administration secured funding from the ministry and from the Yamashina Medical Association (YMA) to develop the Cooperation through Medical Technology (CoMet) system. The YMA formed committees transcending the usual organizational boundaries that typically stagnate information exchange by working with their respective governance bodies and IT vendors to define the type of data transfer, guidance for use of the HIT, requirements for patient consent, information security measures, and accountability regarding possible network hacks or the improper use of the system and data contained therein.

CoMet functioned mainly as a comprehensive electronic health record (EHR), enabling health care organizations and health care professionals outside of the hospital to not only access but also to enter the following important information: (1) patient-level data stored in the hospital's EMR, (2) laboratory data for test requests, (3) various results and clinical documentation, (4) prescription orders, (5) nursing home documentation, and (6) research lab requests.

The Ongoing HIT Operating Funding Model

To balance costs proportionally, the business model for sustaining the HIT solution included the following: (1) ministry funding to cover half of the startup costs for one year to establish the EMR and EHR components, (2) the Otowa Hospital IT budget to cover all of the annual maintenance for the EMR and EHR components used by the hospital, and (3) annual fees for YMA member access to the social/professional networking component of the EHR and CoMet as well as to cover all of the CoMet annual maintenance costs.

Observed Returns on the HIT Investment after Just One Year

Multifaceted Cost Benefits

There were a number of reported benefits for Otowa observed within just one year of the initial HIT implementation in 2005, all of which contributed to quality and operational improvements. For example, the hospital experienced a 75–85% reduction in calls for lab results from the hospital physicians and community physicians, a 63% reduction in manual procedures for preparing and sending outpatient charts for referral visits, and a 33% reduction in manual procedures for inpatient charts. Furthermore, time spent on scheduling appointments was minimized. These time savings allowed health care providers across the spectrum to be more productive, reducing the severity of the shortage of physicians in the community. Also, there was a 40% decrease in lost charge captures realized as a result of the availability of a computer at the point of care.

Improvements in Both Organizational Culture and Physician Professional Development

By enabling improved communications between care providers, HIT changed the culture of Otowa Hospital from one that was highly competitive to one that was highly cooperative. The single objective of drawing patients away from community medical providers was replaced with a culture of cooperation among the community physicians. This new objective then supported the cooperative learning of physicians across organizational boundaries, across government-sponsored health care facilities, and across non-government-sponsored health care facilities. It has also served as a basis for physicians in the community to discuss relevant epidemiological issues that needed addressing.

Improvements in Patient Satisfaction and Health Care Quality

Within just one year of HIT implementation, there was a marked improvement in patient satisfaction and health care quality delivery. For example, there was a 32% increase in patient satisfaction regarding the thoroughness of the consultations between patients and the physicians, resulting in patients not only having a better understanding of their own medical conditions but empowering them to be much more compliant with physician-prescribed medical regimens. Also, there was an incredible 45% reduction in wait times for emergency room services—again associated with higher patient satisfaction. There was also a 56% reduction in wait times for clinical services and a 12% decrease in the length of stay—allowing for 100 more patients per month to receive care, thereby increasing the hospital's overall financial performance.

The Research Team's Study Conclusions Regarding HIT Policy Implications

Policy Implications Known Prior to the Otowa Hospital Study

Prior to analyzing the positive outcomes of HIT implementation at Otowa Hospital, what was already known from a policy perspective was that HIT has the potential to increase the quality of care that patients receive by improving communication among health care providers on multiple levels. To this end, government-sponsored health reform efforts in Japan emphasized HIT implementation as a strategy to reduce costs and to more effectively and efficiently handle an increasingly aging population with intense demands for health care delivery. With the online medical system implementation startup phase were conjectured to be high initial costs, significant data security concerns, and a lack of system standards—all presenting as significant barriers to HIT implementation on a larger scale.

Policy Implications from the Otowa Hospital Study

The research team of Chon, Nishiharab, and Akiyamac said that their study added the following key points to IT health system strategy and policy in Japan:

- HIT can improve patient–physician relationships by promoting communications, enhancing patient and physician knowledge, and increasing time available for face-to-face interactions with patients—factors all strained in health care systems operating beyond an effective and efficient resource capacity.
- There are promising indicators that HIT not only reduces costs and compensates for staff shortages in the short-term, but over the longer term HIT promotes the recruitment and retention of highly skilled staff because of the attractiveness of technology implementation on a systemwide basis—especially in understaffed rural and urban communities.

- Government funding is a catalyst for HIT adoption. However, the funding should be used in conjunction with a broad set of standards for information exchange. Importantly, the latter should not be so restrictive that they prevent parties from adopting EMR and EHR because of a perceived lack of IT capabilities or make the existing system IT capabilities require massive changes in order to meet standards compliance.
- Government-sponsored, community-based IT systems should ensure that there is proper and committed IT leadership, critical for the success of such initiatives. Where there is a shortage of IT leadership, hospitals can employ industry support from IT consultants but with specifications and stated penalties in place beforehand regarding acceptable consultant conduct.
- Community-level IT systems, compared to larger-scale or regional initiatives, can relieve some key issues of concern regarding trust among stakeholders in the information exchange.
- Use of community based IT systems can raise the medical acumen of the entire community and significantly improve the quality of medical care for patients, especially for seniors, who place significant resource demands on the health care system.
- Systemwide IT systems can transform a health care organization's culture to more highly value cooperation among health care providers, especially across both medical specialties and organizational boundaries.

The Research Team's Conclusions

Insights from this research study suggest a possible outcome measure for HIT success in Japan and, possibly, in the United States to reduce national health care expenditures for manageable chronic diseases like congestive heart failure, high blood pressure, diabetes, and wound or skin disorders that are often elderly patient–related. These kinds of diseases can be cared for in less costly non–acute care environments like community clinics or in patients' homes rather than in hospital emergency wards. To bridge the information needed across the different types of health care environments, HIT can increase the quality and access, as well as reduce the costs associated with medical services unnecessarily delivered in a hospital setting. That way, physicians can focus on more critical care activities for patients requiring them.

Another measure of HIT success regarding governance initiatives is the extent to which both Japan and, presumably, the United States could legislate caps on vendor costs for at least the EMR software. The latter often involve customization fees ranging from hundreds of thousands of dollars to tens of millions of dollars (U.S. equivalent) per jurisdiction.

For Japan and for the large-scale health care IT efforts in the United States, governments can sponsor "best practice" research to determine sustainable business models for short-term and long-term IT system implementation; to specify milestones and requirements for demonstrated success of EMR and EHR similar to those found in Japan's HITECH meaningful-use stages; and to schedule funding support for HIT projects extending beyond the one-time startup costs to aid in long-term implementation success.

In summary, national governance and considerable grassroots efforts that are regionally based and community-based are key to creating viable policy, engaging health care staff and patients in the transformation process, and progressing toward the effective infusion of HIT in a health care system to promote technology-enabled health care practices.

CONCLUSION

This chapter had a sizable mission: to accept information technology and the online environment in the health field in terms of online patient records and online health services advancement. We explored at the start of this chapter the excitement of Steven Keating, an advanced university student at MIT's Media Lab, about how information access could help him "keep a handle" on his own brain tumor issue. We then moved to the promise of IT in assisting patients on a broader basis: in terms of their online personal medical records, their online health services, and online provisions for the elderly, for teens, and for those experiencing mental health issues. We closed the chapter realizing that there was considerable resistance by both health care practitioners and patients to accept the online environment as a viable field for health care intervention, despite governments in the United States, the European Union, Japan, Australia, and elsewhere proposing otherwise. Yet, there was hope for advancement by the majority of study respondents on all of these fronts. Realistically, movement from the real world to the virtual world in terms of medical health intervention seems to be a longer-term rather than a shorter-term reality because of users' and practitioners' concerns regarding privacy, security, trust, and confidentiality in an online environment—all of which cause resistance to change.

To gather further insights on this future, readers are referred to the Interview with an Expert sidebar with Dr. Patrick Hung, an expert specializing in the safe passage of information in an online health care environment. As Dr. Hung discusses, and as shown in Table 8.1, there has been a major paradigm shift in the health care service mode in recent years.

Table 8.1 Paradigm Shift in Health Care Service Mode

	Past	Present
Subject		
Doctor and patient relationship	One-on-one	Not limited to one-on-one
Legitimate users for health data	Doctors and workers in the clinic	Doctors, patients, nurses, practitioners, researchers, and insurers in distributed locations
Legitimate users for financial data	Doctors, patients, and workers in the clinic	Doctors, patients, nurses, practitioners, insurers, and medical personnel in distributed locations
Legitimate users for user/data administration	Doctors and workers in the clinic	Nurses, computer operators, database administrators, and medical personnel in distributed locations
Health care system	Isolated	Cooperative environment
Object		
Data format	Paper-based	Electronic-based
Data location	Centralized, usually located in the doctor's clinic	Distributed, but legitimate users should be able to access the data
Data storage medium	Paper-based	Electronic-based (e.g., Internet, CD-ROM, diskettes, and so on)
Policies in governing security and privacy requirements	Diversified	Standardized to Health Insurance Portability and Accountability Act compliance

INTERVIEW WITH AN EXPERT

Dr. Patrick Hung, Information Systems Expert

Dr. Patrick C. K. Hung is an associate professor at the Faculty of Business and Information Technology at the University of Ontario Institute of Technology, Canada. He has been working with Boeing Research and Technology on aviation services–related research, with two patents on mobile network dynamic workflow systems. He is an Honorary International Chair professor at the National Taipei University of Technology and a visiting professor at the University of São Paulo, Brazil. He is a founding committee member of the IEEE International Conference of Web Services (ICWS), the IEEE

International Conference on Services Computing (SCC), and the IEEE BigData Congress (BigData Congress). He is also an associate editor of *IEEE Transactions on Services Computing International* as well as a coordinating editor of *Information Systems Frontiers*. His PhD and master of philosophy science in computer science are from the Hong Kong University of Science and Technology.

Q On February 17, 2009, U.S. President Obama signed into law the Health Information Technology for Economic and Clinical Health (HITECH) Act as a means of stimulating in the United States the adoption of electronic health records (EHRs) rather than continued reliance on paper health records. Similar laws have been passed in the European Union, Japan, and Australia. What do you see as the major gains and the major obstacles that are likely to occur as a result of compliance with these high-tech laws in the health care field?

A There have been in recent years considerable paradigm shifts in the modes of health care services, as shown in the main chapter text. In short, doctor-patient relationships were on a one-on-one basis in the past. Traditionally, the personal health information (PHI) was paper-based and kept in the doctor's clinic. Doctors and nurses were the only users who retained access to patients' PHI. As a result, achieving confidentiality and protecting privacy was relatively easy because the system was isolated.

Nowadays, doctor-patient relationships are no longer limited to a one-on-one basis but may include referral physicians, specialists, and financial staff in insurance companies, to name just a few. In addition, the introduction of electronic medical records (EMRs) has gradually shifted the storage medium away from paper-based to electronic-based. The storage of PHI has, thus, become distributed among many health care–involved parties. In recent years, physicians, researchers, and patients have begun to use the Internet for gathering health data (e.g., viewing medical records), distributing data (e.g., electronic billing), and exchanging health information (e.g., e-mail). From the prospective of patients and doctors, being able to access patients' health data over the Internet is becoming easier and more common throughout the world. However, the major obstacle remaining is that health institutes need a huge amount of resources to support this emerging technological scenario in a manner that is both private and secure.

Q The Health Insurance Portability and Accountability Act (HIPAA) of 1996 focuses on health protections for U.S. employees in a number of ways. The developers of HIPAA felt that such standards would improve the efficiency and effectiveness of the U.S. health care system by demanding secure and private handling of electronic data. Can you comment on whether HIPAA seems to have been effective—why or why not?

A The Health Insurance Portability and Accountability Act of 1996 (HIPAA) defines a set of security and privacy rules to be followed by health care providers in the United States. It provides a set of national standards that health care providers must follow to protect a patient's privacy. The rules ensure that organizations collecting personal health information (PHI) can only use, store, and disclose the relevant health care information for specific purposes. For example, a doctor can access his or her patient's PHI for treatment purposes. PHI includes individually identifiable health information and health care of an individual related to past, present, and future physical and mental health conditions. A major contribution of HIPAA is that it provides a standard format for health care–related transactions. HIPAA is effective because the regulations are divided into four standards or rules: (1) privacy, (2) security, (3) identifiers, and (4) transactions and code sets. These rules are a set of standards for how PHI "in any form or medium" should be controlled and handled. The rules cover all medical records (paper and electronic). According to the U.S. Department of Health and Human Services, HIPAA privacy rule compliance has been compulsory in the United States since April 14, 2004, for covered entities, including health care providers, insurers, health plan providers, and clearinghouses. Failing to comply with the HIPAA rules results in both monetary penalties and suffering loss of reputation and goodwill when noncompliance is publicized.

Before the introduction of the HIPAA legislation, there was no standard organization that addressed all aspects of health care information security and confidentiality. As a result, HIPAA defines the security standard as a set of implementation requirements in electronic transaction formats. It can be said that digitalizing the PHI provides significant efficiency and economic impact when compared to the traditional methods, especially when HIPAA was first mandated.

However, the privacy issues in Web-based applications still need to be addressed properly to avoid economic, legal, and commercial damage. Instead of using expensive proprietary systems, adopting an open standard transaction format, such as Web services, can reduce the costs of development and employment.

The HIPAA privacy rules define and limit the circumstances in which an individual's PHI may be used or disclosed by his or her corresponding service provider. The basic principle of HIPAA states that a service provider should not use or disclose protected health information, except either (1) as the HIPAA privacy rule permits or requires, or (2) as the individual who is the owner of the PHI authorizes.

Q There was an interesting media story about a young man named Steven Keating, who saved his own life by doing research about brain tumors through years of Internet searches. He then requested special medical tests be done by his doctors. In the end, he commented, "The person with the least access to data in the system is the patient. You can get it, but the burden is always on the patient. And it is scattered across many different silos of patient data." How do you think that health care systems can remedy this problem?

A The six rights that HIPAA gives patients regarding their PHI should remedy this problem from the perspective of a patient, as follows:

1. *The right to access, copy, and inspect a patient's own PHI*, allowing patients to access their PHI and related information, such as insurance claims. In the past, a handling fee was often charged for making copies of medical records. This fee helped to offset the cost of labor and copying.
2. *The right to request the correction of inaccurate health information*, allowing patients to ask for an update of their PHI if it is incomplete or incorrect. In the past, patients had to go back to their physician or other providers if they discovered mistakes in their records, which took time and money.
3. *The right to find out where PHI has been used and shared for purposes other than care, payment, or health care operations*, allowing patients to know how their PHI is used and shared by health care providers or health insurers. In the past, health care providers sometimes provided patients' health information to other institutions for research purposes. Despite HIPAA, it is still impossible for patients to stop the unauthorized use of their health care records.
4. *The right to request special restrictions on the use or disclosure of PHI*, protecting patients from having their PHI being used or shared

for any illegitimate purposes unless their express permission (consent) is given. Even if patients have given their permission, they still have the right to revoke it.

5. *The right to request confidential communications of PHI,* allowing patients to request their health care providers contact them at a certain address or by other communication channels (such as through a particular telephone number). In the past, requests for confidential information were very time-consuming and often involved office appointments, so it was difficult for the health care providers to handle every communication request in a timely fashion.
6. *The right to file complaints*, allowing patients to file complaints to their health care providers if their PHI has been used or shared in an illegitimate way, or if the patients were not able to exercise any of their rights. In the past, there was no such complaint mechanism put into place. This meant that patients might not be able to collect any evidence to prove any violation of privacy laws.

Q What new areas regarding electronic health records and online health care services do you think that IT security scholars will focus their research energy on in the near future and why?

A The most important research area IT security scholars will focus on is big data analytics. Big data analytics employ software tools from advanced analytics disciplines such as data mining, predictive analytics, and machine learning to resolve specific problems for clinical, quality/compliance, and operational areas. For example, researchers at the Johns Hopkins University School of Medicine in Baltimore used big data to track trends of influenza with Google's Flu Trends tool and found a strong correlation between the rise in Internet flu search information and the number of patients with flu-like symptoms coming into urban hospital emergency rooms.

Such data analytic information can prove exceptionally helpful to hospitals in effectively planning for large volumes of patients during peak influenza outbreak times. In short, huge numbers of health datasets can be used in conjunction with other datasets to track patients' future behaviors. However, the security and privacy issues of such strategy-planning scenarios is an important topic for future research.

REFERENCES

Chon, C., Nishiharab, E., & Akiyamac, M. (2011). Transforming healthcare with information technology in Japan: A review of policy, people, and progress. *International Journal of Medical Informatics, 80,* 157–170.

Corrigan, J., Donaldson, M., & Kohn, L. (2001). *Crossing the quality chasm: A new health system for the 21st century.* Washington, DC: National Academy Press.

Cross, M. (2011). BMA warns against letting patients have access to their electronic records. *British Medical Journal, 342,* d206.

Department of Health. (2012). *The mandate: A mandate from the government to the NHS Commissioning Board: April 2013 to March 2015.* London: Department of Health.

Dutton, W. H., & Blank, G. (2011). Next generation users: The Internet in Britain. *Oxford Internet survey 2011*, Oxford Internet Institute. Oxford, U.K.: University of Oxford.

Fisher, B., Bhavnani, V., & Winfield, M. (2009). How patients use access to their full health records: A qualitative study of patients in general practice. *Journal Review of Social Medicine, 102*, 539–544.

Fuji, K. T, Galt, K. A., & Serocca, A. B. (2008). Personal health record use by patients as perceived by ambulatory care physicians in Nebraska and South Dakota: A cross-sectional study. *Perspectives in Health Information Management, 5,* 1–16.

Greenhalgh, T., Wood, G. W., Bratan, T., Stramer, K., & Hinder, S. (2008). Patients' attitudes to the summary care record and HealthSpace: Qualitative study. *British Medical Journal, 336,* 1290–1295.

Hoerbst, A., Kohl, C. D., Knaup, P., & Ammenwerth, E. (2010). Attitudes and behaviors related to the introduction of electronic health records among Austrian and German citizens. *International Journal of Medical Informatics, 79,* 81–89.

Humer, C., & Finkle, J. (2014). Your medical record is worth more to hackers than your credit card. Retrieved from http://www.reuters.com/article/2014/09/24/us-cybersecurity-hospitals-idUSKCN0HJ21I20140924

Jones, R. B., & Ashurst, E. J. (2013). Online anonymous discussion between service users and health professionals to ascertain stakeholder concerns in using e-health services in mental health. *Health Informatics Journal, 19,* 281–299.

Landro, L. (2005). Parents barred from teen health files. Retrieved from http://www.wsj.com/articles/SB112484137114721288

Lohr, S. (2015, April 3). Data sharing moves into the medical field. *The Globe and Mail*, p. L7.

Markle Foundation. (2008). Americans overwhelmingly believe electronic personal health records could improve their health. Retrieved from http://www.connectingforhealth.org/resources/ResearchBrief-200806.pdf

McCann, E. (2013). 275K HIPAA breach settlement for Prime. Retrieved from http://www.healthcareitnews.com/news/prime-healthcare-pays-275k-breach

Medicine Io. (2003). *Key capabilities of an electronic health record.* Washington, DC: National Academies Press.

Moreno, M. A., Ralston, R. D., & Grossman, D. C. (2009). Adolescent access to online health services: Perils and promise. *Journal of Adolescent Health, 44,* 244–251.

Pagliari, C., Detmer, D., & Singleton, P. (2007). Potential of electronic personal health records. *British Medical Journal, 335,* 330–333.

Pew Research Center. (2015). Health fact sheet. Retrieved from http://www.pewinternet.org/fact-sheets/health-fact-sheet/

Rouse, M. (2009). HITECH Act (Health Information Technology for Economic and Clinical Health Act). Retrieved from http://searchhealthit.techtarget.com/definition/HITECH-Act

Royal College of General Practitioners. (2010). *Enabling patients to access electronic health records. Guidance for health professionals.* London: Royal College of General Practitioners.

Royal College of General Practitioners. (2012). *Patients' access to records.* London: Royal College of General Practitioners. Retrieved from http://www.rcgp.org.uk/clinical-andresearch/practice-management-resources/healthinformatics-group/patient-access-to-records.aspx

Schell, B. H. (2014). *Contemporary world issues: Internet censorship.* Santa Barbara, CA: ABC-CLIO.

Schell, B. H., & Martin, C. (2006). *Webster's new world hacker dictionary.* Indianapolis, IN: Wiley.

Shah, S. G. S., Fitton, R., Hannan, A., Fisher, B., Young, T., & Barnett, J. (2015). Accessing personal medical records online: A means to what ends? *International Journal of Medical Informatics, 84,* 111–118.

Witry, M. J., Doucette, W. R., Daly, J. M., Levy, B. T., & Chrischilies, E. A. (2010). Family physician perceptions of personal health records. *Perspectives of Health Information Management, 7.* Retrieved from http://www.ncbi.nlm.nih.gov/pmc/articles/PMC2805556/

Directory of Resources

This directory has been compiled to give readers additional resources to consult regarding the topics covered in this book. Resources are arranged according to the chapter titles.

INTERNET AND GAMING ADDICTIONS

Books

American Psychiatric Association. (2000). *Diagnostic and statistical manual of mental disorders*. Text Revised. 4th ed. Washington, DC: American Psychiatric Publishing. The primary medical consultation text used by mental health practitioners for diagnosing Internet and gaming addictions.

Livingstone, S. M., & Haddon, L. (2013). *Children, risk and safety on the Internet: Research and policy challenges in comparative perspective*. Bristol: Policy. From a broad perspective, discusses a theoretical framework for children's Internet use, and then details more specific topics such as public and personal privacy in social networking sites, online bullying, and sexting addictions.

Tamyko, Y. (2014). *Governance of addictions: European public policies*. Oxford: Oxford University Press. Covers such material as the social services, welfare, and criminology approaches to governance on addictions in Europe.

Web Site

http://www.Netaddiction.com. Dr. Kimberly Young's very informative Web site on Internet addictions, which is a valuable educational resource providing online users academic articles, books for further reading, and self-assessment tools for helping readers determine if they have an Internet addiction problem.

CYBERBULLYING AND CYBERSTALKING

Books and Book Chapters

Budd, T., & Mattinson, J. (2000). *The extent and nature of stalking: Findings from the 1998 British Crime Survey*. London: Home Office. Discusses the phases of stalking and implications for policy development around this troubling area in today's on-land and online environments.

Chadwick, S. (2014). *Impacts of cyberbullying, building social and emotional resilience in schools*. Cham: Springer. Details social-emotional resilience in children facing cyberbullying and then discusses strategic and policy implications for dealing with this online problem.

Henson, B. (2010). Cyberstalking. In B. S. Fisher & S. P. Lab (Eds.), *Encyclopedia of victimology and crime prevention* (pp. 253–256). Thousand Oaks, CA: Sage. Takes a criminology perspective on cyberstalking and experiences of victims.

Schell, B. H., & Lanteigne, N. B. (2000). *Stalking, Harassment, and Murder in the Workplace: Guidelines for Protection and Prevention*. Westport, CT: Quorum. A key reference textbook in the field of workplace stalking and cyberstalking, this book shares real-world cases and offers expert opinions on ways to effectively deal with these.

Web Sites

Sites on cyberbullying and on cyberstalking, primarily as self-help sites for victims:

http://www.minormonitor.com/resource/cyber-bullying-cyberbullying/
http://www.ncpc.org/topics/cyberbullying/what-is-cyberbullying
http://www.minormonitor.com/resource/cyber-bullying-cyberbullying/
http://www.fightcyberstalking.org/
https://www.getsafeonline.org/protecting-yourself/cyberstalking/

ONLINE PREDATORS

Books and Book Chapters

Singer, A. (2010). *Alexis: My true story of being seduced by an online predator (louder than words)*. Deerfield Beach, FL: Health Communications. This is a true story about a lonely high school girl who was communicated with by an older man online and was convinced to put personal things of herself on the Internet that she later very much regretted.

Taylor, M., & Quayle, E. (2003). *Child pornography: An Internet crime*. New York, NY: Brunner-Routledge. This book discusses how online predation and child pornography often are related and must be attended to by academics, the authorities, and mental health professionals.

Taylor, M., & Quayle, E. (2010). Internet sexual offending. In J. M. E. Brown & E. A. E. Campbell (Eds.), *The Cambridge handbook of forensic psychology* (pp. 520–526). New York, NY: Cambridge University Press. An excellent forensic psychology approach to understanding the process and outcomes of Internet sexual offending and online predation.

Web Sites

Kids Internet Safety Alliance (KINSA). http://kinsa.net/ Funded by private donations, KINSA, a Canadian not-for-profit organization, is proactive in fighting online predation. KINSA is led by CEO Paul Gillespie, a former Toronto police officer who is now actively engaged in training police and prosecutors around the world in best practices for exchanging information to save children victimized by child predators.

www.abusehurts.ca. Started in 1993, the Canadian Centre for Abuse Awareness (CCAA)'s mission is to significantly reduce the incidence and adverse impact of abuse through education and public awareness. The CCAA is deemed to be a Canadian leader in creating programs to prevent abuse.

www.internet101.ca. This Web site's motto speaks volumes: "Police and partners working together to web-proof our communities." This Web site was created and is operated by a committee of police forces, including the Royal Canadian Mounted Police (RCMP). This site includes safety tips, helpful presentations, and links to other police-approved resources to help minors and their parents surf safely online.

www.isafe.org. Founded in 1998 and endorsed by the U.S. Congress, i-SAFE is a nonprofit foundation whose mission is to protect young people everywhere while online. i-SAFE incorporates classroom curriculum with community outreach to empower students, their teachers, their parents, and law enforcement to safeguard the online environment.

www.virtualglobaltaskforce.com. The Virtual Global Taskforce (VGT) is comprised of law enforcement agencies from around the world working as a cooperative team to fight child abuse online. The mission of the VGT is to build an effective, international partnership of law enforcement agencies to protect children from online child abuse.

www.bewebaware.ca. Be Web Aware is a national, bilingual (English-French) public education program on Internet safety, housed in Canada. The mission is to ensure young Canadians benefit from the assets of the Internet, but remain safe and responsible while engaged in online activities.

www.wiredsafety.org. WiredSafety.org provides Internet safety information for adults and children of all ages. In fact, it has the largest online safety, education, and help group in the world. Their network has more than 9,000 volunteers.

www.boostforkids.org. BOOST offers programs and services to more than 1,000 children, youth, and their families to prevent abuse or provide support when abuse or violence has occurred—on land or online.

www.kidsintheknow.ca. Kids in the Know is a safety curriculum designed to empower children and reduce their risk of victimization while online by helping them build self-esteem by teaching them critical problem-solving skills. The program uses a community-based approach to heighten safety awareness in children.

www.cybertip.ca. Cybertip.ca is Canada's national tip line for reports of online sexual exploitation of children. Thus, its mission is to be a centralized Web portal receiving and addressing reports from the public regarding child pornography, luring, child sex tourism, and minors being exploited through prostitution.

CORPORATE/GOVERNMENT NETWORK HACKS, IDENTITY THEFT, AND INTERNET FRAUD

Books and Book Chapters

Clarke, R. A., & Knake, R. (2012). *Cyber war: The next threat to national security and what to do about it*. New York: Ecco. The authors, one an international security expert who worked for the U.S. government and the other a cyber expert, talk about the role of the Internet in cyberwars—hostile attempts by one nation to penetrate the networks of another nation for critical information. Recent past and present-day cyberwars are detailed in this very interesting and well-written book.

Davidoff, S., & Ham, J. (2012). *Network forensics: Tracking hackers through cyberspace*. Upper Saddle River, NJ: Prentice Hall. This book provides a nice foundation and roadmap for those trying to get the gist of cloud computing, advantages for businesses to move to the cloud, and concerns about IT security in the cloud. The book details the various kinds of footprints that hackers leave when they exploit networks.

Holt, T. J., & Schell, B. H. (2011). *Corporate hacking and technology-driven crime: Social dynamics and implications*. Hershey: Information Science Reference. Covers a full range of topics written by experts in the field. Topics include the general theory of crime and computer hacking, policing of movie and music piracy, deciphering the hacker underground, examining the language of carders, and cyberconflict as an emergent social phenomenon.

Holt, T. J., & Schell, B. H. (2013). *Contemporary world issues: Hackers and hacking*. Santa Barbara, CA: ABC-CLIO. Discusses such topics as the growth and adoption of the Internet, getting unauthorized network access, the key elements of criminal liability, hacker predispositions, network hacks: recent surveys on the survey and types of harm caused, and laws created to keep abreast of the evolving Internet.

Newman, J. Q. (1999). *Identity theft: The cybercrime of the millennium*. Port Townsend, WA: Loompanics Unlimited. Describes why identity theft is such a feared phenomenon post-2000.

Olson, P. (2012). *We are Anonymous: Inside the hacker world of LulzSec, Anonymous, and the global cyber insurgency*. Boston, MA: Little, Brown. The author documents the interesting hacktivist attempts of the LulzSec and Anonymous hacker cells operating on the Internet. Interesting attacks on Sony, Visa, and PayPal networks in retaliation for their poor treatment of WikiLeaks are described in detail.

Web Sites

http://www.2600.com. This is the Web site of the popular hacker magazine *2600: The Hacker Quarterly* and home of the Hackers on Planet Earth (HOPE) hacker conference.

http://wikileaks.org/. This is the controversial Web site for the hacking cell known as WikiLeaks, whose members, including Julian Assange, have a passion for publishing government and industry secrets online with the alleged goal of bringing important news and information to the public.

TECHNOLOGY AND SOCIAL BEHAVIOR: THE RISE OF SOCIAL MEDIA WEB SITES

Books and Book Chapters

Congressional Executive Commission on China. (2012). *China's Censorship of the Internet and Social Media: The Human Toll and Trade*. Seattle, WA: CreateSpace.

This book presents the results of a hearing on China's predisposition to violate human rights and disregard the Internet laws and international standards that authorities say they believe in and uphold. Yet, they have not only increased censorship and control over the Internet, but they have been known to violate their citizens' human rights and dignity after citizens have exercised their freedom to speak out on social media Web sites.

Livingston, S., & Gorzig, A. "Sexting": The exchange of sexual messages online among European youth. In S. Livingstone, L. Haddon, & A. Gorzing (Eds.), *Children, risk and safety on the Internet* (pp. 151–164). Bristol: The Policy Press. Discusses the risks involved to children of sexting with others in social media Web sites.

Tuten, L. T. (2008). *Advertising 2.0: Social media marketing in a Web 2.0 world.* Westport, CT: Praeger. Discusses the intricate and positive connection between social media marketing in a Web 2.0 world and the rapid rise in popularity of social media Web sites.

Web Sites (Top 10)

1. Facebook (www.facebook.com)
   900,000,000 estimated unique monthly visitors
2. Twitter (www.twitter.com)
   310,000,000 estimated unique monthly visitors
3. LinkedIn (www.linkedin.com)
   255,000,000 estimated unique monthly visitors
4. Pinterest (www.pinterest.com)
   250,000,000 estimated unique monthly visitors
5. Google Plus+ (http://plus.google.com)
   120,000,000 estimated unique monthly visitors
6. Tumblr (www.tumblr.com)
   110,000,000 estimated unique monthly visitors
7. Instagram (www.instagram.com)
   100,000,000 estimated unique monthly visitors
8. VK (www.vk.com)
   80,000,000 estimated unique monthly visitors
9. Flickr (www.flickr.com)
   65,000,000 estimated unique monthly visitors
10. Vine (www.vine.com)
    42,000,000 estimated unique monthly visitors

COPYRIGHT INFRINGEMENT, FILE SHARING, AND PEER-TO-PEER (P2P) NETWORKS

Books

Ammori, M. (2013). *On Internet freedom.* Washington, DC: Elkat Books. An Internet freedom advocate, lawyer, and scholar focusing on the First Amendment, Marvin Ammori comprehensively discusses why freedom of the Internet is under constant threat— because of power struggles by corporations, governments, and hacker cells.

Kulesza, J. (2012). *International Internet law.* Routledge. This book looks at critical international legal issues and debates related to Internet governance. Topics include international copyright protection, cyberterrorism, identify theft, fake Internet Web sites, and so on. The author looks at how various jurisdictions view these issues, including China, the United States, the European Union, and Singapore.

MacKinnon, R. (2012). *Consent of the networked: The worldwide struggle for Internet freedom.* New York, NY: Basic Books. The author, a journalist and Internet policy analyst, says that while the Internet was meant to liberate online users so that they could say what they want and share files at their leisure with others online, for every media piece talking about how empowering the Internet is, there is a media piece talking about how companies and governments collect personal information on online citizens without their permission. This book addresses the important question of how technology should be governed to uphold the rights and liberties of online users worldwide.

OBSCENE AND OFFENSIVE CONTENT AND ONLINE CENSORSHIP

Books

Cohen, N. M. (2012). *You can't read this book: Censorship in an age of freedom.* New York: HarperCollins. This book talks about censorship in countries that purport to be active on the Internet and supporters of an age of freedom. The author explores the present-day Internet reality in Iran, China, and elsewhere. The Great Firewall of China is discussed, along with the importance of religion, power, and dictatorships in keeping censorship alive and well in some key jurisdictions connected to the Internet.

Duthel, H. (2011). *Freedom of the press report: Censorship—Internet censorship.* Seattle, WA: CreateSpace. Freedom of the press and Internet censorship are closely related. The author details why in this book and compares and contrasts jurisdictions where the press is most free (such as Finland, Iceland, the Netherlands, Norway, and Sweden) and where the press is least free (such as Eritrea, North Korea, Turkmenistan, Iran, and Myanmar).

Greenberg, A. (2012). *This machine kills secrets: How WikiLeakers, Cypherpunks, and Hacktivists aim to free the world's information*. New York, NY: Dutton Adult (Penguin Books). Greenberg gives readers insights into why Manning, Assange, and Snowden likely did what they did as believers that the world's information is free.

Lankford, R. D. (2010). *Censorship (issues that concern you).* Farmington Hills, MI: Greenhaven Press. This book examines a lot of important topics on censorship, including if censorship is ever acceptable, whether parents and the government should restrict content on the Internet, and the role of Internet service providers (ISPs) in censoring online content. It also looks at workplace infringements on free expression online.

Travis, H. (2013). *Cyberspace law: Censorship and regulation of the Internet.* London: Routledge. This book discusses in detail what the American Civil Liberties Union has labeled "the third era in cyberspace," whereby filters change the Internet's architectural structure, reducing online free speech. Although the courts and other organizations insist that liberties online must be defended, the author says that large, multinational companies have produced tools and strategies enhancing Internet censorship.

Web Sites (Internet Openness Advocacy Groups)

http://www.aclu.org/. American Civil Liberties Union (ACLU). The founder of the ACLU, Roger Baldwin, once said, "So long as we have enough people in this country willing to fight for their rights, we'll be called a democracy." ACLU members are found in the courts, legislatures, and communities defending individual rights and liberties that are guaranteed by the U.S. Constitution and various U.S. laws. The ACLU defends the First Amendment and is headquartered on Broad Street in New York City. The ACLU has been active since 1920.

https://www.eff.org/. Electronic Frontier Foundation (EFF). With their main office in San Francisco, California, the EFF is an organization that was rooted in the summer of 1990, primarily as a reaction to threats against free speech. The EFF continues to defend parties whose rights they believe have been infringed in cyberspace.

www.freedomhouse.org. Freedom House. With offices on Wall Street in New York and on Connecticut Avenue in Washington, D.C., Freedom House is a prestigious, independent private organization supporting the expansion of freedom throughout the world. Their members believe that freedom—whether it be on land or online—is possible only in democratic political systems in which governments are accountable to their own people.

ONLINE PERSONAL HEALTH RECORDS AND HEALTH SERVICES

Books

Medicine Io. (2003). *Key capabilities of an electronic health record*. Washington, DC: National Academies Press. Explores the capabilities of and the increasing demand by patients for ready access to their electronic health records.

Royal College of General Practitioners. (2010). *Enabling patients to access electronic health records. Guidance for health professionals*. London: Royal College of General Practitioners. Discusses precautions that physicians need to take when enabling patients to access their electronic health records.

Sinacore, A. L., & Ginsberg, F. (2015). *Canadian counselling and counselling psychology in the 21st century*. Montreal, Quebec, and Kingston, Ontario: McGill–Queen's University Press. This interesting book looks at how mental health practitioners view changing trends regarding counseling psychology in the Internet age, including clients' wanting Internet access to counselors rather than just office visits.

Vickerstaff, S., Phillipson, C., & Wilkie, R. (2012). *Work, health and wellbeing: The challenges of managing health at work*. Bristol: Policy. This book looks at the modern-day challenges of employees wanting to maintain their health and wellness in the workplace through multiple means, including being involved with online self-help and employment-based personal health components.

Index

About the Author

Bernadette H. Schell is well published in the hacking and IT domain. She has co-authored books such as *The Hacking of America* (2002), *Cybercrime* (2004), *The Internet and Society* (2007), and *The Webster's New World Hacker Dictionary* (2006). Her most recent book was *Internet Censorship* (2014). She has also coauthored two books with Dr. Tom Holt: *Corporate Hacking and Technology-Driven Crime* (2011) and *Hackers and Hacking* (2013). She is currently a Full Professor in the Faculty of Management and in Science, Engineering and Architecture at Laurentian University in Ontario, Canada. She also is the Director of Cybercrime Initiatives there.

About the Author